The Collected Works of Theodore Parker: a Discourse of Matter Pertaining to Religion
by Theodore Parker

Address:
HardPress
8345 NW 66TH ST #2561
MIAMI FL 33166-2626
USA
Email: info@hardpress.net

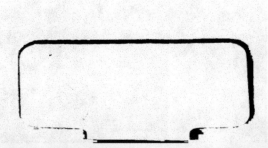

Saulini del   Rome 1859   Vincent Brooks lith

THEODORE PARKER

THE

COLLECTED WORKS

OF

THEODORE PARKER,

MINISTER OF THE TWENTY-EIGHTH CONGREGATIONAL
SOCIETY AT BOSTON, U.S.

CONTAINING HIS

THEOLOGICAL, POLEMICAL, AND CRITICAL WRITINGS,
SERMONS, SPEECHES, AND ADDRESSES,
AND LITERARY MISCELLANIES.

EDITED BY

FRANCES POWER COBBE.

VOL. I.

A DISCOURSE OF MATTERS PERTAINING TO RELIGION.

LONDON:
TRÜBNER & CO., 60, PATERNOSTER ROW.
1863.

March 22.

...y School.

JOHN CHILDS AND SON, PRINTERS.

A

DISCOURSE

OF

MATTERS PERTAINING TO RELIGION.

BY

THEODORE PARKER.

" If an offence come out of the Truth, better is it that the offence come, than the Truth
be concealed."—JEROME.

LONDON:
TRÜBNER & CO., 60, PATERNOSTER ROW.
1863.

ADVERTISEMENT.

THE present volume forms the first of a series intended to include all the published Works of Theodore Parker. A second volume will be issued immediately, containing his "Ten Sermons of Religion," and "Prayers."

The drawing from which the Frontispiece is taken was executed by Saulini in Rome in the spring of 1859, a few months before Mr Parker's death.

F. P. C.

Belgrave House,
    Durdnam Down, Bristol.

" It is perhaps God's will that we should be taught in this our day, among other precious lessons, not to build up our faith upon a book, though it be the Bible itself, but to realize more truly the blessedness of knowing that He, Himself, the Living God, our Father and Friend, is nearer and closer to us than any book can be,—that His voice within the heart may be heard continually by the obedient child that listens for it, and that *that* shall be our Teacher and Guide in the path of duty, which is the path of life, when all other helpers— even the words of the best of Books—may fail us."—*The Pentateuch critically examined, by the Right Rev. J. W. Colenso, D.D., Bishop of Natal.*

PREFACE

BY THE EDITOR.

THE progress of religious belief, from a lesser to a more enlightened stage, is carried on apparently by a series of waves of thought, which sweep over the minds of men at distant intervals. There are periods of comparative calm and stagnation, and then times of gradual swelling and upheaving of the deep, till some great billow slowly rears its crest above the surface higher and still higher to the last; when, with a mighty convulsion, amid foam and spray, and "noise of many waters," it topples over and bursts in thunder up the beach, bearing the flood-line higher than it had ever reached before. A great national reformation has been accomplished.

In the eyes of those who have watched intelligently the signs of the times, it seems that some such wave as this is even now gathering beneath us, a broader and a deeper wave than yet has ever arisen. No partial and temporary rippling of the surface is it now, but the whole mass of living thought seems slowly and steadily upheaved, and the ocean is moved to its depths. Such a phenomenon, if true, bears the highest promise ever held out to humanity, and we cannot but hail it with faith and joy, conscious that the sudden uprising of even the purest reforming sect, carrying us forward for the moment with earthquake violence, would afford no such reason for hopeful confidence in the future.

But this universal upheaving of thought, along with its vast promise of good, brings with it also forebodings of changes which it is impossible to contemplate without grave anxiety. When *this* wave breaks, if break it will, it will reach a point which has never been disturbed hitherto, and in whose conservation or engulfment some of the most sacred interests of the human race are concerned. The old temple of Traditional

Religion, the religion which rests primarily on external evidence of certain supernatural events, stands front to front with the advancing waters, and needs must bear the whole force of their incalculable weight. Already the venerable fane in which our fathers worshipped so long, seems menaced with destruction, while one after another its bulwarks and corner-stones are sapped and submerged, and the sands on which it is built are shifting on every side. In the judgment of many its doom seems inevitable, unless not merely some partial lull and subsidence of the waves takes place, but the whole tide of human thought for ages turns back and sets in an opposite direction.

These solemn forebodings are not unnaturally scorned by those whose trust in the old creed has remained hitherto undisturbed. Every man's peculiar Church must needs be to *his* mind "founded on a rock," and impregnable to "the gates of hell." But to others equally naturally the creed they have themselves found untenable seems sure to prove in the end untenable to all who bring to its examination equal freedom and earnestness, and they note how as years go on every advance in philosophy and every discovery in science seems to bear in one and the same direction. Looking back over a few decades, the change in the state of all controversies on religion becomes remarkable, and the wild raids of professed "infidels" and timid attacks of latitudinarians in past times were found to be superseded by an orderly and resolute invasion, all the more formidable that the hostile bands approach from the most opposite quarters. It seems to be but a question of time, when the leaguer will be complete, and after outposts and trenches have fallen one by one into the hands of the enemy, the old towers themselves will fall, undermined by a deeper philosophy than their builders knew, and shattered by shot and shell from every cohort in the camp of knowledge. Underground, there works the ever-progressing conviction that a supernatural revelation, miracles, prophecies, infallible books, and infallible churches, are things *in themselves* nearly, if not utterly, incredible. And overhead there hurtle in the air (so fast that we can scarce note them as they pass) the missiles from every battalion of science, striking deadly blows wherever they can be brought to bear on the defences of the supposed revelation. The astronomy, the geology, the chronology, and ethnology of our time have at least *seemed* always to contradict, and never to corroborate, the Book which is yet claimed to come directly from the Great Author of Nature; and instead of external authentications and internal verifications of its various parts, every critical explorer brings us back new specimens of anachronisms, contradictions, and difficulties without number, till the authorship and date of all the more important histories are involved in hopeless obscurity. Everywhere and on all sides the results of inquiry are the same, or if now and then the besieged regain with much shouting some vantage ground too lightly claimed by the enemy, they are soon driven back from whole lines of trenches in another direction. Though books appear every month to assure us that "Scripture and science" are "not at variance," and that the "Testimony of the Rocks" is in favour of the Mosaic Cosmogony; yet the urgency with which the asseveration is reiterated and the wildness of the hypotheses to which their authors have recourse to reconcile what ought to require no reconciliation, leave us an impression the direct contrary to that which they intend. Why are there, we ask, no volumes pouring from the press, corresponding to the rapid stream of advancing knowledge, and calling on us to observe "triumphant verifications of Scripture from the recent discoveries" in this, that, or the other science? It is certainly not for lack of will that no such books are written, or written only to bring corroboration to histories no more doubted than that of Thucydides.

The truth is, after all, simple enough. Those grand and noble books which make up the Bible and constitute the "Great Sheaf" in the whole harvest of human thought, even those books cannot be weighed in the balance, or measured by the standard of God's omniscience. Call them human and fallible, and they seem *almost* divine. But call them divine and infallible, and seek to find in them that knowledge of nature which, when they were written, only Nature's God possessed, and we do them wrong and despite, and obscure all their rightful claims to admiration. Nay, to try them as even historically accurate, *according to our philosophy of history*, is an injustice and anachronism. It is an anachronism to expect that men, who in the very extreme of their piety and reverence attributed every remarkable occurrence, every thunder-storm, or victory, or cure of disease, or wise legislation, or composition of noble poetry, to direct Divine interposition—men to whom secondary causes were nothing and first causes everything, should, in the capacity of historians, supply us with statements of facts unrefracted by the coloured media of their imaginations; and detail for our cautious scepticism evidences which they never dreamed of requiring for their own simple-minded and ever ready belief. And passing beyond the Bible to the creeds of the churches, we find it equally impracticable to fit the thoughts of one age into the faith of another. The theological scheme which men composed when they believed the earth to be a plane, the centre of the universe, finds no place for itself in our modern cosmology, and the tremendous drama supposed to have been acted on that mighty stage, before the appalled and gazing Hosts of Heaven, becomes inconceivable played upon our little planet, one of the smallest of the many worlds revolving round one of the millions of suns of the unknown myriads of starry clusters. Modern Astronomy has not so much contradicted isolated statements in the Hebrew Scriptures as left the whole Nicene Theology without standing-room.

In every direction it would seem as if the battle of Traditionalism were lost, nor will the one great compromise offered by its noblest defenders suffice to save it. It will not be enough to abandon the infallibility of sacred books, and claim only Divine Inspiration and perfection for the moral and spiritual part of Christianity. Divinely true, divinely perfect as is much of that moral and spiritual part; *there* also the human and the fallible are to be found, and weightier than the blows which are struck at either the philosophy or the science of the Bible are those directed against doctrines offensive to the conscience and paralyzing to the heart. Nor are these morally objectionable doctrines only matters of unimportance and detail, such as Old Testament stories and precepts of earlier ages, corrected afterwards by a purer teaching. The deepest denial of all rises from the heart of humanity against fundamental dogmas, whose elimination from Christianity would almost identify it with Theism——the dogmas of the Fall, the Atonement, a Personal Devil, and an Eternal Hell.

So wide and vast is this upheaving wave of thought of which we have spoken, that other traditional creeds beside Christianity seem simultaneously threatened by its advance. Mahometanism is visibly running out the last sands of its existence; Judaism itself is undergoing a change; and the vast faith of India, whose origin is lost in the night of time, will probably before another century is over have fallen to rise no more. Not from *external* causes are these and the other religions of the East perishing away. The outward energies at work against them, the European missions and efforts at proselytism, are almost ludicrously inefficient to move a feather of their gigantic weight. But from *within* the change everywhere appears; the old life is gone, a new one is gradually arising, and that not by the formation of purer sects,[1] but by the gradual enlightenment of the masses. Now, this vast movement throughout the world may *possibly* be of a more transitory nature than it now appears. The wave by which we are ourselves upborne is hardly in our power to measure aright, and it may be within the compass of events that it may subside ere long, leaving things everywhere nearly as they have been in the centuries gone by. In particular, as regards Christianity and the English branch thereof, it may be that all that is true in modern criticism and philosophy may be capable of adaptation, in ways we see not now, to its fundamental ideas; and the Church, by enlarging its formularies, may be found capable of absorbing them all, and arising with renewed life like a giant refreshed. These things *may* be so, we say, but it must be admitted that it is hard for us to see how any such reconciliation can take place. The tendency observable is all the other way. At the very utmost, so vast a modification of the popular creed must in such case ensue, as to render it hardly recognizable by its present adherents, while the interval of transition must be one of danger and difficulty, almost equal to that of the entire destruction of the old and reconstruction of a new belief. To enable men to pass through such transition with safety, an independent standing ground for faith in God and duty would be as needful as in the case of the most complete cataclysm and reformation.

But if the contrary prove true, if (as to all human prevision seems most probable) it be found impossible to achieve any compromise between the old and the new, then it is clear that a catastrophe of vast importance is inevitably approaching. The Churches of Christendom, and above all the Protestant Churches, have hitherto stood upon the honest belief of intelligent men. Whatever hypocrisy or pious frauds may at

---

[1] A remarkable exception, however, is the extension of the "Brahmo Somaj," or "Church of the One God," in Bengal, founded by Rammohun Roy, and now numbering 14 branch churches, holding the purest Theistic Creed, and applying it with noble energy to the moral progress of the nation, to the obliteration of caste, the instruction of the lower orders, and the elevation of woman.

any time have been used for their support, we are persuaded
they have hurt rather than helped them.   But if the time ever
come when this state of things can go on no longer, when
there must be a defect either in the honesty or the intelligence
of the adherents of the Churches, then a fatal change will pass
over them.   The tree whose root is dead, or whose stem is
hollow, may continue to put forth leaves for a few years, but
it must wither at last.   The symptoms of such approaching
decay in the Christian Churches will doubtless follow in natural
sequence ; and the refusal of the higher class of minds to adopt
the ministry as a profession will be succeeded rapidly by the
further and further depreciation of the mental status of the
Church, and by a growing public sense of its hollowness and
incapacity to meet the problems of the age.   When this de-
teriorating process has reached a certain length, all the public
and private interests involved in the Churches' conservation,
all the vast *vis inertia* of such an institution, so long solidly
established on English soil, and rooted alike in English prejudices and English sacred affections—all these securities, so
often quoted as guaranteeing its immutable maintenance, must
give way at last and fail.   There is no durable foundation for
a religion whatsoever, save the sincere belief of its adherents.

If these things be true of Traditional Christianity, then, as
we have said, a solemn catastrophe is slowly, but surely, approaching.   The great Ship which has been the Ark of humanity so long, and which even now unfurls its sails so proudly to
the winds, that great and noble ship is, perhaps, in our own
time settling slowly down and sinking under the waters of an
unfathomable sea.   A mournful and a terrible sight it would
be, were we not assured that all the souls it bears are for ever
safe, and that all its freight of precious truths will float up
again with unerring safety, even from the forgotten depths of
time.

The task of him who would most essentially benefit his race
in a time like this, must be to prepare men to meet unharmed
the inevitable future.   He must supply them with a faith
which will remain undisturbed when the great change arrives.

The perils of finding ourselves standing alone without a
God to love or a law to obey, while the frail structure of the
creed of our youth fell around us, like a tent on Lebanon, before the blast of the storm—these perils may be known to
many of us, and happy are they who have survived them in full

spiritual and moral life. Happy are they who slowly and painfully have built up stone by stone for themselves from the foundation a shelter for their souls ; who have begun perchance with naught, save the resolution

> " I will be just and wise and mild,
> Since in me lies such power,"

and then have found that in the hard struggles of the higher self after victory over temptation, they have become conscious that there was ONE present at the fight—One who could aid them with Almighty help, " strengthening them with might by His Spirit in the inner man "—One who when the battle was done would take His soldier to an eternal home. Happy are they who have learned such things ; but *they* know best through what dangers they have passed, and to which they were consigned by the teachers who bade them hold by a creed full of contradictions and difficulties, or else abandon all hope that God would hear their prayers. To them, above all, it will seem terrible that the masses of men, the uneducated, the over-tried sons of toil, should have to pass through such perils ; not one by one as now, but, as it may soon be, by thousands and millions, enhancing all each others' difficulties, and liable to the most fearful aberrations. In view of such a cataclysm, many would fain, with cowardly hearts, strive to put off the evil day and keep away from men's minds all such questions. But it is not in their hands to do so. The tide cannot be stopped by any Canute's decree. It is the great divinely-ordered progress of thought which has brought us to this pass, and we may take courage from the knowledge that He who caused it will guide us through. We must not, dare not, doubt that it will be to a larger, higher, purer truth the human race is being led onward ; and that that truth is *safer* even than all the well-tried errors of the past. The old Ragnarok, the " Twilight of the Gods," in which our heathen forefathers believed, may be coming now ; but there will be a glorious sunrise afterwards. The true " Ages of Faith " are not behind us, but before.

The task, then, as we have said, of the religious teacher of our time, is to prepare and strengthen men for the future ; to give them such faith in God and reverence for His law, *independently* of traditional creeds, as shall avail when these creeds are overwhelmed. He must enable every man to say with the brave Bishop of Natal, " I should tremble at the results of my

inquiries, were it not that I believe firmly in a God of righteousness and truth and love. Should all else give way beneath
me, I feel that His everlasting arms are still under me. *That*
truth I see with my spirit's eyes, once opened to the light of it,
as plainly as I see the sun in the heavens; and that truth, more
or less distinctly apprehended, has been the food of living men,
the strength of brave souls that yearn for light, and battle for
the right and true, the support of struggling and sorrow-
stricken hearts, in all ages of the world, in all climes, under
all religions." The lesson for ever repeated by Christian
teachers that, save within the shadow of their churches, no
prayer can be offered with hope of acceptance on high—that
false and fatal lesson must be disproved and for ever discarded.
The very opposite teaching must be given,—that in the solemn
search for truth, to which every strong soul must sooner or
later betake itself, the help of God, regarded as simply the
LORD OF TRUTH, and not the Patron of this or that theological
system, is the one thing needful for our success. When we most
of all *want* God's spirit to guide us, and God's law to keep us
in that path of duty wherein alone the mental eye is unclouded,
we shall not then be left to lament that we have lost them
hopelessly. We shall rather find, on the contrary, with relief
indescribable, that the hands from which the fetters have fallen
for ever are those which rise the most freely in supplication to
heaven. Our teacher must do this for us, he must accomplish the task which Rénan lays down as the especial one
of our age, " Transporter la religion par delà le surnaturel,
séparer la cause à jamais triomphante de la religion, de la
cause perdue du miracle." [1] In a word, the teacher whom we
need must find for us the true foundation of faith, and must
build thereon a fortress within, and behind the old tottering
walls of tradition, so that whensoever these may crumble and fall
the souls of men may dwell secure, viewing the ruin around
them without dismay, while their faith in God and in His
righteous law remains undisturbed for ever. Thus shall that
teacher prove himself a Preserver and Renovator of Faith, a
BUILDER, not a Destroyer. Incidentally, and to make his work
secure, he must needs dig deep and clear away much rubbish;
but he does it for the purpose of restoration. The destructives
are his antagonists, who would fain leave humanity with no
faith, save the one which all their efforts can never repair, and

[1] La Chaire d'Hébreu au Collége de France. Par Ernest Rénan, p. 30.

who for its maintenance would deprive us of that reliance on conscience and the religious sentiment whereon alone the ultimate ground of *any* faith, even of their own, is to be found.

While contemplating, however, the noble task which might belong to such a teacher as we have supposed, we are arrested by a singular difficulty which it is clear would meet him from the side of those who ought naturally to be his allies. The wide-spread upheaving of thought of which we have spoken has brought out, along with its great and deep benefits, a phase of feeling which may now be traced pervading the higher order of minds of all nominal sections of opinion, orthodox no less than heterodox. Beside the counter-revolution of those who hold tenaciously by the past in proportion as they perceive it to be slipping away from them; beside the far more deplorable error of those who in every religious reformation of the world make an advancing creed the pretext for a retrograde morality; beside all these, there exists a class of minds who have impatiently carried beyond the limits of reason the tendencies of the age, who have abandoned, not only a definite faith, but the hopes of finding any definite faith whatever. Very great and very true is the impression which has been felt in our day of the mystery which surrounds human life on all sides, of the fallibility of all human knowledge, and of the ineffable, impenetrable Majesty of that awful Being whose nature our forefathers presumed to parcel out and analyze as a chemist might do the water or the air. We no longer look on the different creeds of the world, as the martyrs did of old, as being absolutely true or absolutely false, the service of God himself or of the Devil himself. We perceive them to be only steps upward in an infinite ascent, only the substitution for a lower of a higher but still all imperfect ideal of the Holy One. Doubtless we are nearer to the true judgment now. Doubtless also it was well that of old, in the days of the stake and the rack, men should have seen these things differently, for few indeed could have borne to die clearly discerning their persecutors to be only partially mistaken in their own creed; the creed for which they were enduring torture and agony,—only one of the thousand "little systems" of earth

" Which have their day, and cease to be,"

a "broken light" from the inaccessible Sun of Truth. If a

few sublime Socratic souls might have been found contented thus to bear all things sooner than renounce that one ray of purer light which had been granted to them, yet never could ordinary men and timid women, the rank and file of the army of martyrs, have fought the good fight under such banners.   It was needful for them to discern in outward objective dogmas a distinction of good and evil, which in truth existed subjectively in the fidelity or unfaithfulness of their own souls to such light as they possessed.   For them our modern breadth of thought would have seemed culpable latitudinarianism, and our habit of pouring the new wine of our own ideas into the old bottles of sacred formulæ a mockery and a snare. Ignatius and Polycarp, Latimer and Hooper, would have bitterly despised the alchemy which can "distil Astral Spirits out of dead churches," and find something in Paganism and something in Popery transmutable at will into Christianity and Protestantism.   But we in our day have reached a different pass.   We seem to have quitted the region of light and darkness, truth and falsehood, and to have come to a land

> "Where it is always afternoon."

There is among the highest order of minds a disposition to accept finally a condition which may be designated as one of reverential scepticism.   They doubt not only whether any true religious creed has yet been found, but whether a mind penetrated with due modesty should seek to find one.   While the age vaunts itself of being peculiarly one of religious earnestness, it has thus come to pass that it is peculiarly one of religious despair.   We have ceased to think that a great intellect can possess a great faith.

A sort of direful fashion has set in to praise whatever seems vaguest in doctrine and weakest in faith, as if *therefore* it were necessarily wisest and most philosophic.   We look distrustfully on any one who has not dissolved away in some mental crucible all solid belief in a Personal God, and a conscious immortality into certain fluid and gaseous ideas of Eternities and Immensities.   We assume it contentedly as proven that the "limitations of religious thought" make it as hopeless for us to find a faith which will keep alive our souls as an elixir vitæ to keep alive our bodies.   We wander to and fro hopelessly through the wilderness of doubt, and if any come to tell us of a land flowing with milk and honey, the glory of all lands, which they have found beyond, we dismiss them with a complacent sigh, even if they bring back from their Canaan the noblest fruits.

There is surely great error in this state of feeling. Though infallible knowledge is not for man, though we have neither faculties to receive it nor language to convey it, yet it is far indeed from established, that our powers fall short of attaining such a share of knowledge of Divine things as may suffice for the primary wants of our souls. We need such knowledge for the higher part of our nature, as much as we need bread and clothing for the lower. It is the greatest want of the greatest creature, and if it indeed have no supply, then is the analogy of the universe broken off. There is a presumption of incalculable force, that these cravings which arise in the profoundest depths of our souls, which we can never put away, and on which all our moral health depends, are not to be for ever denied their natural satisfaction, while the ravens are fed and the grass of the field drinks in the dew. We have, indeed, asked hitherto for too much. We have called for whole systems of theology, dissecting with blasphemous audacity the mysteries of our awful Maker's nature and attributes. We have cried like children for the moon of an unattainable infallibility. But because these things are denied us, are we therefore to despair of knowing those fundamental truths which we must either gain or else morally and spiritually die? It would be to assume the main point in question, to argue that a Father in Heaven must needs make Himself and His righteous law known to His children. But it is a simple induction from the order of the universe, to conclude that the soul of man is not the only thing left without its food, its light, its guide, its sole-sufficing end and aim.

If, then, it be not improbable that a religion is to be found supplying us with such knowledge, but on the contrary, a thing to be predicted from man's nature and the order of the world; then, he who comes forward to tell us he has found this needful knowledge is not to be hastily dismissed as a dreamer. His special faith may be true or false, but some such faith as his is what we have to look for with well-grounded hope of success.

It is in this light, then, as a teacher of those cardinal truths of religion which are needful for our souls' higher life—those truths which we have reason to trust are within our powers to

know,—as a builder up of faith—that faith which will remain
unshaken upon the rock of human nature itself, when time
shall have levelled every edifice built on the shifting sands of
tradition; it is thus that Theodore Parker claims to be heard.

A few brief words concerning his doctrines and his life may,
perhaps, be useful, by enabling the reader hitherto unac-
quainted with his writings to apprehend their bearing more
perfectly.   These writings, however, are so clear and honest,
and that noble life was so simple in its absolute devotion to its
holy purpose, that small space will suffice to speak for both.

There are four bases logically possible for a religion,—a
living inspired Head, an infallible Church, an authoritative
Book, an individual Consciousness.   Of these four, Parker
chose the last, leaving such creeds as Mormonism and Lamaism
on the first, Romanism on the second, Calvinism on the third,
and scores of intermediate churches shifting illogically between all four.   The reasons for his rejection of the first three
bases of religion are set forth at length in his writings, as also
for his reliance on the veracity of Consciousness, corroborated
for the individual by the consciousness of the wise and good
of all ages.[1]

Standing on this ground of Consciousness, he preached the
great doctrine of Theism, the ABSOLUTE GOODNESS OF GOD.
Every man is conscious of revering and loving certain moral
characteristics, and of hating and despising certain others.
Here, then, we find the assurance that He who made us to feel
such reverence on one side and such contempt on the other,

---

[1] It is, perhaps, needful to guard against the accusation so constantly reiterated against the adherents of Consciousness as a basis of religious faith, that they
actually stand on the lessons of Christianity, while *professedly* disavowing their
authority.   The truth is, that the hypothesis of Darwin (whether true or false,
as regards the genesis of animal species) very aptly represents the natural history
of the various creeds of mankind.   Each one rises out of another, which chrono-
logically preceded it—the strongest and noblest types being the parents of off-
spring, which reproduce in still higher forms their special excellencies.   He who
would pretend in our day to stand free from all obligations to Christianity,
would boast as absurdly as he who should deny his obligations to his parents,
his ancestors, and all the antecedents of his family and nation.   But, in like
manner, he who thinks that St John could have written his Gospel without a
Plato before him, or St Paul his Epistles without a Zeno, would think also that
Newton might have written the Principia had no Pythagoras or Euclid preceded him.   Consciousness, as a basis of theology, is *strengthened*, not discredited,
by every evidence that the greatest saints and sages of all time have corroborated
its truths.   The highest philosophy asks no man to *originate or invent* the
truths of theology, but only when such truths are presented to him in any mode,
to possess the consciousness of their veracity.

is Himself all that He has caused us to revere and love, and never has been or can be aught that by the constitution of our nature we hate or despise. The difference between the characters ascribed to God by traditional creeds and by Theism lies in this, that the traditional creeds, though attributing every *epithet* of honour to Him, yet in effect neutralize them all by delineations of His dealings with mankind wholly at variance with the natural sense of such epithets, insomuch that the words " Good " and " Merciful," when applied to God, have often come to bear as conventional a sense as the titles of honour appropriated to the petty royalties of earth. Theism, on the contrary, confessedly rests its conception of the Divine character on such consciousness as He has Himself given us of what is Good and Just. This consciousness is as yet all imperfect and incomplete. God must be *more* good than our conception of goodness, as the heavens are higher than the earth. But *so far as it goes*, our consciousness is true, and *negatively* it must be absolutely true. God's character—could all its awful splendours be revealed to us, God's dealings with His creatures—could all their scope and purport from eternity to eternity be unveiled before our eyes, might never bear one blot or contain one act which in our heart of hearts we could regard as cruel or unjust,—nay, that we could fail to adore as infinitely good and merciful.

Thus Theism teaches that God is absolutely, infinitely, eternally good, *in our sense of goodness;* not good only to angels, Jews, and Christians,—a few elect out of a lost world ; not good only in Time, and tremendous in the Day of Wrath, when Time shall be no more,—but good to all, good for ever, able and willing to bring back every creature He has made to be folded at last in His eternal love.

And in the most awful of all mysteries, the mystery of Sin and its forgiveness, this same Absolute Goodness of God is our hope and our refuge. We need no other, and (as Channing said well) " a broader and a surer the universe cannot supply." Theism teaches that God, the Just Ruler, must punish sin, but it also assures us that God, the Good One, can only do so in the highest love. In His government, Retribution and Correction are one and the same. The sins of a finite being—finite in number and graduated in degree—are necessarily finite also, and deserving of finite retribution. The sins of a creature of God, made by Him in His own image, are necessarily capable of correction and susceptible of final purification. The repentant sinner seeks the restoration of his soul to the peace of Divine love, but he leaves the punishment of his offences to God's wisdom and God's justice. No "substitute" can ever bear it for him, no "conversion" of his own can evade it. The doom of sin is not an infinite *risk* with a large margin for escape. It is the *certainty* of a complete, albeit finite, retribution.

In God, the "Parent of Good, Almighty," we have both parents in One. All the power and care and forethought and inexorable loving severity which we attribute to the Fatherly character is fulfilled in Him. And all the inexhaustible forgiving love and tenderness which a mother's heart reveals, is His also. Like a father, He supplies our bodily wants and the spiritual food for the higher needs of our souls. Like a mother, He bestows on us the flowers and fruits of earth and all the thousand innocent joys, which are needless for mere existence, but are given to make us happy, to win our hearts to confidence and thankfulness. Too long has the Catholic Church separated off this *Mother Side* of Deity into another object of worship ; and more fatal still has been the error of the Reformed Churches, who in rejecting the Madonna, have rejected all that she imaged forth of the Divine mansuetude and tenderness. God is Himself and alone (as Parker often rightly addressed Him in his prayers) "THE FATHER AND MOTHER OF THE WORLD." Theism bids us adore Him with the mingled sentiments of reverence and love due to both relations. Nay, it bids us behold in His sole ineffable Unity all that men have dimly shadowed out in the creeds of the past, the "Lord of Light," the "Mover" of all things, the "Greatly Wise Lord," the "All-Father," the "Eternal One," and, above all, the triune God of Christendom, the God who in Himself alone is to us Creating, Redeeming, and Sanctifying God.

Such is the first great doctrine of Theism, THE ABSOLUTE GOODNESS OF GOD.

And the second is like it and flows out of it.

God is ever present in the souls of His creatures. He presides over and governs the world of matter, and He is no less present and active in the world of spirit. As He influences and constrains unconscious matter, so He inspires and helps free and conscious man. There is but one *kind* of inspiration possible, albeit many *degrees* thereof. It is the action of the

Holiest on the souls of His creatures, affording moral help through the conscience, and spiritual light through the intellect. We call the first *Grace*, the second *Inspiration*, but they are one and the same; "the light which lighteth every man that cometh into the world"—the power by which we are "strengthened with might by God's Spirit in the inner man." This Divine action cannot be accidental or miraculous, but normal and universal as gravitation itself; the most natural of all things, a fact implied in the relation of the Father of Spirits to His children; of the Creator to the creature which lives and moves and has its being in Him.

This is the second great doctrine of Theism, THE IMMANENCE OF GOD IN THE SOUL, or, in other words, the normal character of Inspiration. It is the key-stone of Parker's peculiar theology, and from it he deduced all his further propositions.

Thirdly, Inspiration being natural and universal, it is a thing of all nations and ages. *Every* good and perfect gift has come down from the Father of Lights, whether it was bestowed three thousand years ago or to-day, in Palestine or England. It was a real inspiration of God which taught Isaiah and Paul; and we may accept all their holy words which touch our consciences and kindle our piety as being truly God's teaching, worthy of all reverence and love. And it was also a real inspiration which taught Plato and Milton; and whatever words of theirs were great and holy, and touch our consciences and kindle our piety, they also we may take as God's teaching with reverence and love.

> " The same great Inspiration through all the ages roll'd,
> Breaking through Moses' tardy lips and Plato's mouth of gold."

Thus the world is not robbed of its Divine Scriptures, but *every* good and true and helpful book becomes for us a Divine Scripture.

Fourthly, Inspiration is limited by the capacity and by the faithfulness of the souls which receive it. "As we draw nigh to Him so He draws nigh to us," said Seneca. As the soul is large by nature and education, so large can its inspiration be. "The cup of ocean is full as the harebell." But none can be infallibly, universally, absolutely inspired. Perfect inspiration could be received only by perfect beings fulfilling absolutely all the laws of mind and morals. In man there must always remain somewhat merely human, personal, fallible. The light

which comes pure from the Sun of Truth is refracted as it
enters the atmosphere of our thoughts, and receives from it
colours of all kinds—doubly refracted when it is reproduced
in human language.   There is somewhat of Divine and somewhat of human in the noblest thoughts and words of man.
As God aids him morally by His grace, and yet never makes
him *impeccable*, so He aids him intellectually by inspiration,
yet never makes him *infallible*.   Thus all the limitations and
errors of the Bible are explained without either destroying its
value or forcing us to do violence to reason and our moral
instincts ; they are recognized as the human element which
inevitably blended with the Divine.   And thus also is it explained how he, who of all the human race most perfectly
fulfilled the conditions under which inspiration is granted to
man ; he, the best beloved of all the sons of God, whose coming
was to the life of humanity what regeneration is to the life of
the individual, may have erred concerning many things, concerning demoniacs, and the end of the world, and the prophecies he connected with himself, and yet may have spoken,
on the Mount of Olives and by the well-side of Samaria, the
deepest truths God ever taught to His creatures ; lessons as
immediately Divine as any voice of thunder from the sky could
have proclaimed.

   Fifthly, From the universality of Inspiration, Parker deduced
the corollary of the trustworthiness of all facts of consciousness, which can be shown to be common to the human race
under normal conditions of development.   Such truths are
necessarily given to the consciousness by Divine aid, they are
written on the soul of man by that hand which writes no
falsehood.

   Thus, our Moral Intuitions are Divine.   They reveal to
us the immutable and eternal laws which are resumed in the
righteous will of God, and which He has taught to His rational
creatures, that through voluntary obedience to them we may attain to the highest end of our being, even an eternal approach
to holiness and to Himself.

   And the idea of an Immortal Life is Divine.   It is a fact of
consciousness given in the nature of man, and appearing
under every circumstance of race and creed and age.   We
may trust to it as God's implanting, the promise of a world
wherein our ideal of God's goodness, so often tried with

mysteries of evil and sin and suffering here, will be fulfilled and overpassed beyond our highest dreams.

Sixthly and lastly, From the doctrine that God is for ever present and active in the souls of His creatures, it follows that it is possible for man to obtain communion with Him at all times. Prayer (for spiritual blessings) is no self-acting delusion. It is a real drawing nigh of the soul to God. There *is* " One who heareth prayer," and who is ever near us waiting to hear and bless it. The relation between the creature and the Creator, unconscious in the material part, and at best a dim sympathy in the intellectual love of truth and the æsthetic sense of beauty, becomes conscious and vivid in the moral and spiritual when the will of man bows itself freely before the will of God, and the finite and infinite spirits meet in the awful communion of intense Prayer. It is the most sacred of all mysteries,—the most solemn thing in all man's life, the greatest reality of his existence. The help and light to be gained through such prayer is a natural thing, not a miraculous one. We do not ask God to change His laws, but to fulfil them. It is the law of spirit, that as we draw to Him so He draws to us. The magnetic bar which has lost its power, regains it when we hang it in the plane of the meridian. The plant which was sickly, weak, and white, growing in the shade, acquires health and verdure in the sunshine. If we bring our pale, faded souls within the rays of God's warmth we may say with confidence, " Heal us, O Father! for we *know* that it is Thy will."

The creed which we have now summed up so briefly has few articles :

AN EVER PRESENT GOD WHO IS ABSOLUTELY GOOD.

A MORAL LAW WRITTEN IN THE CONSCIOUSNESS OF MAN.

THE IMMORTALITY OF THE SOUL.

THE REALITY OF SPIRITUAL PRAYER.

This is the entire theology of Theodore Parker. It contains no doctrines of a Fall, an Incarnation, a Trinity, an Atonement, a Devil, or a Hell,—no Original Sin, and no Imputed Righteousness. Its Morality is summed up in the Two Great Commandments of the Law, and its " Theory of Reconciliation " in the parable of the " Prodigal Son."

To this religion, at once spiritual and rational, Parker gave the name of THEISM,—a name antithetic to Atheism alone, and comprehensive of every worshipper of God ; a name not understood, like the elder Deism, to signify the exclusion of Christianity, but the inclusion of it in one great Absolute Religion.

Theism differs thus, on the one hand, from all such Atheistic, Pantheistic, or Deistic systems as either tell us that there is no God, or that He is an Impersonal Power, or that He is a Great First Cause removed from all reach of human prayers. All such systems as these, even such as admit the existence of God and assume the name of Religions, yet eliminate from religion that which is its vital element—the belief in a real intercourse of prayer and assistance, of repentance and forgiveness, of obedience and guidance, between man and God.

And Theism differs, on the other hand, from all such Christian creeds as profess to tell us of an ever present God, yet affirm all our certain knowledge of Him to be derived from the evidence of tradition concerning long past supernatural events. All such creeds, while admitting a spiritual intercourse between God and the soul, distort and trammel such intercourse by false and unnatural representations of our relation to Him, and by setting at variance the emotions of piety and the dictates of reason.   Thus while the popular creed (albeit nourishing in its disciples the purest spirituality) opposes itself continually to their intellects and moral instincts, and Pantheism and Deism (albeit professedly meeting the claims of the intellect and moral instincts) exclude spirituality—the religion which Parker taught combines all that is noblest in both systems,—the spirituality which springs from belief in a real intercourse between God and the soul, and the intellectual and moral harmony of a creed confessedly founded on human consciousness.

In so far as it can be proved to do this, in so far does Parker's creed command our highest consideration, for it is precisely to the union of a Rational and a Spiritual faith that the hopes of men are directed now in a manner hitherto unknown. We have learned, at last, to recognize that the Intellect is a Divine gift, even as the Religious Feelings are Divine gifts, and that it is not only a senseless but an *impious* endeavour to sacrifice the one for the other.   And, on the other hand, we have learned that a conscious communion between man and God is the essence of religion, and that any creed which excludes it,—be it never so philosophic in all beside,—is of less value than any creed which enables men to attain it,—be it

never so poor and irrational in all beside.   Thus then, for religion's own sake, we ask for an intellectual faith ; and for all
the dearest interests of the soul, we ask that that intellectual
faith shall ratify the spiritual part of our religion.   Hitherto,
with the exception of a few philosophers, men have commonly
sought and found in their traditional creeds the means of attaining such spirituality as they desired, and have been content
to give up reason for their sakes.   Every religion, perhaps, has
enabled some of its votaries to attain to a real intercourse with
God, and, like the churches of Latin and Copt, Greek and
Maronite, clustered around the Holy Sepulchre, each *opens into*
the true sanctuary, which not one of them all can claim as its
own, or monopolize for itself.   But for us, in our time, it has
come to pass that there is no entrance possible into the
fane, save through the vestibule of a creed which shall preserve inviolate all the rights of the intellect and the moral
instincts.   When we have found *this* way to the Holy Place,
we may press forward with God's saints of every age and
creed, even into the innermost shrine of a conscious communion
with Him.   When we have arrived *there*, even the way we
came will become indifferent.

Such then, in brief, is the Theology expounded in these
volumes.   Parker never claimed for it, and none will claim for
him, that it is a perfect system, absolutely true and complete
in all its parts.   Such things are not for man, and the sooner
we dismiss the pretenders to them the better.   It will still be
the best and wisest of existing theologies if it afford us a chart
of the great ocean of thought, to be more and more fully filled
up by explorers for ages to come, and yet sufficient now to
enable us to steer our barks to the haven.   We believe that
there are signs enough within the churches, and without them,
to justify the anticipation that such a theology will do a noble
work ; that those who have abandoned all existing creeds in
despair, will be able here to find a reasonable and a welcome faith ; and that it will legitimatize to their own minds
the aspirations of thousands more, who are yet within the pale
of traditionalism, but daily find that it is the THEISM IN
CHRISTIANITY which is their bread of life ; and that all beyond
is a difficulty and a stumblingblock.   Reville says well, " Pour
nous aussi, au moment où les edifices et les traditions sécu-
laires menacent de s'écrouler, quand on se demande avec anxiété

s'ils n'écraseront pas sous leurs décombres et ceux qui les ébranlent et ceux qui les défendent, un homme tel que Parker est un prophète de consolation et d'espérance." [1]

In the hope that thus it may prove, these Works of Theodore Parker are published in England.

The chief interest of these books is, of course, a theological one ; and to discourses immediately directed to that subject, the first three volumes of the present series are devoted.   It was, however, a leading principle of their author, that religion was no concern for the church and sabbath-day alone, but for all the pursuits and affairs of man.   Accordingly, we find him applying his faith to every good work which his hand found to do.   In his own pulpit, and over the whole country, he laboured to arouse the consciences of his countrymen to their national sins, their unjust wars, their unrighteous politics, the miseries of the poor, the degradation of women, and above all, the one monster crime of slavery, from which America is now purging herself through seas of blood.   Among the sermons and lectures he delivered on these topics, three volumes of the present series have been arranged as Discourses of Politics, of Slavery, and of Sociology.   Beyond these, again, as a man of vast learning and fine literary taste, Parker wrote a variety of papers on matters of scholarship and history, collected in two volumes of Critical and Miscellaneous Writings.   The first of these is already known in England ; the second will consist of articles now first collected from various sources, many of them of great interest and beauty.

As in this long series of works the greater part consists of detached addresses, it will be anticipated that the great fundamental truths, which it was the task of his life to enforce, were frequently reproduced.   A large portion of the matter now collected was taken down by shorthand writers from extempore sermons and orations. These facts will account for occasional repetitions, and for the expressions, perhaps, sometimes all too vivid, of sarcasm and scorn, against the errors of Calvinistic theology and pro-slavery politics.   To the congregation, whose prayers he had led with profoundest reverence, the eloquent outbursts of his subsequent discourse would naturally assume a wholly different character from that they bear to us, who read coldly the notes

[1] Revue des Deux Mondes, 1 Octobre, 1861, p. 746.

of the same discourses, unaware how it was the very greatness
of his reverence for things truly holy, which inflamed his
Luther-like soul with iconoclastic zeal.

As to the extraordinary clearness and didactic lucidity of
Parker's style (strangely resembling that of old Hugh de St Victor, in his monkish Latin), there is no need to apologize for it.
"I always think," said he, "that I am addressing, *not* the highest minds, but the simplest and most uneducated among my
congregation ; and I strive to say everything so that *they* may
understand me." Thus truly did he preach his great gospel
of God's goodness to the poor ; and in a way, perhaps, which
would be safe to few theologians. Always we find him stating
the major term of his syllogism, "God is infinitely good.
Now, what follows ?"

It would seem as if there were two forms of the love of
truth among men. In the one it is an affirmative love, a
forcible grasp thereof, which affords a fulcrum strong enough
to move the world ; yet often leaving the holder without any
accurate sense of the limitations of his creed, and without
much power to appreciate the creeds of others. In the other,
it is a negative love of truth, which takes the form of a hatred
of error, and induces the man to spend his life in stripping his
own creed leaf by leaf, like a rose, of its external and more
questionable doctrines, while he sees vividly the collateral
truths in the creeds of others. Theodore Parker belonged
essentially to the first order of minds. None have preached
with nobler, manlier faith the affirmative truths of absolute religion. In treating of the popular theology, it must be avowed
that, to the majority of Englishmen, his wide human sympathies
will seem to fall short in this one point, and that he has sometimes
appeared to confound the Christianity of the churches generally
with Calvinism, and to have drawn Calvinism itself either from
the grim treatises of the old Puritan divines, or from living
exponents of their doctrine, not to be paralleled on this side
the Atlantic. It is due to one so great in his simple in-
tegrity as Parker, that even those who owe him most of gratitude should thus avow where they find his limitations.

On the side of some of the deeper mysteries of experimental
religion, of repentance and regeneration, Parker said and wrote
but little. He ever strove to give his hearers the fullest, richest faith in the infinite love and goodness of God ; and then
he left that divine alchemy to do its work and infuse a holier

and purer life into their souls. Even to those who came to
him for counsel he commonly acted thus; he lifted their eyes
to God, and then bade them in His light behold their duties.

Happily for those who might regret that he had told us no
more of his thoughts on these matters, we possess in Newman's Book of the Soul, the noblest exposition of the practical
doctrines of a deeply spiritual Theism.

Such, then, are the writings of Theodore Parker now presented to the public. It will be for the reader to judge for
himself of their prophetic power and truth, their glowing eloquence, their profound and varied learning, and of that supreme
honesty of purpose which made Lowell say of him,

> "Every word that he speaks has been fierily furnaced
> In the blast of a life which has struggled in earnest."

Of the life and actions of Parker little need here be said.
The concluding volume of this series will contain his few
autobiographical remains, and possibly the Memoir shortly to
be published by his friends in America. A few words may,
however, be not inappropriately prefixed to his writings; for
of him, more than of most men, might it be said that his doctrines and his life were one. What he preached to the world
he had first found in the depth of his own consciousness, and
that which he preached he lived out in his own noble life.
The great lessons of the Absolute Religion truly penetrated
his whole being. He seemed always to live in the light of
God's love, and to be able to work for his fellows with the un-
wavering faith and tireless energy of one who actually beheld
in vision the foregleams of an immortality, wherein all souls
shall be redeemed and glorified.

Theodore Parker was born in 1810, near Lexington, Mas-
sachusetts. His parents were of the yeoman class, and old
Puritan stock. His grandfather had fired the first shot in the
war of Independence. From childhood he was a laborious
student; at twenty-four, after passing through Harvard Uni-
versity, he knew ten languages, and before his death he is said
to have acquired no less than twenty. His vocation was little
doubtful. "In my early boyhood," he says, "I *felt* I was to be
a minister." In 1837 he was ordained and appointed to the
Unitarian Church at West Roxbury, near Boston. Very soon

the emancipation from all fetters of thought which he had always sought, brought him to conclusions far beyond his fellow-Unitarians. "The worship of the Bible as a Fetish hindered me at every step." He wrote two sermons of the Historical and Moral Contradictions in the Bible, but hesitated for a year to preach them, lest he should "weaken men's respect for true religion by rudely showing them that they worshipped an idol." But at length he could wait no longer, and to ease his conscience preached his two sermons. His hearers told him "of the great comfort they had given them." "I continued," he says after this, "my humble studies, and as fast as I found a new truth I preached it. At length, in 1841, I preached a discourse of the Transient and Permanent in Christianity." This was the crisis. The other ministers, both Trinitarian and Unitarian, were profoundly indignant, and so far as in them lay excommunicated him. "Some of them would not speak to me in the street, and in their public meetings they left the benches where I sat down." Then he delivered in Boston the lectures which eventually were published in an enlarged form as "Discourses of Matters Pertaining to Religion,"—the book of which the present volume is a reprint of the fourth edition.

In September, 1843, Parker came to Europe, and after a year's travel returned to Boston, strengthened in heart and health. On the 16th February, 1845, he entered on the ministry of that congregation (the 28th Congregational Society), which he served with unwearied energy till that fatal morning, fourteen years afterwards, when his excessive labours brought on bleeding from the lungs, and his place knew him no more.

The present volumes will convey but a partial idea of the extent of Parker's labours during the years of his ministry, the sermons he preached, the orations and lectures he delivered through the States, the books he wrote, the studies he prosecuted, and, above all, the philanthropic and anti-slavery labours which he originated and aided. His congregation, which eventually became the largest in Boston, was foremost in every project of social improvement in the city, and the most outspoken and daring of the abolition party. They formed, under Parker's presidency, a committee of vigilance for the aid of slaves, and in the course of a year succeeded in passing four hundred coloured men and women into Canada. The Fugitive

Slave Bill he openly announced he would resist by force, and in 1851 he sheltered in his house a man and wife who formed part of his congregation, and whose master sought to reclaim them. He wrote his sermon that week with his pistol in his desk before him! In the same year another negro, named Sims, was arrested in Boston, and Parker's efforts for his relief, his attendance on him to the vessel in which he was borne back to slavery, and his discourses afterwards, roused so much animosity, that a prosecution against him was commenced, and only relinquished when it was found that his imprisonment would be a triumph for his cause. It was on this occasion he prepared the elaborate "Defence" to be reprinted in the 10th volume of this series,—also the splendid sermons "on Conscience," and on "the Laws of God and the Statutes of Man."

His courage in the anti-slavery cause, and indeed in every cause he had at heart, was such as might be expected of the preacher of such a faith. Obnoxious beyond any other man in America, both on account of his religion and his politics, he never once failed to go wherever his voice or his presence could be of use, delivering lectures in all parts of the country, and entering meetings where he was an object of bitterest rancour. On one such an occasion we have been told by an eye-witness that he was standing in a gallery at a large pro-slavery meeting in New York, when one of the orators tauntingly remarked, "I should like to know what Theodore Parker would say to this!" "Would you like to know?" cried he, starting forward into view,—"I'll tell you what Theodore Parker says to it!" Of course there instantly arose a tremendous clamour and threats of killing him and throwing him over. Parker simply squared his broad chest, and looking to the right and the left, said, undauntedly, "Kill me? Throw me over? you shall do no such thing. Now I'll tell you what I say to this matter." His bravery quelled the riot at once.

Parker's intellectual endowments were of the highest class, and enabled him to defend his religious creed with the power of a clear head and an eloquent tongue. The peculiar characteristic of his mental faculties seemed to be a singular lucidity and clearness of arrangement of facts and ideas. These great natural gifts, combined with so much daring originality of thought, would have been perilous had he not laboured to supply himself with such a ballast of deep and solid learning as served to keep his mind steadily balanced. It has been already said that he understood ten languages. Of their literature, ancient and modern, his amazing knowledge will be sufficiently proved by the notes appended to the present volume. It would probably be difficult to parallel, save in Germany, a scholarship at once so varied and so recondite. For the carefulness and minuteness thereof also, let his recension of De Wette's treatise on the Old Testament testify.

But if God had endowed Parker with a noble intellect and he had honestly multiplied his five talents to ten, there was yet a greater gift which he possessed in still richer measure. The strong, clear head was second to the warm, true heart. Parker loved his friends with a devotion of which men in our day so rarely give proof, that we claim it as the privilege of a woman to know its happiness, albeit such love becomes as much the manliness of a man as the womanliness of a woman. His tenderness to his wife and to all around him broke out in a thousand little gentle cares and delicate thoughtfulnesses continually. No man was ever more beloved in the happy circle admitted to the intimacy of his home, and every mail brought him from far away lands letters of gratitude and affection. His immense power of human sympathy made itself felt so strongly, that it is said no clergyman of any creed, in our day, ever received so many confidences and confessions. No wonder that when the end of that loving life drew near he said to the writer, "I would fain be allowed to stay a little longer here if it pleased God,—the world is so interesting and friends so dear!" At the last of all, when his noble intellect was sinking under the clouds of approaching night, his tender affections were still lingering, anxiously careful for the gentle wife weeping by his side, and he dreamed that he had found comfort for her, telling us with brightening looks that though he was dying in Florence there was another Theodore Parker in America who would carry on his work and be her support and consolation.

Parker was brave, eloquent, learned, and warm-hearted all in an exceptional degree. He was also a man of fine poetic taste and love of art, and of the most refined and winning manners. There seemed no one human pursuit of an elevated kind in which he could not take interest. The element of pure joyous wit and humour was overflowing in him. Even in his graver writings this sometimes breaks out in freaks of sarcasm irrepressible, as where he argues that there can be no Devil since no print of his hoofs has been found in the Old Red Sandstone,—and that men are after all more well-disposed than the contrary, since " even South Carolina senators are *sober all the forenoon!* "   But of course it was in private life that his playful humour naturally overflowed.   We have seen letters to his intimate friends as full of pure drollery as Sydney Smith could have penned.   One we remember, for instance, in which he answered his correspondent's accounts of a journey from Rome to Naples by *his* remarkable discoveries and ethnological and antiquarian speculations on a trip down the railway two stations from Boston.   In another epistle he parodied some foolish over-illustrated biography then in vogue by extracting all the little woodcuts of advertisements of houses, steamers, &c., from the newspapers, and introducing them solemnly as " The House he was born in," " His berceaunette," " His perambulator,"—and finally " His Mother," being the well-known lady with half her hair dyed and the remainder grey !

All this versatility gave an inexpressible charm to Parker's character.   In conversing with him one chord after another was struck, and each seemed richer and sweeter than the last.   At one moment perhaps he was told of some moral results of his labours, or some poor backwoodsman wrote him a letter (we have seen a few out of many such), saying how his sermons were the food of the higher life to the writer and the rough comrades assembled weekly to hear them in their log-huts in the forests of the Far West.   Then Parker's eyes would brighten, and the tears start into them, till he turned the subject to hide his emotion, and in a moment he would jest like a boy at some passing trifle with peals of richest laughter. And growing grave again, as some deeper subject opened, he would pour out his strange hoards of learning, all arranged in his own orderly fashion, as if he had constructed a table of it, beforehand, in his memory.   Never far away were noble, sacred words of love and faith.   One of the most religious women we ever knew, said to us, " It was good only *to see* Mr Parker in his church on Sunday, before we heard him.   It made us all know that he felt the presence of God.   We saw it in his face, so full of solemn joy as he rose to lead our prayers."

Perhaps we have dwelt somewhat too fully on these details

of Parker's character; but as it is impossible for mankind wholly to refrain from forming an estimate of the root of a man's faith by the product of life which it may bear, it has seemed well thus to display, in some degree, how singularly complete and rounded was that nature which this teacher of Theism displayed. All religions, which have importantly influenced the world, have probably been qualified to produce some special virtue in eminent perfection. But the one which shall approve itself as truly divine, must nourish not only isolated merits, but all the possible virtues and faculties of human nature, such as it has been constituted by the Creator. The creeds stand self-condemned, which dwarf or kill any stem or branch, or flower or even leaflet of true humanity,—which make men emaciate and lacerate the bodies God has so wonderfully made;—or prefer hideous and monotonous churches and edifices of charity to the example of a world of endless beauty and variety;—or regard distrustfully every fresh discovery of science, instead of resting satisfied that all truth is God's truth, and to nothing but error can it be dangerous;—or check and crush their natural domestic affections, instead of regarding each one of them as a step, lent to help us up from earth to heaven;—all these creeds stand self-condemned. They may be the service of some unknown being, but they assuredly do not succeed in harmonizing the soul with the Creator of *this* world, the Divine Author of Human Nature. Nay more, the creed which should freeze all the joyous flow of wit and jest, and teach (without shadow of historical authority) that its Ideal Man " seldom smiled and never laughed "—that creed also is condemned. God who has made the playful lamb and singing lark, the whispering winds which rustle in the summer trees, and the ocean waves' " immeasurable laugh "—that same God gave, in His mercy, jest and glee and merriment to man; and here also, as in the joys of the senses and the intellect and the affections, " to enjoy is to obey." Theodore Parker's faith, at least, bore this result,—it brought out in him one of the noblest and most complete developments of our nature which the world has seen; a splendid devotion, even to death, for the holiest cause, and none the less a most perfect fulfilment of the minor duties and obligations of humanity. Though the last man in the world to claim faultlessness for himself, he was yet to all mortal eyes absolutely faithful to the resolution of his boyhood to devote himself to God's immediate service. Living in a land of special personal inquisition, and the mark for thousands of inimical scrutinies, he yet lived out his allotted time, beyond the arrows of calumny, and those who knew him best said that the words they heard over his grave seemed intended for him; "Blessed are the pure in heart, for they shall see God!" The lilies, which were his favourite flowers, and which loving hands laid on his coffin, were not misplaced thereon. Truly if men *cannot* gather grapes of thorns nor figs of thistles, then must the root of that most fruitful life have been a sound one.

At last the end came. The eloquent orations he had poured forth so freely for every righteous cause, and the incessant travelling at all seasons to deliver them, wheresoever he was called, brought out the tendencies of hereditary disease. The last journey he ever made in America was in the midst of a northern winter, and when he was already ill, to perform a funeral service in a friend's family, or rather to comfort the mourners with his sympathy, and speak to them (as he knew so well how to do) of God's great love in their affliction. He returned home much worse, but refused to give up working, and prepared as usual his sermon for the week. He had never spared himself at any time. The words of a hymn he often called for in his church fitted well his brave unwearied spirit:

> " Shall I be carried to the skies
>   On flowery beds of ease,
> While others fought to win the prize,
>   Or sail'd through bloody seas ? "

Or another, of Whittier's, which he liked equally well.

> " Hast thou through life's empty noises
>   Heard the solemn steps of time,
> And the low mysterious voices
>   Of another clime ?
> Not to ease and aimless quiet
>   Doth the inward answer tend,
> But to works of love and duty
>   As thy being's end ;
> Earnest toil and strong endeavour
>   Of a spirit, which within
> Wrestles with familiar evil
>   And besetting sin,
> And without with tireless vigour,
>   Steadfast heart and purpose strong,
> In the power of faith assaileth
>   Every form of wrong."

. Had he understood the gravity of his danger he would doubtless have accepted the duty, however dissonant to his habits, of greater care for himself. But it was hard for the strong heart lodged in the powerful frame to believe that its beatings were already numbered, or that it was needful *yet* to check labours whose full harvest daily filled his bosom. How often this same mistake is made by the choicest spirits of the world, and how inexorable is the law which stops the hand *too* ready for its holy work, we need not pause to repeat. The Life Beyond must explain it all. At best a man only finds his place and fits himself to fill it, either in the company of the Prophets or the humbler ranks of philanthropy, when he has gained almost the summit of mortal life, and all beyond must be declivity and decay. It is little marvel then if those whose hearts are truest to their labours " work while it is called the day," even with self-wasteful energy, dreading the inevitable approach of *Age*—if not yet of Death, of the day when our " windows shall be darkened and the grasshopper a burden," even before the final closing of that night " when no man can work."

Theodore Parker's fourteen years of apostleship were over. On Sunday morning, January 9th, 1859, he wrote to his congregation,—" I shall not speak to you to-day, for this morning a little after four o'clock I had a slight attack of bleeding in the lungs or throat. I hope you will not forget the contribution to the poor. I don't know when I shall again look upon your welcome faces, which have so often cheered my spirit when my flesh was weak." He *never* saw them (at least from his pulpit) again. Compelled to seek a warmer climate, he sailed with his wife and friends for Santa Cruz, where he spent the winter, and then passed through England on his way to Switzerland, where he sojourned awhile with his friend Professor Desor of Neufchâtel, and then passed on to Rome as the cold weather drew near. Friends gathered round him, dear and congenial friends whom he had known and loved at home, and for a while he seemed to do well. But as the spring drew near it became evident that the sands of life were running out ; he sank rapidly and hopelessly. His horror of the oppression and turpitude of the Papal government was so great that he could not endure to die in Rome, and made his friends (among whom was a physician, Dr Appleton, devoted altogether to his care) carry him away to pass his last hours in a free country.

As he passed out of the Roman territory and saw the Italian tricolor waving by the road-side, the dying man raised himself feebly in his carriage and lifted his hat to the emblem of liberty. By the time he had reached Florence the fatigue of the journey had left him but a little residue of days to live. He knew it. He had wished to be spared, and felt, as he had said years before in his Sermon of the Immortal Life, "It is selfish to wish for death when there is so much need of us here." But when the time came he was calm as a child. The writer, who, although aided by his words and honoured by his friendship for many years, had never seen him till that hour, found him on his bed of death, conscious of the inevitable future, but looking at it as peacefully as if it had been a summons to his home across the ocean. "You know I am not afraid to die," he said; and here a smile, the most beautiful we ever saw on a human countenance, broke over his face. "You know I am not afraid to die, but I would fain have lived a little longer to finish my work. God gave me large powers, and I have but half used them." *Half* used them! And he said this on his death-bed, whither he had been brought in the prime of manhood by *over* use of them, by the utter sacrifice of his health and strength in the cause of Truth and Right! He lingered on a few days, gently falling asleep, as it seemed, and dreaming, after the wont of the dying, that he was going on a journey, going home after his long wanderings, and only wakening, at intervals, to give a few parting gifts to friends (among others the bronze inkstand, from which these pages are written), and to comfort his wife, and say tenderest words of thanks for the little offerings of flowers, or aught beside we brought him. Now and then he would rouse himself, and speak his old brave thoughts, answering, as if to a familiar and welcome voice, if we named sacred things. Once, for example, when he asked the day of the week, and we said, "It is Sunday, a blessed day, is it not, dear friend?" "Yes!" he said, with sudden energy; "when one has got over the superstition of it, a *most* blessed day." Gradually and without pain the end came on, and on the 10th of May, 1860, he passed away from earth in perfect peace.

We cannot regard such an end otherwise than with solemn thankfulness, that God allows such men to live and work and die among us, to show us what man may do and be in this life, and to raise our thoughts to what *must* be the life to come,

for souls which have made earth itself a holy place. His most
gifted countrywoman reached Florence too late to pay to her
great fellow-abolitionist a last tribute of the respect and regard which outstripped all limits of creed. At her request the
writer gave her all the details of his last hours, and repeated
(doubtless with faithless tears) the words above quoted, concerning his unfinished labours, adding, "To think that life is
over—that work is stopped!" "And do you think," said she,
raising her eyes with a flash of rebuke, "do *you* think ;—did
he think that Theodore Parker has no work to do for God
now ? "

It must be so. He who recalled his soldier in the heat of
the battle must have a nobler command for him on high ; yet
we must miss him here, and sorely his country misses him in
her hour of trial. He was a great and a good man ; the greatest and best, perhaps, which America has produced. He was
great in many ways,—in original genius, in learning. in eloquence, and in a courage and honesty which no danger could
daunt or check. In time to come his country will glory in his
name, and the world will acknowledge all his gifts and powers.
His true greatness, however, will in future ages rest on this—
that God revealed Himself to his faithful soul, in His most
adorable aspect—that he preached with undying faith, and
lived out in his consecrated life, the lesson he had thus been
taught—that he was worthy to be the *Prophet* of the greatest
of all truths, the ABSOLUTE GOODNESS OF GOD, the central
truth of the universe.

When it was all over, and the great soul had gone home to
God, we saw him lying, as it were, asleep, a pale flush still on
his face, and his head (that noble head!) resting under a crown
of the rich pink and white roses of Tuscany. The strong man,
dead in the flower of manhood, seemed only slumbering on a
warm summer day. Never was the "rapture of repose" more
legible upon the face of death. It seemed as if God had said,
"Well done, good and faithful servant! Well hast thou spent
thy talents ten times ten!" A few days later we followed him,
to hear, as he had desired, the Beatitudes of the Gospels read
for his sole funeral service, over his grave, in the beautiful
Campo Santo of Florence. It seemed well that he should
sleep in such a spot, under a sky as cloudless as his faith, and
where the cypresses of Italy, like nature's spires, stand pointing from a bright world below to a yet brighter heaven. As

we passed along the streets of the grand old city we perceived
that the tricolor banners were hung from every window for
some victory or festival, and the people were passing in
throngs to the churches, whose bells were pealing joyfully.
At first it struck like a dissonance to our hearts, and then we
remembered what Theodore Parker had been and still must be
in a higher life than ours; and we said one to another, "For
us, too, this is a festa-day, the solemn Feast of an Ascension."

PREFACE

TO THE FIRST EDITION.

THE following pages contain the substance of a series of five lectures delivered in Boston, during the last autumn, at the request of several gentlemen. In preparing the work for the press I have enlarged on many subjects, which could be but slightly touched in a brief lecture. It was with much diffidence that I then gave my opinions to the public in that form; but considering the state of theological learning amongst us, and the frequent abuse of the name of Religion, I can no longer withhold my humble mite.

It is the design of this work to recall men from the transient shows of time, to the permanent substance of Religion; from a worship of Creeds and empty Belief, to a worship in the Spirit and in Life. If it satisfy the doubting soul, and help the serious inquirer to true views of God, Man, the Relation between them, and the Duties which come of that relation; if it make Religion appear more congenial and attractive, and a Divine Life more beautiful and sweet than heretofore—my end is answered. I have not sought to pull down, but to build up; to remove the rubbish of human inventions from the fair temple of Divine Truth, that men may enter its shining gates and be blessed now and for ever.

I have found it necessary, though painful, to speak of many popular delusions, and expose their fallacy and dangerous character, but have not, I trust, been blind to "the soul of goodness in things evil," though I have taken no great pains to speak smooth things, or say Peace, Peace, when there was no peace. The subject of Book IV. might seem to require a greater space than I have allowed it, but a cursory examination of many points there hinted at would require a volume, and I did not wish to repeat what is said elsewhere, and therefore have referred to an "Introduction to the Old Testament on the basis of De Wette," which is now in the press, and will probably come before the public in a few months. Some of the thoughts here set forth have also appeared in the Dial for 1840—1842. I can only wish that the Errors of this book may find no favour, but perish speedily, and that the Truths it humbly aims to set forth may do their good and beautiful work.

West Roxbury, Mass.
    7th May, 1842.

PREFACE

TO THE FOURTH EDITION.

It is now fourteen years since I prepared the first edition of this volume. In that time laborious Germans, some of them men of great genius, have investigated the history of the first and second centuries of the Christian Era with an amount of learning, patience, sagacity, and freedom of thought never before directed to that inquiry. Partly by their help, and partly by my own investigations, I have been led to conclude that the fourth Gospel is not the work of John the Disciple of Jesus, but belongs to a later period, and is of small historical value. This conclusion and its consequences will appear in some alterations made in this volume, which I have carefully revised in the light of the theological science of the present day. I know there are Truths in the Book which must prevail; the Errors connected therewith I invite men to expose and leave them to perish, that the Truths may the more readily do their work. I commit both to the Justice of Mankind.

    Boston, Dec. 25, 1855.

CONTENTS.

PAGE

THE INTRODUCTION xli

BOOK I.

OF RELIGION IN GENERAL : OR A DISCOURSE OF THE RELIGIOUS ELE-
MENT AND ITS MANIFESTATIONS.

CHAP. I. An Examination of the Religious Element in Man, and
the Existence of its Object 1
II. Of the Sentiment, Idea, and Conception of God ... 7
III. Power of the Religious Element 13
IV. The Idea of Religion connected with Science and Life 23
V. The three great Historical Forms of Religion ... 28
VI. Of certain Doctrines connected with Religion. I. Of the
Primitive State of Mankind. II. Of the Immortality
of the Soul 70
VII. The Influence of the Religious Element on Life ... 84

BOOK II.

THE RELATION OF THE RELIGIOUS SENTIMENT TO GOD, OR A DISCOURSE
OF INSPIRATION.

CHAP. I. The Idea and Conception of God 103
II. The Relation of Nature to God 110
III. Statement of the Analogy drawn from God's Relation to
Nature 117
IV. The General Relation of Supply to Want 118
V. Statement of the Analogy from this Relation ... 122
VI. The Rationalistic View, or Naturalism 126
VII. The Anti-rationalistic View, or Supernaturalism ... 133
VIII. The Natural-Religious View, or Spiritualism ... 138

BOOK III.

THE RELATION OF THE RELIGIOUS ELEMENT TO JESUS OF NAZARETH,
OR A DISCOURSE OF CHRISTIANITY.

PAGE

CHAP. I. Statement of the Question and the Method of Inquiry   153
     II. Removal of some Difficulties. Character of the Christian
         Records   158
    III. The Main Features of Christianity   163
     IV. The Authority of Jesus, its Real and Pretended Source   172
      V. The Essential Excellence of the Christian Religion   ...   187
     VI. The Moral and Religious Character of Jesus of Naza-
         reth   192
    VII. Mistakes about Jesus—his Reception and Influence   ...   198

BOOK IV.

THE RELATION OF THE RELIGIOUS ELEMENT TO THE GREATEST OF
BOOKS, OR A DISCOURSE OF THE BIBLE.

CHAP. I. Position of the Bible—Claims made for it—Statement of
         the Question   211
     II. An Examination of the Claims of the Old Testament to be
         a Divine, Miraculous, or Infallible Composition   ...   218
    III. An Examination of the Claims of the New Testament to
         be a Divine, Miraculous, or Infallible Composition   ...   234
     IV. The Absolute Religion independent of Historical Docu-
         ments—The Bible as it is   242
      V. Cause of the False and the Real Veneration for the Bible   245

BOOK V.

THE RELATION OF THE RELIGIOUS ELEMENT TO THE GREATEST OF
HUMAN INSTITUTIONS, OR A DISCOURSE OF THE CHURCH.

CHAP. I. Claims of the Christian Church   253
     II. The Gradual Formation of the Christian Church   ...   258
    III. The Fundamental and Distinctive Idea of the Christian
         Church—Division of the Christian Sects   269
     IV. The Catholic Party   271
      V. The Protestant Party   289
     VI. Of the Party that are neither Catholics nor Protestants   316
    VII. The Final Answer to the Question   319

THE CONCLUSION   325

THE INTRODUCTION.

"To false Religion we are indebted for persecutors, zealots, and bigots; and perhaps human depravity has assumed no forms, at once more odious and despicable, than those in which it has appeared in such men. I will say nothing of persecution; it has passed away, I trust, for ever; and torture will be no more inflicted, and murder no more committed, under pretence of extending the spirit and influence of Christianity. But the temper which produced it still remains; its parent bigotry is still in existence; and what is there more adapted to excite thorough disgust, than the disposition, the feelings, the motives, the kind of intellect and degree of knowledge, discovered by some of those, who are pretending to be the sole defenders and patrons of religious truth in this unhappy world, and the true and exclusive heirs of all the mercy of God? It is a particular misfortune, that when gross errors in religion prevail, the vices of which I speak show themselves especially in the clergy; and that we find them ignorant, narrow-minded, presumptuous, and, as far as they have it in their power, oppressive and imperious. The disgust which this character in those who appear as ministers of religion naturally produces, is often transferred to Christianity itself. It ought to be associated only with that form of religion by which those vices are occasioned."— ANDREWS NORTON, *Thoughts on true and false Religion*, second edition, p. 15, 16.

THE INTRODUCTION.

The history of the world shows clearly that Religion is the highest of all human concerns. Yet the greatest good is often subject to the worst abuse. The doctrines and ceremonies that represent the popular religion at this time, offer a strange mingling of truth and error. Theology is often confounded with Religion; men exhaust their strength in believing, and so have little Reason to inquire with, or solid Piety to live by. It requires no prophet to see that what is popularly taught and accepted as Religion is no very divine thing; not fitted to make the world purer, and men more worthy to live in it. In the popular belief of the present, as of all time, there is something mutable and fleeting; something also which is eternally the same. The former lies on the surface, and all can see it; the latter lies deep, and often escapes observation. Our popular theology is mainly based on the superficial and transient element. It stands by the forbearance of the sceptic. They who rely on it, are always in danger and always in dread. A doubt strongly put, shakes the pulpits of New England, and wakens the thunder of the churches; the more reasonable the doubt the greater the alarm. Do men fear lest the mountains fall: Tradition is always uncertain. "Perhaps yes, perhaps no," is all we can say of it. Yet it is made the basis of Religion. Authority is taken for Truth, and not Truth for Authority. Belief is made the Substance of Religion, as Authority its Sanction and Tradition its Ground. The name of Infidel is applied to the best of men; the wisest, the most spiritual and heavenly of our brothers. The bad and the foolish naturally ask, If the name be deserved, what is the use of Religion, as good men and wise men can be good and wise, heavenly and spiritual, without it? The answer is plain—but not to the blind.

Practical Religion implies both a Sentiment and a Life. We honour a phantom which is neither life nor sentiment. Yes, we have two Spectres that often take the place of Religion with us. The one is a Shadow of the Sentiment; that is our creed, belief, theology, by whatever name we call it. The other is the Ghost of Life; this is our ceremonies, forms, devout practices. The two Spectres by turns act the part of Religion, and we are called Christians because we assist at the show. Real Piety is expected of but few. He is called a Christian that bows to the Idol of his Tribe, and sets up also a lesser, but orthodox Idol in his own Den. One word of the Prophet is true of our religion—Its voice is not heard in the streets. Our theology is full of confusion. They who admit Reason to look upon it confound the matter still more, for a great revolution of thought can set affairs right.

Religion is separated from Life; divorced from bed and board. We think to be religious without love for men, and pious with none for God; or, which is the same thing, that we can love our neighbour without helping him, and God without having an idea of Him. The prevailing theology represents God as a being whom a good man must hate; Religion is something alien to our nature, which can only rise as Reason falls. A despair of Man pervades our Theology. Pious men mourn at the famine in our churches; we do not believe in the inspiration of goodness now; only in the tradition of goodness long ago. For all theological purposes, God might have been buried after the ascension of Jesus. We dare not approach the Infinite One face to face; we whine and whimper in our brother's name, as if we could only appear before the Omnipresent by Attorney.

Our reverence for the Past is just in proportion to our ignorance of it. We think God was once everywhere in the World and in the Soul; but has now crept into a corner, as good as dead; that the Bible was his last word. Instead of the Father of All for our God, we have two

Idols; the Bible, a record of men's words and works; and Jesus of Nazareth, a man who lived divinely some centuries ago. These are the Idols of the religious; our standard of truth; the gods in whom we trust. Mammon, the great Idol of men not religious—who overtops them both, and has the sincerest worshippers—need not now be named. His votaries *know* they are idolaters; the other worship in ignorance, their faith fixed mainly on transient things.

I know there are exceptions to this rule. Saints never fail from the earth. Reason will claim some deserted niche in every church. But wise men grieve over our notions of Religion—so poor, so alien to Reason. Pious men weep over our practice of Religion—so far from Christianity. What passes for Christianity in our times is not reasonable; no man pretends it. It can only be defended by forbidding a reasonable man to open his mouth. We go from the street to the church. What a change! Reason and good sense and manly energy, which do their work in the world, have here little·to do; their voice is not heard. The morality, however, is the same in both places; it has only laid off its working dress, smoothed its face, put on its Sunday clothes.

The popular theology is hostile to man; tells us he is an outcast; not a child of God, but a spurious issue of the devil. He must not even pray in his own name. His duty is an impossible thing. No man can do it. He deserves nothing but damnation. Theology tells him that is all he is sure of. It teaches the doctrine of immortality; but in such guise that, if true, it is a misfortune to mankind. Its Heaven is a place no man has a right to. Would a good man willingly accept what is not his? Pray for it? This theology rests on a lie. Men have made it out of assumptions. The conclusions came from the premises; but the premises were made for the sake of the conclusions. Each vouches for the other's truth. But what else will vouch for either? The historical basis of popular doctrines, such as Depravity, Redemption, Resurrection, the Incarnation—is it formed of Facts or of No-Facts? Who shall tell us? Do not the wise men look after these things? One must needs blush for the patience of mankind.

But has Religion only the bubble of Tradition to rest on; no other sanction than Authority; no substance but Belief? They know little of the matter who say it. Did Religion begin with what we call Christianity? Were there no saints before Peter? Religion is the first spiritual thing man learned; the last thing he will abandon. There is but one Religion, as one Ocean; though we call it Faith in our church, and Infidelity out of our church.

It is my design in these pages to recall men from the transient Form to the eternal Substance; from outward and false Belief to real and Inward Life; from this partial Theology and its Idols of human device, to that universal Religion and its ever-living Infinite God; from the temples of human Folly and Sin, which every day crumble and fall, to the inner Sanctuary of the Heart, where the still small voice will never cease to speak. I would show men Religion as she is—most fair of all God's fairest children. If I fail in this, it is the head that is weak, not the heart that is wanting.

BOOK I.

" Who is there almost that has not opinions planted in him by education time out of mind; which by that means came to be as the municipal laws of the country, which must not be questioned, but are then looked on with reverence, as the standard of right and wrong, truth and falsehood, when perhaps these so sacred opinions are but the oracles of the nursery, or the traditional grave talk of those who pretend to inform our childhood; who receive them from hand to hand without ever examining them? . . . . These ancient pre-occupations of our minds, these several and almost sacred opinions, are to be examined if we will make way for truth, and put our minds in that freedom which belongs and is necessary to them. A mistake is not the less so, and will never grow into a truth, because we have believed it a long time, though perhaps it be the harder to part with; and an error is not the less dangerous, nor the less contrary to truth, because it is cried up and had in veneration by any party."—LOCKE, *in* KING'S *Life of him*, second edition, Vol. I. p. 188, 192.

BOOK I.

OF RELIGION IN GENERAL: OR A DISCOURSE OF THE
RELIGIOUS ELEMENT AND ITS MANIFESTATIONS.

CHAPTER I.

AN EXAMINATION OF THE RELIGIOUS ELEMENT IN MAN,
AND THE EXISTENCE OF ITS OBJECT.

As we look on the world which Man has added to that
which came from the hand of its Maker, we are struck
with the variety of its objects, and the contradiction between them. There are institutions to prevent crime; institutions that of necessity perpetuate crime. This is built
on Selfishness; would stand by the downfall of Justice and
Truth. Side by side therewith is another, whose broad
foundation is universal Love,—love for all that are of
woman born. Thus we see palaces and hovels, jails and
asylums for the weak, arsenals and churches, huddled together in the strangest and most intricate confusion. How
shall we bring order out of this chaos; account for the existence of these contradictions? It is serious work to decom-
pose these phenomena, so various and conflicting; to detect
the one cause in the many results. But in doing this, we find
the root of all in Man himself. In him is the same per-
plexing antithesis which we meet in all his works. These
conflicting things existed as ideas in him before they took
their present and concrete shape. Discordant causes have
produced effects not harmonious. Out of Man these institutions have grown; out of his passions, or his judgment; his senses, or his soul. Taken together they are

the exponent which indicates the character and degree of development the race has now attained; they are both the result of the Past and the prophecy of the Future.

From a survey of Society, and an examination of human nature, we come at once to the conclusion, that for every institution out of Man except that of Religion, there is a cause within him, either fleeting or permanent; that the natural wants of the body, the desire of food and raiment, comfort and shelter, have organized themselves, and instituted agriculture and the mechanic arts; that the more delicate principles of our nature, love of the Beautiful, the True, the Good, have their organization also; that the passions have their artillery, and all the gentler emotions somewhat external to represent themselves, and reflect their image. Thus the institution of Laws, with their concomitants, the Court-house and the Jail, we refer to the Moral Sense of mankind, combining with the despotic selfishness of the strong, whose might often usurps the place of Justice. Factories and Commerce, Railroads and Banks, Schools and Shops, Armies and Newspapers, are quite easily referred to something analogous in the wants of Man; to a lasting principle, or a transient desire which has projected them out of itself. Thus we see that these institutions out of Man are but the exhibitions of what is in him, and must be referred either to eternal principles, or momentary passions. Society is the work of Man. There is nothing in society which is not also in him.

Now there is one vast institution, which extends more widely than human statutes; claims the larger place in human affairs; takes a deeper hold on men than the terrible pomp of War, the machinery of Science, the panoply of Comfort. This is the institution of Religion, coeval and co-extensive with the human race. Whence comes this? Is there an eternal principle in us all, which legitimately and of necessity leads to this; or does it come, like Piracy, War, the Slave-trade, and so much other business of Society, from the abuse, misdirection, and disease of human nature? Shall we refer this vast institution to a passing passion which the advancing race will outgrow, or does it come from a principle in us deep and lasting as Man? To this question, for many ages, two answers have been given—one foolish and one wise. The foolish answer, which may be read in Lucretius and elsewhere, is, that Religion is not a necessity of Man's nature, which comes from the action of eternal demands within him, but is the result of spiritual disease, so to say; the effect of fear, of ignorance, combining with selfishness; that hypocritical Priests and knavish Kings, practising on the ignorance, the credulity, the passions, and the fears of men, invented for their own sake, and got up a religion, in which they put no belief and felt no spiritual concern. But judging from a superficial view, it might as well be said that food and comfort were not necessities of our nature, but only cunning devices of butchers, mechanics, and artists, to gain wealth and power. Besides, it is not given to hypocrites under the mitre, nor over the throne, to lay hold on the world and move it. Honest conviction and living faith are needed for that work. To move the world of men firm footing is needed. The hypocrite deceives few but himself, as the attempts at pious frauds, in ancient and modern times, abundantly prove.

The wise answer is, that this institution of Religion, like Society, Friendship, and Marriage, comes out of a principle deep and permanent in the constitution of man; that as humble, and transient, and partial institutions come out of humble, transient, and partial wants, and are to be traced to the senses and the phenomena of life; so this sublime, permanent, and universal institution came out from sublime, permanent, and universal wants, and must be referred to the Soul, the religious Faculty, and so belongs among the unchanging realities of life. Looking, even superficially, but with earnestness, upon human affairs, we are driven to confess, that there is in us a spiritual nature, which directly and legitimately leads to Religion; that as Man's body is connected with the world of Matter; rooted in it; has bodily wants, bodily senses to minister thereto, and a fund of external materials wherewith to gratify these senses and appease these wants; so Man's soul is connected with the world of Spirit; rooted in God; has spiritual wants, and spiritual senses, and a fund of materials wherewith to gratify these spiritual senses and appease these spiritual wants. If this be so, then do not religious institutions come equally from Man?

1 *

Must it not be that there is nothing in Religion, more than in Society, which is not implied in him?

Now the existence of a religious element in us, is not a matter of hazardous and random conjecture, nor attested only by a superficial glance at the history of Man, but this principle is found out, and its existence demonstrated in several legitimate ways.

We see the phenomena of worship and religious observances; of religious wants and actions to supply those wants. Work implies a hand that did, and a head that planned it. A sound induction from these facts carries us back to a religious principle in Man, though the induction does not determine the nature of this principle, except that it is the cause of these phenomena. This common and notorious fact of religious phenomena being found everywhere, can be explained only on the supposition that Man is, by the necessity of his nature, inclined to Religion; that worship, in some form, gross or refined, in act, or word, or thought, or life, is natural and quite indispensable to the race. If the opposite view be taken, that there is no religious principle in Man, then there are permanent and universal phenomena without a corresponding cause, and the fact remains unexplained and unaccountable.

Again, we feel conscious of this element within us. We are not sufficient for ourselves; not self-originated; not self-sustained. A few years ago, and we were not; a few years hence, and our bodies shall not be. A mystery is gathered about our little life. We have but small control over things around us; are limited and hemmed in on all sides. Our schemes fail. Our plans miscarry. One after another our lights go out. Our realities prove dreams. Our hopes waste away. We are not where we would be, nor what we would be. After much experience, men powerful as Napoleon, victorious as Cæsar, confess, what simpler men knew by instinct long before, that it is not in Man that walketh to direct his steps. We find our circumference very near the centre, everywhere. An exceedingly short radius measures all our strength. We can know little of material things; nothing but their phenomena. As the circle of our knowledge widens its ring, we feel our ignorance on more numerous points, and the Unknown seems greater than before. At the end of a toilsome life, we confess, with a great man of modern times, that we have wandered on the shore, and gathered here a bright pebble, and there a shining shell—but an ocean of Truth, boundless and unfathomed, lies before us, and all unknown. The wisest Ancient knew only this, that he knew nothing. We feel an irresistible tendency to refer all outward things, and ourselves with them, to a Power beyond us, sublime and mysterious, which we cannot measure, nor even comprehend. We are filled with reverence at the thought of this power. Outward matters give us the occasion which awakens consciousness, and spontaneous nature leads us to something higher than ourselves, and greater than all the eyes behold. We are bowed down at the thought. Thus the sentiment of something superhuman comes natural as breath. This primitive spiritual sensation comes over the soul, when a sudden calamity throws us from our habitual state ; when joy fills our cup to its brim ; at "a wedding or a funeral, a mourning or a festival ; " when we stand beside a great work of nature, a mountain, a waterfall ; when the twilight gloom of a primitive forest sends awe into the heart ; when we sit alone with ourselves, and turn in the eye, and ask, What am I ? Whence came I ? Whither shall I go ? There is no man who has not felt this sensation ; this mysterious sentiment of something unbounded.

Still further, we arrive at the same result from a philosophical analysis of Man's nature. We set aside the Body with its senses as the man's house, having doors and windows ; we examine the Understanding, which is his handmaid ; we separate the Affections, which unite man with man ; we discover the Moral Sense, by which we can discern between right and wrong, as by the body's eye between black and white, or night and day ; and behind all these, and deeper down, beneath all the shifting phenomena of life, we discover the RELIGIOUS ELEMENT OF MAN. Looking carefully at this element ; separating this as a cause from its actions, and these from their effects ; stripping this faculty of all accidental circumstances peculiar to the age, nation, sect, or individual, and pursuing a sharp and final analysis till the subject and predicate can no longer be separated ; we find as the ultimate fact, that the religious element first manifests itself in our consciousness by a feeling of need, of want; in one word, by A SENSE OF DEPENDENCE.[1] This primitive feeling does not itself disclose the character, and still less the nature and essence, of the Object on which it depends; no more than the senses disclose the nature of their objects; no more than the eye or ear discovers the essence of light or sound. Like them, it acts spontaneously and unconsciously, soon as the outward occasion offers, with no effort of will, forethought, or making up the mind.

Thus, then, it appears that induction from notorious facts, consciousness spontaneously active, and a philosophical analysis of our nature, all lead equally to some religious element or principle as an essential part of Man's constitution. Now, when it is stated thus nakedly and abstractedly that Man has in his nature a permanent religious element, it is not easy to see on what grounds this primary faculty can be denied by any thinking man, who will notice the religious phenomena in history, trust his own consciousness, or examine and analyze the combined elements of his own being. It is true, men do not often say to themselves, "Go to now. Lo, I have a religious element in the bottom of my heart." But neither do they often say, "Behold, I have hands and feet, and am the same being that I was last night or forty years ago." In a natural and healthy state of mind, men rarely speak or think of what is felt unconsciously to be most true, and the basis of all spiritual action. It is, indeed, most abundantly established, that there is a religious element in Man.

[1] The religious and moral elements mutually involve each other in practice; neither can attain a perfect development without the other; but they are yet as distinct from one another as the faculties of sight and hearing, or memory and imagination. Perhaps all will not agree with that analysis which makes a *sense of dependence* the ultimate fact of consciousness in the case. This is the statement of Schleiermacher, not to mention more ancient authorities. See his Christliche Glaube nach der Grundsätzen der ev. Kirche, B. I. § 4, p. 15, et seq. in his Works, 1 Abt. B. III., Berlin, 1835. Of course a sense of infinite as well as finite dependence is intended. Others may call it a *consciousness of the Infinite;* I contend more for the *fact* of a religious element in man than for the above analysis of that element. This theory has been assailed by several philosophers, amongst others by Hegel. See his Philosophie der Religion, 2nd improved edition, B. I. p. 87, et seq., in B. XI. of his Works, Berlin, 1840, B. XVII. p. 279, et seq.; Rosenkranz, Leben Hegels, Berlin, 1844, p. 341, et seq. See also Bretschneider, Handbuch der Dogmatik, Leip. 1838, Vol. I., § 12, 6. See Studien und Kritiken, für Oct. 1846, p. 845, et seq. for a defence of the opinion of Schleiermacher.

CHAPTER II.

OF THE SENTIMENT, IDEA, AND CONCEPTION OF GOD.

Now the existence of this religious element, our experience of this sense of dependence, this sentiment of something without bounds, is itself a proof by implication of the existence of its object,—something on which dependence rests. A belief in this relation between the feeling in us and its object independent of us, comes unavoidably from the laws of Man's nature; there is nothing of which we can be more certain.[1] A natural want in Man's constitution implies satisfaction in some quarter, just as the faculty of seeing implies something to correspond to this faculty, namely, objects to be seen, and a medium of light to see by. As the tendency to love implies something lovely for its object, so the religious consciousness implies its object. If it is regarded as a sense of absolute dependence, it implies the Absolute on which this dependence rests, independent of ourselves.

Spiritual, like bodily faculties, act jointly and not one at a time, and when the occasion is given from without us, the Reason, spontaneously, independent of our forethought and volition, acting by its own laws, gives us by intuition an IDEA of that on which we depend. To this idea we give the name of GOD or GODS, as it is represented by one or several separate conceptions. Thus the existence of God is implied by the natural sense of dependence; implied in

[1] The truth of the human faculties must be assumed in all arguments, and if this be admitted we have then the same evidence for spiritual facts as for the maxims or the demonstrations of Geometry. On this point see some good remarks in Cudworth's Intellectual System, Andover, 1838, 2 vols. 8vo, Vol. II. p. 135, et seq. If any one denies the trustworthiness of the human faculties, there can be no argument with him; the axioms of morals and of mathematics are alike nonsense to such a reasoner. Demonstration presupposes something so certain it requires no demonstrating. So *Reasoning* presupposes the trustworthiness of *Reason*.

the religious element itself; it is expressed by the spontaneous intuition of Reason.

Now men come to this Idea early. It is the logical condition of all other ideas; without this as an element of our consciousness, or lying latent, as it were, and unrecognized in us, we could have no *ideas* at all. The senses reveal to us something external to the body, and independent thereof, on which it depends; they tell not what it is. Consciousness reveals something in like manner, not the human spirit, in me, but its absolute ground, on which the spirit depends.[1] Outward circumstances furnish the occasion by which we approach and discover the Idea of God; but they do not furnish the Idea itself. That is a fact given by the nature of Man. Hence some philosophers have called it an innate idea; others, a reminiscence of what the spirit knew in a higher state of life before it took the body. Both opinions may be regarded as rhetorical statements of the truth that the Idea of God is a fact given by Man's nature, and not an invention or device of ours. The belief in God's existence therefore is natural, not against nature. It comes unavoidably from the legitimate action of the intellectual and the religious faculties, just as the belief in light comes from using the eyes, and belief in our existence from mere existing. The knowledge of God's existence, therefore, may be called in the language of Philosophy, an INTUITION OF REASON; or in the mythological language of the elder Theology,[2] a REVELATION FROM GOD.

If the above statement be correct, then our belief in God's existence does not depend on the *à posteriori* argument,

---

[1] I use the word Spirit to denote all the faculties not material—as distinguished from Body.

[2] English writers have rarely attempted to account philosophically for the origin of the Idea of God. They have usually assumed this, and then defended it by the various arguments. See Locke's Essay on the Human Understanding, Book I. ch. IV.; and Cousin's Psychology, Henry's Translation, Hartford, 1834, p. 46, et seq., and 181, et seq. See some valuable remarks in Cudworth's Intellectual System, &c., Vol. II. p. 143, et seq. See the Christian Examiner for January, 1840, p. 309, et seq., and the works there cited. See also the article of President Hopkins in American Quarterly Observer, No. II., Boston, 1833; and Ripley's Philosophical Miscellanies, Vol. I. p. 40, et seq., and 203, et seq. Some valuable thoughts on this subject may also be found in De Wette, Das Wesen des Christlichen Glaubens, vom Standpunkte des Glaubens dargestellt, Basel, 1846. § 4, et ant. See too Wirth, die speculative Idee Gottes, Stuttgart, 1845; and Sengler, die Idee Gottes, Heidelberg, 1845.

on considerations drawn from the order, fitness, and beauty discovered by observations made in the material world; nor yet on the *à priori* argument, on considerations drawn from the eternal nature of things, and observations made in the spiritual world. It depends primarily on no *argument* whatever; not on *reasoning* but *Reason*. The fact is given outright, as it were, and comes to the man, as soon and as naturally as the consciousness of his own existence, and is indeed logically inseparable from it, for we cannot be conscious of ourselves except as *dependent* beings.[1]

This intuitive perception of God is afterwards fundamentally and logically established by the *à priori* argument, and beautifully confirmed by the *à posteriori* argument; but we are not left without the Idea of God till we become metaphysicians and naturalists, and so can discover it by much thinking. It comes spontaneously, by a law, of whose action we are, at first, not conscious. The belief always precedes the proof, intuition giving the thing to be reasoned about. Unless this intuitive function be performed, it is not possible to attain a knowledge of God. For all arguments to that end must be addressed to a faculty which cannot originate the Idea of God, but only confirm it when given from some other quarter. Any argument is vain when the logical condition of all argument has not been complied with.[2] If the reasoner, as Dr. Clarke has done,[3] presuppose that his opponent has "no transcendent idea of God," all his reasoning could never produce it, howsoever capable of confirming and legitimating that idea if already existing in the consciousness. As we may speak of sights to the blind, and sounds to the deaf, and convince them that things called sights and sounds actually exist,

---

[1] This doctrine seems to be implied in the writings of the Alexandrian fathers.

[2] Kant has abundantly shown the insufficiency of all the *philosophical arguments* for the existence of God, the physico-theological, the cosmological, and the ontological. See the Kritik der reinen Vernunft, 7th edition, p. 444, et seq. But the fact of the Idea given in man's nature cannot be got rid of. It is not a little curious that none of the Christian writers seem to have attempted an *ontological* proof of the existence of God till the eleventh century, when Anselm led the way. See Bouchitté Histoire des Preuves de l'Existence de Dieu dépuis les Temps les plus réculés jusqu'au Monologium d'Anselme, in the Mem. de l'Acad. des Sciences Morales, &c., Tom. I. Savants Etrangères, Paris, 1841, p. 395, et seq., and his second Mémoire, p. 461, et seq., which brings the history down to that time. Tom. II. p. 59, et seq., 77, et seq.

[3] In his Demonstration of the Being and Attributes of God.

but can furnish no *Idea* of those things when there is no
corresponding sensation, so we may convince a man's understanding of the soundness of our argumentation, but
yet give him no Idea of God unless he have previously an
intuitive sense thereof.   Without the intuitive perception,
the metaphysical argument gives us only an idea of abstract
Power and Wisdom ; the argument from design gives only
a limited and imperfect Cause for the limited and imperfect
effects.   Neither reveals to us the Infinite God.

The Idea of God then transcends all possible external
experience, and is given by intuition, or natural revelation,
which comes of the joint and spontaneous action of reason
and the religious element.[1]   Now *theoretically* this Idea involves no contradiction and is perfect : that is, when the
proper conditions are complied with, and nothing disturbs
the free action of the spirit, we receive the Idea of a Being,
infinite in Power, Wisdom, and Goodness ; that is, infinite,
or perfect, in all possible relations.[2]   But *practically*, in the
majority of cases, these conditions are not observed; men attempt to form a complex and definite *conception* of God. The
primitive Idea, eternal in Man, is lost sight of.   The conception of God, as men express it in their language, is
always imperfect ; sometimes self-contradictory and impossible.   Human actions, human thoughts, human feelings,
yes, human passions and all the limitations of mortal men,
are collected about the Idea of God.   Its primitive simplicity
and beauty are lost.   It becomes self-destructive ; and the
conception of God, as many minds set it forth, like that of
a Griffin, or Centaur, or "men whose heads do grow beneath their shoulders," is self-contradictory ; the notion of
a being who, from the very nature of things, could not exist.   They for the most part have been called Atheists who
denied the popular conception of God, showed its inconsistency, and proved that such a being could not be.[3]   The

---

[1] The Idea of God, like that of Liberty and Immortality, may be called a
judgment à priori, and from the necessity of the case, transcends all objective
experience, as it is logically anterior to it.
[2] See Cudworth's Intellectual System, Chap. IV. § 8—10, Vol. I. p. 213, et
seq.
[3] The best men have often been branded as Atheists.   The following benefac-
tors of the world have borne that stigma : Thales, Anaxagoras, Pythagoras, Socrates, Plato, Aristotle, Xenophanes, and both the Zenos; Cicero, Seneca, Abelard, Galileo, Kepler, Des Cartes, Leibnitz, Wolf, Locke, Cudworth, Samuel

early Christians and all the most distinguished and religious philosophers have borne that name, simply because they were too far before men for their sympathy, too far above them for their comprehension, and because, therefore, their Idea of God was sublimer and nearer the truth than that held by their opponents.

Now the *conception* we form of God, under the most perfect circumstances, must, from the nature of things, fall short of the reality. The Finite can form no adequate conception or imagination of the Infinite. All the conceptions of the human mind are conceived under the limitation of Time and Space; of dependence on a cause exterior to itself;

Clarke, Jacob Böhme; Kant, and Fichte, and Schelling, and Hegel, are still under the ban. See some curious details of this subject in Reimmann's Historia Atheismi, &c., 1725, a dull book but profitable. See also a Dissertation by Buchwaldius, De Controversiis recentioribus de Atheismo, Viteb. 1716, 1 vol. quarto, and "Historical Sketch of Atheism," by Dr Pond, in American Biblical Repository, for Oct. 1839, p. 320, et seq.

Possevin, in his Bibliotheca, puts Luther and Melancthon among the Atheists. Mersenne (in his Comment. in Geneseos) says, that in 1622 there were 50,000 Atheists in Paris alone, often a dozen in a single house. Biographie Universelle, Tom. XXVIII. p. 390. See some curious details respecting the literary treatment of the subject in J. G. Walch's Philosophisches Lexicon, 2d ed., Leip. 1733, pp. 134—146. Dr Woods, in his translation of Knapp's Theology (New York, 1831, 2 vols. 8vo), in a note borrowed from Hahn's Lehrbuch des Christ. Glaubens, p. 175, et seq., places DR PRIESTLEY among the modern Atheists, where also he puts De La Mettrie, Von Holbach (or LaGrange), Helvetius, Diderot, and d'Alembert. Such catalogues are instructive. But see Clarke's Classification of Atheists at the beginning of the discourse, in his Works, Vol. II. p. 521, et seq.

The charge of impiety is always brought against such as differ from the public faith, especially if they rise above it. Thus Hicks declared Tillotson "*the gravest Atheist that ever was.*" Discourse on Tillotson and Burnet in Lechler, Gesch. Englischen Deismus, Stuttgart, 1841, p. 150, et seq. In 1697, Peter Browne, for a similar abuse of Toland, was rewarded with the office of a Bishop. —Ib. p. 195. A curious old writer says, "among the Grecians of old, those Secretaries of Nature, which first made a tender of the natural causes of lightnings and tempests to the rude ears of men, were blasted with the reproach of Atheists, and fell under the hatred of the untutored rabble, because they did not, like them, receive every extraordinary in nature as an immediate expression of the power and displeasure of the Deity." Spencer, Preface to his Discourse concerning Prodigies, London, 1665. Diodorus Siculus, Lib. 1, p. 75 (ed. Rhodoman), relates an instructive case. A Roman soldier, in Egypt, accidentally *killed a cat* —killed a god, for the cat was a popular object of worship. The people rose upon him, and nothing could save him from a violent death at the hands of the mob. All religious persecutions, if it be allowed to compare the little with the great, may be reduced to this one denomination. *The heretic*, actually or by implication, *killed a consecrated cat, and the Orthodox would fain kill him.* But as the same thing is not sacred in all countries (for even asses have their worshippers), the cat-killer, though an abomination in Egypt, would be a great saint in some lands where *dogs* are worshipped.

while the Infinite is necessarily free from these limitations. A man can comprehend no form of being but his own finite form, which answers to the Supreme Being even less than a grain of dust to the world itself. There is no conceivable ratio between Finite and Infinite.[1] Our human personality[2] gives a false modification to all our conceptions of the Infinite. But if, not resting in a merely sentimental consciousness of God, which is vague, and alone leads rather to pantheistic mysticism than to a *reasonable* faith, we take the fact given in our nature—the primitive Idea of God, as a Being of infinite Power, Wisdom, and Goodness, involves no contradiction. This is, perhaps, the most faithful expression of the Idea that words can convey. This language does not define the nature of God, but distinguishes our Idea of him from all other ideas and conceptions whatever. Some great religious souls have been content with this native Idea; have found it satisfactory both to Faith and Reason, and confessed with the ancients, that no man by searching could perfectly find out God. Others project their own limitations upon their conception of God, making him to appear such an one as themselves; thus they reverse the saying of Scripture, and creating a phantom in their own image, call it God. Thus, while the Idea of God, as a fact given in man's nature, and affording a consistent representation of its Object, is permanent and alike in all; while a merely sentimental consciousness or feeling of God, though vague and mysterious, is always the same in itself; the popular Conception of God is of the most various and evanescent character, and is not the same in any two ages or men. The Idea is the substance; the concep-

---

[1] M. Cousin thinks God is comprehensible by the human spirit, and even attempts to construct the " intellectual existence " of God. Creation he makes the easiest thing in the world to conceive of! See his Introduction to the History of Philosophy, Linberg's Translation, pp. 132—143. See also Ripley, l. c. Vol. I. p. 271, et seq. One would naturally think human presumption could go no further; but this pleasing illusion is dispelled by the perusal of some of his opponents.

[2] Zenophanes saw further into the secret than some others, when he said, that if Horses or Lions had hands and were to represent each his Deity, it would be a *Horse* or a *Lion*, for these animals would impose their limitations on the Godhead just as man has done. See the passage in Eusebius, Præp. Ev. XIII. 13, and Clemens Alex. Strom. V. 14.

The late excellent Dr Arnold goes to the other extreme, and says, " *It is only of God in Christ that I can, in my present state of being, conceive anything at all.*" (!) Life, &c., New York, 1845, Chap. VII. Letter 61, p. 212.

tion is a transient phenomenon, which at best only imperfectly represents the substance. To possess the Idea of God, though latent in us, is unavoidable; to feel its comfort is natural; to dwell in the Sentiment of God is delightful; but to frame an adequate Conception of Deity, and set this forth in words, is not only above human capability, but impossible in the nature of things. The abyss of God is not to be fathomed save by Him who is All-in-all.[1]

CHAPTER III.

POWER OF THE RELIGIOUS ELEMENT.

Now this inborn religious Faculty is the basis and cause of all Religion. Without this internal religious element, either Man could not have any religious notions, nor become religious at all, or else religion would be something foreign to his nature, which he might yet be taught mechanically from without, as bears are taught to dance, and parrots to talk; but which, like this acquired and unnatural accomplishment of the beast and the bird, would divert him from his true nature and perfection, rendering him a monster, but less of a man than he would be without the superfetation of this Religion upon him. Without a moral faculty, we could have no duties in respect to men; without a religious faculty, no duties in respect of God. The foundation of each is in Man, not out of him. If man have not a religious element in his nature, miraculous or other "revelations" can no more render him religious than fragments of sermons and leaves of the Bible can make a Lamb religious when mixed and eaten with its daily food. The Law, the Duty, and the Destiny of Man, as of all God's creatures, are writ in himself, and by the Almighty's hand.[2]

[1] See Parker's Sermons of Theism, Atheism, and the Popular Theology, Boston, 1853, Serm. I.
[2] See the treatise of Cicero on the foundation of duties in the essay De Legi-

The religious element existing within us, and this alone, renders Religion the duty, the privilege, and the welfare of mankind. Thus Religion is not a superinduction upon the race, as some would make it appear; not an after-thought of God interpolated in human affairs, when the work was otherwise complete; but it is an original necessity of our nature; the religious element is deep and essentially laid in the very constitution of Man.

I. Now this religious element is universal. This may be proved in several ways. Whatever exists in the fundamental nature of one man, exists likewise in all men, though in different degrees and variously modified by different circumstances. Human nature is the same in the men of all races, ages, and countries. Man remains always identical, only the differing circumstances of climate, condition, culture, race, nation, and individual, modify the manifestations of what is at bottom the same. Races, ages, nations, and individuals, differ only in the various degrees they possess of particular faculties, and in the development or the neglect of these faculties. When, therefore, it is shown that the religious sentiment exists as a natural principle in any one man, its existence in all other men, that are, were, or shall be, follows unavoidably from the unity of human nature.

Again, the universality of the religious element is confirmed by historical arguments, which also have some force. We discover religious phenomena in all lands, wherever Man has advanced above the primitive condition of mere animal wildness. Of course there must have been a period in his development when the religious faculties had not come to conscious activity : but after that state of spiritual infancy is passed by, religious emotions appear in the rudest and most civilized state; among the cannibals of New Zealand and the refined voluptuaries of old Babylon ; in the Esquimaux fisherman and the Parisian philosopher. The subsequent history of men shows no period in which

bus, Lib. I. It may surprise some men that a Pagan should come at the truth which lies at the bottom of all moral obligation, while so many Christian moralists have shot wide of the mark. See the discussion of the same subject, and a very different conclusion, in Paley's Moral Philosophy, and Dymond's Essays. See the heathen witnesses collected in Taylor, Elements of the Civil Law ; Lond. 1786, p. 100, et seq.

'these phenomena do not appear; Man worships, feels dependence and accountability, religious fear or hope, and gives signs of these spiritual emotions all the world over. No nation with fire and garments has been found so savage that they have not attained this; none so refined as to outgrow it. The widest observation, therefore, as well as a philosophical deduction from the nature of Man, warrants the conclusion that this sentiment is universal.[1]

But at first glance there are some apparent exceptions to this rule. A few persons from time to time arise and claim the name of Atheist. But even these admit they feel this religious tendency; they acknowledge a sense of dependence, which they refer, not to the sound action of a natural element in their constitution, but to a disease thereof, to the influence of culture, or the instruction of their nurses, and count it an obstinate disease of their mind, or else a prejudice early imbibed and not easily removed.[2] Even if some one could be found who denied that he ever felt any religious emotion whatever, however feebly—this would prove nothing against the universality of its existence, and no more against the general rule of its manifestation, than the rare fact of a child born with a single arm proves against the general rule, that Man by nature has two arms.[3]

Again, travellers tell us some nations with considerable civilization have no God, no priests, no worship, and therefore give no sign of the existence of the religious element in them. Admitting they state a fact, we are not to conclude the religious element is wanting in the savages; only that they, like infants, have not attained the proper stage, when we could discover signs of its action. But

[1] Empirical observation alone would not teach the *universality* of this element, unless it were detected *in each man*, for a generalization can never go beyond the facts it embraces; but observation, so far as it goes, confirms the abstract conclusion which we reach independent of observation.

[2] See Hume's Natural History of Religion, Introduction. Essays; Lond. 1822, Vol. II. p. 379.

[3] One of the most remarkable Atheists of the present day is M. Comte, author of the valuable and sometimes profound work Cours de l'Philosophie positive; Paris, 1830—42, 6 vols. 8vo. He glories in the name, but in many places gives evidence of the religious element existing in him in no small power. See Cudworth's Intellectual System, &c., Ch. IV. § 1—5. Some one says "No man is a consistent Atheist—if such be possible—who admits the existence of any general law."

these travellers are often mistaken.[1] Their observations have, in such cases, been superficial, made with but a slight knowledge of the manners and customs of the nation they treat. And, besides, their prejudice blinded their eyes. They looked for a regular worship, doctrines of religion, priests, temples, images, forms, and ceremonies. But there is one stage of religious consciousness in which none of these signs appear ; and yet the religious element is at its work. The travellers, not finding the usual signs of worship, denied the existence of worship itself, and even of any religious consciousness in the nation. But if they had found a people ignorant of cookery and without the implements of that art, it would be quite as wise to conclude from this negative testimony that the nation never ate nor drank. On such evidence, the early Christians were convicted of Atheism by the Pagans, and subsequently the Pagans by the Christians.[2]

---

[1] It seems surprising that so acute a philosopher as Locke (Essays, B. I. ch. 4, § 8) should *prove a negative by hearsay*, and assert on such evidence as Rhoe, Jo. de Léry, Martinière, Torry, Ovington, &c., that there were " whole nations amongst whom there was to be found no notion of a God, no religion." See the able remarks of his friend Shaftesbury—who is most unrighteously reckoned a speculative enemy to religion—against this opinion, in his Characteristics, Lond. 1758, Vol. IV. p. 81, et seq. ; 8th Letter to a Student, &c. Steller declares the Kamschatkans have no idea of a Supreme Being, yet gives an account of their mythology ! See Pritchard, Researches into the Physical History of Mankind, Lond. 1841, et seq., Vol. IV. p. 499. So intelligent a writer as Mr Norton says that " *in the popular religion of the Greeks and Romans there was no recognition of God.*" Evidences of the Genuineness of the Gospels, Boston, 1837, et seq., Vol. III. p. 13. This example shows the caution with which we are to read less exact writers, who deny that certain savages have any religion. See examples of this sort collected, for a different purpose, in Monboddo, Origin and Progress of Language, 2nd ed., Edinburgh, 1774, Vol. I. book ii. chap. 3, where see *much more evidence to show that races of men exist with tails*. Some writers seem to think Christianity is never safe until they have shown, as they fancy, that man cannot, by the natural exercise of his faculties, attain a knowledge of even the simplest and most obvious religious truths. Some foolish books have been based on this idea, which is yet the staple of many sermons. See on this head the valuable remarks of M. Comte ubi supra, Vol. V. p. 32, et seq.
It is not long since the whole nation of the Chinese were accused of Atheism, and that by writers so respectable as Le Père de Sainte Marie, and Le Père Longobardi. See, who will, Leibnitz's refutation of the charge, Opp. ed. Dutens, Vol. IV. part i. p. 170, et seq.
[2] Winslow, with others, at first declared the American Indians had no religion or knowledge of God, but he afterwards corrected his mistake. See Francis's Life of Eliot, p. 32, et seq. See also Catlin's Letters, &c., on the North American Indians, New York, 1841, Vol. I. p. 156. Even Meiners, Kritische Geschichte der Religionen, Vol. I. p. 11, 12, admits there is no nation without

There is still one other case of apparent exception to the rule. Some persons have been found, who in early childhood were separated from human society and grew up towards the years of maturity in an isolated state, having no contact with their fellow-mortals. These give no signs of any religious element in their nature. But other universal faculties of the race, the tendency to laugh, and to speak articulate words, give quite as little sign of their existence.[1] Yet when these unfortunate persons are exposed to the ordinary influence of life, the religious, like other faculties, does its work. Hence we may conclude it existed, though dormant until the proper conditions of its development were supplied.

These three apparent exceptions serve only to confirm the rule that the religious sentiment, like the power of attention, thought, and love, is universal in the race. Yet it is plain that there was a period in which the primitive wild man, without language or self-consciousness, gave no sign of any religious faculty at all, still the original element lay in this baby-man.

However, like other faculties, this is possessed in different degrees by different races, nations, and individuals, and at particular epochs of the world's or the individual's history acquires a predominance it has not at other times. It seems God never creates two races, nations, or men, with precisely the same endowments. There is a difference, more or less striking, between the intellectual, æsthetic, and moral development of two races, or nations, or even between two men of the same race and nation. This difference seems to be the effect, not merely of the

religious observances. See in Pritchard, l. c. Vol. I. p. 188, the statements relative to the Esquimaux, and his correction of the erroneous and ill-natured accounts of others. If any nation is destitute of religious opinions and observances, it must be the Esquimaux, and the Bushmans of South Africa, who seem to be the lowest of the human race. But it is clear, from the statement of travellers and missionaries, that both have religious sentiments and opinions. The Heathen philosophers admitted it as a fact *universally acknowledged* that there was a God.

[1] See a collection of the most remarkable of these cases in Jahn's Appendix Hermeneuticæ, &c., Viennæ, 1815, Vol. II. p. 208, et seq., and the authors there cited. Monboddo, Ancient Metaphysics, &c., Edinburgh, 1779, et seq., Vol. III. book ii. chap. 1, and Appendix, chap. 3. Col. Sleeman's account of "Wolves nurturing Children in their Dens," Plymouth, England, 1852. Windsor's Papuans, Lond. 1853. Capt. Gibson's communication to the American Geog. Soc., Dec. 1853.

different circumstances whereto they are exposed, but also
of the different endowments with which they set out.   If
we watch in history the gradual development and evolu-
lution of the human race, we see that one nation takes the
lead in the march of mind, pursues science, literature, and
the arts ; another in war, and the practical business of
political thrift, while a third nation, prominent neither for
science nor political skill, takes the lead in Religion, and
in the comparative strength of its religious consciousness
surpasses both.

Three forms of monotheistic Religion have, at various
times, come up in the world's history.   Two of them at
this moment perhaps outnumber the votaries of all other
religions, and divide between them the more advanced
civilization of mankind.   These three are the Mosaic, the
Christian, and the Mahometan ; all recognizing the unity
of God, the religious nature of Man, and the relation between God and Man.   All of these, surprising as it is,
came from one family of men, the Shemitic, who spoke, in
substance, the same language, lived in the same country,
and had the same customs and political institutions.   Even
that wide-spread and more monstrous form of Religion,
which our fathers had in the wilds of Europe, betrays its
likeness to this Oriental stock ; and that form, still earlier,
which dotted Greece all over with its temples, filling the
isles of the Mediterranean with its solemn and mysterious
chant, came apparently from the same source.[1]   The beautiful spirit of the Greek, modified, enlarged, and embellished
what Oriental piety at first called down from the Empy-
rean.   The nations now at the head of modern civilization
have not developed independently their power of creative
religious genius, so to say ; for each form of worship that
has prevailed with them was originally derived from some
other race.   These nations are more scientific than religious ; reflective rather than spontaneous ; utilitarian
more than reverential ; and, so far as history relates, have
never yet created a permanent form of Religion which has
extended to other families of men.   Their faith, like their

---

[1] This Orientalism of the religious opinions among the Europeans has led to
some very absurd conceits ; see a notorious instance in Davie's Mythology of the
Druids.   See also La Religion des Gaulois, &c., par le R. P. Dom [Jacques
Martin] ; Paris, 1727, 2 vols. 4to.

choicer fruits, is an importation from abroad, not an indigenous plant, though now happily naturalized, and rendered productive in their soil. Of all nations hitherto known, these are the most disposed to reflection, literature, science, and the practical arts; while the Shemitish tribes in their early age were above all others religious, and have had an influence in religious history entirely disproportionate to their numbers, their art, their science, or their laws. Out of the heart of this ancient family of nations flowed forth that triple stream of pious life, which even now gives energy to the pulsations of the world. Egypt and Greece have stirred the intellect of mankind; and spoken to our love of the Grand, the Beautiful, the True, to faculties that lie deep in us. But this Oriental people have touched the Soul of men, and awakened reverence for the Good, the Holy, the Altogether Beautiful, which lies in the profoundest deep of all. The religious element appears least conspicuous, it may be, in some nations of Australia—perhaps the most barbarous of men. With savages in general it is in its infancy, like all the nobler attributes of Man,[1] but as they develope their nature, this faculty becomes more and more apparent.

II. Again; this element is indestructible in human nature. It is not in the power of caprice within, nor external circumstances, war or peace, freedom or slavery, ignorance or refinement, wholly to abolish or destroy it. Its growth may be retarded, or quickened; its power misdirected, or suffered to flow in its proper channel. But no violence from within, no violence from without, can ever destroy this element. It were as easy to extirpate hunger and thirst from the sound living body, as this element from the spirit. It may sleep. It never dies. Kept down by external force to-day, it flames up to heaven in streams of light to-morrow. When perverted from its natural course, it writes, in devastation, its chronicles of wrongs,—a horrid page of human history, which proves its awful power, as the strength of the human muscle is proved by the distortions of the maniac. Sensual men, who hate the restraints of Religion, who know nothing of its en-

[1] M. Comte takes a very different view of the matter, and has both fact and philosophy against him.

couragements, strive to pluck up by the roots this plant
which God has set in the midst of the garden.   But there
it stands—the tree of Knowledge, the tree of Life.   Even
such as boast the name of Infidel and Atheist find, unconsciously, repose in its wide shadow, and refreshment in its
fruit.   It blesses obedient men.   He who violates the
divine law, and thus would wring this feeling from his
heart, feels it, like a heated iron, in the marrow of his
bones.

III. Still further; this religious element is the strongest and deepest in human nature.   It depends on nothing
outside, conventional or artificial.   It is identical in all
men; not a similar thing, but the same.   Superficially,
man differs from man, in the less and more; but in the
nature of the primitive religious element all agree, as in
whatever is deepest.   Out of the profoundest abyss in man
proceed his worship, his prayer, his hymn of praise.   The
history of the world shows us what a space Religion fills.
She is the mother of philosophy and the arts; has presided
over the greatest wars.   She holds now all nations with
her unseen hand; restrains their passions, more powerful
than all the cunning statutes of the lawgiver; awakens
their virtue; allays their sorrows with a mild comfort, all
her own; brightens their hopes with the purple ray of
faith, shed through the sombre curtains of necessity.

Religious emotion often controls society, inspires the
lawgiver and the artist—is the deep-moving principle; it
has called forth the greatest heroism of past ages; the
proudest deeds of daring and endurance have been done
in its name. Without Religion, all the sages of a kingdom
cannot build a city; but with it, how a rude fanatic sways
the mass of men.   The greatest works of human art have
risen only at Religion's call.   The marble is pliant at her
magic touch, and seems to breathe a pious life.   The
chiselled stone is instinct with a living soul, and stands
there, silent, yet full of hymns and prayers; an embodied
aspiration, a thought with wings that mock at space and
time.   The Temples of the East, the Cathedrals of the
West; Altar and Column and Statue and Image,—these
are the tribute Art pays to her.   Whence did Michael An-
gelo, Phidias, Praxiteles, and all the mighty sons of Art,

who chronicled their awful thoughts in stone, shaping brute matter to a divine form, building up the Pyramid and Parthenon, or forcing the hard elements to swell into the arch, aspire into the dome or the fantastic tower,— whence did they.draw their inspiration ? All their greatest wonders are wrought in Religion's name. In the very dawn of time, Genius looks through the clouds and lifts up his voice in hymns and songs and stories of the Gods; and the Angel of Music carves out her thanksgiving, her penitence, her prayers for Man, on the unseen air, as a votive gift for her. Her sweetest note, her most majestic chant, she breathes only at Religion's call. Thus it has always been. A thousand men will readily become celibate monks for Religion. Would they for Gold, or Ease, or Fame ?

The greatest sacrifices ever made are offered in the name of Religion. For this a man will forego ease, peace, friends, society, wife, and child, all that mortal flesh holds dearest; no danger is too dangerous, no suffering too stern to bear, if Religion say the word. Simeon the Stylite will stay years long on his pillar's top; the devotee of Budha tear off his palpitating flesh to serve his God. The Pagan idolater, bowing down to a false image of stone, renounces his possessions, submits to barbarous and cruel rites, shameful mutilation of his limbs; gives the firstborn of his body for the sin of his soul; casts his own person to destruction, because he dreams Baal, or Saturn, Jehovah, or Moloch, demands the sacrifice. The Christian idolater, doing equal homage to a lying thought, gives up Common Sense, Reason, Conscience, Love of his brother, at the same fancied mandate; is ready to credit most obvious absurdities; accept contradictions; do what conflicts with the moral sense; believe dogmas that make life dark, eternity dreadful, Man a worm, and God a tyrant; dogmas that make him count as cursed half his brother men, because told such is his duty, in the name of Religion. In this name Thomas More, the ablest head of his times, will believe a bit of bread becomes the Almighty God, when a lewd priest but mumbles his juggling Latin and lifts up his hands. In our day, heads as able as Thomas More's believe doctrines quite as absurd, because taught as Religion and God's command. In its behalf, the

foolishest teaching becomes acceptable; the foulest doctrines, the grossest conduct, crimes that, like the fabled
banquet of Thyestes, might make the sun sicken at the
sight and turn back affrighted in his course,—these things
are counted as beautiful, superior to Reason, acceptable to
God.   The wicked man may bless his brother in crime;
the unrighteous blast the holy with his curse, and devotees
shall shout "Amen," to both the blessing and the ban.

On what other authority have rites so bloody been accepted; or doctrines so false to reason, so libellous of God?   For
what else has Man achieved such works, and made such
sacrifice?   In what name but this, will the man of vast
and far outstretching mind, the counsellor, the chief, the
sage, the native king of men, forego the vastness of his
thought, put out his spirit's eyes, and bow him to a drivel-
ling wretch who knows nothing but treacherous mummery
and juggling tricks?   In Religion this has been done from
the first false prophet to the last false priest, and the pride of
the Understanding is abashed; the supremacy of Reason degraded; the majesty of Conscience trampled on; the beau-
tifulness of Faith and Love trodden down into the mire of
the streets.   The hand, the foot, the eye, the ear, the
tongue, the most sacred members of the body; judgment,
imagination, the overmastering faculties of mind; justice,
mercy, and love, the fairest affections of the soul,—all
these have been reckoned a poor and paltry sacrifice, and
lopped off at the shrine of God as things unholy.   This
has been done, not only by Pagan polytheists, and savage
idolaters, but by Christian devotees, accomplished scholars,
the enlightened men of enlightened times.

These melancholy results, which are but aberrations of
the religious element, the disease of the baby, not the
soundness of mankind, have often been confounded with
Religion itself, regarded as the legitimate fruit of the religious faculty.   Hence men have said, Such results prove
that Religion itself is a popular fury; the foolishness of
the people; the madness of mankind.   They prove a very
different thing.   They show the depth, the strength, the
awful power of that element which thus can overmaster all
the rest of Man—Passion and Conscience, Reason and
Love.   Tell a man his interest requires a sacrifice, he hesi-
tates; convince him his Religion demands it, and crowds

rush at once, and joyful, to a martyr's fiery death. It is
the best things that are capable of the worst abuse; the
very abuse may test the value.[1]

CHAPTER IV.

THE IDEA OF RELIGION CONNECTED WITH SCIENCE AND LIFE.

THE legitimate action of the religious element produces
reverence. This reverence may ascend into Trust, Hope,
and Love, which is according to its nature; or descend
into Doubt, Fear, and Hate, which is against its nature:
it thus rises or falls, as it coexists in the individual, with
wisdom and goodness, or with ignorance and vice. However, the legitimate and normal action of the religious element leads ultimately, and of necessity, to reverence,
absolute trust, and perfect love of God. These are the
result only of its sound and healthy action.

Now there can be but one kind of Religion, as there can
be but one kind of time and space. It may exist in different
degrees, weak or powerful; in combination with other
emotions, love or hate, with wisdom or folly, and thus it
is superficially modified, just as Love, which is always the
same thing, is modified by the character of the man who
feels it, and by that of the object to which it is directed.
Of course, then, there is no difference but of words between *revealed* Religion and *natural* Religion, for all actual
Religion is revealed in us, or it could not be felt, and all
revealed Religion is natural, or it would be of no use.[2]

[1] On this theme, see the forcible and eloquent remarks of Professor Whewell,
in his Sermons on the Foundation of Morals, 2nd edition, p. 28, et seq., a work
well worthy, in its spirit and general tone, of his illustrious predecessors, "the
Latitude men about Cambridge." See also Mr Parker's Sermon Of the Relation between the Ecclesiastical Institutions, and the Religious Consciousness of
the American People, 1855; and that Of the Function of a Teacher of Religion, 1855; Sermons of Theism, Atheism, and the Popular Theology, 1855,
Sermons III., IV., V., VI.

[2] This distinction between natural and revealed religion is very old; at least

What is of use to a man comes upon the plane of his consciousness, not merely above it, or below it. We may regard Religion from different points of view, and give corresponding names to our partial conceptions, which we have purposely limited, and so speak of natural and revealed Religion; Monotheistic, Polytheistic, or Pantheistic, Pagan, Jewish, Christian, Mahometan Religion. But in these cases the distinction, indicated by the terms, belongs to the thinker's mind, not to Religion itself, the object of thought. Historical phenomena of Religion vary in the more and less. Some express it purely and beautifully; others mingle foreign emotions with it, and but feebly represent the pious feeling.

To determine the question what is Absolute, that is, perfect Religion, Religion with no limitation, we are not to gather to a focus the scattered rays of all the various forms under which Religion has appeared in history, for we can never collect the Absolute from any number of imperfect phenomena; and, besides, in making the search and forming an eclecticism from all the historical religious phenomena, we presuppose in ourselves the criterion by which they are judged, namely, the Absolute itself, which we seek to construct, and thus move only in a circle, and end where we began. To answer the question, we must go back to the primitive facts of religious consciousness within us. Then we find religion is VOLUNTARY OBEDIENCE TO THE LAW OF GOD, INWARD AND OUTWARD OBEDIENCE to that law he has written on our nature, revealed in various ways through Instinct, Reason, Conscience, and the Religious emotions. Through it we regard Him as the absolute object of Reverence, Faith, and Love.[1] This obedience may be unconsci-

---

as old as the time of Origen. But it is evidently a distinction in *form* not in *substance*. The terms seem to have risen from taking an exclusive view of some *positive* and *historical* form of religion. All *religions* claim to have been *miraculously revealed*.

[1] The above definition or Idea of Religion is not given as the only or the best that can possibly be given, but simply as my own, the best I can find. If others have a better I shall rejoice at it. I will give some of the more striking definitions that have been set forth by others. Plato: "A Likeness to God, according to our ability." John Smith: "God is First Truth and Primitive Goodness. True Religion is a vigorous efflux and emanation of both upon the Spirit of man, and therefore is called a Participation of the Divine Nature. . . . . Religion is a heaven-born thing; the seed of God in the spirits of men whereby they

ous, as in little children who have known no contradiction between duty and desire; and perhaps involuntary in the perfect saint, to whom all duties are desirable, who has ended the contradiction by willing himself God's will, and thus becoming one with God. It may be conscious, as with many men whose strife is not yet over. It seems the highest and completest mode of Religion must be self-conscious,—free goodness, free piety, and free, self-conscious trust in God.[1]

Now there are two tendencies connected with Religion; one is speculative : here the man is intellectually employed in matters pertaining to Religion, to God, to Man's religious nature, and his relation and connection with God. The result of this tendency is Theology. This is not Religion itself. It is men's Thought about Religion; the Philosophy of divine things; the Science of Religion. Its sphere is the mind of men. Religion and Theology are no more to be confounded than the stars with astronomy.[2]

While the religious element, like the intellectual or the moral, or human nature itself, remains ever the same, the Religious Consciousness of mankind is continually progressive; and so Theology, which is the intellectual expression

are formed to a similitude and likeness of Himself." Kant : " Reverence for the moral law as a divine command." Schelling : " The union of the Finite and the Infinite." Fichte: " Faith in a moral government of the world." Hegel : "Morality becoming conscious of the free universality of its concrete essence." This will convey no idea to one not acquainted with the peculiar phraseology of Hegel. It seems to mean, Perfect mind becoming conscious of itself. Schleiermacher : " Immediate self-consciousness of the absolute dependence of all the finite on the infinite." Hase : " Striving after the Absolute, which is in itself unattainable ; but by love of it man participates of the divine perfection." Wollaston : "An obligation to *do* what ought not to be omitted, and to *forbear* what ought not to be done." Jeremy Taylor : " The whole duty of man, comprehending in it justice, charity, and sobriety." For the opinions of the ancients, see a treatise of Nitzsch, in Studien und Kritiken for 1828, p. 527, et seq.

[1] See Parker's Sermons of Theism, &c., Serm. V. and VI.

[2] Much difficulty has arisen from this confusion of Religion and Theology ; it is one proximate cause of that rancorous hatred which exists between the *theological* parties of the present day. Each connects Religion exclusively with its own sectarian theology. But there were great men before Agamemnon ; good men before Moses. Theology is a natural product of the human mind. Each man has some notion of divine things—that is, a *theology ;* if he collect them into a system, it is a *system of theology*, which differs in some points from that of every other man living. There is but one Religion, though many theologies. See de Wette, Ueber Religion und Theologie, Part I. Ch. I.—III. ; Part II. Ch. I.—III. ; his Dogmatik, § 4—8.

thereof, advances, like all other science, from age to age.
The most various theological doctrines exist in connection
with religious emotions, helping or hindering man's general
development.   The highest notion I can form of Religion
is this, which I called the Absolute Religion : conscious
service of the Infinite God by keeping every law he has
enacted into the constitution of the Universe,—service of
Him by the normal use, discipline, development, and delight of every limb of the body, every faculty of the spirit,
and so of all the powers we possess.

The other tendency is practical; here the man is employed in acts of obedience to Religion.   The result of this
tendency is Morality.   This alone is not Religion itself,
but one part of the life Religion demands.   There may be
Morality deep and true with little or no purely religious
consciousness, for a sharp analysis separates between the
religious and moral elements in a man.[1]   Morality is the
harmony between man's action and the natural law of God.
It is a part of Religion which includes it " as the Sea her
waves."   In its highest form Morality doubtless implies
Religious emotions, but not necessarily the self-consciousness thereof.   For though Piety, the love of God, and
Benevolence, the love of Man, do logically involve each
other, yet experience shows that a man may see and observe the distinction between right and wrong, clearly and
disinterestedly, without consciously feeling, as such, reverence, or love of God ; that is, he may be truly moral up to
a certain point, without being consciously religious, though
he cannot be truly religious without at the same time being
moral also.   But in a harmonious man, the two are practically inseparable as substance and form.   The merely
moral man, in the actions, thoughts, and feelings which
relate to his fellow-mortal, obeys the eternal law of duty,
revealed in his nature, as such, and from love of that law,

---

[1] It seems plain that the ethical and religious element in Man are not the
same ; at least, they are as unlike as Memory and Imagination, though, like
these, they act most harmoniously when in conjunction.   It is true we cannot
draw a line between them as between Sight and Hearing, but this inability to
tell where one begins and the other ends is no argument against the separate
existence of the faculties themselves.   See Kant, Religion innerhalb der Grenzen
der blossen Vernunft ; 2nd ed. 1794, Pref. p. iii., et seq.   Still Religion and
Morality are to be distinguished by their *centre* rather than their *circumference ;* by their *type* more than their *limit.*

without regard to its Author. The religious man obeys the same law, but regards it as the will of God. One rests in the law, the other only in its Author.[1]

Now in all forms of Religion there must be a common element which is the same thing in each man ; not a similar thing, but just the same thing, different only in degree, not in kind, and in its direction towards one or many objects, in both of which particulars it is influenced in some measure by external circumstances. Then since men exist under most various conditions, and in widely different degrees of civilization, it is plain that the religious consciousness must appear under various forms, accompanied with various doctrines, as to the number and nature of its Objects, the Deities ; with various rites, forms, and ceremonies, as it means to appease, propitiate, and serve these Objects ; with various organizations, designed to accomplish the purposes which it is supposed to demand ; and, in short, with apparently various and even opposite effects upon life and character. As all men are at bottom the same, but as no two nations or ages are exactly alike in character, circumstances, or development, so, therefore, though the religious element be the same in all, we must expect to find that its manifestations are never exactly alike in any two ages or nations, though they give the same name to their form of worship. If we look still more minutely, we see that no two men are exactly alike in character, circumstances, and development, and therefore that no two men can exhibit their Religion in just the same way, though they kneel at the same altar, and pronounce the same creed. From the difference between men, it follows that there must be as many different subjective conceptions of God, and forms of Religion, as there are men and women who think about God, and apply their thoughts and feelings to life. Hence, though the religious faculty be always the same in all, the Doctrines of Religion, or theology ; the Forms of Religion, or mode of worship ; and the Practice of Religion, which is Morality, cannot be the same thing in any two men, though one mother bore them, and they were educated in the same way. The conception we form of God ; our notion about

[1] See Mr Parker's Ten Sermons, Sermons I. to V.

Man; of the relation between him and God; of the duties which grow out of that relation, may be taken as the exponent of all the man's thoughts, feelings, and life. They are therefore alike the measure and the result of the total development of a man, an age, or race. If these things are so, then the phenomena of Religion—like those of Science and Art—must vary from land to land, and age to age, with the varying civilization of mankind; must be one thing in New Zealand, and the first century, and something quite different in New England, and the fifty-ninth century. They must be one thing in the wise man, and another in the foolish man. They must vary also in the same individual, for a man's wisdom, goodness, and general character, affect the phenomena of his Religion. The Religion of the boy and the man, of Saul the youth, and Paul the aged, how unlike they appear. The boy's prayer will not fill the man's heart; nor can the stripling son of Zebedee comprehend that devotion and life which he shall enjoy when he becomes the Saint mature in years.

CHAPTER V.

THE THREE GREAT HISTORICAL FORMS OF RELIGION.

Looking at the religious history of mankind, and especially at that portion of the human race which has risen highest in the scale of progress, we see that the various phenomena of Religion may, for the present purpose, be summed up in three distinct classes or types, corresponding to three distinct degrees of civilization, and almost inseparable from them. These are FETICHISM, POLYTHEISM, and MONOTHEISM. But this classification is imperfect, and wholly external, though of use for the present purpose. It must be borne in mind that we never find a nation in which either mode prevails alone. Nothing is truer than this, that minds of the same spiritual growth see the same spiritual truth. Thus, a savage Saint, living in a nation of Idolaters or Polytheists, worships the one true God, as Jesus of Nazareth has done. In a Christian land superstitious men may be found, who are as much Idolaters as Nebuchadnezzar or Jeroboam.

I. Fetichism denotes the worship of visible objects, such as beasts, birds, fish, insects, trees, mountains, the stars, the sun, the moon, the earth, the sea, and air, as types of the infinite Spirit. It is the worship of Nature.[1] It includes many forms of religious observances that prevailed widely in ancient days, and still continue among savage tribes. It belongs to a period in the progress of the individual, or society, when civilization is low, the manners wild and barbarous, and the intellect acts in ignorance of the causes at work around it; when Man neither understands nature nor himself. Some writers suppose the human race started at first with a pure Theism; for the knowledge of truth, say they, must be older than the perception of error in this respect. It seems the sentiment of Man would lead him to the ONE GOD. Doubtless it would if the conditions of its highest action were perfectly fulfilled. But as this is not done in a state of ignorance and barbarism, therefore the religious sentiment mistakes its object, and sometimes worships the symbol more than the thing it stands for.

In this stage of growth, not only the common objects above enumerated, but gems, metals, stones that fell from heaven,[2] images, carved bits of wood, stuffed skins of

---

[1] It will probably be denied by some, that these objects were worshipped as symbols of the Deity. It seems, however, that even the most savage nations regarded their Idols only as Types of God. On this subject, see Constant, Religion, &c., Paris, 1824, 5 vols. 8vo; Philip Van Limburg Brauwer, Histoire de la Civilization morale et religieuse des Grecs, &c., Groningues, 1833—42, 8 vols. 8vo, Vol. II. Ch. IX. X. et alibi; Oldendorp, Geschichte der Mission—auf—St Thomas, &c., Barby. 1777, p. 318, et seq.; Du Culte des Dieux fétiches [par De Brosses, Paris], 1770, 1 vol. 12mo; Movers, Untersuchung über die Religion und der Gottheiten der Phönizier, Bonn, 1841, 2 vols. 8vo; Comte, Cours de Philosophie positive, Vol. V.; Stuhr, Allg. Gesch. der Religionsformen, Berlin, 1838, 2 vols. 8vo; Meimers, ubi supra; and the numerous accounts of the savage nations, by missionaries, travellers, &c. Catlin, ubi supra, Vol. I. p. 35, et seq., p. 88, et seq., p. 156, et seq., &c.

[2] These *Stone-fetiches* are called *Baetylia* by the learned. Cybele was worshipped in the form of a black stone, in Asia Minor. Theophrast. Charact. 16. Lucian, Pseudomant. § 30. The ancient Laplanders also worshipped large

beasts, like the *medicine-bags* of the North-American Indians, are reckoned as divinities, and so become objects of adoration.[1] But in this case the visible object is idealized; not worshipped as the brute thing it really is, but as the type and symbol of God. Nature is an Apparition of the Deity, God in a mask. Brute matter was never an object of adoration. Thus the Egyptians who worshipped the Crocodile, did not worship it as a Crocodile, but as a symbol of God, " an appropriate one," says Plutarch, " for it alone, of all animals, has no tongue, and God needs none to speak his power and glory." Similar causes, it may be, led to the worship of other animals. Thus the Hawk was a type of divine foresight; the Bull of strength; the Serpent of mystery. The Savage did not worship the Buffalo, but the Manitou of all Buffaloes, the universal cause of each particular effect. Still more, there is something mysterious about the animals. Their instinctive knowledge of coming storms, and other events; the wondrous foresight of the Beaver, the Bee; the sagacity of the Dog; the obscurity attending all their emotions, helped, no doubt, to procure them a place among powers greater than human. It is the Unknown which men worship in common things; at this stage, man, whose emotions are understood, is never an object of adoration.[2]

Fetichism is the infancy of Religion. Here the religious

stones called *Seiteh*. See Scheffer's Lappland. In the time of Pausanias, at Phoræ, in Achaia, there were nearly thirty square stones, called by the names of the Gods, and worshipped. Opp., ed. Lips. 1838, Vol. II. Lib. vii. ch. 22, p. 618. Rough stones, he adds, formerly received divine honours universally in Greece. The erection of such is forbidden in Levit. xxvi. 1, et al. On this form of worship, see some curious facts collected by Michelet, Hist. de France, Liv. I. Eclaircissements, Oeuvres, Ed. Bruxelles, 1840, Tom. III. p. 51, 55, 61, seq. 93 (note i.). The erection of *Baetylia* is forbidden by several councils of the Church, e. g. C. *Arelat*, II. Can. 23; C. *Autoisiod*. Can. 3; C. *Tolet*. XII. Can. 11.

[1] See Catlin, ubi supra. See also Legis, Fundgruben des Alten Nordens, Leip., 1829, 2 vols. 8vo, and his Alkuna, Nordische und Nord-Slawische Mythologie, Leip., 1831, Vol. I. 8vo. Mone, Geschichte der Heidenthums in Nordlichen Europa, Leip., 1822, 2 vols. 8vo. See Grimm, Deutsche Mythologie, Gött. 1835, for this worship of Nature in the North.

[2] But see the causes of Animal worship assigned by Diod. Sic. Lib. I. p. 76, ed. Rhodoman; the remarks of Cicero, De Nat. Deorum, Tusc. V. et al.; Plutarch, De Iside et Osir., p. 72, et seq., et al.; Wilkinson, Manners, &c., of Ancient Egypt, 2nd Series, Vol. I. p. 104, seq., and Porphyry, De Abst. IV. 9, cited by him. Jean Paul says, that "in the beast men see the Isis-veil of a Deity," a thought which Hegel has expanded in his Philos. der Religion. See Creutzer, Symbol. 3rd ed. Vol. I. p. 30, et seq.

consciousness is still in the arms of rude, savage life, where sensation prevails over reflection. It is a deification of Nature, "All is God, but God himself." It loses the Infinite in the finite ; worships the creature more than the Creator. Its lowest form—for in this lowest deep there is a lower deep—is the worship of beasts ; the highest the sublime, but deceitful, reverence which the old Sabæan paid the host of Heaven, or which some Grecian or Indian philosopher offered to the Universe personified, and called Pan, or Brahma. Then all the mass of created things was a Fetiche. God was worshipped in a sublime and devout, but bewildering, Pantheism. He was not considered as distinct from the Universe. (Pantheism and Fetichism are nearly allied.[1])

In the lowest form of this worship, so far as we can gather from the savage tribes, each individual has his own peculiar Fetiche, a beast, an image, a stone, a mountain, or a star, a concrete and visible type of God. For it seems in this state that all, or most, external things, are supposed to have a life analogous in kind to ours, but more or less intense in degree. The concrete form is but the veil of God, like that before Isis in Egypt. There are no priests, for each man has access to his own Deity at will. Worship and prayer are personal, and without mediators. The age of the priesthood, as a distinct class, has not come. Worship is entirely free ; there is no rite, estab-

---

[1] In consequence of the opinion in fetichistic nations, that external things have a mysterious life, M. Comte, ubi supra, Vol. V. p. 36, et seq., *discovers traces of it in animals.* When a savage, a child, or a dog, first hears a watch tick, each supposes it endowed with life, " whence results, by natural *consequence*, a Fetichism, which, at bottom, is common to all three!" Here he confounds the *sign* with the *cause.*

Pliny has a curious passage in which he ascribes to the Elephant Æquitas, Religio quoque Siderum ; Solisque ac Lunæ Veneratio. Nat. Hist. Lib. VIII. ch. 1. The notion that beasts had a moral sense appears frequently among the ancients. Ulpian says jus naturale is common to all animals. Origen says that Celsus taught that there was no difference between the Soul of a man and that of Emmets, Bees, &c., Lib. II. Cels. Cont. Clement of Alex. (Stromt. VI. 14, p. 705, 706, ed. Potter) says God gave the Heathen the sun, moon, and stars, that they might worship them, such worship being the way to that of God himself. Perhaps he was led to this opinion by following the LXX. in Deut. iv. 19.

Fetichism continued in Europe long after the introduction of Christianity. The councils of the Church forbid its various forms in numerous decrees, e. g. C. *Turg.* II. Can. 22 ; C. *Autoisiod.* Can. 1. 4 ; C. *Quinisext.* Can. 62, 65, 79 ; *Narbon.* Can. 15 ; C. *Rothomag.* Can. 4, 14. See in Stäudlin, Gesch. Theol. Vol. III. 371, et seq.

lished and fixed. Public theological doctrines are not yet
formed. There are no mysteries in which each may not
share.

This state of Fetichism continues as long as Man is in
the gross state of ignorance which renders it possible.
Next, as the power of abstraction and generalization becomes enlarged, and the qualities of external nature are
understood, there are concrete and visible Gods for the
Family ; next for the Tribe ; then for the Nation. But
their power is supposed to be limited within certain
bounds. A subsequent generalization gives an invisible
but still concrete Deity for each department of Nature—
the earth, the sea, the sky.

Now as soon as there is a Fetiche for the family, or the
tribe, a mediator becomes needed to interpret the will and
insure the favour of that Fetiche, to bring rain, or plenty,
or success, and to avert impending evils. Such are the
angekoks of the Esquimaux, the *medicine-men* of the Mandans, the *jugglers* of the Negroes. Then a priesthood
gradually springs up, at first possessing none but spiritual
powers ; at length it surrounds its God with mysteries ;
excludes him from the public eye ; establishes forms, sacrifices, and doctrines ; limits access to the Gods ; becomes
tyrannical ; aspires after political power ; and founds a
theocracy, the worst of despotisms, the earliest, and the
most lasting.[1] Still it has occupied a high and indispensable position in the development of the human race.

The highest form of Fetichism is the worship of the
stars, or of the universe.[2] Here it easily branches off into
Polytheism. Indeed, it is impossible to tell where one
begins and the other ends, for traces of each of the three
forms are found in all the others ; the two must be distinguished by their centre, not their circumference. The

[1] See at the end of Hodges's "Elihu." &c., London, 1750, 1 vol. 4to, a
striking account of the manner in which religious forms are established, taken
from a French publication which was burned by the common hangman at Paris.
See also on the establishment and influence of the priesthood upon religion.
Constant, ubi sup., Vol. II. Liv. iii. iv., Vol. IV. passim. His judgment of
the priesthood, though often just, is sometimes too severe. Comte, ubi sup.,
Vol. V. p. 57, et seq. ·On the priesthood among savage nations, see Pritchard,
ubi sup., Vol. I. p. 206, et seq. ; Meiners, ubi sup., Vol. II. p. 481—602.

[2] See Strabo's remarkable account of the worship of the Ancient Persians,
Opp. ed. Siebenkees, Vol. VI. Lib. xv. § 13, p. 221. See too the remarks of
Herbert, De Religione Gentilitium, Amst. 1663, 1 vol. 4to, Ch. II., XIV., et al.

GREAT SPIRIT is worshipped, perhaps, in all stages of Fetichism. The Fetiche and the Manitou, visible types, are not the Great Spirit. But even in the worship of many Gods, or of ONE alone, traces of the ruder form still linger. The Fetiche of the individual is preserved in the Amulet, worn as a charm; in the figure of an animal painted on the dress, the armour, or the flesh of the worshipper. The Family Fetiche survives in the household Gods; the Penates of the Romans; the Teraphim of Laban; the Idol of Micah. The Fetiche of the Tribe still lives in the Lares of the Roman; in the patron God of each Grecian people; in some animal treated with great respect, or idealized in art, as the Bull Apis, the brazen Serpent, Horses consecrated to the Sun in Solomon's Temple;[1] in an image of Deity, like the old wooden statues of Minerva, always religiously kept, or the magnificent figures of the Gods in marble, ivory, or gold, the productions of maturest art; in some chosen symbol, the Palladium, the Ancilia, the Ark of the Covenant. The Fetiche of the Nation, almost inseparably connected with the former, is still remembered in the mystical Cherubim and Most Holy Place among the Jews; in the Olympian Jove of Greece, and the Capitoline Jupiter of Rome; in the image of "the Great Goddess Diana, which fell down from Jupiter." It appears also in reverence for particular places formerly deemed the local and exclusive residence of the Fetiche,—such as the Caaba at Mecca; Hebron, Moriah, and Bethel in Judea; Delphi in Greece, and the great gathering places of the North-men in Europe, spots deemed holy by the superstitious even now, and therefore made the site of Christian Churches.[2]

Other and more general vestiges of Fetichism remain in the popular superstitions; in the belief of signs, omens,

[1] Vatke, Biblische Theologie, Berlin, 1835, Vol. I., attempts to trace out the connection of Fetichism with the Jewish ritual.

[2] See Mone, ubi supra, Vol. I. p. 23, et seq., p. 43, et seq., p. 113, et seq., p. 249, et seq., and elsewhere. Wilkinson, ubi sup. Vol. I., Ch. xii.; Vol. II. Ch. ii. and xiv. His theory, however, differs widely from the above. Whatever was extraordinary was deemed eminently divine. Thus with the Hebrews a great cedar was the *cedar of God.* Other nations had their Dê-wa-dâ-ru, God Timber, &c. See Grimm, Deutsche Mythologie, p. 41, et seq. Lucan, Pharsal., Lib. III. 399, et seq. Mithridates, at the siege of Patara, dared not cut down the sacred trees. Appian, De Bello Mith. Ch. XXVII. Opp. ed. Schweighauser, I. p. 679, 680.

auguries, divination by the flight of birds, and other accidental occurrences; in the notion that unusual events,
thunder, and earthquakes, and pestilence, are peculiar
manifestations of God; that he is more specially present
in a certain place, as a church, or time, as the sabbath, or
the hour of death; is pleased with actions not natural,
sacrifices, fasts, penance, and the like.[1]   Perhaps no form
of religion has yet been adopted which has not the stain
of Fetichism upon it.   The popular Christian theology is
full of it.   The names of the constellations are records of
Fetichism that will long endure.[2]

Under this form Religion has the smallest sound influence upon life; the religious does not aid the moral
element.[3]   The supposed demands of Religion seem capricious to the last degree, unnatural and absurd.   The imperfect priesthood of necromancers and jugglers,—which
belongs to this period,—enhances the evil by multiplying
rites; encouraging asceticism; laying heavy burdens upon
the people; demanding odious mutilations and horrible
sacrifices, often of human victims, in the name of God, and
in helping to keep Religion in its infant state, by forbidding the secular eye to look upon its mysterious jugglery,
and prohibiting the banns between Faith and Knowledge.
Still this class, devoted to speculation and study, does
great immediate service to the race, by promoting science
and art, and indirectly and against its will contributes to
overturn the form it designs to support.   The priesthood
comes unavoidably.[4]

In a low form of Fetichism, a Law of Nature seems
scarce ever recognized.   All things are thought to have a
life of their own; all phenomena, growth, decay, and reproduction.   The seasons of the year, the changes in the

[1] The great religious festivals of the Christians, Yule and Easter, are easily
traced back to such an occasion, at least to analogous festivals of fetichistic or
polytheistic people.   The festival of John the Baptist must be put in this class.
See some details on this subject in a very poor book of Nork's, Der Mystagog,
&c.

[2] See Creutzer, Symbolik und Mythologie, 3rd ed. Vol. I. p. 30, et seq.

[3] The Guaycarus Indians of South America put to death all children born
before the 30th year of their mother.   Bartlett's Progress of Ethnology, N. Y.
1847, p. 28.

[4] See the remarks of Lafitau, Mœurs des sauvages Ameriquains, &c., 2 vols.
4to, Paris, 1734, Vol. I. p. 108—456.   His work is amazingly superficial, but
contains now and then a good thing.

sky, and similar things, depend on the caprice of the Deities. The jugglers can make it rain ; a witch can split the moon ; a magician heal the sick. Law is resolved into miracle. The most cunning men, who understand the Laws of Nature better than others, are miracle-workers, magicians, priests, necromancers, astrologers, soothsayers, physicians, general mediators and interpreters of the Gods ; as the Mandans called them "great medicine-men." [1]

Then as men experience both joy and grief, pain and pleasure, and as they are too rude in thought to see that both are but different phases of the same thing, and affliction is but success in a mask, it is supposed they cannot be the work of the same Divinity. Hence comes the wide division into good and evil Gods, a distinction found in all religions, and carefully preserved in the theological doctrines of the Christian Church. Worship is paid both to the good and evil Deity. A sacrifice is offered to avert the wrath of the one, and secure the favour of the other. The sacrifice corresponds to the character ascribed to the Deity, and this depends again on the national and personal character of the devotee.[2]

Now in that stage of civilization where every man has his own personal Deity, and no two perhaps the same, the bond that unites man to man is exceedingly slight. Each man's hand is, in some measure, against his brother's. Opposition, or unlikeness, among the Gods, leads to hostility among men. Thus family is arrayed against family, tribe against tribe, nation against nation, because the peculiar God of the one family, tribe, or nation, is deemed hostile to all others. Therefore among cruel nations, whose Gods of course are conceived of as cruel, the most

---

[1] Mr. Catlin, ubi sup., relates anecdotes that illustrate the state of thought and feeling in the state of Fetichism. Much also may be found in Marco Polo's Travels in the Eastern parts of the World, London, 1818, and in Marsden's Notes to that edition. The early Voyagers, likewise, are full of facts that belong here.

[2] The worship of *evil beings* is a curious phenomenon in human history. The literature of the subject is copious and instructive. Some famous men think the existence of the Devil cannot be found out by the light of Nature and unaided Reason; others make it a doctrine of *natural* religion. Some think him incapable of Atheism, though only a *speculative theist.* The doctrine is a disgrace to the Christian Church, and well fitted to excite the disgust of thinking and pious men. But see what may be said for the doctrine by Mayer, Historia Diaboli, 2nd edition, 1780. See the literature in Wegscheider, Institutiones, § 104, 105.

acceptable sacrifice to the Fetiche is the blood of his enemies.   A stranger whom accident or design brings to the
devotee is a choice offering.   The Saint is a murderer.
War is a constant and normal state of men, not an exception as it afterwards becomes ; the captives are sacrificed
as a matter of course.   The energies of the race are devoted to destruction ; not to creative industry.   It is the
business of a man to war ; of a slave and a woman, to till
the soil.   The fancied God guides the deepening battle ;
presides over the butchery, and canonizes the bloody hand.
He is the God of Battles, teaches men to war, inspires
them to fight.

It is, unfortunately, but too easy to find historical verifications of this phase of human nature.   The Jews, in
their early and remarkable passage from Fetichism to
Polytheism and Monotheism—if we may trust the tale—
resolve to exterminate all the Canaanites, millions of men,
unoffending and peaceful, because the two nations worshipped different Gods, and Jehovah, the peculiar Deity of
the Jews, a jealous God, demanded the destruction of the
other nation, who did not worship him.   Men, women,
and children must be slain.[1]   The Spaniards found cannibalism in the name of God, prevailing at Mexico, and elsewhere.   In our day it still continues in the South Sea
Islands, under forms horrible almost as of old in the Holy
Land.[2]

But the intense demands which war makes on all the
energies of men help to unfold the thinking faculty, to
elevate the race and thus indirectly to promote truer no-

[1] See a dreadful example of human sacrifice in 2 Kings iii. 27.   This prevailed in many parts of America when first discovered by the Christians, who
continued it in a different form, not offering to God but Mammon.   See Bancroft, History of the United States, Vol. III. p. 296, 297, for some forms of this.
The whole of Chap. XXII. is replete with philosophical and historical instruction, and one of the most valuable and brilliant even in *that* series of shining
pages.

[2] On this passage in human history, see Comte, Vol. V. p. 90, et seq., p. 132,
et seq., and p. 186, et seq.

See F. W. Chillani, Die Menschen-Opf. der alten Hebräer, Nürmberg, 1842,
1 vol. 8vo.   He strongly maintains that human sacrifice was not forbidden by
Moses, but continued a legal and essential part of the national worship till the
separation of the two kingdoms.   Vestiges of this he thinks appear in the conse-
cration of the first-born, in circumcision, in the Paschal Lamb, &c. &c.   He
cites many curious facts.   See p. 376.   Daumer Geheimnitze des Christlichen
Altarthums, Hamb. 1847, ch. 3, 5, 9—16, 74, 75, et al.

tions of Religion. Thus War, cruel and hideous monster as he is, has yet rocked Art and Science in his bloody arms. God makes the wrath of man to praise him;

" From seeming evil still educing good,
   And better thence again, and better still
   In infinite progression."

As civilization goes forward in this rough way, the voice of humanity begins to speak more loudly, Morality is wedded to Religion, and a new progeny is born to bless the world. It begins to be felt that if the captive consents to serve his conqueror's God, the service will be more acceptable than his death. Hence he is spared; still worships his own Deity perhaps, but confesses the superiority of the victorious God. The God of the conquered party becomes a Devil, or a strange God, or a servant of the controlling Deity. Thus the Gibeonites and the Helots who once would have been sacrificed to the conquering God, became hewers of wood and drawers of water to the Hebrews and the Spartans, and served to develope the directly useful and creative faculties of man. The Gods demand the service, not the life-blood, of the stranger and captive. No doubt the anointed priesthood opposed this refinement with a " Thus saith the Lord," and condemned such as received the blessing of men ready to perish. But it would not do. Samuel hews Agag in pieces, though Saul would have saved him; but the days of Samuel also are numbered, and the theocratic power pales its ineffectual ray before a rising light.

II. POLYTHEISM is the next stage in the religious development of mankind. Here reflection begins to predominate over sensation. As the laws of Nature, the habits and organization of animals, begin to be understood, they cease to represent the true object of worship. No man ever deified Weight and Solidity. But as men change slowly from form to form, and more slowly still from the form to the substance, coarse and material Fetichism must be idealized before it could pass away. No doubt men, for the sake of example, bowed to the old stock and stone when they knew an idol was nothing. It might offend the weak to give up the lie all at once.

Polytheism is the worship of many Gods without the worship of animals. It may be referred to two sources, worship of the Powers of material nature and of the Powers of spiritual nature. Its history is that of a conflict between the two.[1] In the earliest epoch of Greek Polytheism, the former prevails; the latter at a subsequent period. The early deities are children of the Earth, the Sky, the Ocean. These objects themselves are Gods.[2] In a word, the Saturnian Gods of the older mythology are deified powers of Nature: but in the mythology of the later philosophers, it is absolute spiritual power that rules the world from the top of Olympus, and the subordinate deities are the spiritual faculties of Man personified and embellished.[3] Matter, no longer worshipped, is passive, powerless, and dishonoured. The animals are driven off from Olympus. Man is idealized and worshipped. The Supreme wears the personality of men. Anthropomorphism takes the place of a deification of Nature. The popular Gods are of the same origin as their worshippers, born, nursed, bred, but immortal and not growing old.[4] They are married like men and women, and become parents. They preside over each department of Nature and each province of art.[5] Pluto rules over the abodes of the departed; Neptune

[1] In what relates to this subject, I shall consider Polytheism as it appeared to the great mass of its votaries. Its most obvious phenomena are the most valuable. Some, as Bryant, take the speculations of naturalists and make it only a system of Physics: others, as Cudworth, following the refinements of later philosophers, would prove it to be a system of Monotheism in disguise. But to the mass Apollo was not the Sun nor the beautiful influence of God, whatsoever he might appear to the mystic sage.

[2] Julius Firmicus maintains that the heathen deities were simply deified natural objects. De Errore prof. Religionum, Ch. I.—V. But Clement of Alexandria more wisely refers them to seven distinct sources. Cohortatio ad Gentes, Opp. I., ed. Potter, p. 21, 22. Earth and Heaven are the oldest Gods of Greece.

[3] See for example the contest of Eros and Anacreon, Carm. XIV. p. 18, 19, ed. Möbius.

[4] See Heyne, Excursus VIII., in Iliad, I. 494, p. 189; Hegel, Philosophie der Rel., Vol. II. p. 96—141; Werke, Vol. XII.; Pindar, Nem. VI. 1, et seq., Olymp. XII. et seq., &c.

[5] See Aristotle, Metaphysica, Opp., ed. Baker, Oxford, 1837, VIII. Lib. XI. § 8, p. 233, et seq. In the old Pelasgic Polytheism, it seems there were no proper names for the individual Gods. The general term *Gods* was all. Herodotus, Lib. II. ch. 52, Opp., ed. Baehr., I. p. 606, et seq. Plato mentions the two classes of Gods, one derived from the *worship of Nature*, the other from that of *man*. Legg. Lib. XI., Opp. ed. Ast. VII. p. 344. See Plutarch cited in Eusebius, P. E. III. 1, p. 57, Vers. Lat., ed. 1579.

over the ocean; Jove over the land and sky. One divinity wakes the olive and the corn, another has charge of
the vine. One guides the day from his chariot with
golden wheels. A sister Deity walks in brightness
through the nocturnal sky. A fountain in the shade, a
brook leaping down the hills, or curling through the
plains; a mountain walled with savage rocks; a seques-
tered vale fringed with romantic trees,—each was the
residence of a God. Demons dwelt in dark caves, and
shook the woods at night with hideous rout, breaking
even the cedars. They sat on the rocks—fair virgins
above the water, but hideous shapes below—to decoy
sailors to their destruction. The mysterious sounds of
Nature, the religious music of the wind playing among
the pines at eventide, or stirring the hot palm tree at
noonday, was the melody of the God of sounds.[1] A beautiful form of man or woman was a shrine of God.[2] The
storms had a deity. Witches rode the rack of night. A
God offended roused nations to war, or drove Ulysses
over many lands. A pestilence, drought, famine, inunda-
tion, an army of locusts was the special work of a God.[3]

[1] See the beautiful lines of Wordsworth, Excursion, Boston, 1824, Book IV.
p. 159, et seq. See also Creutzer, ubi sup., Vol. I. p. 8—29.
[2] See Herodotus, V. 47. The Greeks erected an altar on the grave of Phi-
lippos, the most beautiful of the Greeks, and offered sacrifice. See Wachsmuth,
Antiquities of Greece, Vol. II. 2, p. 315, on the general adoration of Beauty
amongst the Greeks. Hegel calls this worship *the Religion of Beauty*.
Phil. der Religion, Vol. II. p. 96, et seq. National character marks the religious form.
[3] A *disease* was sometimes personified and worshipped, as Fever at Rome.
See Ælian, Var. Hist. XII. 11, p. 734, et seq., ed. Gronovius; Valerius Maximus, Lib. II. Ch. V. 6, Vol. I. p. 126, et seq., ed. Hase. Some say a certain
ruin at Tivoli is the remnant of a Temple to *Tussis*, a cough. Cicero speaks of
a temple to *Fever* on the Palatine. Nat. Deorum, III. 15, Opp. ed. Lemaira,
XII. p. 333, where see the note. Nero erected a monument to the Manes of a
crystal vase that got broken. Temples were erected to *Shame* and *Impudence*,
Fear, *Death*, *Laughter*, and *Gluttony*, among the Heathen, as shrines to the
Saints among Christians. Pausanias, Lib. IV. Ch. XVII., says, the Athenians
alone of all the Greeks had a Temple for Modesty and Mercy. See, however,
the ingenious remark of Cousin, Journal des Savans, March, 1835, p. 136, et
seq., and Creutzer's animadversions thereon, ubi sup. Vol. I. p. 135, 136. Brouwer, Vol. I. p. 357. In India, each natural object is the seat of a God. But
in Greece the worship of nature passed into the higher form. See some fanciful
remarks of Hermann on the most ancient mythology of the Greeks in his Opuscula, Vol. II. p. 167. It is a noticeable fact that some of the old Polytheistic
theogonies spoke of a *gradual and progressive devolopment of the Gods ;* the *creator*
keeps even pace with the *creation*. The explanation of a fact so singular as the
self-contradictory opinion that the Infinite is not always the same may be found

No ship is called by the name of Glaucus because he offended a deity.[1]

Arts also have their patron divinity. Phœbus-Apollo inspires the Poet and Artist; the Muses—Daughters of Memory and Jove—fire the bosom from their golden urn of truth;[2] Thor, Ares, Mars, have power in war; a sober virgin-goddess directs the useful arts of life; a deity presides over agriculture, the labours of the smith, the shepherd, the weaver, and each art of Man. He defends men engaged in these concerns. Every nation, city, or family has its favourite God—a Zeus, Athena, Juno, Odin, Baal, Jehovah, Osiris, or Melkartha, who is supposed to be partial to the nation which is his "chosen people." Now perhaps no nation ever believed in many separate, independent, absolute deities. All the Gods are not of equal might. One is King of all, the God of Gods, who holds the others with an iron sway. Sometimes he is the All-Father; sometimes the All-Fate, which, in some ages, seems to be made a substitute for the one true God.[3] Each nation thinks its own chief God greater than the Gods of all other nations; or, in time of war, seeks to seduce the hostile Gods by sacrifice, promise of temples and cere-

in the history of *human conceptions* of God, for these are necessarily progressive. See Aristotle, Metaphysica, XIV. p. 1000, et seq., Opp. II., ed. Duval, Par. 1629. See Hesiod's Theogony everywhere, and note the *progress of the divine species* from Chaos and Earth to the moral divinities, Eunomia, Dike, Eirene, &c. In some of the Oriental theogonies, the rule was inverted, the first *emanation* was the best. See Warton, History of English Poetry, Lond. 1824, Vol. I., Pref. by the Editor.

[1] Herodotus, Lib. VI. 86, relates the beautiful story of Glaucus, so full of moral truth. Compare with it, Zechariah v. 3, 4, Job xv. 20, et seq., xviii. et seq., where the same beautiful and natural sentiment appears.

[2] See the strange pantheistic account of the origin and history of Gods and all things in the Orphic poems and Mythology. These have been collected and treated of with great discrimination by Lobeck, Aglaophamus, Vol. I. p. 473, et seq. See the more summary account in Brandis, Geschichte der Philosophie, Vol. I. p. 60, et seq. There are some valuable thoughts in Creutzer's Review of the new edition of *Cornutus*, De Nat. Deorum, in Theol. Stud. und Kritiken für 1846, p. 208, et seq.

[3] Men must believe in somewhat that to them is Absolute; if their conception of the Deity be imperfect, they unavoidably retreat to a somewhat Superior to the Deity. Thus for every defect in the popular conception of Zeus, some new power is added to Fate. "It is impossible even for God to escape Fate," said Herodotus. See also Cudworth, Ch. I. § 1—3, Zenophanes makes a sharp distinction between *God* and the *Gods*. See in Clem. Alex. Strom. V. p. 601, and the remarks of Brandis, ubi sup., Vol. I. p. 361, et seq. note; see also Vol. II. p. 340, et seq. See too Cornutus (or Phurnutus) De Nat. Deorum in Gale, Opusc. Mythologica, &c., Amst. 1688.

monies, a pilgrimage, or a vow. Thus the Romans invoked the Gods of their enemy to come out of the beleaguered city, and join with them, the conquerors of the world. The Gods were to be had at a bargain. Jacob drives a trade with Elohim; the God receives a human service as adequate return for his own divine service.[1] The promise of each is only "for value received."

In this stage of religious development each Deity does not answer to the Idea of God, as mentioned above; it is not the Being of infinite power, wisdom, and love. Neither the Zeus of the Iliad, nor the Elohim of Genesis, nor the Jupiter of the Pharsalia, nor even the Jehovah of the Jewish Prophets, is always this. A transient and complex conception takes the place of the eternal Idea of God. Hence his limitations; those of a man. Jehovah is narrow; Zeus is licentious; Hermes will lie and steal; Juno is a shrew.[2]

The Gods of polytheistic nations are in part deified men.[3] The actions of many men, of different ages and countries, are united into one man's achievement, and we have a Hercules, or an Apollo, a thrice-great Hermes, a Jupiter, or an Odin. The inventors of useful arts, as agriculture, navigation; of the plough, the loom, laws, fire, and letters, subsequently became Gods. Great men, wise men, good men, were honoured while living; they are deified when they decease. As they judged or governed the living once, so now the dead. Their actions are idealized; the good lives after them; their faults are buried. Statues, altars, temples are erected to them. He who was first honoured as a man is now worshipped as a God.[4] To these personal deities are added the attributes of the old Fetiches, and still more the powers of Nature. The attributes of the moon, the sun, the lightning, the ocean, or the stars are

---

[1] Genesis xxviii. 10—22.
[2] Sermons of Theism, &c. Sermon III. and IV.
[3] Tertullian, De Anima, Ch. 33. See Meiners, ubi sup., Vol. I. p. 290, et seq.; Pindar, Olymp. II. 68, et seq., ed Dissen., and his remarks, Vol. II. p. 36, et seq. This Anthropomorphism took various forms in Greece, Egypt, and India. In the former it was the *elevation of a man to the Gods;* in the latter the *descent of a God to man.* This feature of Oriental worship furnishes a fruitful hint as to the origin of the doctrine of *the Incarnation* and its value. The doctrine of some Christians unites the two in the *God-man.*
[4] See the origin of Idolatry laid down in Wisdom of Solomon, Ch. xiv. 17—19. Warburton, Divine Legation, Book V. § ii. [iii.]

transferred to a personal being, conceived as a man. To
be made strong he is made monstrous, with many hands,
or heads.   In a polytheistic nation, if we trace the history
of the popular conception of any God, that of Zeus among
the Grecians, for example, we see a gradual advance, till
their highest God becomes their conception of the Absolute.   Then the others are insignificant ; merely his servants ; like colonels and corporals in an army, they are
parts of his state machinery.   The passage to Monotheism
is then easy.[1]   The spiritual leaders of every nation,—
obedient souls into whom the spirit enters and makes them
Sons of God and prophets,—see the meaning which the
popular notion hides ; they expose what is false, proclaim
the eternal truth, and as their recompense are stoned,
exiled, or slain.   But the march of mankind is over the
tombs of the prophets.   The world is saved only by crucified redeemers.   The truth is not silenced with Aristotle ;
nor exiled with Anaxagoras ; nor slain with Socrates.   It
enters the soul of its veriest foes, and their children build
up the monuments of the murdered Seer.

We cannot enter into the feelings of a polytheist ; nor
see how Morality was fostered by his religion.   Ours
would be a similar puzzle to him.   But Polytheism has
played a great part in the development of mankind—yes,
in the deveolpment of Morality and Religion.[2]   Its aim
was to "raise a mortal to the skies ;" to infinitize the
finite ; to bridge over the great gulf between Man and
God.   Let us look briefly at some of its features.

I. In Polytheism we find a regular priesthood.   This is
sometimes exclusive and hereditary, as in Egypt and India,
where it establishes castes, and founds a theocracy ; sometimes not hereditary, but open, free, as in Greece.[3]   When

[1] There are two strongly marked tendencies in all polytheistic religions—one
towards pure Monotheism, the other to Pantheism. See an expression of the
latter in Orpheus, ed. Hermann, p. 457, " Zeus is the first, Zeus the last," &c.
&c., cited also in Cudworth, ubi sup., Vol. I. p. 404. See Zeno, in Diogenes
Laertius, ed Hübner, Lib. VII. Ch. 73, Vol. II. p. 186, et seq. ; Clemens
Alexand. Stromat. VII. 12. See also Cudworth, Ch. IV. § 17, et seq., and
Mosheim's Annotations.

[2] M. Comte thinks this the period of the greatest religious activity ! The
facts look the other way.

[3] Even in Greece some sacerdotal functions vested by descent in certain families, for example, in the Iambides, Branchides, Eumolpides, Asclepiades, Cery-

"every clove of garlic is a God," as in Fetichism, each man is his own priest; but when a troop of Fetiches are condensed into a single God, and he is invisible, all cannot have equal access to him, for he is not infinite, but partial; chooses his own place and time. Some mediator, therefore, must stand between the God and common men.[1] This was the function of the priest. Perhaps his office became hereditary at a very early period, for as we trace backward the progress of mankind the law of inheritance has a wider range. The priesthood, separated from the actual cares of war, and of providing for material wants—the two sole departments of human activity in a barbarous age—have leisure to study the will of the Gods. Hence arises a learned class, who gradually foster the higher concerns of mankind. The effort to learn the will of the Gods, leads to the study of Nature, and therefore to Science. The attempt to please them by images, ceremonies, and the like, leads to architecture, statues, music, poetry, and hymns—to the elegant arts. The priesthood fostered all these. It took different forms to suit the genius of different nations; established castes and founded the most odious despotism in Egypt and the East, and perhaps the North, but in Greece left public opinion comparatively free. In the one, change of opinion was violent and caused commotion, as the fabled Giant buried under Ætna shakes the island when he turns; in the other it was natural, easy as for Endymion to turn the other cheek to the Moon. Taken in the whole, it has been a heavy rider on the neck of the nations. Its virtue has been, in a rude age to promote Science, Art, Patriotism, Piety to the Gods, and, in a certain fashion, Love to men. But its vice has been to grasp at the throat of mankind, control their thoughts and govern their life, aspiring to be the Will of the World. When it has been free, as in the philosophic age in Greece, its influence has been deep, silent, and unseen; blessed and beautiful. But when it is hered-

cides, Clitiades. See them in Wachsmuth, Vol. I. P. i. p. 152. See Grimm, Deutsche Mythologie, Ch. V.; Meiners, Vol. II. Book xii.; Brouwer, Vol. I.

[1] See Montesquieu, Esprit des Lois, Liv. XXV. Ch. iv. See Priestley's Comparison of the Institutions of Moses with those of the Hindoos, &c., Northumberland, 1799, § X. for the esteem in which the sacerdotal class was held in India. Brouwer, Vol. III. Ch. xviii., xix. Also Von Bohlen, Das alte Indien, Vol. I. p. 45, et seq.; Vol. II. p. 12, et seq.

itary and exclusive, it preserves the form, ritual, and creed of barbarous times in the midst of civilization; separates Morality from Religion, life from belief, good sense from theology; demands horrible sacrifices of the body, or the soul; and, like the angry God in the old Pelasgic fable, chains for eternal damnation the bold free spirit which, learning the riddle of the world, brings down the fire of Heaven to bless poor mortal men. It were useless to quote examples of the influence of the priesthood. It has been the burthen of Fate upon the human race. Each age has its Levites; instruments of cruelty are in their habitations. In many nations their story is a tale of blood; the tragedy of Sin and Woe.[1]

II. In the polytheistic period, war is a normal state and almost constant. Religion then unites men of the same tribe and nation; but severs one people from another. The Gods are hostile; Jehovah and Baal cannot agree. Their worshippers must bite and devour one another. It is high treason for a citizen to communicate the form of the national Religion to a foreigner; Jehovah is a jealous God. Strangers are sacrificed in Tauris and Egypt, and the captives in war put to death at the command of the Priest. But war at that period had also a civilizing influence. It was to the ancient world what Trade is to modern times: another form of the same selfishness. It was the chief method of extending a nation's influence. The remnant of the conquered nation was added to the victorious empire; became its slaves or tributaries, and at last shared its civilization, adding the sum of its own excellence to the moral treasury of its master. Conquered Greece gave Arts and Philosophy to Rome; the exiled Jews brought back from Babylon the great doctrine of eternal life. The Goths conquered Rome, but Roman Christianity subdued the Goths. Religion, allied with the fiercest animal passions, demanded war; this led to science. It was soon seen that one head which thinks is worth a

[1] See the one-sided view of Constant, which pervades his entire work on Religion. See his Essay on the "Progressive Development of Religious Ideas," in Ripley's Philosophical Miscellanies, Vol. II. p. 292, et seq. Virgil, in his description of the Elysian fields, assigns the first place to *Legislators*, the magnanimous Heroes who civilized mankind; the next to *Patriots*, and the third to *Priests*. Æn. VI. 661, et seq.

hundred hands. Science elevates the mass of men, they perceive the folly of bloodshed, and its sin. Thus War, by a fatal necessity, digs its own grave. The art of production surpasses the art to destroy.[1]

All the wars of polytheistic nations have more or less a religious character. Their worship, however, favoured less the extermination of enemies than their subjugation, while Monotheism, denying the existence of all deities but one, when it is superinduced upon a nation, in a rude state, like Fetichism itself, butchers its captives, as the Jews, the Mahometans, and the Christians have often done—a sacrifice to the blood-thirsty phantom they call a God.[2] In the ruder stages of Polytheism, war is the principal occupation of men. The Military and the Priestly powers, strength of Body and strength of Thought, are the two Scales of Society; Science and Art are chiefly devoted to kill men and honour the Gods. The same weapons which conquer the spoil, sacrifice it to the Deity.[3]

III. But as Polytheism leads men to spare the life of the captive, so it leads to a demand for his service. Slavery, therefore, like war, comes unavoidably from this form of Religion, and the social system which grows out of it. At this day, under the influence of Monotheism, we are filled with deep horror at the thought of one man invading the personality of another, to make him a thing—a slave. The flesh of a religious man creeps at the thought of it. But yet slavery was an indispensable adjunct of this rough form of society. Between that Fetichism which bade a man slay his captive, eating his body and drinking his blood as indispensable elements of his communion with God, and that Polytheism which only makes him a slave, there is a great gulf which it required long centuries to fill up and pass over. Anger slowly gave place to interest; perhaps to Mercy. Without this change, with the advance of the art to destroy, the human race must have perished.

[1] M. Montgéry, a French captain, touchingly complains "that the art to destroy, though the easiest of all from its very nature, is now much less advanced than the art of production, in spite of the superior difficulty of the latter." Quoted in Comte, ubi sup., Vol. V. p. 167.
[2] Here is the explanation of the given facts collected by Daumer and others.
[3] M. Comte, Vol. V. p. 165, et seq., has some valuable remarks on this stage of human civilization. See also Vico, Scienza nuova, Bib. II. Cap. I.—IV.

By means of slavery the art of production was advanced. The Gibeonite and the Helot must work and not fight. Thus by forced labour, the repugnance against work which is so powerful among the barbarous and half-civilized, is overcome ; systematic industry is developed ; the human race is helped forward in this mysterious way.   Both the theocratic and the military caste demanded a servile class, inseparable from the spirit of barbarism, and the worship of many Gods, which falls as that spirit dies out, and the recognition of one God, Father of all, drives selfishness out of the heart.   In an age of Polytheism, Slavery and War were in harmony with the institutions of society and the spirit of the age.   Murder and Cannibalism, two other shoots from the same stock, had enjoyed their day.   All are revolting to the spirit of Monotheism ; at variance with its idea of life ; uncertain and dangerous ; monstrous anomalies full of deadly peril.   The Priesthood of Poly-theism—like all castes based on a lie—upheld the system of slavery, which rested on the same foundation with itself. The slavery of sacerdotal governments is more oppressive and degrading than that of a military despotism.   It binds the Soul—makes distinctions in the nature of men.   The Prophet would free men ; but the priest enslaves.   As Polytheism does its work, and Man developes his nature higher than the selfish, the condition of the slave is made better.   It becomes a religious duty to free the bondsmen at their master's death, as formerly the priests had burned them on his funeral pile, or buried them alive in his tomb to attend him in the realm of shades.[1]   Just as civilization

[1] See, who will, the mingling of profound and superficial remarks on this subject in Montesquieu, ubi sup., Liv. XV.   Grotius, De jure Belli ac Pacis, Lib. III. Ch. vii. viii.   Selden, De jure naturali, &c., ed. 1680, Lib. I. Ch. v. p. 174, and Lib. VII. VIII. XII. et al.   See the valuable treatise of Charles Comte, Traité de la Législation, ou Exposition des Lois générales suivant lesquelles les Peuples prospèrent, dépérissent ou restent stationaire, &c. &c., 3rd ed., Bruxelles, 1837, Liv. V., the whole of which is devoted to the subject of slavery and its influence in ancient and modern times.   We need only compare the popular opinion respecting slavery among the Jews, with that of the Greeks or Romans, in their best days, to see the influences of Monotheism and Polytheism in regard to this subject.   See some remarks on the Jewish slavery in Michaelis's Laws of Moses.   Slavery in the East has in general been of a much milder character than in any other portion of the world.   Wolf somewhere says the Greeks received this relic of barbarism from the Asiatics.   If so, they made the evil institution worse than they found it.   According to Burckhardt, it exists in a very mild form among the Mahometans, everywhere.   Of course his remarks do not apply to the Turks, the most cruel of Mussulmen.   Perhaps

advanced and the form of Religion therewith, it was found difficult to preserve the institution of ancient crime, which sensuality and sin clung to and embraced.[1]

IV. Another striking feature of polytheistic influence, was the union of power over the Body with power over the Soul ; the divine right to prescribe actions and prohibit thoughts. This is the fundamental principle of all theocracies. The Priests were the speculative class ; their superior knowledge was natural power ; superstition in the people and selfishness in the Priest, converted that power into despotic tyranny. The military were the active caste ; superior strength and skill gave them also a natural power. But he who alone in an age of barbarism can foretell an eclipse, or poison a flock of sheep, can subdue an army by these means. At an early stage of polytheism, we find the political subject to the priestly power. The latter holds communion with the Gods, whom none dare disobey. Romulus, Æacus, Minos, Moses, profess to receive their laws from God. To disobey them, therefore, is to incur the wrath of the powers that hold the thunder and lightning. Thus manners and laws, opinions and actions, are subject to the same external authority. The theocratic governor controls the conscience and the passions of the people. Thus the radical evil arising from the confusion between the Priests of different Gods was partially removed, for the spiritual and temporal power was lodged in the same hand.

In some nations the Priesthood was inferior to the political power, as in Greece. Here the sacerdotal class held an inferior rank, from Homer's time to that of Laertius.[2]

no code of *ancient* laws (to say nothing of modern legislation) was more humane than the Jewish in this respect.

[1] See Comte, Phil. positive, Vol. V. p. 186, et seq. On this subject of slavery in Polytheistic nations, see Gibbon, Decline and Fall. ed. Paris, 1840, Vol. I. Ch. ii. p. 37, et seq., and the valuable notes of Milman and Guizot. For the influence of Monotheism on this frightful evil, compare Schlosser, Geschichte der Alten Welt, Vol. III. Part III. Ch. ix. § 2, et al. ; in particular the story of Paulinus, and Deogratias, p. 284, et seq., and p. 334, et seq., p. 427, et seq. ; and compare it with the conduct of Cato (as given by Plutarch, Life of Cato the Censor, and Schlosser, ubi sup., Vol. II. Part II. p. 189, et seq., Charles Comte, ubi sup., Liv. V.), and alas, with the conduct of the American Government and the commercial churches of our large towns in 1850—1855.

[2] See Demosthenes, Cont. Near. Ch. XX. in Oratores Attici, Lond. 1828,

The Genius of the nation demanded it ; accordingly there sprang up a body of men, neither political, sacerdotal, nor military—the philosophers.[1] They could have found no place in any theocratic government, but have done the world great religious service, building "wiser than they knew." It was comparatively easy for Art, Science, and all the great works of men, to go forward under such circumstances. Hence comes that wonderful development of mind in the country of Homer, Socrates, and Phidias. But in countries where the temporal was subject to the spiritual power, the reverse followed ; there was no change without a violent revolution. The character of the nation becomes monotonous ; science, literature, morals, cease to improve. When the nation goes down, it "falls like Lucifer, never to hope again." The story of Samuel affords us an instance, among the Jews, of the sacerdotal class resisting, and successfully, the attempt to take away its power. Here the Priest, finding there must be a King, succeeded at length in placing on the throne a "man after God's own heart," that is, one who would sacrifice as the Priest allowed. The effort to separate the temporal from the spiritual power, to disenthral mankind from the tyranny of sacerdotal corporations, is one of the great battles for the souls of the world. It begins early, and continues long. The contest shakes the earth in its time.

V. Another trait of the polytheistic period is the deification of men.[2] Fetichism makes gods of cattle; Polytheism of men. This exaltation of men exerted great influence in the early stage of polytheism, when it was a

Vol. VIII. p. 391, et seq. ; Aristot. Rep. III. 14, Opp. ed. Bekker, X. p. 87. See also César Cantu, Histoire Universelle, Paris, 1841—1844, Vol. I. Ch. xxviii. xxix.; Constant, Liv. V. Ch. v., and Brouwer's remarks thereon, p. 363, note.

[1] Perhaps none of the polytheistic nations offers an instance of the spiritual and temporal power existing in separate hands, when one party was entirely independent of the other. The separation of the two was reserved for a different age, and will be treated of in its place.

[2] See Farmer on the Worship of Human Spirits, London, 1783. Plutarch (Isis and Osiris) denies that human spirits were ever worshipped, but he is opposed by notorious facts. See Creutzer, ubi sup., p. 137, et seq. The deification of human beings of course implied a belief in the immortality of the human soul, and is one of the many standing proofs of that belief. See Heyne's remarks on Iliad, XXIII. 64 and 104, Vol. VIII. p. 368, 378, et seq.

real belief of the people and the priest, and not a verbal form, as in the decline of the old worship. Stout hearts could look forward to a wider sphere in the untrod world of spirit, where they should wield the sceptre of command and sit down with the immortal Gods, renewed in never-ending youth. The examples of Æacus, Minos, Rhadamanthus, of Bacchus and Hercules—mortals promoted to the Godhead by merit, and not birth—crowned the ambition of the aspiring.[1] The kindred belief that the soul, dislodged from its "fleshly nook," still had an influence on the affairs of men, and came, a guardian spirit, to bless mankind, was a powerful auxiliary in a rude state of religious growth—a notion which has not yet faded out of the civilized world.[2] This worship seems unaccountable in our times; but when such men were supposed to be descendants of the Gods, or born miraculously, and sustained by superhuman beings; or mediators between them and the human race; when it was believed they in life had possessed celestial powers, or were incarnations of some deity or heavenly spirit, the transition to their Apotheosis is less violent and absurd; it follows as a natural result. The divine being is more glorious when he has shaken off the robe of flesh.[3] Certain it is, this belief was clung to with astonishing tenacity, and, under several forms, still retains its place in the Christian church.[4]

The moral effect of Polytheism, on the whole, is difficult to understand. However, it is safe to say it is greater than that of Fetichism. The constant evil of war in public, and slavery in private; the arbitrary character assigned to the Gods; the influence of the priesthood, laying more stress on the ritual and the creed than on the life; the exceeding outwardness of many popular forms of worship; the constant separation made between Religion

[1] Pausanias touchingly complains that in his day mortals no longer became gods. See Lib. VII. Ch. ii. Opp. ed. Schubert and Walz. III. p. 9.

[2] The Christians began at an early age to imitate this, as well as other parts of the old polytheistic system. Eusebius, P. E. XIII. 11; Augustine, De Civ. Dei, VIII. 27.

[3] On this subject, see Meiners, ubi sup., Vol. I. B. III. Ch. i. and ii.

[4] See in Gibbon, Decline and Fall, Ch. XLVII. § iii., the lament of Serapion at the loss of his *concrete Gods*. But it was only the *Arian* notions that deprived him of his finite God. Jerome condemns the Anthropomorphism of the Polytheists as *stultissimam hæresin*, but believed the divine incarnation in Jesus. See also Prudentius Apotheosis, Opp. I. p. 430, et seq., London, 1824.

and Morality ; the indifference of the priesthood in Greece, their despotism in India,—do not offer a very favourable picture of the influence of Polytheism in producing a beautiful life. Yet, on the other hand, the high tone of Morality which pervades much of the literature of Greece, the reverential piety displayed by poets and philosophers, and still more the undeniable fact of characters in her story rarely surpassed in nobleness of aim and loftiness of attainment, —these things lead to the opinion that the moral influence of this worship, when free from the shackles of a sacerdotal caste, has been vastly underrated by Christian scholars.[1]

To trace the connection between the public virtue and the popular theology, is a great and difficult matter, not to be attempted here. But this fact is plain, that in a rude state of life this connection is slight, scarce perceptible ; the popular worship represents Fear, Reverence it may be ; perhaps a Hope ; or even Trust. But the services it demands are rites and offerings, not a divine life. As civilization is advanced, Religion claims a more reasonable service, and we find enlightened men, whom the spirit of God made wise, demanding only a divine life as an offering to Him. Spiritual men, of the same elevation, see always the same spiritual truth. We notice a gradual ascent in the scale of moral ideas, from the time of Homer, through Solon, Theognis, the seven wise men, Pindar, Æschylus, Sophocles, and the philosophers of their day.[2] The philosophers and sages of Greece and Rome recommend Absolute Goodness as the only perfect service of God. With them Sin is the disease of the soul ; Virtue is health ; a divine Life the true good of mankind ; Perfection the aim. None have set forth this more ably.[3]

---

[1] The special influence of Polytheism upon morals, differed with the different forms it assumed. In India it sometimes led to rigid asceticism and lofty contemplative quietism ; in Rome, to great public activity and manly vigour ; in Greece, to a gay abandonment to the natural emotions ; in Persia, to ascetic purity and formal devotion. On this subject see the curious and able, but onesided and partial, treatise of Tholuck on the Moral Influence of Heathenism, in the American Biblical Repository, Vol. II. He has shown up the dark side of Heathenism, but seems to have no true conception of ancient manners and life. See Ackermann, das Christliche in Plato, &c., Ch. I. (See below, note [2] and [3])

[2] See the proof of this in Brandis, Geschichte der Philosophie, Vol. I. § 24, 25.

[3] See, on the moral culture of the Greeks in special, Jacobs, Vermischte

In the higher stages of Polytheism, Man is regarded as fallen. He felt his alienation from his Father. Religion looks back longingly to the Golden Age, when Gods dwelt familiar with men. It seeks to restore the links broken out of the divine chain. Hence its sacrifices, and above all its mysteries,[1] both of which were often abused, and made substitutes for holiness, and not symbols thereof.

When War is a normal state, and Slavery is common, the condition of one half the human race is soon told. Woman is a tool or a toy. Her story is hitherto the dark side of the world. If a distinction be made between public morality, private morality, and domestic morality, it may safely be said that Polytheism did much for the outward regulation of the two first, but little for the last. However, since there were Gods that watched over the affairs of the household, a limit was theoretically set to domestic immorality, spite of the temptations which both slavery and public opinion spread in the way. When there were Gods, whose special vocation was to guard the craftsmen of a certain trade, protect travellers and defenceless men; when there were general, never-dying avengers of wrong, who stopped at no goal but justice,—a bound was fixed, in some measure, to private oppression. Man, however, was not honoured as Man. Even in Plato's ideal State, the strong tyrannized over the weak; human selfishness wore a bloody robe; Patriotism was greater than Philanthropy. The popular view of sin and holiness was low. It was absurd for Mercury to conduct men to hell for adultery and lies. Heal thyself, the Shade might say. All Pagan antiquity offers nothing akin to our lives of pious men.[2] It is true, as St Augustine has well said, "that matter which is now called the Christian religion, was in existence among the

---

Schriften, Vol. III. p. 374. He has perhaps done justice to both sides of this difficult subject.

[1] Cicero, De Legg. II. See on this subject of the Mysteries in general, Lobeck, Aglaophamus, sive de Theologiæ mysticæ Causis, &c., Pars III., Ch. iii. iv. The mysteries seem sometimes to have offered beautiful symbols to aid man in returning to union with the Gods. Warburton, in spite of his erroneous views, has collected much useful information on this subject: Divine Legation. Book II. § iv. But he sometimes sees out of him what existed only in himself.

[2] But see in Plutarch the singular story of Thespesius, his miraculous conversion, &c. De sera Numinis Vindicta, Opp. II. Ch. xxvii. p. 563, et seq., ed. Xyiander.

ancients ; it has never been wanting, from the beginning
of the human race."[1]   There is but one Religion, and it
can never die out.   Unquestionably there were souls
beautifully pious, and devoutly moral, who felt the Kingdom of Heaven in their bosom, and lived it out in their
lowly life.   Still, it must be confessed the beneficial influence of the public Worship of Polytheists on public and
private virtue, was sadly weak.[2]   The popular life is determined, in some measure, by the popular Conception of
God, and that was low, and did not correspond to the
pure Idea of Him ;[3] still the Sentiment was at its work.

But worship was more obviously woven up with public
life under this form than under that which subsequently
took its place.   A wedding or a funeral, peace and war,
seed-time and harvest, had each its religious rite.   It was
the mother of philosophy, of art, and science, though, like
Saturn in the fable, she sought to devour her own children, and met a similar and well-merited fate.   Classic
Polytheism led to contentedness with the world as it was,
and a sound cheerful enjoyment of its goodness and delight.   Religion itself was glad and beautiful.[4]   But its
idea of life was little higher than its fact.   However, that
weakish cant and snivelling sentimentality of worship,
which disgrace our day, were unknown at that stage.[5]
The popular faith oscillated between Unbelief and Superstition.   Plato wisely excluded the mythological poets
from his ideal commonwealth.   The character of the Gods
as it was painted by the popular mythology of Egypt,

---

[1] Retract. I. 13.   See also Civ. Dei, VIII. and Cont. Acad. III. 20.
[2] On the influence of the national *cultus*, see Athenaeus, Deipnosoph. VII.
65, 66, XIV. 24, et al. ; Homeric Hymns I. vs. 147, et seq.
[3] Plato is seldom surpassed, in our day, in his conception of some of the
qualities of the Divine Being.   He was mainly free from that anthropomorphic
tendency which Christians have derived from the ruder portions of the Old Testament.   See Rep. Lib. IV. passim.   But neither he nor Aristotle—a yet greater
man—ever attained the idea of a God who is the Author, or even the Master,
of the material world.   God and Matter were antagonistic forces, mutually
hostile.
[4] See the pleasant remarks of Plutarch on the cheerful character of public
worship, Opp. Vol. II. p. 1101, et seq., ed. Xylander ; Strabo, Lib. X. Ch. iii.
iv. Opp. iv. p. 167, et seq., ed. Siebenkees and Tschucke.
[5] Many beautiful traits of Polytheism may be seen in Plutarch's Moral
Works, especially the treatises on Superstition ; That it is not possible to live
well according to Epicurus ; of Isis and Osiris ; of the tardy Vengeance of God.
See the English Version, Lond. 1691, 4 vols. 8vo.

Greece, and India, like some of the legends of the Old Testament, served to confound moral distinctions, and encourage crime. Polytheists themselves confess it.[1] Yet a distinction seems often to have been made between the private and the official character of the deities. There was no devil, no pandemonium, in ancient classic Polytheism as in the modern Church. Antiquity has no such disgrace to bear. Perhaps the poetic fictions about the Gods were regarded always as fictions, and no more. Still this influence must have been pernicious.[2] It would seem, at first glance, that only strong intellectual insight, or great moral purity, or a happy combination of external circumstances, could free men from the evil. However, in forming the morals of a people, it is not so much the doctrine that penetrates and moves the nation's soul as it is the feeling of that sublimity which resides only in God, and of that enchanting loveliness which alone belongs to what is filled with God. Isocrates well called the mythological tales blasphemies against the Gods. Aristophanes exposes in public the absurdities which were honoured in the recesses of the temples. The priesthood in Greece has no armour of offence against ridicule.[3] But goodness never dies out of man's heart.

Mankind pass slowly from stage to stage :—

> " Slowly as spreads the green of Earth
> O'er the receding Ocean's bed,
> Dim as the distant Stars come forth,
> Uncertain as a vision fled,"

seems the gradual progress of the race. But in the midst of the absurd doctrines of the priests, and the immoral tales wherewith mistaken poets sought to adorn their conception of God, pure hearts beat, and lofty minds rose

[1] Xenophanes, a contemporary of Pythagoras, censures Homer and Hesiod for their narratives of the Gods, imputing to them what it was shameful for a man to think of. See Karsten, Phil. vett. Reliquia, Vol. I. p. 43, et seq. See Plato, Repub. II. p. 377 ; Pindar, Olymp. I. 28. But no religion was ever *designed* to favour impurity, even when it allows it in the Gods. See the fine remarks of Seneca, De Vita beata, Ch. XXVI. § 5, 6. Even the Gods were subject to the eternal laws. Fate punished Zeus for each offence. He smarted at home for his infidelity abroad.

[2] See the classic passages in Aristophanes, Clouds, 1065, et seq.

[3] It still remains unexplained how the Athenians, on a religious festival, could applaud the exhibitions of the comic drama, which exposed the popular mythology to ridicule, as it is done in the Birds of Aristophanes—to mention a single example—and still continue the popular worship.

above the grovelling ideas of the temple and the market-place. The people who know not the law, are often better off than the sage or the soothsayer; for they know only what it is needed to know. "He is oft the wisest man that is not wise at all." Religion lies so close to men, that a pure heart and mind, free from prejudice, see its truths, its duties, and hopes. But before mankind passes from Fetichism to pure Monotheism, at a certain stage of religious progress, there are two subordinate forms of religious speculation which claim the attention of the race, namely, Dualism and Pantheism. The one is the highest form of Polytheism; the other a degenerate expression of Monotheism, and both together form the logical tie between the two.

Dualism is the deification of two principles, the Absolute Good and the Greatest Evil. The origin of this form of religious speculation has been already hinted at.[1] Philosophically stated, it is the recognition of two absolute beings, the one Supreme Good, the other Supreme Evil. But this involves a contradiction; for if the Good be absolute, Evil is not, and the reverse. Another form, therefore, was invented. The Good Being was absolute and infinite; the Evil Principle was originally good, but did not keep his first estate. Here also was another difficulty: an independent and divine being cannot be mutable and frail, therefore the evil principle must of necessity be a dependent creature, and not divine in the proper sense. So a third form takes place, in which it is supposed that both the Good and the Evil are emanations from one Absolute Being, that Evil is only negative, and will at last end; that all wicked, as all good, principles are subject to the Infinite God. At this point Dualism coalesces with the doctrine of one God, and dies its death. This system of Dualism, in its various forms, has extended widely. It seems to have been most fully developed in Persia. It came early into the Christian Church, and still retains its hold throughout the greater part of Christendom, though it is fast dying away before the advance of Reason and Faith.[2]

[1] See above, Ch. IV.
[2] The doctrine of two principles is older than the time of Zoroaster. Hyde,

Pantheism has, perhaps, never been altogether a stranger to the world. It makes all things God, and God all things. This view seems at first congenial to a poetic and religious mind. If the world be regarded as a collection of powers,—the awful force of the storm, of the thunder, the earthquake; the huge magnificence of the ocean, in its slumber or its wrath; the sublimity of the ever-during hills; the rocks, which resist all but the unseen hand of Time; these might lead to the thought that matter is God. If men looked at the order, fitness, beauty, love, everywhere apparent in Nature, the impression is confirmed. The All of things appears so beautiful to the comprehensive eye, that we almost think it is its own Cause and Creator. , The animals find their support and their pleasure; the painted leopard and the snowy swan, each living by its own law; the bird of passage that pursues, from zone to zone, its unmarked path; the summer warbler which sings out its melodious existence in the woodbine; the flowers that come unasked, charming the youthful year; the golden fruit maturing in its wilderness of green; the dew and the rainbow; the frost flake and the mountain snow; the glories that wait upon the morning, or sing the sun to his ambrosial rest; the pomp of the sun at noon, amid the clouds of a June day; the awful majesty of night, when all the stars with a serene step come out, and tread their round, and seem to watch in blest tranquillity about the slumbering world; the moon waning and waxing, walking in beauty through the night:—daily the water is rough with the winds; they come or abide at no man's bidding, and roll the yellow corn, or wake religious music at nightfall in the pines — these

Hist. Religion, vet. Persarum, Ch. IX. and XX. XXII. Bayle's Dictionary, article Zoroaster, Vol. V. p. 636. See also Cudworth, Ch. IV. § 13, p. 289, et. seq , and Mosheim's Notes, Vol. I. p. 320. et seq.; Rhode, Heilige Sage der Zendvolks, B. II. Ch. ix. x. xii.; Brucker, Historia Philosophiæ, Vol. I. p. 176, et seq. Plutarch was a Dualist, though in a modified sense. See his Isis and Osiris, and Psychogonia. Marcion, among the early Christians, was accused of this belief, and indeed the existence of a Devil is still believed by most Christian divines to be second only in importance to the belief of a God; at the very least, a *scriptural doctrine, and of great value.* See a curious book of Mayer, (Historia Diaboli,) who thinks it a matter of *divine revelation.* See also the ingenious remarks of Professor Woods, in his translation of Knapp's Theology, New York, 1831, Vol. I. § 62—66, et seq. See the early form of Dualism among the Christians in Beausobre, Histoire de Manichée et du Manichéisme, 2 vols. 4to.

things are all so fair, so wondrous, so wrapt in mystery, it
is no marvel that men say, This is divine; yes, the All is
God; he is the light of the morning, the beauty of the
noon, and the strength of the sun. The little grass
grows by his presence. He preserveth the cedars. The
stars are serene because he is in them. The lilies are redolent of God. He is the One; the All. God is the
mind of man. The soul of all; more moving than motion; more stable than rest; fairer than beauty, and
stronger than strength. The power of Nature is God;
the universe, broad and deep and high, a handful of dust,
which God enchants. He is the mysterious magic that
possesses the world. Yes, he is the All; the Reality of
all phenomena.

But an old writer thus pleasantly rebukes this conclusion: "Surely, vain are all men by nature, who are ignorant of God, and could not out of the good things that are
seen, know him that is . . . but deemed either Fire, or Wind,
or the swift Air, or the Circle of the Stars, or the violent
Water, or the Lights of Heaven, to be the Gods which govern
the world. With whose beauty if they being delighted took
them to be Gods; let them know how much better the Lord
of them is, for the first Author of beauty had created them."[1]

To view the subject in a philosophical and abstract way,
Pantheism is the worship of All as God. He is the One
and All; not conceived as distinct from the Universe, nor
independent of it. It is said to have prevailed widely in
ancient times, and, if we may believe what is reported, it
has not ended with Spinoza. It may be divided into two

[1] Wisdom of Solomon, Ch. xiii. 1, et seq. At the present day Pantheism
seems to be the bugbear of some excellent persons. They see it everywhere
except on the dark walls of their own churches. The disciples of Locke find it in all
schools of philosophy but the Sensual; the followers of Calvin see it in the
liberal churches. It has become dangerous to say "*God is Spirit;*" a *definite*
God, whose *personality we understand*, is the orthodox article. M. Maret, in
his Essai sur le Panthéisme dans les Sociétés modernes, Paris, 1840, 1 vol. 8vo,
finds it the natural result of Protestantism, and places before us the pleasant
alternatives, either the Catholic Church or Pantheism! Preface, p. xv. et al.
The rationalism of the nineteenth century must end in scepticism, or leap over
to Pantheism! According to him all the philosophers of the Spiritual School in
our day are Pantheists.—Formerly divines condemned Philosophy because it had
too little of God; now because it has *too much*. It would seem difficult to get
the orthodox medium; too much and too little are found equally dangerous.
See the pleasant remarks of Hegel on this charge of Pantheism, Encyclopädie
der philosoph. Wissenchaften, &c., third edition, § 573.

forms, Material Pantheism, sometimes called Hylozoism, and Spiritual Pantheism, or Psycho-zoism. Material Pantheism affirms the existence of Matter, but denies the existence of Spirit, or anything besides matter. Creation is not possible; the Phenomena of Nature and Life are not the result of a "fortuitous concourse of atoms," as in Atheism, but of Laws in Nature itself. Matter is in a constant flux; but it changes only by laws which are themselves immutable. Of course this does not admit God as the Absolute or Infinite, but the sum-total of material things; He is limited both to the extension and the qualities of matter; He is merely immanent therein, but does not transcend material forms. This seems to have been the Pantheism of Strato of Lampsacus, of Democritus, perhaps of Hippocrates, and, as some think, though erroneously, of Xenophanes, Parmenides, and, in general, of the Eleatic Philosophers in Greece,[1] and of many others whose tendency is more spiritual.[2] Its philosophic form is the last result of an attempt to form an adequate *Conception* of God. It has sometimes been called Kosmo-theism, (World-Divinity,) but it gives us a world without a God.

Spiritual Pantheism affirms the existence of Spirit, and sometimes, either expressly or by implication, denies the existence of Matter. This makes all Spirit God; always the same, but ever unfolding into new forms, and therefore a perpetual *Becoming;* God is the absolute substance, with these two attributes—Thought and Extension. He is self-conscious in men; without self-consciousness in animals. Before the creation of men he was not *self*-conscious. All beside God is devoid of Substantiality. It is not but only APPEARS; its *being* is its *being seen*. This is Psycho-theism (Soul-Divinity). It gives us a God without a World, and He is the only cause that exists, the

---

[1] See Karsten, ubi sup., Vol. I. and II. See the opinions of these men ably summed up by Ritter, Geschichte der Philosophie, Vol. I. B. v., and Brandis, ubi sup., Vol. I. § 66—72. Cudworth has many fine observations on this sort of pantheism, Vol. I. Ch. iv. § 15—26, and elsewhere. He denies that this school make the deity corporeal, and charges this upon others. See Ch. III.

[2] See Jäsche, Der Pantheismus, &c., Vols. II. and III. passim, and the histories of Philosophy. If a man is curious to detect a pantheistic tendency he will find it in the *Soul of-the-world*, among the ancients, in the *Plastic Nature* of Cudworth, or the *Hylarchic Principle* of Henry More.

Sum-total of Spirit; immanent in Spirit but not transcending spiritual manifestations. This was the Pantheism of Spinoza and some others. It lies at the bottom of many mystical discourses, and appears, more or less, in most of the pious and spiritual writers of the middle ages, who confound the Divine Being with their own personality, and yet find some support for their doctrines in the language, more or less figurative, of the New Testament.

This system appears more or less in the writings of John the Evangelist, in Dionysius the Areopagite, and the many authors who have drawn from him. It tinges in some measure the spiritual philosophy of the present day.[1] But the charge of Pantheism is very vague, and is usually urged most by such as know little of its meaning. He who conceives of God, as transcending creation indeed, but yet at the same time as the Immanent Cause of all things, as infinitely present, and infinitely active, with no limitations, is sure to be called a Pantheist in these days, as he would have passed for an Atheist two centuries ago. Some who have been called by this easy but obnoxious name, both in ancient and modern times, have been philosophical defenders of the doctrine of one God, but have given him the historical form neither of Brahma nor Jehovah.[2]

---

[1] See the curious forms this assumes in Theologia Mystica . . . speculativa . . . et affectiva, per Henric. Harph. &c., Colon. 1538. Jäsche and Maret find it in all the modern spiritual philosophy. Indeed, the two rocks that threaten theology seem to be a Theosophy which resolves all into God, and Anthropomorphism, which in fact denies the Infinite. This mystical tendency, popularly denominated Pantheism, appears in the ancient religions of the East; it enters largely into the doctrine of the *Sufis*, a Mahometan sect. See Tholuck, Blüthensamlung aus der morgenlandischen Mystik, p. 33, et seq., and passim. Von Hammer also, in his Geschichte der schönen Redekunste Persens, &c., p. 340, et seq., 347, et seq., et al., gives extracts from these Oriental speculators who are more or less justly charged with Pantheism.

[2] The writings of Spinoza have hitherto been supposed to contain the most pernicious form of Pantheism; but of late, the poison has been detected also in the works of Schleiermacher, Fichte, Schelling, Hegel, Cousin, not to mention others of less note. Pantheism is a word of convenient ambiguity, and serves as well to express the *theological odium* as the more ancient word Atheism, which has been deemed by some synonymous with Philosophy. See the recent controversial writings of Mr Norton and Mr Ripley, respecting the Pantheism of Spinoza and Schleiermacher. It has been well said, the question between the alleged Pantheist and the pure Theist is simply this : *Is God the immanent cause of the World, or is he not ?* See Sengler, Die Idee Gottes, B. I. p. 10, 107, 899.

III. Monotheism is the worship of one Supreme God. It may admit numerous divine beings superior to men, yet beneath the Supreme Divinity, as the Jews, the Mahometans, and the Christians have done; or it may deny these subsidiary beings, as some philosophers have taught. The Idea of God to which Monotheism ultimately attains, is that of a Being infinitely powerful, wise, and good. He may, however, be supposed to manifest himself in *one form* only, as the Jehovah of the Hebrews, and the Allah of the Mahometans; in *three forms*, as the Triune God of most Christians; or in *all forms*, as the Pan and Brahma of the Greek and Indian—for it is indifferent whether we ascribe no form or all forms to the Infinite.

Since the form of Monotheism prevails at this day, little need be said to portray its most important features.[1] It annihilates all distinction of nations, tribes, and men. There is one God for all mankind. He has no favourites, but is the equal Father of them all. War and slavery are repugnant to its spirit, for men are brothers. There is no envy, strife, or confusion in the divine consciousness, to justify hostility among men; He hears equally the prayer of all, and gives them infinite good at last. No priesthood is needed to serve Him. Under Fetichism every man could have access to his God, for divine symbols were more numerous than men; miracles were performed every day; inspiration was common, but of little value; the favour of the Gods was supposed to give a wonderful and miraculous command over Nature. Under Polytheism, only a chosen few had direct access to God; an appointed Priesthood; a sacerdotal caste. They stood between men and the Gods. Divine symbols became more rare. Inspiration was not usual; a miracle was a most uncommon thing; the favourites of heaven were children born of the Gods; admitted to intercourse with them, or enabled by them to do wonderful works. Now Monotheism would restore inspiration to all. By representing God as spiritual and omnipresent, it brings him within every man's reach; by making Him infinitely perfect, it shows his Wisdom, Love, and Will always the same. Therefore, it annihilates favouritism and all capricious miracles. Inspiration, like the sunlight, awaits all who will accept its

[1] Sermons of Theism, &c., Sermon V. and VI.

conditions. All are Sons of God; they only are his favoured ones who serve him best. No day, nor spot, nor deed, is exclusively sacred; but all time, and each place, and every noble act. The created All is a Symbol of God.

But here also human perversity and ignorance have done their work; have attempted to lessen the symbols of the Deity; to make him of difficult access; to bar up the fountain of Truth and source of Light still more than under Polytheism, by the establishment of places and times, of rituals and creeds; by the appointment of exclusive priests to mediate, where no mediator is needed or possible; by the notion that God is capricious, revengeful, uncertain, partial to individuals or nations; by taking a few doctrines and insisting on exclusive belief; by selecting a few from the many alleged miracles, insisting that these, and these alone, shall be accepted, and thus making the religious duty of men arbitrary and almost contemptible. Still, however, no human ignorance, no perversity, no pride of priest or king, can long prevent this doctrine from doing its vast and beautiful work. It struggles mightily with the Sin and Superstition of the world, and at last will overcome them.

The history of this doctrine is instructive. It was said above there were three elements to be considered in this matter, namely, the Sentiment of God; the Idea of God; and the Conception of God. The Sentiment is vague and mysterious, but always the same thing in kind, only felt more or less strongly, and with more or less admixture of foreign elements. The Idea is always the same in itself, as it is implied and writ in man's constitution; but is seen with more or less of a distinct consciousness. Both of these lead to Unity,[1] to Monotheism, and accordingly, in

---

[1] Meiners, in his work, Historia Doctrinæ de vero Deo, &c., 1 vol. 12mo, 1780, (which, though celebrated, is a passionate and one-sided book, altogether unworthy of the subject, and "behind the times" of its composition,) maintains that the Heathens knew nothing of the one God till about 3554 years after the creation of the world, when Anaxagoras helped them to this doctrine. See, on the other hand, the broad and philosophical views of Cudworth, Ch. IV. passim, who, however, seems sometimes to push his hypothesis too far. A history of Monotheism is still to be desired, though Tenneman, Ritter, Brandis, and even Brucker, have collected many facts, and formed valuable contributions to such a work. Münscher has collected valuable passages from the Fathers, relating to the history of the doctrine among the Christians, and their controversies with the Heathen, in his Lehrbuch der Christlichen Dogmengeschichte, 3rd ed., by Von Cöln, Vol. I. Ch. vi. § 52, et seq. But Warburton, who wrote like an

the prayers and hymns, the festivals and fasts, of Fetichists and Polytheists we find often as clear and definite intimations of Monotheism, as in the devotional writings of professed Monotheists. In this sense the doctrine is old as human civilization, and has never been lost sight of. This is so plain it requires no proof. But the Conception of God, which men superadd to the Sentiment and Idea of Him, is continually changing with the advance of the world, of the nation, or the man. We can trace its historical development in the writings of Priests, and Philosophers, and Poets, though it is impossible to say when and where it was first taught with distinct philosophical consciousness, that there is one God; one only. The history of this subject demands a treatise by itself.[1] This, however, is certain, that we find signs and proofs of its existence among the earliest poets and philosophers of Greece; in the dim remnants of Egyptian splendour; in the uncertain records of the East; in the spontaneous effusions of savage hearts, and in the most ancient writings of the Jews. The latter have produced such an influence on the world, that their doctrine requires a few words on this point.

The Deity was conceived of by the Hebrews as entirely separate from Nature; this distinguishes Judaism from all forms which had a pantheistic tendency, and which deified matter or men. He was the primitive ground and cause of all. But the Jewish Religion did not, with logical consistency, deny the existence of other Gods, inferior to the highest. Here we must consider the doctrine of the *Jewish books*, and that of the *Jewish people*. In the first the reality of other deities is generally assumed. The first commandment of the decalogue implies the existence of other Gods. The mention of Sons of God who visited the daughters of men;[2] of the divine council or Host of Heaven;[3] the contract Jacob makes with Jehovah;[4] the frequent reference to strange Gods; the preëminence claimed for Jehovah above all the deities of the other

attorney, gives the most erroneous judgments upon the ancient heathen doctrine respecting the unity of God. See the temperate remarks of Mosheim, De Recusante Constant, &c., p. 17, et seq.

[1] See note, p. 60.   [2] Gen. vi. 2.
[3] Gen. iii. 22; 1 Kings xxii. 19; Job ii. 1.
[4] Gen. xxviii. 20, 22: comp. Herodotus, IV. 179.

nations[1]—these things show that the mind of the writers was not decided in favour of the exclusive existence of Jehovah. The people and their kings before the exile were strongly inclined to a mingled worship of Fetichism and Polytheism, a medium between the ideal religion of Moses and the actual worship of the Canaanites. It is difficult in the present state of critical investigation, to determine nicely the date of all the different books of the Jews, but this may be safely said, that the early books have more of a polytheistic tendency than the writings of the later prophets, for at length, both the learned and the unlearned became pure Monotheists.[2] At first Jehovah and the Elohim seem to be recognized as joint Gods;[3] but at the end Jehovah is the *only* God.

But the character assigned him is fluctuating. He is always the Creator and Lord of Heaven and Earth, yet is not always represented as the Father of all nations, but of the Jews only, who will punish the Heathens with the most awful severity.[4] In some parts of the Old Testament he is almighty, omnipresent, and omniscient; eternal and unalterable. But in others he is represented with limitations in respect to all these attributes. Not only are the sensual perceptions of a man ascribed to him, for this is unavoidable in popular speech, but he walks on the earth, eats with Abraham, wrestles with Jacob, appears in a visible form to Moses, tempts men, speaks in human speech, is pleased with the fragrant sacrifice, sleeps and awakes, rises early in the morning; is jealous, passionate, revengeful.[5] However, in other passages the loftiest

---

[1] See the numerous passages where Jehovah is spoken of as the chief of the Gods: 2 Chr. ii. 5; Ps. xcv. xcvii. 7, et seq.: Ex. xii. 12, xv. 11, xviii. 11, &c. &c. Strabo, ubi sup., Lib. XVI. Ch. ii. § 35, gives a strange account of the Jewish theology.

[2] Compare with the former passages, Jer. ii. 26—28; Isa. xliv. 6—20; Deut. iv. 28, et seq., xxxii. 16, 17, 39; Ps. cxv. cxxxv., and Ecclesiasticus xxxiii. 5, xliii. 28; Wisdom of Sol. xii. 13; Baruch iii. 35. See de Wette, Bib. Dogmatik, § 97, et seq., and 149, et seq., who has collected some of the most important passages. See too his Wesen des Glaubens, &c., § 14, p. 72, et seq.

[3] See Bauer, Dicta, Classica, V. T. &c., 1798, Vol. I. § 41, et seq. See also the treatise of Stahl on the Appearances of God, &c., in Eichhorn, Bibliothek der Bib. Lit. Vol. VII. p. 156, et seq.

[4] See an able article on "the Relation of Jehovah to the Heathen," in Eichhorn, ubi sup., Vol. VIII. p. 222, et seq. See Ammon, Fortbildung des Christenthums, Leip. 1836, et seq., Vol. I. Book i. Ch. i.

[5] Lessing well says, the Hebrews proceeded from the conception of the *most*

attributes are assigned him. He is the God of infinite Love; Father of all, who possesses the Earth and Heavens.

The conception which a man forms of God, depends on the character and attainment of the man himself; this differed with individual Jews as with the Greeks, the Christians, and the Mahometans. However, this must be confessed, that under the guidance of Divine Providence, the great and beautiful doctrine of one God for the Hebrews seems very early embraced by the great Jewish Lawgiver; incorporated in his national legislation; and defended with rigorous enactions. At our day it is difficult to understand the service rendered to the human race by the mighty soul of Moses, and that a thousand years before Anaxagoras.[1] His name is ploughed into the history of the world. His influence can never die. It must have been a vast soul, endowed with moral and religious genius to a degree extraordinary among men, which at that early age could attempt to found a State on the doctrine and worship of one national God.

Was he the first of the come-outers? Or had others, too far before the age for its acceptance, perished before him in the greatness of their endeavour? History is silent.[2] But the bodies of many Prophets must be rolled

powerful God to that of the *only* God, but remained for a long time far below the true transcendent notion of the one true God. "Education of the human race," Werke, ed. 1824, Vol. XXIV. p. 43, 44. See also on this subject of Hebrew Theism, the valuable but somewhat one-sided views of Vatke, Bib. Theologie, Vol. I. § 44, et seq. But see also Salvador, Hist. des Institutions de Möise, &c., Brussels, 1830, Vol. III. p. 175, et seq.

At first Christian Artists found it in bad taste and even heathenish to paint the Almighty in any form. Then, in decorating churches and MSS. with pictures drawn from O. S. stories, they often put only a *hand* for God, or omitting that, put Christ for the Father. See Didron, Iconographie Chrétienne, Paris, 1843, p. 174, et seq. See the nice distinction made by John of Damascus in regard to images of God, Orat. I. in Imaginibus, Opp. ed. Basil, 1574, p. 701, et seq. et al. Before the twelfth century it seems there were no pictures of God from Christian Artists. Afterwards the Italians painted him as a *Pope*, the Germans as an *Emperor*, the French and English as a *King*. Didron, ubi sup., p. 230, et seq.

[1] Constant, Liv. IV. Ch. xi., has some just remarks on the excellence of the Hebrew Theology.

[2] It is difficult to determine accurately the date of events in Chinese history, such are the pretensions of Chinese scholars on the one hand, and such the bigoted scepticism of dogmatists on the other; but see the Chinese Classical Work, commonly called the Four Books, translated by David Pollie; Malacca, 1829, 1 vol. 8vo. See Cantu, ubi sup., Vol. III. Ch. xxi. et seq.

into the gulf that yawns wide and deep between the Ideal and the Actual, before the successful man comes in the fulness of time, at God's command, to lead men into the promised land, reaping what they did not sow. These men have risen up in all countries and every time. In the rudest ages as in the most refined, they look through the glass of Nature, seeing clearly the invisible things of God, and by the things that are made and the feelings felt, understanding his eternal power and Godhead. They adored Him as the Spirit who dwells in the sun, looks through the stars, speaks in the wind, controls the world, is chief of all powers, animal, material, spiritual, and Father of all men —their dear and blessed God. In his light they loved to live, nor feared to die.

There is a great advance from the Fetichism of the Canaanite to the Theism of Moses ; from the rude conceptions of the New Zealander to the refined notions of an enlightened Christian. Ages of progress and revolution seem to separate them, so different is their theology. Yet the Religion of each is the same, distinguished only by the more and less. The change from one of these three religious types to the other is slow ; but attended with tumult, war, and suffering. In the ancient civilized nations, little is known of their passage from Fetichism to Polytheism. It took place at an early age of the world, before written documents were common. We have, therefore, no records to verify this passage in the history of the Greeks, Egyptians, or Hebrews. Yet in the earliest periods of each of these nations we find monuments which show that Fetichism was not far off, and furnish a lingering but imperfect evidence of the fierce struggle which had gone on. The wrecks of Fetichism strew the shores of Greece and Egypt. Judea furnishes us with some familiar examples.[1]

¹ The legendary character of the Pentateuch renders it unsafe to depend entirely on its historical statements. Many passages seem to have been originally designed, or at least retouched, by some one who sought to enhance the difference between Moses and the people. Still, the "general drift" of the tradition is not to be mistaken, and can scarcely be wrong. The testimony of the prophets respecting the early state of the nation is more valuable than that of the Pentateuch itself. See De Wette, Introduction to the O. T., tr. by Theo. Parker, Boston. 1843, Vol. II. passim. See too, Ewald, Geschichte des Volks Israel, Vol I., Gött., 1843.

In the patriarchal times, if we may trust the mythical stories in Genesis, we find sacred stones which seem to be Fetiches, Stone-pillars,[1] Idolatry,[2] worship of Ramphan and Chiun while in Egypt and the desert ;[3] the Golden Calf of Aaron and that of Jeroboam ;[4] and the Goats that were worshipped in the wilderness.[5] Besides, we find the worship of the serpent,[6] a relic of the superstition of Egypt or Phœnicia; the worship of Baal in its various forms ;[7] of Astarte, "Heaven's Queen and Mother ;" of Thammuz, and Moloch ;[8] all of which seem to be remains of Fetichism.[9] In the very Law itself we find traces of Fetichism. The prohibition of certain kinds of food, garments, and sacrifices ; the forms of divination, the altars, feasts, sacrifices, scape-goat, the ornaments of the priest's dress, all seem to have grown out of the rude worship that formerly prevailed. The old Idolatry was spiritualized, its forms modified and made to serve for the worship of Jehovah. The frequent relapses of king and people prove, on the one hand, that the nation was slowly emerging out of a state of great darkness and superstition, and, on the other, that lofty minds and noble hearts were toiling for their civilization.

For many centuries a most bloody contention went on between the ideal Monotheism and the actual Idolatry ; at times it was a war of extermination. This shows how difficult it is to introduce Monotheism before the people are

---

[1] Gen. xxviii. 18, xxxv. 14.
[2] Gen. xxxi. 19, xxxv. 1—4.
[3] See Josh. xxiv. 14; Ezek. xx. 7, et seq., xxiii. 3; Amos v. 25, 26 ; Exod. xxxii. 1; Lev. xvii.
[4] Exod. xxxii. 1—6; 1 Kings xii. 28 ; Ezek. i. 10, and x. 14.
[5] Levit. xvii. 7. *Devils*, in our version.
[6] Numb. xxi. 4—9 ; 2 Kings xvii. 4.
[7] 1 Kings xviii. 23, 26, 28, xix. 18; Jerem. xix. 5 ; 2 Kings i. 2 ; Judges viii. 32, ix. 4, 46; Numb. xxv. 1, et seq.
[8] 1 Kings xi. 33 ; Jerem. vii. 18 ; Judges ii. 13, x. 6 ; 2 Kings xxiii. 7; Levit. xix. 29; Deut. xxiii. 18 ; Ezek. viii. 14 ; 2 Kings xxiii. 5, xvii. 16, xxi. 3, 5 ; Deut. iv. 19, xvii. 3 ; 2 Kings xxiii. 10; Levit. xviii. 21, xx. 2, et seq. ; Deut. xviii. 10 ; Jerem. vii. 31, xix. 5, xxxii. 35. See the testimony of the ancients and remarks of the learned on this subject in De Wette, Archäologie, &c., § 191, et seq., and § 231, et seq. Vatke goes too far in his explanations, § 21—27 ; but his book is full of valuable thoughts.
[9] There is a remarkable passage, though of but four words, in Hosea xiii. 2, which shows that one of the worst vices of Fetichism still prevailed in his time, saying, "*They that sacrifice a man shall kiss the calves,*" i. e. the Idols of the People. This is not the common translation—but it seems to me the true one.

ready to receive it. They must wait till they attain the requisite moral and intellectual growth. Before this is reached, they can receive it but in name, and are detained from the ruder, and to them more congenial, form, only at the expense of most rigorous laws, suffering, and bloodshed. Before the Exile the Hebrews constantly revolted; afterwards they never returned to the ruder worship, but ten tribes of the nation were gone for ever.[1]

In the more recent conflict of Monotheism and Polytheism, the history of the Christian and Mahometan religions shows what suffering is endured first by the advocates of the new, and next by those of the old faith, before the rude doctrine could give place to the better. War and extermination do their work, and remove the unbelieving. Many a country has been Christianized or Mahometanized by the sword. These things have taken place within a few centuries; when the conquering religion was called Christianity. Are the wars of Charlemagne forgotten? Go back thousands of years, to the strife between sacerdotal Polytheism and Fetichism, when each was a more bloody faith, and imagination cannot paint the horrors of the struggle.

Now, each of these forms represented an Idea of the popular consciousness which passed for a truth, or it could not be embraced; for a great truth, or it would not prevail widely; yes, for all of truth the man could receive at the time he embraced it. We creep before walking. Mankind has likewise an infancy, though it will at length put away childish things. Each of these forms did the world service in its day. Its truth was permanent; its error, the result of the imperfect development of man's faculties. It happens in religious as in scientific matters, that a doctrine contains both truth and falsehood. It is accepted for its truth or the appearance of truth. At first the falsehood does little harm, for it comes in contact with no active faculty in man which detects it.[2] But gradually

---

[1] See Newman's Hebrew Monarchy, Lond. 1847, Ch. IX. Ewald, ubi sup. B. II. p. 92, et seq. Anhang zum 2ten Band. III. (1) p. 197, et seq.

[2] We often see the most strange inconsistency between a man's conduct and his creed. Roman Lucretia sacrificed to Venus. The worshipper of Jupiter did not imitate his vices; nor does the modern devotee of some unholy creed, with a Christian name, become what the creed logically demands. A man may hold

the truth does its work; elevates those who receive it; new faculties awake; the falsehood is seen to be false. The free man would gladly reject it. But the Priesthood, whom interest chains to the old form, though false; or the People, not yet elevated enough to see the truth,— will not allow a man to separate the false from the true. They say to the Prophet and the Sage, "Thou shalt accept the old doctrine as we and our fathers. It is from God; the only Rule. Unless thou accept it on the same authority and in the same way as ourselves, we will burn thee and thy children with fire. Thou mayest live as likest thee; thou shalt believe with us." The free man replies, "Burn then if thou wilt; but Truth thou canst not burn down. A lie thou canst not build up. God does not die with his children, nor Truth with its martyrs."

Then, as Truth is stronger than every lie, and he that has her is mightier than all men, so the fagot of martyrdom proves the fire-pillar of the human race, guiding them from the bondage and darkness of Egypt to the land of liberty and light. Truth, armed with her arrows to smite, her olive to bless, spreads wide her wings amid the outcry of the Priest and the King. At last Error goes down to the ground, but because honoured beyond her time, takes with her temple and tower in her fall.

The Truth represented by Fetichism is this: The un-

doctrines which render virtue nugatory, which make the flesh creep with horror, and yet live a divine life, or be gay even to frivolity. The late Dr Hopkins was a striking illustration of this statement. So long as the religious sentiment preponderates, the false doctrine fails of its legitimate effect. See some judicious observations on this theme in Constant, Liv. I. Ch. iii. iv., and Polytnéisme Rom. Vol. I. p. 59—81.

M. Comte, Vol. V. p. 280, thinks the doctrine of pure Monotheism is perfectly sterile and incapable of becoming the basis of a true religious system! Judging only from experience, his conclusion is utterly false. But such as might be expected from one who is, as he *boasts*, "equally free from Fetichistic, Polytheistic, and Monotheistic prejudices." He looks longingly to a time when all theism shall have passed away, and the "hypothesis of a God" become exploded! But the true man of science is of all men most modest and reverent. He who has followed Newton through the wondrous soaring of his genius comes grateful to that swan-song, beautiful as it is sublime, with which he finishes his flight, and sings of the ONE CAUSE ETERNAL and INFINITE, who rules the all. It cannot be read without a tear of joy. Principia, ed. 1833, Vol. IV. p. 199, 201. "*Et hi omnes*," &c. &c. See too the beautiful and pious conclusion of Mr. Whewell to his Philosophy of the Inductive Sciences, Vol. II. p. 582, 583. And the remarks of Descartes, Meditations, Med. 3, ad finem. It was worthy of Linnæus to say, as he looked at a little flower, *Deum Sempiternum, omniscium, omnipotentem, à tergo transeuntem vidi et obstupui.*

5 *

known God is present in Matter; spiritual power is the strongest of forces. Its error was to make Matter God. The truth of Polytheism is: God is present, and active, everywhere; in Space, in Spirit; breathes in the wind; speaks in the storm; inspires to acts of virtue; helps the efforts of all true men. Its falsehood was, that it divided God, and gave but a chaos of Deity. When the falsehood was seen and felt to be such, and its truth believed in for itself, on its own authority, then was the time for Fetichism and Polytheism to fall. So they fell, never to hope again, for mankind never apostatizes. One generation takes up the Ark of Religion where another let it fall, and carries forward the hope of the world. The old form never passes away, till all its truth is transferred to the new. These types of religious progress are but the frames on which the artist spreads the canvas, while he paints his piece. The frame may perish when this is done. Fetichism and Polytheism did good, not because they were Fetichism and Polytheism, but because Religion was in them and they were steps in the spiritual progress of mankind—indispensable steps.

Such, then, are the three great forms of manifestation assumed by this religious Element. We cannot understand the mental and religious state of men who saw the Divine in a serpent, a cat, or an enchanted ring; not even that of superstitious Christians, who make earth a demonland, and the one God but a King of Devils. Yet each religious doctrine has sometimes stood for a truth. It was devised to help pious hearts, and has imperfectly accomplished its purpose. It could not have been but as it was. Looking carelessly at the past, the history of man's religious consciousness appears but a series of revolutions. What is to-day built up with prayers and tears, is to-morrow pulled down with shouting and bloodshed, giving place to a new fabric equally transient. Prophets were mistaken, and saints confounded. Religious history is the tale of confusion. But looking deeper, we see it is a series of developments, all tending towards one great and beautiful end, the harmonious perfection of Man; that in theology as in other science, in morals as in theology, the circle of his vision becomes wider continually; his opinions more true; his ideal more fair and sublime. Each form that has been, bore its justification in itself; an evil that "God winked at," to use the bold figure of a great man. It was natural and indispensable in its time and place; a part of the scheme of agencies provided from before the foundation of the world. Each form may perish; but its truth nevers dies. Nations pass away. A handful of red dust alone marks the spot where a metropolis opened its hundred gates; but Religion does not perish. Cities and nations mark the steps of her progress. A nation, at the head of the civilized world, organizes Religion as well as it can; perpetuates and diffuses its truth, and thus preaches the advent of a higher faith, and prepares its way. Each failure is a prophecy of the Perfect. But the change from faith to faith is attended with persecution on the one side, and martyrdom on the other. A little philosophy turns men from Religion. Much knowledge restores them to their faith, to the bosom of Piety. The great men of the world, men gifted with the deepest insight, and living the most royal life, have been Man's pioneers in these steps of progress. Moses, Hermes, Confucius, Budha, Zoroaster, Anaxagoras, Socrates, Plato, have lent their holy hands in Man's greatest work. Religion filled their soul with strength and light. It is only little men, that make wide the mouth and draw out the tongue at pure and genuine piety and nobleness of heart. Shall we not judge the world, as a rose, by its best side? God, of his wisdom, raises up men of religious genius; heaven-sent prophets; born fully armed and fitted for their fearful work. They have an eye to see through the reverend hulls of falsity; to detect the truth a long way off. They send their eagle gaze far down into the heart; far on into the future, thinking for ages not yet born. The word comes from God with blessed radiance upon their mind. They must speak the tidings from on high, and shed its beamy light on men around, till the heavy lids are opened, and the sleepy eye beholds. But alas for him who moves in such work. If there be not superhuman might to sustain him; if his soul be not naked of selfishness, he will say often, "Alas for me! Would God my mother had died or ever I was born to bear all the burdens of the world, and right its wrongs." He that feareth the Lord—when was not he a prey? He must take his life in his hand, and become as a stranger to men. But if he fall and perish it is his gain. Is it not also the world's? It is the burning wood that warms men.

In passing judgment on these different religious states, we are never to forget, that there is no monopoly of religious emotion by any nation or any age. He that worships truly, by whatever form, worships the Only God; He hears the prayer, whether called Brahma, Jehovah, Pan, or Lord; or called by no name at all. Each people has its Prophets and its Saints; and many a swarthy Indian, who bowed down to wood and stone; many a grim-faced Calmuck, who worshipped the great God of Storms; many a Grecian peasant, who did homage to Phœbus-Apollo when the Sun rose or went down; yes, many a savage, his hands smeared all over with human sacrifice, shall come from the East and the West, and sit down in the Kingdom of God, with Moses and Zoroaster, with Socrates and Jesus,—while men, who called daily on the only living God, who paid their tribute and bowed at the name of Christ, shall be cast out, because they did no more. Men are to be judged by what is given, not what is withheld.

CHAPTER VI.

OF CERTAIN DOCTRINES CONNECTED WITH RELIGION. I. OF THE PRIMITIVE STATE OF MANKIND. II. OF THE IMMORTALITY OF THE SOUL.

I. *Of the Primitive State of Mankind.*

VARIOUS theories have been connected with Religion, respecting the origin and primitive condition of the human race. Many nations have claimed to be the primitive possessors of their native soil; Autochthones, who sprang miraculously out of the ground, were descended from stones, grasshoppers, emmets, or other created things.

Others call themselves Children of the Gods.[1] Some nations trace back their descent to a time of utter barbarism, whence the Gods recalled them; others start from a golden age, as the primitive condition of men.[2] The latter opinion prevailed with the Hebrews, from whom the Christians have derived it. According to them, the primitive state was one of the highest felicity, from which men fell; the primitive worship, therefore, must have been the normal Religion of mankind.[3]

This question then presents itself, From what point did the human race set out; from civilization and the true worship of one God, or from cannibalism and the deification of Nature? Has the human race fallen or risen? The question is purely historical, and to be answered by historical witnesses. But in the presence, and still more in the absence, of such witnesses, the à priori doctrines of the man's philosophy affect his decision. Reasoning with no facts is easy, as all motion in vacuo. The analogy of the geological formation of the earth; its gradual preparation, so to say, for the reception of plants and animals, the ruder first, and then the more complex and beautiful, till at last she opens her bosom to man,—this, in connection with many similar analogies, would tend to show that a similar order was to be expected in the affairs of men; development from the lower to the higher, and not the reverse.[4] In strict accordance with this analogy, some have taught that Man was created in the lowest stage of savage life; his Religion the rudest worship of nature;

---

[1] Diodorus Siculus says, somewhere, all ancient nations claim to be the *most ancient*.

[2] See the heathen view of this in Hesiod. Opera et Dies; Lucretius, V. 923, et seq.; Virgil, Georg. I. 125, et seq., Ecl. IV.; Ovid, Met. I. 89, et seq.; Plato, Polit. p. 271, et seq. See Heyne, Opusc. Vol. III. p. 24, et seq.; Hesiod's Theog. 521—579. See other parallels in Bauer's Mythologie des A. T. &c, Vol. I. p. 85, et seq. See also the curious speculations of Eichhorn (Urgeschichte ed. Gabler.), Büttmann (Mythologus), and Hartmann (über des Pentateuch). Compare Rosenmüller, Alterthumskunde, Vol. I. Part i. p. 180, et seq., and the striking passage in Kleuker's Zendavesta, Vol. II. p. 211, 227, et seq.; III. p. 85. See Rhode's remarks upon the passages, ubi sup., p. 388, et seq. See Bauer, Dicta Classica, § 52.

[3] See the opinions of *Zoroaster* on this point collected by Bretschneider, Darstellung der Dogmatik, &c., der Apoc. Schriften, Vol. I. § 52, p. 286, et seq.

[4] See Vestiges of the Natural History of Creation, Lond., 1844, 1st ed. p. 277, et seq., for some curious remarks.

his Morality that of the cannibal; that all of the civilized races have risen from this point, and gradually passed through Fetichism and Polytheism, before they reached refinement and true Religion; the spiritual man is the gradual development of germs latent in the natural man.[1]

Another party, consisting more of poets and dogmatists than of philosophers, teaches the opposite doctrine, that a single human pair was created in the full majority of their powers, with a perfect Morality and Religion; that they *fell* from this state, and while some few kept alive the lamp of Truth, and passed it on from hand to hand, that the mass sunk into barbarity and sin, whence they are slowly emerging, aided of course by the traditional torch of Truth, still kept by their more fortunate brothers.[2]

[1] See Comte, Vol. V. p. 32, et al. Here arises the kindred question, Have all the human race descended from a single pair, or started up in the various parts of the earth where we find them? The first opinion has been defended by the Christian Church, in general with more obstinacy than argument. Pritchard, ubi sup., derives all from one stock, and collects many interesting facts relative to the human race in various conditions. But the unity of the race is not to be made out *genealogically*. It is *essential to the nature* of mankind. Augustine has some curious speculations on this head, De Civitate Dei, XII. 21, XIII. 19—23, XIV. 10—12, 16—26. Lactantius, Institut. II. 11, VII. 4. See the opinions of Buddeus, and the curious literature he cites, Hist. Ecclesiast. V. T. Vol. I. p. 92, et seq. On the other hand, Palfrey's Academical Lectures, Vol. II. Lect. xxi., xxii.; Kant, von der Racen der Menschen, Werke, Vol. VI. p. 313, et seq. ; Begriff einer Menschenrace, ib. p. 33, et seq.; Muthmaaslicher Anfang der Menschengeschichte, ib. Vol. VII. p. 363, et seq. Even Schleiermacher departs from the common view. Christliche Glaube, § 60—61. See, likewise, the ingenious observations of Samuel S. Smith, Inquiry into the causes of different Complexions, &c., of the human Race. To make out the case, that all men are descended from a primitive power, it is only necessary to assume, *philosophically*, a principle in the first man, whence all varieties may be derived, and then, *historically*, to assume the derivation, and the vicious circle is complete. Kames has some disingenuous remarks in his History of Man, Preliminary Discourse. See Mémoires de l'Académie royale des Sciences morales et politiques, (Paris,) 1841, Tom. III. p. xxiii. et seq., and the literature referred to.

[2] See this, which is the prevalent opinion, set forth by Knapp, ubi sup., Vol. I. § 54—57. Hahn, Lehrbuch des Christ. Glaub. § 74, 75. Tholuck, in Biblical Repository, Vol. II. p. 119, et seq.; Hopkins's System of Doctrines, &c., 2nd ed. Vol. I. Part. i. Chap. 5, 8.—Bretschneider, Dogmatik, 4th ed. Vol. I. § 112, et seq., gives the Lutheran view of this subject, *but thinks Oken no heretic for maintaining* (in the Isis for 1819, Vol. II. p. 1118) *that man may have arisen from an embryo, with human qualities, in the slime of the sea !* p. 812. See Jeremy Taylor, Doctrine and Practice of Repentance, Chap. VI., and the conflicting remarks in the Sermon at the Funeral of Sir George Dalston; Jonathan Edwards, Original Sin, Part II. Chap. i., and Notes on Bible, Works, Lond. 1839, Vol. II. p. 689, et seq. More on the same subject may be seen in Faber's Horæ Mosaicæ ; Edwards, On the Truth and Authority of the Scrip-

Now in favour of this latter opinion there is no direct historical testimony except the legendary and mythological writings of the Hebrews, which have no more authority in the premises than the similar narratives of the Phœnicians, the Persians, and Chinese. If we assume the miraculous authority of these legends, the matter ends—in an assumption. The indirect testimony in favour of this doctrine is this: The opinion found in many nations that there had once been a golden age. Now, if this opinion were universal, it would not prove the fact alleged, for it can easily be explained from the notorious tendency of men, in a low state of civilization, to aggrandize the past; the senses delight to remember. That opinion only serves to illustrate this tendency. The sensual Greek often looked longingly backward to the Golden Age; but the more spiritual prophet of the Hebrews looks forward to the Kingdom of Heaven yet to be. But the opinion prevails among many nations, that they have slowly advanced from a ruder state.[1]

Again, it is often alleged, that no nation has ever risen out of the savage state except under the influence of tribes previously enlightened—an historical thesis which has never been proved. No one knows whence the Chinese, the Mexicans, the Peruvians, derived assistance. We have yet to be told who taught the Greenlander to build his boat; the Otaheitan to fashion his war club; the Sacs and Pawnees to handle the hatchet, cook the flesh of the buffalo, and wear his skin. Besides, it is begging the question, to say the civilization of Rome, Athens, Tyre, Judea, Egypt, Babylon, Nineveh, came from the traditionary knowledge of some primitive people. If a savage nation in seven centuries can learn to use oil and tallow for light, in a time sufficiently long it may write the Iliad, and build the Parthenon.

tures; Collier's Lectures on Scripture Facts; Gray's Connection between Sacred and Profane Literature; Cormack's Inquiry; Fletcher's Appeal; Deane's Worship of the Serpent, &c. &c.; Sénac, Christianisme dans ses Rapports avec la Civilization moderne, Paris, 1837, Vol. I. Part i. ch. 2. See the opinions of the Ancients on the creation and primitive state of Man, collected in Grotius, De Veritate, ed. Clericus, Lib. I. § 16.

[1] Strauss, Die Christ. Glaubenslehre, 1840-1, Vol. I. § 45, et seq., decides against the hypothesis of a single pair, and even ascribes the origin of man to the power of *equivocal generation*. But his arguments in favour of the latter have little or no weight. See Kames, ubi sup.

Again, it is said that traces of Monotheism are found
even in the low stages of our religious history. This must
necessarily follow from the identity of the human race;
from the Sentiment and Idea of God, expressing themselves
spontaneously. If Man is the same in all ages, differing
only in degree of development, and this element is natural
to him, then we must expect to find such expressions of it
in the poets and philosophers; in the religion of India,
Greece, and Rome. Men of the same spiritual elevation
see everywhere the same spiritual truth. If this doctrine
of Monotheism proceed from tradition alone, then it must
be more clear and distinct as we approach the source of
the tradition. But this is notoriously contrary to facts.[1]

The opposite doctrine has no more of *direct* historical
testimony in its favour; but is supported by many indirect testimonies: by the fact, that the greater part of
the human race are still in the condition of Fetichism and
Polytheism, and that the further we go back in history
the worse is this state, and the ruder their religion. In
the days of Herodotus, the proportion of rude and savage
people was far greater than at this day. Even in that
nation alleged to be most highly favoured, we find their
social, moral, and religious condition is more rude the
further we trace it back. They and other nations, at the
time we first meet them in history, bordered close upon the
Fetichistic state to which their mythology refers. No
nation has ever been found in a normal state of religious
culture.

If we reason only from established facts, we must conclude, that the hypothesis of a golden age, a garden of
Eden, a perfect condition of man on the earth in ancient
times, is purely gratuitous. The Kingdom of Heaven is
not behind but before us. No one can determine, by historical evidence, what was the primitive state of the
human race, or when, or where, or how mankind, at the
command of God, came into existence. Here our conclusions can be only negative.[2]

---

[1] Voltaire, Essai sur les Mœurs, &c., edit. 1785, Vol. I. p. 17, et seq., 20,
et seq., has many just remarks on the ruder periods of society.
[2] Constant, Liv. I. Ch. vi. and x. Ch. vi. treats this subject with a superficial-
ity unusual even with him. He thinks the doctrine of a Fall is a device of the
Priesthood, at least, that it owes its importance and continuation to the sacer-

II. *On the Immortality of the Soul.*

The doctrine that Man lives for ever seems almost as general as the belief in a God. Like that, it comes naturally from an eternal desire in the human heart; a longing after the Infinite. In the rudest nations and the most civilized, this doctrine appears. Perhaps there has never been but a single form of Religion among civilized men under which it was not taught plainly and distinctly, and here it was continually implied. It seems we have by nature a sentiment of immortality; an instinctive belief therein. Rude nations, in whom instinct seems to predominate, trust the spontaneous belief. They construct an ideal world, in which the shade of the departed pursues his calling and finds justice at the last; recompense for his toil; right for his earthly wrongs. The conception of the form of future life depends on the condition and character of the believer. Hence it is a state of war or peace; of sensual or spiritual delight; of reform or progress, with different nations. The notion formed of the next world is the index of man's state in this. Here the Idolater and the Pantheist, the Mahometan and the Christian, express their conflicting views of life. The Sentiment and Idea of immortality may be true, but the definite conception must be mainly subjective, and therefore false. In a low stage of civilization the doctrine, like the religious feelings themselves, seems to have but little moral influence on life. It presents no motive to virtue, and therefore does not receive the same place in their system as at a subsequent period.

In rude ages men reason but little. As they begin to be civilized they ask proofs of Immortality, not satisfied with the instinctive feeling; not convinced that infinite Goodness will do what is best for all and each of his creatures. Hence come doubts on this head; inquiries; attempts to prove the doctrine; a denial of it. There seems an antithesis between instinct and understanding. The *reasoning*

dotal class. See some admirable remarks on the savage state in de Maistre, Soirées de St Petersburg, Vol. I. See also Leroux's criticism on the opinions of Jouffroy and Pascal in his Réfutation de l'Eclecticism, 1840, p. 330, et seq. Leroux believes in the progress of all species, Man, the Beaver, and the Bee. M. Maret, ubi sup., p. 30, et seq., and 240, et seq., makes some very judicious observations.

of men is then against it, but when an accident drives them to somewhat more fundamental than processes of logic, the instinctive belief does its work. Here then are three distinct things : a Belief in a future and immortal state ; a. Definite Conception of that state ; and a Proof of the fact of a future and immortal state. The two latter may be fluctuating and inadequate, while the former remains secure.

Now it may be considered as pretty well fixed, that all nations of the earth, above the mere wild man, believe this doctrine ; at least, the exceptions are so rare, that they only confirm the rule. However, it is often difficult, and sometimes impossible, to determine the popular conception, and the influence of this belief at a particular time and place. But the subject demands a more special and detailed examination. Let us look at the opinion of the ancients.

1. *Opinion of the Hebrews respecting a Future State.*

It has sometimes been taught that this doctrine was perfectly understood, even by the Patriarchs ; and sometimes declared altogether foreign to the Old Testament. Both statements are incorrect. In some parts of the Hebrew Scriptures we find rude notions of a future state, but a firm belief in it ; in others doubt, and even denial thereof. In the early books, at least, it never appears as a motive. It has no sanction in the Law ; no symbol in the Jewish worship. The soul was sometimes placed in the *blood,* as by Empedocles ;[1] sometimes in the *breath ;*[2] the heart, or the bowels, were sometimes considered as its seat.[3] The notion of immortality was indefinite in the early books ; there are cloudy views of a subterranean world,[4] which gradually acquire more distinctness. The state of the departed is a gloomy, joyless consciousness ; the servant is free from his master ; the king has a shadowy grandeur.[5]

[1] Gen. ix. 4; Lev. xvii. 11; Deut. xii. 23. See Cicero, Tusc. Lib. I. Ch. 9, 10.
[2] Gen. ii. 7; Ps. civ. 29, et al.
[3] Deut. xxxii. 46; Ps. vii. 10 ; Ps. xvi. 7 ; Prov. xxiii. 16, et al.
[4] Gen. xxv. 8, xxxvii. 35; Num. xvi. 30, 33. In Job, Isaiab, and the Psalms this becomes more definite. Job x. 21, xxxviii. 17.
[5] Job iii. 13—19; Isaiah xiv.; Ezek. xxxii. ; 1 Sam. xxviii. See Homer, Od. XI. Virgil, Æneid, VI.

The dead prophet can be called back to admonish the living. Enoch and Elijah, like Ganymede with the Greeks, being favourites of the deity,[1] and taken miraculously to him. Other passages deny the doctrine of immortality with great plainness.[2]

After the return from exile, the doctrine appears more definitely. Ezekiel and the pseudo-Isaiah[3] allude to a resurrection of the body, a notion which is perhaps of Zoroastrian origin.[4] Perhaps older than Zoroaster. But it is only a doubtful immortality that is taught in the apocryphal book of Ecclesiasticus, though in the Wisdom of Solomon,[5] and in the fourth book of Maccabees, it is set forth with great clearness.[6] The second book of Maccabees teaches in the plainest terms the resurrection of all ; the righteous to happiness, the wicked to shame.[7] They will find their former friends, and resume their old pursuits.[8] Nothing is plainer.

[1] See also Ps. xvii. 15, lxxiii. 24. See the mistakes of Michaelis respecting this doctrine of immortality, in his Argumenta immortalitate, . . . ex Mose collecta, in his Syntagma Comment. Vol. I. p. 80, et seq. See his notes on Lowth, p. 465, ed. Rosenmüller. Warburton founds his strange hypothesis on the opposite view. See on this point, Bauer, Dicta classica, Vol. II. § 56, et seq. ; De Wette, ubi sup., § 113, et seq. ; Lessing, Beyträgen aus der Wolfenbüttelschen Bibliothek, Vol. IV. p. 484, et seq. See the moderate and judicious remarks of Knapp, ubi sup., Vol. II. § 149. See Henkes Mag. für Religions Philosophie, Vol. V. pt. I. p. 16, et seq., and a treatise in the Studien und Kritiken for 1830, Vol. II. p. 884, et seq.

[2] Eccles. iii. 19—21, ix. 10. In Job xiv. 10—14, et al., Job distinctly denies the immortality which he had previously affirmed, but this shows the exquisite art of the poem. See De Wette, Introduction to O. T., Vol. II. p. 556, 557, note a. Perhaps the opinions put into Job's mouth are not those of the Author, but such only as he thought the circumstances of his hero required.

[3] Ezek. xxxvii. ; Isa. xxvi. 19. See Gesenius in loco.

[4] Rhode, ubi sup., p. 494, Nork, Mythen der alten Perser, 1835, p. 148, et seq. ; Priestley, ubi sup., § XXIII. ; Bretschneider, ubi sup., § 53, p. 325, et seq.

[5] i. 15, 16, ii. 22—iii. et seq., v. 15, vi. 18. It is connected with a preëxistent state, viii. 19, 20. The 2nd Book of Esdras is quite remarkable for the view it presents of this doctrine. See ii. 23, 31, 34, 35, iv. 40, et seq., vii. 13, 27—35, 42, et seq., viii. 1, et seq. et al. But the character and date of the book prevent me from using it in the text.

[6] xv. 3, xvi. 25, xvii. 18, et al. de Wette, ubi sup., § 180. See the remarkable passage in 4th Esdras, which Fabricius has added from the Arabic Version Codex pseudepigraphus, ed alt. Hamb. 1741, Vol. II. p. 235, et seq. However, it may have been added by a Christian. In the Psalter of Solomon, it is said *they that fear the Lord shall rise again to everlasting life.* See Ch. xiv. 2, et seq., and xv. in Fabricius, ubi sup., Vol. I. p. 926, 954, et seq. I do not pretend to determine the date of this apocryphal book.

[7] vii. 9, 11, 14, 23, xii. 43, et seq., xv. 12, et seq.

[8] See in Eichhorn, ubi sup., Vol. IV. p. 653, et seq., a valuable contribution to the History of this doctrine by Frisch. He make an ingenious comparison

At the time of Jesus, the Pharisees believed in the resurrection of the body ; a state of rewards and punishments.[1] Some of them connected it with the common notion of the transmigration of souls ;[2] perhaps with that of preëxistence. The Essenes, still more philosophically, taught the immortality of the soul, and the certainty of retribution, without the resurrection of the body. The soul is formed of the most subtle air, and is confined in the body as in a prison ; death redeems it from a long bondage, and the living soul mounts upward rejoicing.[3] We find similar views in Philo.[4] Perhaps they were common in reflecting minds at the time of Jesus, who always presupposes a belief in immortality. The Sadducees alone opposed it. Such were the beginning and history of this dogma with the Jews. Its progress and formation are obvious.

2. *Of this Doctrine among the Heathen Nations.*

Among savage nations this belief is common. It appears in prayers and offerings for the dead ; in the mode of burial. The savage American deposits in the tomb the bow and the pipe, the dress and the tomahawk of the de-

of passages from the Apocrypha, and the New Testament. The same doctrine is taught in both. See Flatt, in Paulus, Memorabil. st. II. p. 157, et seq. ; Bretschneider, ubi sup., § 53—58.

[1] Acts xxiii. 6—8, xxiv. 15 ; Matth. xxii. 24, et seq. ; Mark xii. 19, et seq.

[2] Josephus, Wars, II. viii. 14. Josephus may have added the metempsychosis to suit the taste of his readers.

[3] Josephus, Wars, II. viii. 11. Josephus himself seems to agree with this opinion, when he "talks like a philosopher," in his pretended speech, Wars, III. viii. 5. See Buddeus, ubi sup., II. p. 1202, et seq. ; Paulus, Memorabil., Vol. II. p. 157, et seq. ; and De Wette, ubi sup., § 178, et seq.

[4] See also the views of Philo, De Somniis, p. 586 ; De Abrah, p. 385 ; De Mundi Opif., p. 31. The soul is immortal by *nature*, but by *grace*. See Dähne, Geschichtliche Darstellung der Judischen,—Alexand. Philosophie, &c., 1834, Vol. I. p. 330, et seq. 405, 485, et seq., who cites the above and other proof passages ; Ritter, ubi sup., Vol. IV. See Weizel on the primitive doctrine of immortality among the Christians, in Theol. Stud. und Kritiken, for 1836, p. 957, et seq. Constant, Liv. IX. Cb. vii., makes some just remarks on this subject. On the state of opinions in the time of Christ, see Gfrörer, Jahrhundert des Heils, 1838, Vol. II. Ch. vii. ; Triglandius de tribus Judæorum sectis, in quo Serarii, Drusii, Scaligeri, Opuscula, &c., 1703, Vol. I. Part I Lib. II. and III., Part II. Lib. II.—IV., and Scaliger's Animadversions ; and the very valuable treatise of Leclerc, Prolegomena ad Hist. EccL Lib. I. Ch. i. See Flügge, Geschichte des Glaubens an Unsterblichkeit, &c. &c., Leip. 1794, Vol. I. p. 112—160, 201—251, et passim ; Bouchitté Mém. de l'Institut. Savans étrangères, Tom. II. p. 621, et seq.

ceased warrior. The Scythian, the Goth, the Indian, and the half-barbarous Greek, burned or buried the horse, or the servant, the wife, or the captive of a great man at his decease, that he might go down royally attended to the realm of shades. Metempsychosis ; the deification of the dead, ceremonies in their honour, gifts left on their tombs, oaths confirmed in their name, are all signs of this belief.[1] The Egyptians, the Gauls, and Scandinavians spoke of death as the object of life.[2] Lucan foolishly thinks the latter are brave because they believe in endless existence.

Each savage people has its place of souls. Death with them is not an extinction, but a change of life. The tomb is a sacred place. No expense is too great for the dead. The picture of Heaven is earth embellished. At first, the next world is not a domain of moral justice ; God has no tribunal of judgment. But with the advance of the present, the conception of a future state rises also. The Pawnees have but one place for all the departed. The Scandinavians have two, Nifleheim and Nastrond ; the Persians seven ; the Hindoos no less than twenty-four, for different degrees of merit.[3] With many savages, the good and evil become angels to bless, or demons to curse mankind.[4]

To come to the civilized states of antiquity, India, Egypt, Persia, we find the doctrine prevalent in the earliest time, even in the ages when Mythology takes the place of History. In India and Egypt it was most often connected with

[1] See Lafitau, ubi sup., Vol. II. p. 387, et seq., 410, et seq., 420, et seq., 444, et seq., Vol I. p. 359, et seq., 507, et seq. ; Catlin, ubi sup., Vol. I. Bancroft's Hist. Vol. III. Ch. xxii. ; Constant, Livre IX. Ch. vii. viii., Livre II. Ch. iv. ; Martin, ubi sup., Vol. I. p. 18, 56, 329 ; Vol. II. p. 212, et seq. ; United States Exploring Expedition, Phil. 1845-6, Vol. VII. p. 63, et seq., 99, et seq., et al. For the Fetichism of the Savages, see p. 16, et seq., 26, et seq., 51, et seq., 97, et seq., 110, et seq.

[2] On the belief of the Scandinavians, the Caledonians, the Parsees, Indians, &c., see Flügge, Vol. II. The ancient Lithuanians had some singular opinions and customs in relation to the dead, for which see Boemus, Omnium Gentium Mores, &c., Friburg, 1540, p. 182.

[3] Constant, ibid. Meiners, ubi sup., Vol. I. Book iii. See Leroux, De l'Humanité, &c., Vol. II. p. 468, et seq.

[4] Meiners, p. 302, et seq. Farmer, On the Worship of Human Spirits, passim. I have mentioned a few books on this subject, which have furnished the facts on which the above conclusions rest. I can refer to books of Travels, Voyages in general, the Lettres Edifiantes, descriptions of foreign countries, which furnish the facts in abundance. The works of Meiners, Constant, and Lafitau are themselves but a compilation from these sources.

transmigration to other bodies. Herodotus says, the
Egyptians first taught the doctrine.[1] But who knows?
Pausanias is nearer the truth when he refers it to India,[2]
where it was taught before the birth of Philosophy in the
West.[3] It begins with the beginning of the nations.

In Greece we find it in a rude form in Homer; connected with Metempsychosis in Orpheus, Pythagoras, and
Pherecydes; assuming a new form in Sophocles and Pindar, and becoming a doctrine fixed and settled with
Socrates, Plato, and his school in general.[4] In Homer the
future state is a joyless existence. Achilles would rather
be king of earthly men for a day, than of spirits for ever.
Like the future state of the Jews, it offers no motive, and
presents no terror. The shades of the weary came together from all lands into their dim sojourn. Enemies forgot
their strife; but friends were joined.[5] The present life
is obscurely renewed in the next world. But the more
especial friends or foes of the Gods are raised to honour,
or condemned to shame. The transmigration of souls is
perhaps derived from the wondrous mutation in the vegetable and animal world, where an acorn unswathed becomes an oak, and an egg discloses an eagle.[6]

In Hesiod, the condition of the dead is improved with
the advance of the nation. The good have a place in the
Isles of the Blest.[7] In the latter poets, the doctrine rises
still higher, while the form is not always definite.[8] Pindar

[1] Lib. II. Chap. 123. See Creutzer's note, in Bähr's edition.
[2] The date of all things is uncertain in the East. I cannot pretend to chrono-
logical accuracy, but see Asiatic Researches, Vol. V. p. 360; VII. 310; VIII.
448, et seq.; Priestley, ubi sup., § XXIII.; Ritter. Vol. I. p. 132.
[3] Stanley's History of Philosophy. Part XIII. Sect. ii. Chap. x. Hyde, ubi
sup.
[4] Brouwer, Vol. II. Ch. xviii.; Wilkinson, Vol. II. p. 440, et seq. Homer
assigns to the Gods a beautiful abode not shaken by the winds, &c., Od. VI.
41, et seq. See the imitation of the passage in Lucretius, III. 18, et seq.
Struchtmeyer, Theologia Mythica, sive de Origine Tartari et Elysii, Libri V.,
Hag. Com. 1753, 1 Vol. 8vo, Lib. I.
[5] See Iliad, XXIII. et seq. et al.; Odyss. XI. and XXIV. passim, and
Heyne, Excursus on Iliad, XXIII. 71 and 104, Vol. VIII. p. 368, et seq.;
Diod. &c., Vol. I. p. 86. See the similar views of the North American Indians,
in Schoolcraft, Algic Researches; Wachsmuth, Vol. II. Part ii. p. 106, 244,
290; Potter, Antiquities; Görres, Mythengeschichte, passim.
[6] See Xenophon, Memorab., ed. Schneider, Lips. 1829, Lib. I. Chap. iii.
§ 7, and the Note of Bornemann.
[7] Opera et Dies, vs. 160, et seq., and the Scholia in Poet. Min., ed. Gaisford,
Lips. 1823, Vol. II. p. 142, et seq.
[8] See the Gnomic poets in general, for the moral views of life; for the

celebrates the condition of the Good in the next life. It is a state where the righteous are rewarded and the wicked punished until sin is consumed from their nature, when they come to the divine abode.[1]

To pass from the Poets to the Philosophers; the Immortality of the Soul was taught continually, from Pherecydes to Plotinus. There were those who doubted, and some that denied; yet it was defended by all the greatest philosophers, Thales, Pythagoras, Socrates, Plato, Aristotle, Cicero, Plutarch, Epictetus,[2] and by the most in-

immortality of the soul, Simonides, Frag. XXX. (XXXIII.); Tyrtaeus III. in Gaisford, Vol. III. p. 160, 242. See the curious passage in Aristophanes, Ranae, vs. 449—460, Opp. ed. Bekker, Lond. 1829, Vol. I p. 535, in which see B.'s note. See Orpheus, as cited by Lobeck, Aglaoph., p. 950; Cudworth, Chap. I. § 21, 22. and Mosheim in loc. See the indifferent book of Priestley, Heathen Philosophy, Part I. § 3, 5; Part II. § 3, 5; also p. 125, et seq., 197, et seq., 265, et seq.

[1] Olymp. II. vs. 104, et seq. (57—92, in Dissen.) See Cowley's wild imitation in his Pindarique Odes, Lond. 1720, Vol. II. p. 160, et seq. See similar thoughts in Propertius, Lib. III. 39, et seq.; and Tibullus, Eleg. III 58; Virgil. Æneid, VI. See also Pindar's Fragment, II. Vol. III. p. 34, ed. Heyne, Lips. 1817, Frag. I. p. 31, et seq., Frag. III. p. 36; and the notes of Dissen, in his edition of Pindar, Vol. II. p. 648, et seq., and Lobeck, ubi sup. See, who will, a treatise in the Acta Eruditorum for August, 1722, de Statu Animæ separatæ post mortem, &c.

[2] Cicero, Tusc. Lib. I. Chap. xvi., says Pherecydes was the first who taught this doctrine. See the note in Lemaire's edition. See also Diogenes Laert. Thales, Lib. I. § 43, p. 27, et seq. and Plutarch, De Placitis Phil., Lib. IV. Ch. ii.—vii., Opp. Vol. II. p. 898, et seq. It has been thought doubtful that Aristotle believed in immortality, and perhaps it is not easy to prove this point. See De Anima, III. 5; but compare Ethic. Nicom. Lib. III. Chap. vi., which denies it. See again De Anima, II. 2; De Gen. Anim. III. 4. Plato teaches immortality with the greatest clearness. See the Phædo, passim; Georgias, p. 524, et seq. et al.; Apolog. Laws, (if they are genuine,) Lib. X. XII.; Epinomis, Timæus, Rep. X. p. 612, et seq. Plato makes the essence of man spiritual; Tim. p. 69, C. et seq., 72, D. et seq., Rep. IV. p. 431, A. He was opposed to the Materialists, Soph p. 246, A. However, he did not condemn the body. His argument in favour of immortality, like many later arguments on the same theme, creates more questions than it answers. The form of the doctrine, its connection with preëxistence and transmigration, like many doctrines still popularly connected with it, serve only to disfigure the doctrine itself, and bring it into reproach. The opinion of Cicero is so well known, that it is almost superfluous to cite passages; but see Frag. de Consolat. 12, et seq., 27, et al.; De Senectute, Chap. XXI., et seq., Tusc. I. C. 16; De Amicit., Ch. 3, 4; Somnium Scipionis, et al. See Seneca, De Ira, I. 3; Consolatio ad Helv., Chap. VI.; De Vita Beata, Chap. XXII. Ep. 50, 102, 117. Sometimes he speaks decidedly, at other times with doubt. See Lipsius Physiol. Stoic. Lib. III. Diss. viii.—xix. See Locke, Essay, Book IV. Chap. iii., and Letters to Bishop of Worcester.

See Plutarch, De Sera Numinis Vindicta, Morals, Lond. 1691, Vol. IV. p. 197, et seq. See too the Story of Soleus the Thespesian, ibid. p. 206, et seq.; Plut. Vit. Quint. Sertorius, Opp. 1. 571, 572, F & B., for an account of the

fluential schools. No doubt it was often connected with absurd notions, in jest or earnest. But when or where has its fate been different? Bishop Warburton thinks it no part of Natural Religion; Dodwell thinks immortality is only coëxtensive with Christian baptism, and is super-induced upon the mortal soul by that dispensation of water.[1] Could a heathen be more absurd? If the popular doctrine of the Christian Church, which dooms the mass of men to endless misery, be true, then were immortality a misfor-tune to the race. The wisest of the Heathen taught such a dogma as little as did Jesus of Nazareth. We must always separate the doctrine from its proof and its form; the latter is often imperfect while the doctrine is true.

Since the time of Bishop Warburton, it has been com-mon to deny that the Heathen were acquainted with this doctrine.[2] "It was one guess among many," has often been said. But a man even slightly acquainted with an-cient thought and life, knows it is not so. God has not made truth so hard to come at, that the world of men con-tinued so many thousand years in ignorance of a future life. Before the time above named, it was taught by scholars, even scholars of the clerical order, that the doc-trine was well known to the Heathen. Cudworth and

Fortunate Islands, with which comp. Diod. Sic. Hist. II. Vol. I. p. 137, et seq. It seems the Priests of Serapis distinctly taught the Immortality of the Soul. Augustine says, "Many of the Philosophers of the Gentiles have written much concerning the immortality of the Soul, and in numerous books have they left it on record that the Soul is immortal. *But when you come to the resurrec-tion of the Flesh, they do not hesitate but openly deny that, contradicting it to such a degree that they declare it impossible for this terrene flesh to rise to Heaven.*" Expos. Psalms, lxxxviii. Justin M. says the doctrine of immortality was *no new thing* in Christ's time—but was taught by Plato and Pythagoras. The new element Christ added to the doctrine he thinks was the *resurrection of the Flesh.* Opp. ed. Otto. ii. p. 540. See the Literature collected on this subject by Kort-holt in his Annotations on Athenagoras, Legat., &c. &c., ed. Oxon. 1704, p. 94, et seq.

[1] Epistolary Discourse, &c., London, 1706. He thinks that *Regular Bishops* have the power of making men immortal through the "*divine baptismal spirit.*" See for the history of opinions among the Christians, Flügge, Vol. III. pt. 1 and 2.

[2] Warburton has the merit of framing an hypothesis so completely original that no one, perhaps, (except Bishop Hurd,) has ever shared it in full with him. Part of his singular theory is this : A belief in a future state was found neces-sary *in heathen countries* to keep the subjects in order ; the philosophers and priests got up a doctrine for that purpose, teaching that the soul was immortal, but not believing a word of it. *Moses, who believed the doctrine, yet never taught it, controlled the people by means of his inspiration, and the perfect Law.*

More, Wilkins, Taylor, and Wollaston, to mention only the most obvious names, bear testimony to the fact.[1]

To sum up in a few words the history of this doctrine, both among Jews and Gentiles : it seems that rude nations, like the Celts and the Sarmatians, clung instinctively to the sentiment of immortality ; that the doctrine was well known to the philosophers, and commonly accepted ; that some doubted, and some denied it altogether. A few had reached an eminence in philosophy, and could in their way demonstrate the proposition, and satisfy their logical doubt, thus reconciling the instinctive and reflective faculty. From the first book of Moses to the last of Maccabees, from Homer to Cicero, there is a great change in the form of the doctrine. All other forms also had changed.

But how far was the doctrine diffused among the people ? We can tell but faintly from history. But what nature demands and Providence affords, lingers longest in the bosom of the mass of men. The doctrine was not strange to the fishermen of Galilee. Was it more so to the peasants of Greece ?[2] The early Apologists of Christianity found no difficulty from the unity of God, and the immortality of the soul ; both are presupposed by Jesus and Paul. How far it moved men in common life can be told neither from the courtiers of Pagan Cæsar Augustus, nor from those of Christian Louis the Well-beloved. A Roman, and a Christian Pontiff—how much are they moved by the tardy terrors of future judgment ?[3] Juvenal could

---

[1] See Cudworth and More, passim ; Wilkins, Principles and Duties of Natural Religion, &c., Book I. Ch. xi. ; see also Ch. iv. and viii. ; Taylor's Sermon, preached at the Funeral of that worthy Knight, Sir George Dalston, &c. ; Wollaston, Religion of Nature, Sect. IX. It would be easy to cite passages from the early Christians, testifying to the truth possessed by the Heathens B. C. I will mention but one from Minucius Felix. "A man might judge either that the present Christians are philosophers, or else that the old philosophers were Christians." See likewise Brougham's Discourse on Natural Theology, Note VI.—IX. in Appendix. Polybius, ubi sup., Lib. VI. c. 53—56, seems to think the legislators got up the doctrine, with no faith in it, except a general belief it would make men submissive. See Timæus, De Anima Mundi, in Gale, ubi sup.

[2] The *resurrection of the body* seems to have been the doctrine that offended Paul's hearers at Athens ; that of *immortality* alone was well known to the Stoics, some of whom believed it, and the Epicureans, who rejected it. Acts xvii. 16, et seq. See Wetstein in loc.

[3] See Horace, Epist. Lib. I. Ep. xvi. ; Juvenal, Satir. XIII. ; Persius, Satir. II. How far do these express the popular sentiment ?

6 *

repeat his biting sneer in more ages than one.[1] Was the argument of the Pagan philosopher unsatisfactory? It was never otherwise. Mr Strauss declares it has not yet been demonstrated ; Mr Locke, that it cannot be proved. The spontaneous sentiment does its work with few words,. Who shall demonstrate for us a fact of consciousness, or prove our personal identity ? But the doctrine was connected with gross errors,—preëxistence and metempsychosis. Has the doctrine ever been free of such connection? in even a single historical case ? It does not appear. The doctrine of inherited sin, of depravity born in the bones of men ; the notion that the mass of men are doomed by the God of Mercy to eternal woe—immortal only to be wretched —is not a strange thing in the nineteenth century. Modern savages have foul notions of God ; ancient civilization has sins enough on its head, hideous sins, unknown even in our day, for the world has been worse,—but both are free from such a stain.[2]

CHAPTER VII.

THE INFLUENCE OF THE RELIGIOUS ELEMENT ON LIFE.

MAN is not a being of isolated faculties which act independently. The religious, like each other element in us, acts jointly with other powers. Its action therefore is helped or hindered by them. The Idea of Religion is only realized by an harmonious action of all the faculties, the intellectual, the moral. Yet the religious faculty must act,

---

[1] Satir. II. 149, et seq.

[2] Leclerc, ubi sup., gives a bird's-eye view of the state of the world at the commencement of the Christian period, perhaps the most faithful that has been given of manners and opinions. The popular mythology was in about the same estimation among cultivated men as the popular theology at the present time with men of piety and good sense. Leroux. de l'Humanité, Vol. I. p. 302, et seq., makes some observations on this doctrine among the ancients, not without interest. See a Sermon of Immortal Life, by Theo. Parker, Bost., 1846.

more or less, though the understanding be not cultivated, and the moral elements sleep in Egyptian night; in connection therefore with Wisdom or Folly, with Hope or Fear, with Love or Hate. Now in all periods of human history Religion demands something of her votaries. The ruder their condition, the more capricious and unreasonable is the demand. Though the Religious instinct itself be ever the same, the form of its expression varies with man's intellectual and moral state. Its influence on life may be considered under its three different manifestations.

I. *Of Superstition.*

Combining with Ignorance and Fear, the Religious Element leads to Superstition. This is the vilification and debasement of men. It may be defined as FEAR BEFORE GOD. Plutarch, though himself religious, pronounced it worse than Atheism. But the latter cannot exist to the same extent; is never an active principle. Superstition is a morbid state of human nature, where the conditions of religious development are not fulfilled; where the functions of the religious faculty are impeded and counteracted. But it must act, as the heart beats in the frenzy of a fever. It has been said with truth, " Perfect love casts out fear." The converse is quite as true. Perfect fear casts out Love. The superstitious man begins by fearing God, not loving him. He goes on, like a timid boy in the darkness, by projecting his own conceptions out of himself; conjuring up a phantom he calls his God ; a Deity capricious, cruel, revengeful, lying in wait for the unwary; a God ugly, morose, and only to be feared. He ends by paying a service meet for such a God, the service of Horror and Fear. Each man's conception of God is his conception of a man carried out to infinity ; the pure idea is eclipsed by a human personality. This conception therefore varies as the men who form it vary. It is the index of their Soul. The superstitious man projects out of himself a creation begotten of his Folly and his Fear; calls the furious phantom God, Moloch, Jehovah; then attempts to please the capricious Being he has conjured up. To do this, the demands his Superstition makes are not to keep the laws which the one God wrote on the walls of Man's being; but to do arbitrary

acts which this fancied God demands. He must give up
to the deity what is dearest to himself. Hence the savage
offers a sacrifice of favourite articles of food; the first-fruits
of the chase, or agriculture; weapons of war which have
done signal service; the nobler animals; the skins of rare
beasts. He conceives the anger of his God may be soothed
like a man's excited passion by libations, incense, the
smoke of plants, the steam of a sacrifice.

Again, the superstitious man would appease his God by
unnatural personal service. He undertakes an enterprise,
almost impossible, and succeeds, for the fire of his purpose subdues and softens the rock that opposes him. He
submits to painful privation of food, rest, clothing; leads
a life of solitude; wears a comfortless dress, that girds and
frets the very flesh; stands in a painful position; shuts
himself in a dungeon; lives in a cave; stands on a pillar's
top; goes unshorn and filthy. He exposes himself to be
scorched by the sun and frozen by the frost. He lacerates
his flesh; punctures his skin to receive sacred figures of
the Gods. He mutilates his body, cutting off the most
useful members. He sacrifices his cattle, his enemies, his
children; defiles the sacred temple of his body; destroys
his mortal life to serve his God. In a state more refined,
Superstition demands abstinence from all the sensual goods
of life. Its present pleasures are a godless thing. The
flesh is damned. To serve God is to mortify the appetites
God gave. Then the superstitious man abstains from com-
fortable food, clothing, and shelter; comes neither eating
nor drinking; watches all night absorbed in holy vigils.
The man of God must be thin and spare. Bernard has but
to show his neck, fleshless and scraggy, to be confessed a
mighty saint. Above all, he must abstain from marriage.
The Devil lurks under the bridal rose. The vow of the celibate can send him howling back to hell. The smothered
volcano is grateful to God. Then comes the assumption
of arbitrary vows; the performance of pilgrimages to distant places, thinly clad and barefoot; the repetition of
prayers, not as a delight, spontaneously poured out, but
as a penance, or work of supererogation. In this state,
Superstition builds convents, monasteries, sends Anthony
to his dwelling in the desert; it founds orders of Mendi-
cants, Rechabites, Nazarites, Encratites, Pilgrims, Flagel-

lants, and similar Moss-troopers of Religion, whom Heaven yet turns to good account. This is the Superstition of the Flesh. It promises the favour of its God on condition of these most useless and arbitrary acts. It dwells on the absurdest of externals.

However, in a later day it goes to still more subtle refinements. The man does not mutilate his body, nor give up the most sacred of his material possessions. This was the Superstition of savage life. But he mutilates his soul; gives up the most sacred of his spiritual treasures. This is the Superstition of refined life. Here the man is ready to forego Reason, Conscience, and Love, God's most precious gifts; the noblest attributes of Man; the tie that softly joins him to the eternal world. He will think against Reason; decide against Conscience; act against Love; because he dreams the God of Reason, Conscience, and Love demands it. It is a slight thing to hack and mutilate the body, though it be the fairest temple God ever made, and to mar its completeness a sin. But to dismember the soul, the very image of God; to lop off most sacred affections; to call Reason a Liar, Conscience a devil's-oracle, and cast Love clean out from the heart, this is the last triumph of Superstition; but one often witnessed, in all three forms of Religion—Fetichism, Polytheism, Monotheism; in all ages before Christ; in all ages after Christ. This is the Superstition of the Soul. The one might be the Superstition of the Hero; this is the Superstition of the Pharisee.

A man rude in spirit must have a rude conception of God. He thinks the Deity like himself. If a Buffalo had a religion, his conception of Deity would probably be a Buffalo, fairer limbed, stronger, and swifter than himself, grazing in the fairest meadows of Heaven. If he were superstitious, his service would consist in offerings of grass, of water, of salt; perhaps in abstinence from the pleasures, comforts, necessities of a bison's life. His devil also would be a Buffalo, but of another colour, lean, vicious, and ugly. Now when a man has these rude conceptions, inseparable from a rude state, offerings and sacrifice are natural. When they come spontaneous, as the expression of a grateful or a penitent heart; the seal of a resolution; the sign of Faith, Hope, and Love, as an outward symbol which strengthens the in-dwelling sentiment—the sacrifice is pleasant and may be beautiful. The child who saw God in the swelling and rounded clouds of a June day, and left on a rock the ribbon-grass and garden roses as mute symbols of gratitude to the Great Spirit who poured out the voluptuous weather; the ancient pagan who bowed prone to the dust, in homage, as the sun looked out from the windows of morning, or offered the smoke of incense at nightfall in gratitude for the day, or kissed his hand to the Moon, thankful for that spectacle of loveliness passing above him; the man who, with reverent thankfulness or penitence, offers a sacrifice of joy or grief, to express what words too poorly tell;—he is no idolater, but Nature's simple child. We rejoice in self-denial for a father, a son, a friend. Love and every strong emotion has its sacrifice. It is rooted deep in the heart of men. God needs nothing. He cannot receive; yet Man needs to give. But if these things are done as substitutes for holiness, as causes and not mere signs of reconciliation with God, as means to coax and wheedle the Deity and bribe the All-powerful, it is Superstition, rank and odious. Examples enough of this are found in all ages. To take two of the most celebrated cases, one from the Hebrews, the other from a Heathen people: Abraham would sacrifice his son to Jehovah, who demanded that offering,[1] Agamemnon his daughter to

---

[1] Gen. xxii. 1—14. The conjectures of the learned about this mythical legend, which may have some fact at its foundation, are numerous, and some of them remarkable for their ingenuity. Some one supposes that Abraham was tempted by the *Elohim*, but *Jehovah* prevented the sacrifice. It is easy to find Heathen parallels. See the story of Cronus in Eusebius, P. E. I. 10; of Aristodemus, of whom Pausanias tells a curious story, IV. 9. See the case of Helena and Valeria Luperca, who were both miraculously saved from sacrifice, in Plutarch. Paralel. Opp. Vol. II. p. 314. The Bulgarian legend of poor Lasar is quite remarkable, and strikingly analogous to that of Abram and Isaac. A stranger comes to Lasar's house, L. has nothing for his guest's supper, and therefore, at his suggestion, kills Jenko, his son; the guest eats; but at midnight cries aloud that he is—the LORD! Jenko is restored to life. See the story in a notice of Paton's Servia, in For. Quart. Review for Oct. 1845, Am. ed. p. 130.

Polybius says we must allow writers *to enlarge in stories of miracles, and in fables of that sort, when they desire to promote piety among the people.* But, he adds, an excess in this line is not to be tolerated. Opp. Lib. XVI. ch. 11, ed. Schweighäuser, Oxon. 1823, III. p. 289. Elsewhere he says, this would not be necessary in a state composed of wise men, but the *people require to be managed with obscure fears and tragical stories.* Ibid. Lib. VI. ch. 56, Vol. II. p. 389. Strabo is of the same opinion, and thinks that *women and the people cannot be led to piety by philosophical discourses,* only by Fables and Myths. Geog. Lib. I. ch. 2, ed. Siebenkees, p. 51-2. Dionysius Hal. speaks more

angry Diana. But a Deity kindly interferes in both cases. The Angel of Jehovah rescues Isaac from the remorseless knife; a ram is found for a sacrifice. Diana delivers the daughter of Agamemnon and leaves a hind in her place. No one doubts the latter is a case of superstition most ghastly and terrible. A father murder his own child—a human sacrifice to the Lord of Life! It is rebellion against Conscience, Reason, Affection; treason against God. Though Calchas, the anointed minister, declared it the will of Heaven—there is an older than Calchas who says, It is a Lie. He that defends the former patriarch, counting it a blameless and beautiful act of piety and faith performed at the command of God—what shall be said of him? He proves the worm of Superstition is not yet dead, nor its fire quenched, and leads weak men to ask, Which then has most of Religion, the Christian, who justifies Abraham, or the Pagan Greeks, who condemned Agamemnon? He leads weak men to ask; the strong make no question of so plain a matter.

But why go back to Patriarchs at Aulis or Moriah; do we not live in New England and the nineteenth century? Have the footsteps of Superstition been effaced from our land? Our books of theology are full thereof; our churches and homes, not empty of it. When a man fears God more than he loves him; when he will forsake Reason, Conscience, Love—the still small voice of God in the heart—for any of the legion voices of Authority, Tradition, Expediency, which come of Ignorance, Selfishness, and Sin; whenever he hopes by a poor prayer, or a listless attendance at church, or an austere observance of Sabbaths and Fast-days, a compliance with forms; when he hopes by professing with his tongue the doctrine he cannot believe in his heart, to atone for wicked actions, wrong thoughts, unholy feelings, a six-days' life of meanness, deception, rottenness, and sin,—then is he superstitious. Are there no fires but those of Moloch; no idols of printed paper, and spoken wind? No false worship but bowing the knee to Baal, Adonis, Priapus, Cybele? Superstition changes its forms, not its substance. If he were superstitious who

wisely. Antiq. II. ch. 18—20, Opp. ed. Reiske, Lips. 1774. I. p. 271, et seq., and properly commends Romulus for rejecting immoral Stories from the public and official theology.

in days of ignorance but made his son's body pass through
the fire to his God, what shall be said of them in an age of
light, who systematically degrade the fairest gifts of men,
God's dearest benefaction; who make life darkness, death
despair, the world a desert, Man a worm, nothing but a
worm, and God an ugly fiend, that made the most of men
for utter wretchedness, death, and eternal hell? Alas for
them. They are blind and see not. They lie down in
their folly. Let Charity cover them up.

II.   *Of Fanaticism.*

There is another morbid state of the religious Element.
It consists in its union with Hatred and other malignant
passions in men. Here it leads to Fanaticism. As the
essence of Superstition is Fear coupled with religious feeling; so the essence of Fanaticism is Malice mingling with
that sentiment. It may be called HATRED BEFORE GOD. The
Superstitious man fears lest God hate him; the Fanatic
thinks he hates not him but his enemies. Is the Fanatic
a Jew?—the Gentiles are hateful to Jehovah; a Mahometan?—all are infidel dogs who do not bow to the prophet,
their end is destruction. Is he a Christian?—he counts
all others as Heathens whom God will damn; of this or
that sect?—he condemns all the rest for their belief, let
their life be divine as the prayer of a saint. Out of his
selfish passion he creates him a God; breathes into it
the breath of his Hatred; he worships and prays to it, and
says "Deliver me, for thou art my God." Then he feels
—so he fancies—inspiration to visit his foes with divine
vengeance. He can curse and smite them in the name of
his God. It is the sword of the Lord, and the fire of the
Most High that drinks up the blood and stifles the groan
of the wretched.

Like Superstition, it is found in all ages of the world.
It is the insanity of mankind. As the richest soils grow
weightiest harvests, or most noxious weeds and poisons
the most baneful; as the strongest bodies take disease the
most sorely; so the deepest natures, the highest forms of
worship, when once infected with this leprosy, go to the
wildest excess of desperation. Thus the fanaticism of
worshippers of one God has no parallel among idolaters

and polytheists. There is a point in human nature where moral distinctions do not appear, as on the earth there are spots where the compass will not traverse, and dens where the sun never shines. This fact is little dwelt on by philosophers; still it is a fact. Seen from this point, Right and Wrong lose their distinctive character and run into each other. Good seems Evil and Evil Good, or both appear the same. The sophistry of the understanding sometimes leagues with appetite, and gradually entices the thoughtless into this pit. The Antinomian of all times turns in thither, to increase his Faith and diminish his Works. It is the very cave of Trophonius; he that enters loses his manhood and walks backward as he returns; his soul, so filled with God, whatever the flesh does, he thinks cannot be wrong, though it break all laws, human and divine. The fanatic dwells continually in this state. God demands of him to persecute his foes. The thought troubles him by day, and stares on him as a spectre at night. God, or his angel, appear to his crazed fancy and bid him to the work with promise of reward, or spurs him with a curse. Then there is no lie too malignant for him to invent and utter; no curse too awful for him to imprecate; no refinement of torture too cruel or exquisitely rending for his fancy to devise, his malice to inflict; Nature is teased for new tortures; Art is racked to extort fresh engines of cruelty. As the jaded Roman offered a reward for the invention of a new pleasure, so the fanatic would renounce Heaven could he give an added pang to hell.

Men of this character have played so great a part in the world's history, they must not be passed over in silence. The ashes of the innocents they have burned, are sown broadcast and abundant in all lands. The earth is quick with this living dust. The blood of prophets and saviours they have shed still cries for justice. The Canaanites, the Jews, the Saracen, the Christian, Polytheist and Idolater, New Zealand and New England, are guilty of this. Let the early Christian and the delaying Heathen tell their tale. Let the voice of the Heretic speak from the dungeon-racks of the Inquisition; that of the " true believer " from the scaffolds of Elizabeth—most Christian Queen; let the voices of the murdered come up from the squares of Paris, the plains of the Low Countries, from the streets of Antioch, Byzantium,

Jerusalem, Alexandria, Damascus, Rome, Mexico; from the wheels, racks, and gibbets of the world; let the men who died in religious wars, always the bloodiest and most remorseless; the women, whom nothing could save from a fate yet more awful; the babes, newly born, who perished in the sack and conflagration of idolatrous and heretical cities, when for the sake of Religion men violated its every precept, and in the name of God broke down his Law, and trampled his image into bloody dust;—let all these speak, to admonish, and to blame.

But it is not well to rest on general terms alone. Paul had no little fanaticism, when he persecuted the Christians; kept the garments of men who stoned Stephen. Moses had much of it, if, as the story goes, he commanded the extirpation of nations of idolaters, millions of men, virtuous as the Jews; Joshua, Samuel, David, had much of it, and executed schemes bloody as a murderer's most sanguine dream. It has been both the foe and the auxiliary of the Christian Church. There is a long line of Fanatics, extending from the time of Jesus, reaching from century to century, marching on from age to age, with the banner of the Cross over their heads, and the Gospel on their tongues, and fire and sword in their hands.[1] The last of that Apocalyptic rabble has not as yet passed by. Let the clouds of darkness hide them. What need to tell of our own fathers; what they suffered, what they inflicted; their crime is fresh and unatoned. Rather let us take the wings of an angel, and fly away from scenes so awful, the slaughter-house of souls.

But the milder forms of Fanaticism we cannot escape. They meet us in the theological war of extermination, which sect now wars with sect, pulpit with pulpit, man with man. If one would seek specimens of Superstition in its milder form, let him open a popular commentary on the Bible, or read much of that weakish matter which circulates in what men call, as if in mockery, " good, pious books." If he would find Fanaticism in its modern and more Pharisaic shape, let him open the sectarian newspapers, or read theological polemics. To what mean uses may we not descend? The spirit of a Caligula and a Dominic, of Alva

---

[1] See the Book of Revelation, passim.

and Ignatius stares at men in the street. It can only bay in the distance; it dares not bite. Poor, craven Fanaticism! fallen like Lucifer, never to hope again. Like Pope and Pagan in the story, he sits chained by the wayside to grin and gibber, and howl and snarl, as the Pilgrim goes by, singing the song of the fearless and free, on the highway to Heaven, with his girdle about him and white robe on. Poor Fanaticism, who was drunk with the blood of the saints, and in his debauch lifted his horn and pushed at the Almighty, and slew the children of God,—he shall revel but in the dreamy remembrance of his ancient crime; his teeth shall be fleshed no more in the limbs of the living.

These two morbid states just past over, represent the most hideous forms of human degradation; where the foulest passions are at their foulest work; where Malice, which a Devil might envy, and which might make Hell darker with its frown; where Hate and Rancour build up their organizations and ply their arts. In man there is a mixture of good and evil. "A being darkly wise and poorly great," he has in him somewhat of the Angel and something of the Devil. In Fanaticism, the Angel sleeps and the Devil drives. But let us leave the hateful theme.[1]

III. *Of Solid Piety.*

The legitimate and perfect action of the Religious Element takes place when it exists in harmonious combination with Reason, Conscience, and Affection. Then it is not Hatred, and not Fear, but LOVE BEFORE GOD. It produces the most beautiful development of human nature; the golden age, the fairest Eden of life, the kingdom of Heaven. Its Deity is the God of Infinite Power, Wisdom, Justice, Love, and Holiness—Fidelity to Himself,—within whose encircling arms it is beautiful to be. The demands it makes are to keep the Law He has written in the heart,

---

[1] A powerful priesthood has usually had great influence in promoting fanaticism of the most desperate character. One need only look over the history of persecutions in all ages to see this. We see it among the Hebrews, the Germans, the Druids; the nations that opposed the spread of Christianity. The Christian Church itself has erected monuments enough to perpetuate the fact. The story of Haman and Mordecai is no bad allegory of the conflict between the orthodox priesthood and the unorganized heretics.

to be good, to do good; to love men, to love God. It may use forms, prayers, dogmas, ceremonies, priests, temples, sabbaths, festivals, and fasts; yes, sacrifices if it will, as means, not ends; symbols of a sentiment, not substitutes for it. Its substance is Love of God; its Piety the form, Morality the Love of men; its temple a pure heart; its sacrifice a divine life. The end it proposes is, to reunite the man with God, till he thinks God's thought, which is Truth; feels God's feeling, which is Love, wills God's will, which is the eternal Right; thus finding God in the sense wherein he is not far from any one of us; becoming one with Him, and so partaking the divine nature. The means to this high end are an extinction of all in man that opposes God's law; a perfect obedience to Him as he speaks in Reason, Conscience, Affection. It leads through active obedience to an absolute trust, a perfect love; to the complete harmony of the finite man with the infinite God, and man's will coalesces in that of Him who is All in All. Then Faith and Knowledge are the same thing, Reason and Revelation do not conflict, Desire and Duty go hand in hand, and strew man's path with flowers. Desire has become dutiful, and Duty desirable. The divine spirit incarnates itself in the man. The riddle of the world is solved. Perfect love casts out fear. Then Religion demands no particular actions, forms, or modes of thought. The man's ploughing is holy as his prayer; his daily bread as the smoke of his sacrifice; his home sacred as his temple; his work-day and his sabbath are alike God's day. His priest is the holy spirit within him; Faith and Works his communion of both kinds. He does not sacrifice Reason to Religon, nor Religion to Reason. Brother and Sister, they dwell together in love. A life harmonious and beautiful, conducted by Righteousness, filled full with Truth and enchanted by Love to men and God,—this is the service he pays to the Father of All. Belief does not take the place of Life. Capricious austerity atones for no duty left undone. He loves Religion as a bride, for her own sake, not for what she brings. He lies low in the hand of God. The breath of the Father is on him.

If Joy comes to this man, he rejoices in its rosy light. His Wealth, his Wisdom, his Power, is not for himself alone, but for all God's children. Nothing is his which a

brother needs more than he. Like God himself, he is kind
to the thankless and unmerciful. Purity without and Piety
within; these are his Heaven, both present and to come.
Is not his flesh as holy as his soul—his body a temple of
God?

If trouble comes on him, which Prudence could not
foresee, nor Strength overcome, nor Wisdom escape from,
he bears it with a heart serene and full of peace. Over
every gloomy cavern, and den of despair, Hope arches her
rainbow; the ambrosial light descends. Religion shows
him that, out of desert rocks, black and savage, where the
Vulture has her home, where the Storm and the Avalanche
are born, and whence they descend, to crush and to kill;
out of these hopeless cliffs, falls the river of Life, which
flows for all, and makes glad the people of God. When
the Storm and the Avalanche sweep from him all that is
dearest to mortal hope, is he comfortless? Out of the
hard marble of Life, the deposition of a few joys and many
sorrows, of birth and death, and smiles and grief, he hews
him the beautiful statue of religious Tranquillity. It stands
ever beside him, with the smile of heavenly satisfaction on
its lip, and its thrusting finger pointing to the sky.

The true religious man, amid all the ills of time, keeps
a serene forehead, and entertains a peaceful heart. Thus
going out and coming in amid all the trials of the city, the
agony of the plague, the horrors of the thirty tyrants, the
fierce democracy abroad, the fiercer ill at home, the Saint,
the Sage of Athens, was still the same. Such an one can
endure hardness; can stand alone and be content; a rock
amid the waves, lonely, but not moved. Around him the
few or many may scream their screams, or cry their
clamours; calumniate or blaspheme. What is it all to him,
but the cawing of the sea-bird about that solitary and
deep-rooted stone? So swarms of summer flies, and spite-
ful wasps, may assail the branches of an oak, which lifts
its head, storm-tried and old, above the hills. They move
a leaf, or bend a twig, by their united weight. Their noise,
fitful and malicious, elsewhere might frighten the sheep in
the meadows. Here it becomes a placid hum. It joins
the wild whisper of the leaves. It swells the breezy music
of the tree, but makes it bear no acorn less.

He fears no evil, God is his armour against fate. I rejoices in his trials, and Jeremiah sings psalms in his tem
geon, and Daniel prays three times a day with his wi will
up, that all may hear, and Nebuchadnezzar cast him bsti
lions if he will; Luther will go to the Diet at Worms th, if it
rain enemies for nine days running; "though the L art perils
be thick as the tiles on the roof." Martyred Stephen sees
God in the clouds. The victim at the stake glories in the
fire he lights, which shall shine all England through. Yes,
Paul, an old man forsaken of his friends, tried by many
perils, daily expecting an awful death, sits comforted in
his dungeon. The Lord stands by and says, Fear not,
Paul, Lo, I am with thee to the world's end. The tranquil
saint can say, I know whom I have served. I have not
the spirit of fear, but joy. I am ready to be sacrificed.
Such trials prove the Soul as Gold is proved. The dross
perishes in the fire; but the virgin metal—it comes
brighter from the flame. What is it for such a man to be
scourged, forsaken, his name a proverb, counted as the
offscouring of the world? There is that in him which
looks down millions. Cast out, he is not in dismay; forsaken, never less alone. Slowly and soft the Soul of Faith
comes into the man. He knows that he is seen by the
pure and terrible eyes of Infinity. He feels the sympathy
of the Soul of All, and says, with modest triumph, I am
not alone, for Thou art with me. Mortal affections may
cease their melody; but the Infinite speaks to his soul
comfort too deep for words, and too divine. What if he
have not the Sun of human affection to cheer him? The
awful faces of the stars look from the serene depths of
divine Love, and seem to say, "Well done." What if the
sweet music of human sympathy vanish before the discordant curse of his brother man? The melody of the
spheres—so sweet we heed it not when tried less sorely—
rolls in upon the soul its tranquil tide, and that same
Word, which was in the beginning, says, "Thou art my
beloved Son, and in thee am I well pleased." Earth is
overcome, and Heaven won.

It is well for mankind that God now and then raises up
a hero of the soul; exposes him to grim trials in the fore-
front of the battle; sustains him there, that we may know
what nobility is in Man, and how near him God; to

show that greatness in the religious man is only needed to be found; that his Charity does not expire with the quiverings of his flesh; that this hero can end his breath with a "Father, forgive them."

Man everywhere is the measure of man. There is nothing which the Flesh and the Devil can inflict in their rage, but the Holy Spirit can bear in its exceeding peace. The Art of the tormentor is less than the Nature of the suffering soul. All the denunciations of all that sat on Moses's seat, or have since climbed to that of the Messiah; the scorn of the contemptuous; the fury of the passionate; the wrath of a monarch, and the roar of his armies; all these are to a religious soul but the buzzing of the flies about that mountain oak. There is nothing that prevails against Truth.

Now in some men Religion is a continual growth. They are always in harmony with God. Silently and unconscious, erect as a palm tree, they grow up to the measure of a man. To them Reason and Religion are of the same birth. They are born saints; Aborigines of Heaven. Betwixt their Idea of Life and their Fact of Life there has at no time been a gulf. But others join themselves to the Armada of Sin, and get scarred all over with wounds as they do thankless battle in that leprous host. Before these men become religious, there must be a change,—well-defined, deeply marked,—a change that will be remembered. The Saints who have been sinners, tell us of the struggle and desperate battle that goes on between the Flesh and the Spirit. It is as if the Devil and the Archangel contended. Well says John Bunyan, The Devil fought with me weeks long, and I with the Devil. To take the leap of Niagara, and stop when half-way down, and by their proper motion reascend, is no slight thing, nor the remembrance thereof like to pass away.

This passage from sin to salvation; this second birth of the Soul, as both Christians and Heathens call it, is one of the many mysteries of Man. Two elements meet in the consciousness. There is a negation of the past; an affirmation of the future. Terror and Hope, Penitence and Faith, rush together in that moment and a new life begins. The character gradually grows over the wounds of sin. With bleeding feet the man retreads his way, but gains at last

the mountain top of Life and wonders at the tortuous track
he left behind.

Shall it be said that Religion is the great refinement of
the world; its tranquil star that never sets? Need it be
told that all Nature works in its behalf; that every mute
and every living thing seems to repeat God's voice, Be perfect; that Nature, which is the *out-ness* of God, favours Religion, which is the *in-ness* of Man, and so God works with
us? Heathens knew it many centuries ago. It has long
been known that Religion—in its true estate—created the
deepest welfare of Man. Socrates, Seneca, Plutarch, An-
toninus, Fenelon can tell us this. It might well be so.
Religion comes from what is strongest, deepest, most
beautiful and divine; lays no rude hand on soul or sense;
condemns no faculty as base. It sets no bounds to Reason
but Truth; none to Affection but Love; none to Desire
but Duty; none to the Soul but Perfection; and these are
not limits, but the charter of infinite freedom.

No doubt there is joy in the success of earthly schemes.
There is joy to the miser as he satiates his prurient palm
with gold: there is joy for the fool of fortune when his
gaming brings a prize. But what is it? His request is
granted; but leanness enters his soul. There is delight
in feasting on the bounties of Earth, the garment in which
God veils the brightness of his face; in being filled with
the fragrant loveliness of flowers; the song of birds; the
hum of bees; the sounds of ocean; the rustle of the summer wind, heard at evening in the pine tops; in the cool
running brooks; in the majestic sweep of undulating hills;
the grandeur of untamed forests; the majesty of the mountain; in the morning's virgin beauty; in the maternal
grace of evening, and the sublime and mystic pomp of
night. Nature's silent sympathy—how beautiful it is!

There is joy, no doubt there is joy, to the mind of Genius, when thought bursts on him as the tropic sun rending
a cloud; when long trains of ideas sweep through his soul,
like constellated orbs before an angel's eye; when sublime
thoughts and burning words rush to the heart; when Nature unveils her secret truth, and some great Law breaks,
all at once, upon a Newton's mind, and chaos ends in light;
when the hour of his inspiration and the joy of his genius

is on him, 't is then that this child of Heaven feels a god-like delight. 'T is sympathy with Truth.

There is a higher and more tranquil bliss when heart communes with heart; when two souls unite in one, like mingling dew-drops on a rose, that scarcely touch the flower, but mirror the heavens in their little orbs; when perfect love transforms two souls, either man's or woman's, each to the other's image; when one heart beats in two bosoms; one spirit speaks with a divided tongue; when the same soul is eloquent in mutual eyes—there is a rapture deep, serene, heart-felt, and abiding in this mysterious fellow-feeling with a congenial soul, which puts to shame the cold sympathy of Nature, and the ecstatic but short-lived bliss of Genius in his high and burning hour.

But the welfare of Religion is more than each or all of these. The glad reliance that comes upon the man; the sense of trust; a rest with God; the soul's exceeding peace; the universal harmony; the infinite within; sympathy with the Soul of All—is bliss that words cannot portray. He only knows, who feels. The speech of a prophet cannot tell the tale. No: not if a seraph touched his lips with fire. In the high hour of religious visitation from the living God, there seems to be no separate thought; the tide of universal life sets through the soul. The thought of self is gone. It is a little accident to be a king or a clown, a parent or a child. Man is at one with God, and He is All in All. Neither the loveliness of Nature, neither the joy of Genius, nor the sweet breathing of congenial hearts, that make delicious music as they beat,—neither one nor all of these can equal the joy of the religious soul that is at one with God, so full of peace that prayer is needless. This deeper joy gives an added charm to the former blessings. Nature undergoes a new transformation. A story tells that when the rising sun fell on Memnon's statue it wakened music in that breast of stone. Religion does the same with Nature. From the shining snake to the waterfall, it is all eloquent of God. As to John in the Apocalypse, there stands an angel in the sun; the seraphim hang over every flower; God speaks in each little grass that fringes a mountain rock. Then even Genius is wedded to a greater bliss. His thoughts shine

7 *

more brilliant, when set in the light of Religion, Friendship and Love it renders infinite. The man loves God
when he but loves his friend. This is the joy Religion
gives ; its perennial rest ; it everlasting life. It comes not
by chance. It is the possession of such as ask and toil
and toil and ask. It is withheld from none, as other gifts.
Nature tells little to the deaf, the blind, the rude. Every
man is not a genius, and has not his joy. Few men can
find a friend that is the world to them. That triune sympathy is not for every one. But this welfare of Religion,
the deepest, truest, the everlasting, the sympathy with
God, lies within the reach of all his Sons.

BOOK II.

" Reason is natural Revelation, whereby the eternal Father of Light and Fountain of all Knowledge communicates to mankind that portion of truth which he has laid within the reach of their natural faculties. Revelation is natural Reason enlarged by a new set of discoveries, communicated by God immediately, which Reason vouches the truth of, by the testimony and proofs it gives that they come from God. So that he that takes away Reason to make way for Revelation puts out the light of both, and does much-what the same as if he would persuade a man to put out his eyes the better to receive the remote light of an invisible star by a telescope."—LOCKE, *Essay,* Book IV. Chap. xix. § 4.

BOOK II.

CHAPTER I.

THE IDEA AND CONCEPTION OF GOD.

Two things are necessary to render Religion possible;
namely, a religious faculty in Man, and God out of Man as
the object of that religious faculty. The existence of these
two things admitted, Religion follows necessarily, as vision
from the existence of a seeing faculty in Man, and that of
light out of him. Now the existence of the religious element, as it was said before, implies its object. We have
naturally a Sentiment of God. Reason gives us an Idea
of Him. But to these we superadd a Conception of Him.
Can this definite conception be adequate? Certainly not.
The Idea of God, as the Infinite, may exhaust the most
transcendent Imagination; it is the highest Idea of which
Man is capable. But is God to be measured by our Idea?
Shall the finite circumscribe the Infinite? The existence
of God is so plainly and deeply writ, both in us and out of
us, in what we are and what we experience, that the humblest and the loftiest minds may be satisfied of this reality,
and may know that there is an absolute Cause; a Ground
of all things; the Infinite of Power, Wisdom, Justice,
Love, whereon we may repose, wherein we may confide.
This conclusion comes alike from the spontaneous Sentiment, and premeditated Reflection; from the intuition of
Reason, and the process of Reasoning. This Idea of God

is clear and distinct; not to be confounded with any other idea.

But when we attempt to go further, to give a logical description of Deity, its nature and essence; to define and classify its attributes; to make a definite Conception of God, as of the finite objects of the senses or the understanding, going into minute details, then we have nothing but our own subjective notions, which do not, of necessity, have an objective reality corresponding thereto. All men may know God as the Infinite. His nature and essence are past finding out. But we know God only in part—from the manifestations of divinity, seen in nature, felt in Man; manifestations of Matter and Spirit. Are these the whole of God; is Man his measure? Then is He exhausted, and not infinite. We affix the terms of human limitation to God, and speak of his Personality; some limiting it to one, others extending it to three, to seven, to thirty, or to many millions of persons. Can such terms apply to the Infinite? We talk of a personal God. If thereby we only deny that he has the limitations of unconscious Matter, no wrong is done. But our conception of Personality is that of finite personality; limited by human imperfections; hemmed in by Time and Space; restricted by partial emotions, displeasure, wrath, ignorance, caprice. Can this be said of God? If Matter were conscious, as Locke thinks it possible, it must predicate Materiality of God as persons predicate Personality of him. We apply the term impersonal. If it mean God has not the limitations of our personality it is well. But if it mean that he has those of unconscious Matter, it is worse than the other term. Can God be personal and conscious, as Joseph and Peter; unconscious and impersonal, as a moss or the celestial ether? No man will say it. Where then is the philosophic value of such terms?

The nature of God is past finding out. "There is no searching of his understanding." As the Absolute Cause, God must contain in himself, potentially, the ground of consciousness, of personality—yes, of unconsciousness and impersonality. But to apply these terms to Him seems to me a vain attempt to fathom the abyss of the Godhead and report the soundings. Will our line reach to the bottom of God? There is nothing on Earth, or in Heaven, to which we can compare him; of course we can have no image of him in the mind.[1]

There has been enough dogmatism respecting the nature, essence, and personality of God—respecting the Metaphysics of the Deity, and that by men who, perhaps, did not thoroughly understand all about the nature, essence, and metaphysics of Man. It avails nothing. Meanwhile the greatest religious souls that have ever been, are content to fall back on the Sentiment and the Idea of God, and confess that none by searching can perfectly find Him out. They can say, therefore, with an old Heathen, "Since he cannot be fully declared by any one name, though compounded of never so many, therefore is he rather to be called by every name, he being both one and all things; so that [to express the whole of God] either everything must be called by his name, or he by the name of everything."[2] "Call him, therefore," says another Pagan, "by all names, for all can express but a whisper of Him; call him rather by no name, for none can declare his Power, Wisdom, and Goodness."

Malebranche says, with as much philosophy as piety, "One ought not so much to call God a Spirit, in order to express positively what he is, as in order to signify that he is not Matter. He is a being infinitely perfect. Of this we cannot doubt. But in the same manner we ought

---

[1] There has been some controversy on this question of the *personality* of God in modern times. The writings of Spinoza, both now and formerly, have caused much discussion of this point. The capital maxim of Spinoza on this head is, all attempts to *determine* the nature of God are a negation of him. *Determinatio negatio est.* See Ep. 50, p. 634, ed. Paulus. He thinks God has *self-conscious personality* only in self-conscious persons, i. e. men. Ethic. II. Prop. 11, and Coroll.

Some have thought to help the matter by the Trinitarian hypothesis. If there were but one man in the universe, he could not indeed, it is said, have our conception of personality, which demands other persons. This condition is fulfilled for the divine Being soon as we admit a trinity in unity. Mystical writers have always inclined to a denial of the personality of God. Thus Plotinus, Dionysius the Areopagite, Scotus Erigena, Meister Eckart, Tauler, and Böhme, to mention no more, deny it. On this subject see Hegel, Lectures on the proofs of the existence of God, at the end of Philosophie der Religion; Encyclopädie, § 562, et seq., 2nd ed. See the subject touched upon by Strauss, Glaubenslehre, § 33. See also Nitzsch's review of Strauss in Studien und Kritiken for Jan. 1, 1842; Sengler, ubi sup., B. I. p. Abs. II.—IV.

In reference to Spinoza, see the controversial writings of Messrs Norton and Ripley, above referred to.

[2] See the Asclepian Dialogue, and also the passages from Seneca and Julian, cited in Cudworth, Vol. II. p. 679, et seq., Ch. IV. § 32.

not to imagine . . . that he is clothed with a human body
. . . under colour that that figure was the most perfect of
any; so neither ought we to imagine that the Spirit of
God has human ideas, or bears any resemblance to our
Spirit, under colour that we know nothing more perfect
than the human mind.   We ought rather to believe that
as he comprehends the perfection of Matter, without being
material, . . . so he comprehends also the perfections of
created spirits without being Spirit, in the manner we
conceive Spirit.   That his true name is, HE THAT IS, or, in
other words, Being without restriction, All Being, the
Being Infinite and Universal."[1]   Still we have a positive
Idea of God.   It is the most positive of all.   It is implied
logically in every idea that we form, so that as God himself is the being of all existence, the background and
cause of all things that are, the reality of all appearance,
so the Idea of God is the central truth, as it were, of all
other ideas whatever.   The objects of all other ideas are
dependent, and not final; the object of this, independent
and ultimate.   This Idea of an Independent and Infinite
Cause, therefore, is necessarily presupposed by the conception of any dependent and finite effect.   For example,
a man forms a notion of his own existence.   This notion
involves that of dependence, which conducts him back to
that on which dependence rests.   He has no complete
notion of his own existence without the notion of dependence; nor of that without the object on which he depends.
Take our stand where we may, and reason, we come back
logically to this which is the primitive fact in all our intellectual conceptions, just as each point in the circumference
of a circle is a point in the radius thereof, and this leads
straightway to the Centre, whence they all proceed.[2]

---

[1] Recherches de la Vérité, Liv. III. Ch. ix., as cited in Hume, Dialogues
concerning Nat. Rel. Vol. II. p. 469.   See Kant, Kritik der reinen Vernunft,
p. 441—540, 7th ed.; Weisse, Die Idee der Gottheit, 1833.   Some have been
unwilling to attribute *being* to the Deity, since we have no conception nor knowledge of *being in itself*, still less of *infinite being*.   Our knowledge of *being* is
only of *being this and that*, a *conditioned being*, which is not predicable of God.

[2] This is not the place to attempt a proof of God's existence.   In Book I.
Ch. ii. I could only hint at the sources of argument.   See in Weisse, Kant, and
Strauss, a criticism on the various means of proof resorted to by different Philo-
sophers.   Weisse divides these proofs into three classes.   I. The *Ontological*
argument, which leads to Pantheism; II. The *Cosmological*, which leads to
Deism; and III. The *Theological*, which leads to pure Theism.   See Leibnitz,

But the Idea of God as a Being of Infinite Power, Wisdom, Love,—in one Word, the Absolute,—does not satisfy. It seems cold; we call it abstract. We are not beings of Reason alone; so are not satisfied with mere Ideas. We have Imagination, Feelings, limited Affections, Understanding, Flesh and Blood. Therefore we want a Conception of God which shall answer to this complex nature of ours. Man may be said to live in the World of Eternity, or abstract truth; that of Time, or historical events; that of Space, or of concrete things. Some men want, therefore, not only an Idea for the first, but a Conception for the second, and a Form for the third. Accordingly the feelings, Fear, Reverence, Devotion, Love, naturally personify God, humanize the deity, and represent the Infinite under the limitations of a finite and imperfect being, whom we " can know all about." He has the thoughts, feelings, passions, limitations of a man; is subject to time and space; sees, remembers, has a form. This is anthropomorphism. It is well in its place. Some rude men seem to require it. They must paint to themselves a deity with a form—the Ancient of days; a venerable monarch seated on a throne, surrounded by troops of followers. But it must be remembered all this is poetry; this personal and anthropomorphitic Conception is a phantom of the brain that has no existence independent of ourselves. A poet personifies a mountain or the moon; addresses it as if it wore the form of man, could see and feel, had human thoughts, sentiments, hopes, and pleasures, and expectations. What the poet's fancy does for the mountain, the feelings of reverence and devotion do for the Idea of God. They clothe it with a human personality, because that is the highest which is known to us. Men would comprehend the deity; they can only apprehend him. A Beaver, or a Reindeer, if possessed of religious faculties, would also conceive of the deity with the limitations of its own personality, as a Beaver or a Reindeer—whose faculties as such were perfect; but the Conception, like our own, must be only subjective, for even Man is no measure of God.[1]

Théodicée, Pt. I. § 7, p. 506, ed. Erdmann, 1840, and his Epist. ad Bierlingium, in his Epp. ad div. Ed. Kortholt, Vol. IV. p. 21 (cited by Strauss, ubi sup.).
[1] See Xenophanes as cited above by Eusebius, P. E. XIII. 13. See Karsten,

Now by reasoning we lay aside the disguises of the Deity, which the feelings have wrapped about the Idea of Him. We separate the substantial from the phenomenal elements in the Conception of God. We divest it of all particular form, all sensual or corporeal attributes, and have no image of God in the mind. He is Spirit,[1] and therefore free from the limitations of Space. He is no-where in particular, but everywhere in general, essentially and vitally omnipresent. Denying all particular form, we must affirm of him Universal Being.

The next step in the analysis is to lay aside all partial action of the Deity. He is equally the cause of the storm and the calm sunshine; of the fierceness of the Lion and the Lamb's gentleness, so long as both obey the laws they are made to keep. All the natural action in the material world is God's action, whether the wind blows a plank and the shipwrecked woman who grasps it to the shore, or scatters a fleet and sends families to the bottom. But Infinite Action or Causation must be attributed to Him.

Then all mental processes, like those of men, are separated from the Idea of Him. We cannot say he thinks, for that is to reason from the known to the unknown, which is impossible to the omniscient; nor that he plans or consults with himself, for that implies the infirmity of not seeing the best way all at once; nor that he remembers or foresees, for that implies a restriction in time, a past and a present, while the Infinite must fill Eternity, all time, as well as Immensity, all space. We cannot attribute to Him reflection, which is after-thought, nor imagination, which is fore-thought, since both imply limited faculties. Judgment, fancy, comparison, induction—these are the operations of finite minds. They are not to be applied to the divine Being except as figures of speech; then they merely represent an unknown emotion. We have got a name but no real thing. But Infinite Knowing must be his.

We go still further in this analysis of the conception of God, and all partial feeling must be denied. We cannot

---

ubi sup., Vol. I. p. 35, et seq. The passage from Seneca, De Superstitione, preserved by Augustine, Civ. Dei, Lib. VI. C. 10; Seneca, Opp. ed. Paris, 1829, IV. p. 39, et seq.

[1] I use the term Spirit simply as a *negation of the limitations of matter*. We cannot tell the *essence* of God.

say that he hates; is angry, or grieved; repents; is moved by the special prayer of James and John; that he is sad to-day and to-morrow joyful; all these are human, limitations of our personality, and are no more to be ascribed to God than the form of the Reindeer, or the shrewdness of the Beaver. But Love implies no finiteness. This we conceive as Infinite.

At the end of the Analysis, what is left? BEING, CAUSE, KNOWLEDGE, LOVE, each with no conceivable limitation. To express it in a word, a being of Infinite Power, Wisdom, Justice, Love, and Holiness, Fidelity to himself. Thus by an analysis of the conception of God, we find in fact, or by implication, just what was given synthetically by the intuition of Reason. But do these qualities exhaust the Deity? Surely not. They only form our Idea of Him. It is idle, impious in men to say, the finite creature of yesterday can measure Him who is the All in All, the True, the Holy, the Good, the Altogether-beautiful. Let a man look into the Milky-way, and strive to conceive of the Mind that is the Cause, the Will, of all those centres to unknown worlds, and ask, What can I know of Him? Nay, let a man turn over in his hand a single crystal of snow, and consider its elements, their history, transformation, influence, and try to grasp up the philosophy of this little atom of matter, and he will learn to bow before the thought of Him, and say there is no searching of his understanding. If there are other orders of beings higher than ourselves, their idea of God must include elements above our reach. The finite approximates, but cannot reach the Infinite.

In criticizing the conception of God, I would not attempt the fool's task, to define and describe God's nature, but to separate our Idea of Him from all other ideas; not to tell all in God that answers to the Idea in Man,— that of course is impossible,—but to separate the eternal Idea from the transient conception; to declare the positive and necessary existence of this Idea in Man, of its Object out of Man, while I deny the existence of any limitations of human personality, or of our anthropomorphitic consciousness in the Deity.

CHAPTER II.

THE RELATION OF NATURE TO GOD.

To determine the relation of Man to God it is well to determine first the relation of God to Nature—the material world—that we may have the force of the analogy of that relation to aid us. Conscious man may be very dissimilar to unconscious matter, but yet their relations to God are analogous. Both depend on him. To make out the point and decide the relation of God to Nature we must start from the Idea of God, which was laid down above, a Being of Infinite Power, Wisdom, Justice, Love, and Holiness. Now to make the matter clear as noonday, God is either present in all space, or not present in all space. If infinite, he must be present everywhere in general, and not limited to any particular spot, as an old writer so beautifully says : "Even Heaven and the Heaven of Heavens cannot contain Him." [1] Heathen writers are full of such expressions.[2] God, then, is universally present in the world of matter. He is the substantiality of matter. The circle of his being in space has an infinite radius. We cannot say, Lo here, or Lo there—for he is everywhere. He fills all Nature with his overflowing currents ; without him it were not. His Presence gives it existence ; his Will its law and force ; his Wisdom its order ; his Goodness its beauty.

It follows unavoidably, from the Idea of God, that he is present everywhere in space ; not transiently present, now and then, but immanently present, always ; his centre here ; his circumference nowhere ; just as present in the eye of an emmet as in the Jewish holy of holies, or the sun itself. We may call common what God has cleansed

---

[1] See, too, the beautiful statement in Ps. cxxxix. 1—13.
[2] See those in Cudworth, Ch. IV. § 28, and elsewhere.

with his presence; but there is no corner of space so small, no atom of matter so despised and little, but God, the Infinite, is there.[1]

Now, to push the inquiry nearer the point. The Nature or Substance of God, as represented by our Idea of him, is divisible or not divisible. If infinite he must be indivisible, a part of God cannot be in this point of space, and another in that; his Power in the sun, his Wisdom in the moon, and his Justice in the earth. He must be wholly, vitally, essentially present, as much in one point as in another point, or all points; as essentially present in each point at any one moment of time as at any other or all moments of time. He is there not idly present but actively, as much now as at creation. Divine omnipotence can neither slumber nor sleep. Was God but transiently active in Matter at creation, his action now passed away? From the Idea of him it follows that He is immanent in the world, however much he also transcends the world. "Our Father worketh hitherto," and for this reason Nature works, and so has done since its creation. There is no spot the foot of hoary Time has trod on, but it is instinct with God's activity. He is the ground of Nature; what is permanent in the passing; what is real in the apparent. All Nature then is but an exhibition of God to the senses; the veil of smoke on which his shadow falls; the dew-drop in which the heaven of his magnificence is poorly imaged. The Sun is but a sparkle of his splendour. Endless and without beginning flows forth the stream of divine influence that encircles and possesses the all of things. From God it comes, to God it goes. The material world is perpetual growth; a continual transfiguration, renewal that never ceases. Is this without God? Is it not because God, who is ever the same, flows into it without end? It is the fulness of God that flows into the crystal of the rock, the juices of the plant, the life of the emmet and the elephant. He penetrates and pervades the World. All things are full of Him, who surrounds the sun, the stars, the universe itself; "goes through all lands, the expanse of oceans, and the profound Heaven."[2]

[1] See the judicious remarks of Lord Brougham, Dialogue on Instinct, Dial. II., near the end. Dr Palfrey, in his Dudleian Lecture, attributes only a qualified omnipresence to the Deity.

[2] Virgil, Georgic IV. 222. See many passages cited by Cudworth, Chap. IV. § 31, p. 664, et seq., 455, et seq.; and the passages collected from Tschaleddin

Inanimate matter, by itself, is dependent; incapable of life, motion, or even existence. To assert the opposite is to make it a God. In its present state it has no will. Yet there is in it existence, motion, life. The smallest molecule in a ray of polarized light and the largest planet in the system exist and move as if possessed of a Will, powerful, regular, irresistible. The powers of Nature, then, that of Gravitation, Electricity, Growth, what are they but modes of God's action? If we look deep into the heart of this mystery, such must be the conclusion. Nature is moved by the first Mover; beautified by him who is the Sum of Beauty; animated by him who is of all the Creator, Defence, and Life.[1]

Such, then, is the relation of God to Matter up to this point. He is immanent therein and perpetually active. Now, to go further, if this be true, it would seem that the various objects and things in Nature were fitted to express and reveal different degrees and measures of the divine influence, so to say; that this degree of manifestation in each depends on the capacity which God has primarily bestowed upon it;[2] that the material but inorganic, the vegetable but inanimate, and the animal but irrational world, received each as high a mode of divine influence as its several nature would allow.

Then, to sum up all in brief, the Material World with its objects sublimely great, or meanly little, as we judge them; its atoms of dust, its orbs of fire; the rock that stands by the sea-shore, the water that wears it away; the worm, a birth of yesterday, which we trample underfoot; the streets of constellations that gleam perennial overhead; the aspiring palm tree, fixed to one spot, and

Rumi by Rückert, in his Gedichte, and Tholuck, Bluthensammlung aus der morgenlandischen Mystik.

[1] Cudworth makes three hypotheses; either, 1. *All things happen* in nature by *the fortuitous concourse of atoms*, and this it is Atheism to suppose; or, 2. There is in Nature a *formative faculty*, " *a plastic nature*," which does the work; or, 3. Each act is done *immediately* by God. He, it is well known, adopts the second alternative. See Chap. III. § 37. See also More's Enchiridion Metaphysicum, Antidote against Atheism, Book II. ; Apol. pro Cartesio, p. 115, et seq. On the *Transcendency* of God, see Descartes, Princip. P. I. No. 21, et al. Leibnitz. Théod, No. 385, et al.

[2] I will not say there is not, in the abstract, as much of divine influence in a *wheat-straw* as in a *world*. But in reference to ourselves there *appear* to be *various degrees* of it

the lions that are sent out free, these incarnate and make visible all of God their several natures will admit. If Man were not spiritual, and could yet conceive of the aggregate of invisible things, he might call it God, for he could go no further.

Now, as God is Infinite, imperfection is not to be spoken of Him. His Will therefore—if we may so use that term —is always the same. As Nature has of itself no power, and God is present and active therein, it must obey and represent his unalterable will. Hence, seeing the uniformity of operation, that things preserve their identity, we say they are governed by a Law that never changes. It is so. But this Law—what is it but the Will of God ? a mode of divine action ? It is this in the last analysis. The apparent secondary causes do not prevent this conclusion.

The things of Nature, having no will, obey this law from necessity.[1] They thus reflect God's image and make real his conception—if we may use such language with this application. They are tools, not Artists. We never in Nature see the smallest departure from Nature's law. The granite, the grass, keep their law ; none go astray from the flock of stars ; fire does not refuse to burn, nor water to be wet. We look backwards and forwards, but the same law records everywhere the obedience that is paid it. Our confidence in the uniformity of Nature's law is complete, in other words, in the fact that God is always the same ; his modes of action always the same. This is true of the inorganic, the vegetable, the animal world.[2] Each thing keeps its law with no attempt at violation of it.[3] From this obedience comes the regularity and

---

[1] I use the term *obedience* figuratively. Of course there is no *real* obedience without *power to disobey*.

[2] M. Leroux, an acute and brilliant but fanciful writer, thinks the capabilities of man change by civilization, and, which is to the present point, that the *animals* advance also ; that the Bee and the Beaver are on the march towards perfection, and have made some progress already. However he may make out the case *metaphysically*, it would be puzzling to settle the matter by facts. But if his hypothesis were admissible, it would not militate with the doctrine in the text.

[3] From this view it does not follow that animals are *mere machines*, with no consciousness, only that they have not free-will. However, in some of the superior animals there is some small degree of freedom apparent. The Dog and the Elephant seem sometimes to exercise a mind, and to become in some

order apparent in Nature. Obeying the law of God, his omnipotence is on its side. To oppose a law of Nature, therefore, is to oppose the Deity. It is sure to redress itself.

But these created things have no consciousness, so far as we know, at least, nothing which is the same with our self-consciousness. They have no moral will; no power in general to do otherwise than as they do. Their action is not the result of forethought, reflection, judgment, voluntary obedience to an acknowledged law. No one supposes the Bison, the Rosebush, and the Moon, reflect in themselves; make up their mind and say, "Go to, now, let us bring up our young, or put forth our blossoms, or give light at nightfall, because it is right to do so, and God's law." Their obedience is unavoidable. They do what they cannot help doing.[1] Their obedience, therefore, is not their merit, but their necessity. It is power they passively yield to; not a duty they voluntarily and consciously perform. All the action, therefore, of the material, inorganic, vegetable, and animal world is mechanical, vital, or, at the utmost, instinctive; not self-conscious, the result of private will.[2] There is, therefore, no room for caprice in this department. The Crystal must form itself after a prescribed pattern; the Leaf presume a given shape; the Bee build her cell with six angles. The man-

measure emancipated from their instincts. On this curious question, see Descartes, Epist. P. I. Ep. 27, 67; Henry More, Epist. ad Cartesium.

[1] This point has been happily touched upon by Hooker, Eccles. Polity, Book I. Chap. iii. § 2. See his curious reflections in the following sections.

[2] I have not the presumption to attempt to draw a line between these three departments of Nature, nor to tell what is the *essence of mechanical, vital*, or *instinctive* action. I would only indicate a distinction that, to my mind, is very plain. But I cannot pretend to say where one ends and the other begins. Again, it may seem unphilosophical to deny consciousness, or even self-consciousness, to the superior animals; but if they possess a self-consciousness, it is something apparently so remote from ours, that it only leads to confusion if both are called by the same term. The functions of a plant we cannot explain by the laws of *mechanical* action; nor the function of an animal, a Dog, for example, by any qualities of body. On this subject, see Whewell, Hist. Inductive Sciences, Book IX. Chap. i.—iii. Cudworth, Chap. III. § 37. No. 17, et seq., has shown that there may be *sentient*, and not mere *mechanical*, life, without consciousness, and therefore without *free-will*. Is not this near the truth, that God alone is *absolutely* free, and man has a *relative* freedom, the degree of which may be constantly increased? Taking a *certain stand-point*, it is true, Freedom and Necessity are the same thing, and may be predicated or denied of Deity indifferently; thus, if God is perfect, all his action is perfect. He can do no otherwise than as he does. Perfection therefore is his *necessity*, but it is his *freedom* none the less. Here the difference is merely in words.

tle of Destiny is girt about these things. To study the laws of Nature, therefore, is to study the modes of God's action. Science becomes sacred, and passes into a sort of devotion. Well says the old sage, "Geometry is the praise of God." It reveals the perfections of the Divine Mind, for God manifests himself in every object of science, in the half-living Molecules of powdered wood; in the Comet with its orbit which imagination cannot surround; in the Cones and Cycloids of the Mathematician, that exist nowhere in the world of concrete things, but which the conscious mind carries thither.

Since all these objects represent, more or less, the divine mind, and are in perfect harmony with it, and so always at one with God, they express, it may be, all of deity which Matter in these three modes can contain, and thus exhibit all of God that can be made manifest to the eye, the ear, and the other senses of man. Since these things are so, Nature is not only strong and beautiful, but has likewise a religious aspect. This fact was noticed in the very earliest times; appears in the rudest worship, which is an adoration of God in Nature. It will move man's heart to the latest day, and exert an influence on souls that are deepest and most holy. Who that looks on the ocean, in its anger or its play; who that walks at twilight under a mountain's brow, listens to the sighing of the pines, touched by the indolent wind of summer, and hears the light tinkle of the brook, murmuring its quiet tune,—who is there but feels the deep Religion of the scene? In the heart of a city we are called away from God. The dust of man's foot and the sooty print of his fingers are on all we see. The very earth is unnatural, and the Heaven scarce seen. In a crowd of busy men which set through its streets, or flow together of a holiday; in the dust and jar, the bustle and strife of business, there is little to remind us of God. Men must build a cathedral for that. But everywhere in nature we are carried straightway back to Him. The fern, green and growing amid the frost, each little grass and lichen, is a silent memento. The first bird of spring, and the last rose of summer; the grandeur or the dulness of evening and morning; the rain, the dew, the sunshine; the stars that come out to watch over the farmer's rising corn; the birds

that nestle contentedly, brooding over their young, quietly
tending the little strugglers with their beak,—all these
have a religious significance to a thinking soul. Every
violet blooms of God, each lily is fragrant with the presence of deity. The awful scenes, of storm, and lightning
and thunder, seem but the sterner sounds of the great
concert, wherewith God speaks to man. Is this an accident? Ay, earth is full of such " accidents." When the
seer rests from religious thought, or when the world's
temptations make his soul tremble, and though the spirit
be willing the flesh is weak; when the perishable body
weighs down the mind, musing on many things; when he
wishes to draw near to God, he goes, not to the city—
there conscious men obstruct him with their works—but
to the meadow, spangled all over with flowers, and sung
to by every bird; to the mountain, " visited all night by
troops of stars;" to the ocean, the undying type of shifting
phenomena and unchanging law; to the forest, stretching
out motherly arms, with its mighty growth and awful
shade, and there, in the obedience these things pay, in their
order, strength, beauty, he is encountered front to front
with the awful presence of Almighty power. A voice cries
to him from the thicket, " God will provide." The bushes
burn with deity. Angels minister to him. There is no
mortal pang, but it is allayed by God's fair voice as it
whispers, in nature, still and small, it may be, but moving on the face of the deep, and bringing light out of
darkness.

> " Oh joy that in our embers
> Is something that doth live,
> That Nature yet remembers
> What was so fugitive."

Now to sum up the result. It seems from the very Idea
of God that he must be infinitely present in each point of
space. This immanence of God in Matter is the basis of
his influence; this is modified by the capacities of the
objects in Nature; all of its action is God's action; its
laws modes of that action. The imposition of a law, then,
which is perfect, and is also perfectly obeyed, though
blindly and without self-consciousness, seems to be the
measure of God's relation to Matter. Its action therefore is only mechanical, vital or instinctive, not voluntary

and self-conscious. From the nature of these things, it must be so.

CHAPTER III.

STATEMENT OF THE ANALOGY DRAWN FROM GOD'S RELATION TO NATURE.

Now if God be present in Matter, the analogy is that he is also present in Man. But to examine this point more closely, let us set out as before from the Idea of God. If he have not the limitations of matter, but is Infinite, as the Idea declares, then he pervades Spirit as well as Space; is in Man as well as out of him. If it follows from the Idea that he is immanent in the Material World—in a moss; it follows also that he must be immanent in the Spiritual world—in a man. If he is immanently active, and thus totally and essentially present, in each corner of Space, and each Atom of creation, then is he as universally present in all Spirit. If the reverse be true, then he is not omnipresent, therefore not Infinite, and of course not God. The Infinite God must fill each point of Spirit as of Space. Here then, in God's presence in the soul, is a basis laid for his direct influence on men; as his presence in Nature is the basis of his direct influence there.

As in Nature his influence was modified only by the capacities of material things, so here must it be modified only by the capabilities of spiritual things; there it assumed the forms of mechanical, vital, and instinctive action; here it must ascend to the form of voluntary and self-conscious action. This conclusion follows undeniably from the analogy of God's presence and activity in Matter. It follows as necessarily from the Idea of God, for as he is the materiality of Matter, so is he the spirituality of Spirit.

CHAPTER IV.

THE GENERAL RELATION OF SUPPLY TO WANT.

WE find in Nature that every want is naturally supplied. That is, there is something external to each created being to answer all the internal wants of that being. This conclusion could have been anticipated without experience, since it follows from the perfections of the Deity, that all his direct works must be perfect. Experience shows this is the rule in nature. We never find a race of animals destitute of what is most needed for them, wandering up and down, seeking rest and finding none. What is most certainly needed for each, is most bountifully provided. The supply answers the demand. The natural circumstances, therefore, attending a race of animals, for example, are perfect. The animal keeps perfectly the law or condition of its nature. The result of these perfect circumstances on the one hand, and perfect obedience on the other, is this,—each animal in its natural state attains its legitimate end, reaches perfection after its kind. Thus every Sparrow in a flock is perfect in the qualities of a Sparrow, at least, such is the general rule ; the exceptions to it are so rare they only seem to confirm that rule.

Now to apply this general maxim to the special case of Man. We are mixed beings, spirits wedded to bodies. Setting aside the religious nature of Man for the moment, and for the present purpose distributing our faculties into the animal, intellectual, affectional, and moral, let us see the relation between our four-fold wants and the supply thereof. We have certain animal wants, such as the desire of food, shelter, and comfort. Our animal welfare, even our animal existence, depends on the relation of the world to these wants, on the condition that they are supplied. Now we find in the world of Nature, exterior to ourselves, a supply for these demands. It is so placed that man can reach it for himself. To speak in general terms, there is not a natural want in our body which has not its corresponding supply, placed out of the body. There is not even a disease of the body, brought upon us by disobedience of its law, but there is somewhere a remedy, at least an alleviation of that disease. The peculiar supply of peculiar wants is provided most abundantly when most needed, and where most needed; furs in the North, spices in the South, antidotes where the poison is found. God is a bountiful parent and no step-father to the body, and does not pay off, to his obedient children, a penny of satisfaction for a pound of want. Natural supply balances natural want the world over.

But this is not all. How shall man find the supply that is provided? It will be useless unless there is some faculty to mediate between it and the want. Now Man is furnished with a faculty to perform his office. It is *instinct* which we have in common with the lower animals, and *understanding* which we have more exclusively, at least no other animal possessing it in the same degree with ourselves. Instinct anticipates experience. It acts spontaneously where we have no previous knowledge, yet as if we were fully possessed of ideas. It shows itself as soon as we are born, in the impulse that prompts the infant to his natural food. It appears complete in all animals. It looks only forward, and is a perfect guide so far as it goes. The young chick pecks adroitly at the tiny worm it meets the first hour it leaves the shell.[1] It needs no instruction. The lower animals have nothing but instinct for their guide. It is sufficient for their purpose. They act, therefore, without reflection, from necessity, and are subordinate to their instinct, and therefore must always remain in the instinctive state.[2] Children and savages—who are in some respects the children of the human race—act chiefly by instinct, but constantly approach the development of the understanding.

[1] See Lord Brougham, Dialogues on Instinct, for some remarkable facts.
[2] Whewell, ubi sup., Vol. II. Pt. i. Book ix. Ch. iii. Man may subdue the instinct of an animal, and apparently improve the creature, by superinducing his own understanding upon it. The pliant nature of dogs and horses enables them to yield to him in this case. But they are not *really* improved in the qualities of a dog or a horse, but only become caricatures of their master's caprice.

This acts in a different way. It generalizes from experience; makes an induction from facts; a deduction from principles. It looks both backwards and forwards. The man of understanding acts from experience, reflection, forethought, and habit. If he had no other impelling principle, all his action must be of this character. But though understanding be capable of indefinite increase, instinct can never be wholly extirpated from this compound being, man. The most artificial or cultivated feels the twinges of instinctive nature. The lower animals rely entirely on instinct; the savage chiefly thereon, while the civilized and matured man depends mostly on understanding for his guide. As the sphere of action enlarges which takes place as the boy outgrows his childhood, and the savage emerges from barbarism, instinct ceases to be an adequate guide, and the understanding spontaneously developes itself to take its place.[1]

In respect, then, to Man's animal nature, this fact remains, that there is an external supply for each internal want, and a guide to conduct from the want to the supply. This guide is adequate to the purpose. When it is followed, and thus the conditions of our animal nature complied with, the want is satisfied, becomes a source of pleasure, a means of development. In this case there is nothing miraculous intervening between the desire and its gratification. Man is hungry. Instinct leads him to the ripened fruit. He eats and is appeased. The satisfaction of the want comes naturally, by a regular law, which God has imposed upon the constitution of Man. He is blessed by obeying, and cursed by violating this law. God himself does not transcend this law, but acts through it, by it, in it. We observe the law and obtain what we need. Thus for every point of natural desire in the body, there is a point of natural satisfaction out of the body. This guide conducts, from one to the other, as a radius connects the centre with the circumference. Our animal welfare is complete when the two are thus brought into contact.

Now the same rule may be shown to hold good in each

---

[1] See some profound remarks on the force of the instinctive life among savages, Bancroft, ubi sup., Ch. XXII.

other department into which we have divided the human faculties. There is something without us to correspond to each want of the Intellect. This is found in the objects of Nature ; in the sublime, the useful, the beautiful, the common things we meet ; in the ideas and conceptions that arise unavoidably when man, the thinking subject, comes intellectually in contact with external things, the object of thought. We turn to these things instinctively, at first,

> " The eye,—it cannot choose but see,
> We cannot bid the ear be still ;
> Our bodies feel, where'er they be,
> Against or with our will."

Man is not sufficient for himself intellectually, more than physically. He cannot rely wholly on what he is. There is at first nothing in Man but Man himself ; a being of multiform tendencies, and many powers lying latent—germ sheathed in germ. Without some external object to rouse the senses, excite curiosity, to stimulate the understanding, induce reflection, exercise reason, judgment, imagination,—all these faculties would sleep in their causes, unused and worthless in the soul. Obeying the instinctive tendency of the mind, which impels to thought, keeping its laws, we gain satisfaction for the intellectual desires. One after another the faculties come into action, grow up to maturity, and intellectual welfare is complete with no miracle, but by obedience to the laws of mind.

The same may be said of the affectional and moral nature of Man. There is something without us to answer the demands of the Affections and the Moral Sense, and we turn instinctively to them. Does God provide for the animal wants and no more ? He is no step-father, but a bountiful parent to the intellectual, affectional, and moral elements of his child. There is a point of satisfaction out of these for each point of desire in them, and a guide to mediate between the two. This general rule may then be laid down, That for each animal, intellectual, affectional, moral want of Man, there is a supply set within his reach, and a guide to connect the two ; that no miracle is needed to supply the want ; but satisfaction is given soon as the guide is followed and the law kept, which instinct or the understanding reveals.

CHAPTER V.

STATEMENT OF THE ANALOGY FROM THIS RELATION.

Now it was said before, that the religious was the deepest, highest, strongest element in Man, and since the wants of the lower faculties are so abundantly provided with natural means of satisfying them, the Analogy leads us irresistibly to conclude, that the higher faculty would not be neglected; that here as elsewhere there must be a natural and not miraculous supply for natural wants, a natural guide to conduct from one to the other, and natural laws, or conditions, to be observed, and natural satisfaction to be obtained in this way; that as God was no step-father, but a bountiful parent to the lower elements, so he must be to the higher; that as there was a point of satisfaction out of the body, mind, and heart, for each desire in it, so there must be a point of satisfaction out of the soul, for each desire in the soul. Is it God's way to take care of oxen and leave men uncared for? In a system where every spot on an insect's wing is rounded as diligently, and as carefully finished off, as a world, are we to suppose the Soul of Man is left without natural protection? If there is a law, a permanent mode of divine action, whereby each atom of dust keeps its place and holds its own, surely we are not to dream the Soul of Man is left with no law for its religious life and satisfaction.

To draw the parallels still closer. By the religious consciousness we feel the want of some assured support to depend on, who has infinite Power to sustain us, infinite Wisdom to provide for us, infinite Goodness to cherish us; as we must know the will of Him on whom we depend, and thus determine what is religious truth and religious duty, in order that we may do that duty, receive that truth, obey that will, and thus obtain rest for the soul, and the highest spiritual welfare, by knowing and fulfilling its conditions, so Analogy teaches that in this, as in the other case, there must be a supply for the wants, and some plain, regular, and not miraculous means, accessible to each man, whereby he can get a knowledge of this Support, discover this Will, and thus, by observing the proper conditions, obtain the highest spiritual welfare.

This argument for a direct connection between Man and God, is only rebutted in one of these two ways: Either, first, by denying that Man has any religious wants; or, secondly, by affirming that he is himself alone a supply to them, without need of reliance on anything independent of himself. The last is contrary to philosophy, for, theoretically speaking, by nature there is nothing in Man, but Man himself, his tendencies and powers of action and reception; in the religious element there is nothing but the religious element, as, theoretically speaking, by nature, there is in the body nothing but the body; in hunger nothing but hunger. To make Man dependent on nothing but Man; the religious element on nothing but the religious element, and therefore sufficient for itself, is quite as absurd as to make the body dependent only on the body; the appetite of hunger on nothing but hunger, sufficient to satisfy itself. Besides, our consciousness, and above all our religious consciousness, is that of dependence. The soul feels its direct dependence on God, as much as the body sees its own direct dependence on matter.

If the one statement is contrary to philosophy, the other is contrary to fact. We feel religious wants; the history of Man is a perpetual expression of these wants; an effort for satisfaction. It cannot be denied that we need something that shall bear the same relation to the religious Element which food bears to the palate, light to the eye, sound to the ear, beauty to the imagination, truth to the understanding, friendship to the heart, and duty to conscience. How shall we pass from the want to its satisfaction? Now the force of the Analogy is this—it leads us to expect such a natural satisfaction for spiritual wants as we have for the humbler wants. The very wants themselves imply the satisfaction; soon as we begin to act, there awakes, by nature, a Sentiment of God. Reason gives us a distinct Idea of Him, and from this Idea also it follows that he must supply these wants.

The question then comes as to the fact : Is there, or is there not, a regular law, that is, a constant mode of operation, by which the religious wants are supplied, as by a regular law the body's wants are met ? Now, animated by the natural trust, or faith, which is the spontaneous action of the religious Element, we should say : Yes, it must be so. God takes care of the sparrow's body ; can he neglect Man's Soul ? Then, reasoning again from the general analogy of God's providence, as before shown, and still more from the Idea of God, as above laid down, we say again : It must be so. Man must, through the religious Element, have a connection with God, as by the senses with Matter. He is, relative to us, the object of the soul, as much as matter is the object of the senses. As God has an influence on passive and unconscious Matter, so he must have on active and conscious Man. As this action in the one case is only modified by the conditions of Matter, so will it be in the other only by the conditions of Man. As no obedient animal is doomed to wander up and down, seeking rest, but finding none ; so no obedient man can be left hopeless, forlorn, without a supply, without a guide.

Now it might be supposed that the spontaneous presentiment of this supply for our spiritual demands, this two-fold argument from the Idea of God and the Analogy of his action in general, would satisfy both the spontaneous and the reflective mind, convincing them of Man's general capability of a connection with God, of receiving truth in a regular and a natural way from him, by revelation, inspiration, suggestion, or by what other name we may call the joint action of the divine and human mind. Such indeed is the belief of nations in an early and simple state. It is attested by the literature, traditions, and monuments of all primitive people. They believed that God held converse with Men. He spoke in the voices of nature ; in signs and omens ; in dreams by night ; in deep, silent thoughts by day ; skill, strength, wisdom, goodness, were referred to Him. The highest function of men was

God's Gift. He made the laws of Minos, Moses, Numa, Rhadamanthus; he inspires the Poet, Artist, Patriot; works with the righteous everywhere. Had Fetichism no meaning? Was Polytheism only a lie with no truth at the bottom? Prayers, sacrifices, fasts, priesthoods, show that men believed in intercourse with God. Good simple-hearted men and women, who live lives of piety, believe it now, and never dream it is a great philosophical truth, which lies in their mind. They wonder anybody should doubt it.

But yet among thinking men, who have thought just enough to distrust instinct, but not enough to see by the understanding the object which instinct discloses, especially it seems among thinking Englishmen and Americans, a general doubt prevails on this point.

The material world is before our eyes; its phenomena are obvious to the senses, and most men having active senses—which develope before the understanding—and the lower faculties of intellect also somewhat active, get pretty clear notions about these phenomena, though not of their cause and philosophy. But as the soul is rarely so active as the senses, as the whole spiritual nature is not often so well developed as the sensual, so spiritual phenomena are little noticed; very few men have clear notions about them. Hence to many men all spiritual and religious matters are vague. "Perhaps yes and perhaps no," is all they can say.

Then again the matter is made worse, for they hear extravagant claims made in relation to spiritual things and intercourse with God. One man says he was healed of a fever, or saved from drowning, not by the medicine, or the boatman, but by the direct interposition of God; another will have it that he has direct and miraculous illuminations, though it is plain he is still sitting in darkness. This bigot would destroy all human knowledge, that there may be clean paper to receive the divine word, miraculously written thereon; that fanatic bids men trust the doctrine which is reputed of miraculous origin and even at variance with human faculties. Both the bigot and the fanatic condemn Science as the "Pride of Reason," and talk boastingly of their special revelations, their new light, the signs and wonders they have seen or heard of to attest this revelation. The sincere man of good sense is disgusted by these things, and asks if there be no Pride of Folly as well as Reason, and no revelation of nonsense from the man's own brain, which is mistaken as an eternal truth coming winged from the Godhead? He rests, therefore, in his notions of mere material things; will see nothing which he cannot see through; believe nothing he cannot handle. These material notions have already become systematized; and so far as there is any philosophy commonly accredited amongst us, it is one which grows mainly out of this sensual way of looking at things; a philosophy which logically denies the possibility of inspiration, or intercourse with God, except through a miracle that shall transcend the faculties of Man.

Now on this subject of inspiration there are but three views possible. Each of these is supported by no one writer exclusively or perfectly, but by many taken in the aggregate. Let us examine each of them as it appears in recent times, with its philosophy and logical consequences. However, it is to be remembered that all conclusions which follow logically, are not to be charged on men who admit the premises.

CHAPTER VI.

THE RATIONALISTIC VIEW, OR NATURALISM.

THIS allows that the original powers of Nature, as shown in the inorganic, the vegetable, and the animal world, all came from God at the first; that he is a principle either material or spiritual, separate from the world, and independent thereof. He made the World, and all things, including Man, and stamped on them certain laws, which they are to keep.[1] He was but transiently present and

---

[1] There is another form of *Naturalism* which denies the existence of a God separate or separable from the universe. Since this system would annihilate

active in Nature at creation ; is not immanently present and active therein.   He has now nothing to do with the world but—to see it go. Here, then, is God on the one side ; on the other, Man and Nature.   But there is a great gulf fixed between them, over which there passes, neither God nor Man.

This theory teaches that Man, in addition to his organs of perception, has certain intellectual faculties by which he can reason from effect to cause ; can discover truth, which is the statement of a fact ; from a number of facts in science can discern a scientific law, the relation of thing to thing ; from a number of facts in morals, can learn the relation of man to man, deduce a moral law, which shall teach the most expedient and profitable way of managing affairs.   Its statement of both scientific and moral facts rests solely on experience, and never goes beyond the precedents.   Still further, it allows that men can find out there is a God, by reasoning experimentally from observations in the material world, and metaphysically also, from the connection of notions in the mind.   But this conclusion is only to be reached, in either case, by a process that is long, complicated, tortuous, and so difficult that but one man in some thousands has the necessary experimental knowledge, and but one in some millions the metaphysical subtlety, requisite to go through it, and become certain that there is a God.   Its notion of God is this—a Being who exists as the Power, Mind, and Will that caused the universe.[1]

The metaphysical philosophy of this system may be briefly stated.   In Man, by nature, there is nothing but man ; there is but one channel by which knowledge can come into man, that is sensation ; perception through the senses.   That is an assumption, nobody pretends it is proved.   This knowledge is modified by reflection—the mind's process of ruminating upon the knowledge which sensation affords.   At any given time, therefore, if we examine what is in Man, we find nothing which has not first been in the senses.   Now the senses converse only with finite phenomena.   Reflection—what can it get out of

all Religion, it may be called *irreligious Naturalism ;* with that I have now nothing to do.   Some have been called Rationalists, who deny that God is separate from the world.   See above, Book I.
    [1] Dr Dewey, writing in the Christian Examiner, says the proposition that there is a God " *is not a certainty.*"   See Examiner for Sept. 1845, p. 197, et seq.

these? The Absolute? The premise does not warrant the conclusion. Something "as good as Infinite?" Let us see. It makes a scientific law a mere generalization from observed facts which it can never go beyond. Its science, therefore, is in the rear of observation; we do not know thereby whether the next stone shall fall to the ground or from it. All it can say of the universality of any law of science, is this, "So far as we have seen, it is so." It cannot pass from the Particular to the Universal. It makes a moral law the result of external experience, merely an induction from moral facts; not the affirmation of Man's moral nature declaring the eternal rule of Right. It learns Morality by seeing what plan succeeds best in the long run. Its Morality, therefore, is Selfishness verified by experiment. A man in a new case, for which he can find no precedents, knows not what to do. He is never certain he is right till he gets the reward. Its moral law at present, like the statute law, is the slowly elaborated product of centuries of experience. It pretends to find out God, as a law in science, solely, by reasoning from effect to cause; from a plan to the designer. Then on what does a man's belief in God depend? On man's nature, acting spontaneously? No; for there is nothing in man but man, and nothing comes in but sensations, which do not directly give us God. It depends on reflection, argument, that process of reasoning mentioned before. Now admitting that sensation affords sufficient premise for the conclusion, there is a difficulty in the way. The man must either depend on his own reasoning, or that of another. In the one case he may be mistaken, in an argument so long, crooked, and difficult. It is at best an inference. The "Hypothesis of a God," as some impiously call it—may thus rest on no better argument than the hypothesis of Vortices, or Epicycles. In the other case, if we trust another man, he may be mistaken; still worse, may design to deceive the inquirer, as, we are told, the Heathen Sages did. Where, then, is the certain conviction of any God at all? This theory allows none. Its "proof of the existence of God" is a proof of the possibility of a God; perhaps of his probability; surely no more.

But the case is yet worse. In any argumentation there must be no more expressed in the conclusion than is logically and confessedly implied in the premises. When finite phenomena are the only premises, whence comes the Idea of Infinite God? It denies that Man has any Idea of the Absolute, Infinite, Perfect. Instead of this, it allows only an accumulative notion, formed from a series of conceptions of what is finite and imperfect. The little we can know of God came from reasoning about objects of sense. Its notion of God is deduced purely from empirical observation; what notion of a God can rest legitimately on that basis? Nature is finite. To infer an infinite Author is false logic. We see but in part, and have not grasped up this sum of things, nor seen how seeming evil consists with real good, nor accounted for the great amount of misery, apparently unliquidated, in the world; therefore Nature is imperfect to men's eyes. Why infer a perfect Author from an imperfect work? Injustice and cruelty are allowed in the world. How then can its Maker be relied on as just and merciful? Let there be nothing in the conclusion which is not in the premises.

This theory gives us only a finite and imperfect God, which is no God at all. He cannot be trusted out of sight; for its faith is only an inference from what is seen. Instead of a religious sentiment in man, which craves all the perfections of the Godhead, reaches out after the Infinite "first Good, first Perfect, and first Fair," it gives us only a tendency to reverence or fear what is superior to ourselves, and above our comprehension; a tendency which the Bat and the Owl have in common with Socrates and Fenelon. It makes a man the slave of his organization. Free-will is not possible. His highest aim is self-preservation; his greatest evil death. It denies the immortality of Man, and foolishly asks "proofs" of the fact—meaning proofs palpable to the senses. Its finite God is not to be trusted, except under his bond and covenant to give us what we ask for.

It makes no difference between Good and Evil; Expedient and Inexpedient are the better words. These are to be learned only by long study and much cunning. All men have not the requisite skill to find out moral and religious doctrines, and no means of proving either in their own heart; therefore they must take the word of their appointed teachers and philosophers, who "have investigated the matter;" found there is "an expedient way" for men to follow, and a "God" to punish them if they do not follow it. In moral and religious matters the mass of men must rely on the authority of their teachers. Millions of men, who never made an astronomical observation, believe the distance between the Earth and the Sun is what Newton or Laplace declares it to be. Why should not men take moral and religious doctrines on the same evidence? It is true, astronomers have differed a little—some making the Earth the centre, some the Sun—and divines still more. But men must learn the moral law as the statute law. The State is above each man's private notions about good and evil, and controls these, as well as their passions. Man must act always from mean and selfish views, never from Love of the Good, the Beautiful, the True.

This system would have religious forms and ceremonies to take up the mind of the people; moral precepts, and religious creeds, "published by authority," to keep men from unprofitable crimes; an established Church, like the Jail and the Gallows, a piece of state-machinery. It is logical in this, for it fears that, without such a provision, the sensual nature would overlay the intellectual; the few religious ideas common men could get, would be so shadowy and uncertain, and men be so blinded by Prejudice, Superstition, and Fancy, or so far misled by Passion and ignorant Selfishness, that nothing but want and anarchy would ensue. It tells men to pray. None can escape the conviction that prayer, vocal or silent, put up as a request, or felt as a sense of supplication, is natural as hunger and thirst, or tears and smiles. Even a self-styled Atheist [1] talks of the important physiological functions of prayer. This theory makes prayer a Soliloquy of the man; a thinking with the upper part of the head; a sort of moral gymnastics. Thereby we get nothing from God. He is the other side of the world. "He is a journeying, or pursuing, or peradventure he sleepeth." Prayer is useful to the worshipper as the poet's frenzy, when he apostrophizes a Mountain, or the Moon, and works himself into a rapture, but gets nothing from the Mountain or the Moon, except what he carried out.

In a word, this theory reduces the Idea of God to that of

[1] M. Comte.

an abstract Cause, and excludes this cause both from Man and the World. It has only a finite God, which is no God at all, for the two terms cancel each other. It has only a selfish Morality, which is no Morality at all, for the same reason. It reduces the Soul to the aggregate functions of the flesh; Providence to a law of matter; Infinity to a dream; Religion to priestcraft; Prayer to an apostrophe; Morality to making a good bargain; Conscience to cunning. It denies the possibility of any connection between God and Man. Revelation and Inspiration it regards as figures of speech, by which we refer to an agency purely ideal what was the result of the Senses and Matter acting thereon. Men calling themselves inspired, speaking in the name of God, were deceivers, or deceived. Prophets, the religious Geniuses of the world, mistook their fancies for revelation; embraced a cloud instead of a Goddess, and produced only misshapen dreams. Judged by this system, Jesus of Nazareth was a pure-minded fanatic, who knew no more about God than Peter Bayle and Pomponatius, but yet did the world service, by teaching the result of his own or others' experience, as revelations from God accompanied with the promise of another life, which is reckoned a pleasant delusion, useful to keep men out of crime, a clever auxiliary of the powers that be.

This System has perhaps never been held in all its parts by any one man,[1] but each portion has often been defended, and all its parts go together and come unavoidably from that notion, that there is nothing in man which was not first in the senses.[2] The best representatives of this school were, it may be, the French Materialists of the last century, and some of the English Deists. The latter term is applied to men of the most various character and ways of thinking. Some of them were most excellent men in all respects; men who did mankind great service by exposing the fanaticism of the Superstitious, and by showing the absurdities

[1] It is instructive to see the influence of this form of philosophy in the various departments of inquiry, as shown in the writings of Bacon, Hobbes, Locke, Collins, Mandeville, Hartley, Hume, Priestley, Paley, Horne-Tooke, Condillac, Helvetius, Darwin, Bentham, &c. But this philosophy could never fully satisfy the English mind. So there were such men as Cudworth, More, Cumberland, Edwards, Wollaston, Clarke, Butler, Berkely, Harris, Price, and more recently, Reid, Stewart, Brown, Coleridge, and Carlyle, not to mention the *more mystical* men like Fox and Penn, with their followers.

[2] See the judicious observations of Shaftesbury, eighth Letter to a Student.

embraced by many of the Christians. Some of them were much more religious and heavenly-minded than their opponents, and had a theology much more Christian, which called Goodness by its proper name, and worshipped God in lowliness of heart, and a divine life. But the spirit of this system takes different forms in different men. It appears in the cold morality and repulsive forms of Religion of Dr Priestley, who was yet one of the best of men; in the scepticism of Hume and his followers, which has been a useful medicine to the Church; in the selfish system of Paley, far more dangerous than the doubts of Hume or the scoffs of Gibbon and Voltaire; in the coarse, vulgar materialism of Hobbes, who may be taken as one of the best representatives of the system.

It is obvious enough, that this system of Naturalism is the Philosophy which lies at the foundation of the popular theology in New England; that it is very little understood by the men, out of pulpits and in pulpits, who adhere to it; who, while they hold fast to the theory of the worst of the English Deists—though of only the worst; while they deny the immanence of God in Matter and Man, and therefore take away the possibility of natural inspiration, and cling to that system of philosophy which justifies the Doubt of Hume, the Selfishness of Paley, the coarse Materialism of Hobbes,—are yet ashamed of their descent, and seek to point out others of a quite different spiritual complexion, as the lineal descendants of that ancient stock.

This system has one negative merit. It can, as such, never lead to fanaticism. Those sects or individuals, who approach most nearly to pure Naturalism, have never been accused, in religious matters, of going too fast or too far. But it has a positive excellence. It lays great stress on the human mind, and cultivates the understanding to the last degree. However, its Philosophy, its Theology, its Worship, are of the senses, and the senses alone.[1]

[1] I have not thought it necessary to refer particularly to the authors representing this system. I have rather taken pains to express their doctrine in my own words, lest individuals should be thought responsible for the sins of the system. One may read many works of divinity, and see that this philosophy lay unconsciously in the writer's mind. I do not mean to insinuate that many persons fully and knowingly believe this doctrine, but that they are yet governed by it, under the modification treated of in the next chapter. Locke has sometimes been charged with follies of this character, but unjustly, as it seems to me, for though the fundamental principles of his philosophy, and many pas-

CHAPTER VII.

THE ANTI-RATIONALISTIC VIEW, OR SUPERNATURALISM.

THIS system differs in many respects from the other; but its philosophy is at bottom the same. It denies that by natural action there can be anything in Man which was not first in the senses; whatever transcends the senses can come to him only by a Miracle. And the Miracle is attended with phenomena obvious to the senses. To develope the natural side of the theory it sets God on the one side and man on the other. However it admits the immanence of God in Matter, and talks very little about the laws of Matter, which it thinks require revision, amendment, and even repeal, as if the nature of things changed, or God grew wiser by experiment. It does not see that if God is always the same, and immanent in Nature, the laws of Nature can neither change nor be changed.[1] It limits the power of Man still further than the former theory. It denies that he can, of himself, discover the existence of God; or find out that it is better to love his brother than to hate him, to subject the Passions to Reason, Desire to Duty, rather than to subject Reason to Passion, Duty to Desire.[2] Man can find out all that is

sages in his works, do certainly look that way, others are of a quite spiritual tendency. See King's Life of Locke, Vol. 1. p. 366, et seq., and his theological writings, passim.

[1] Leibnitz, in a letter to the Princess of Wales, Opp. phil. ed. Erdmann, Berlin, 1840, p. 746-7, amuses himself with ridiculing this view, which he ascribes to Newton and his followers; "according to them," says he, "God must wind up his watch from time to time or it would stop outright. He was not farsighted enough to make a perpetual motion."

[2] Some Supernaturalists admit that Man by nature can find out the most important religious truths, in the way set down before, and some admit a moral sense in man. Others deny both. A recent writer denies that he can find by the light of Nature ANY THEOLOGICAL TRUTH. Natural theology is not possible. See Irons, On the whole Doctrine of Final Causes, Lond. 1836. p. 34, 129, and passim. His introductory chapter on modern Deism is very curious.

needed for his animal and intellectual welfare, with no miracle ; but can learn nothing that is needed for his moral and religious welfare. He can invent the steam engine, and calculate the orbit of Halley's comet ; but cannot tell Good from Evil, nor determine that there is a God. The Unnecessary is given him ; the Indispensable he cannot get by nature. Man, therefore, is the veriest wretch in creation. His mind forces him to inquire on religious matters, but brings him into doubt, and leaves him in the very slough of Despond. He goes up and down sorrowing, seeking rest, but finding none. Nay ; it goes further still, and declares that, by nature, all men's actions are sin, hateful to God.

On the other hand, it teaches that God works a miracle from time to time, and makes to men a positive revelation of moral and religious truth, which they could not otherwise gain. Its history of revelations is this : God revealed his own existence in a visible form to the first man ; taught him religious and moral duties by words orally spoken. The first man communicated this knowledge to his descendants, from whom the tradition of the fact has spread over all the world. Men know there is a God, and a distinction between right and wrong, only by hearsay, as they know there was a Flood in the time of Noah, or Deucalion. The first man sinned, and fell from the state of frequent communion with God. Revelations have since become rare ; exceptions in the history of men. However, as Man having no connection with the Infinite must soon perish, God continued to make miraculous revelations to one single people. To them he gave laws, religious and civil ; made predictions, and accompanied each revelation by some miraculous sign, for without it none could distinguish the truth from a lie. Other nations received reflections of this light, which was directly imparted to the favoured people. At length he made a revelation of all religious and moral truth, by means of his Son, a divine and miraculous being, both God and Man, and confirmed the tidings by miracles the most surprising. As this re-

He has some excellent remarks, for there are two kingdoms of philosophy in him, but wishes to advance what he calls revealed religion, at the expense of the foundation of all Religion. The Ottoman King never thinks himself secure on the throne till he has slain all his brothers.

velation is to last for ever, it has been recorded miraculously, and preserved for all coming time. The persons who received direct communication miraculously from God, are of course mediators between Him and the human race.

Now to live as religious men, we must have a knowledge of religious truth; for this we must depend alone on these mediators. Without them we have no access to God. They have established a new relation between Man and God. But they are mortal, and have deceased. However, their sayings are recorded by miraculous aid. A knowledge of God's will, of Morality and Religion, therefore, is only to be got at, by studying the documents which contain a record of their words and works, for the Word of God has become the letter of Scripture. We can know nothing of God, Religion, or Morals at first hand. God was but transiently present in a small number of the race, and has now left it altogether.

This theory forgets that a verbal revelation can never communicate a simple idea, like that of God, Justice, Love, Religion, more than a word can give a deaf man an idea of sound. It makes inspiration a very rare miracle, confined to one nation, and to some scores of men in that nation, who stand between us and God. We cannot pray in our own name, but in that of the mediator, who hears the prayer, and makes intercession for us. It exalts certain miraculous persons, but degrades Man. In prophets and saints, in Moses and Jesus, it does not see the possibility of the race made real, but only the miraculous work of God. Our duty is not to inquire into the truth of their word. Reason is no judge of that. We must put faith in all which all of them tell us, though they contradict each other never so often. Thus it makes an antithesis between Faith and Knowledge, Reason and Revelation. It denies that common men, in the nineteenth century, can get at Truth, and God, as Paul and John in the first century. It sacrifices Reason, Conscience, and Love to the words of the miraculous men, and thus makes its mediator a tyrant, who rules over the soul by external authority, restricting Reason, Conscience, and Love; not a brother, who acts in the soul, by waking its dormant powers, disclosing truth, and leading others by a divine life to God, the Source of Light. It says the words of Jesus are true because he

spoke them; not that he spoke them because true.   It
relies entirely on past times; does not give us the Absolute Religion, as it exists in Man's nature, and the Ideas
of the Almighty, only a historical mode of worship, as
lived out here or there.   It says the canon of Revelation
is closed; God will no longer act on men as heretofore.
We have come at the end of the feast; are born in the
latter days and dotage of mankind, and can only get light
by raking amid the ashes of the past, and blowing its
brands, now almost extinct.   It denies that God is present
and active in all spirit as in all space—thus it denies that
he is Infinite.   In the miraculous documents it gives us
an objective standard, "the only infallible rule of religious
faith and practice."   These mediators are greater than the
soul; the Bible the master of Reason, Conscience, and the
Religious Sentiment.   They stand in the place of God.
    Men ask of this system: How do you know there is in
Man nothing but the product of sensation, or miraculous
tradition; that he cannot approach God except by miracle;
that these mediators received truth miraculously; taught
all truth; nothing but the truth; that you have their
words pure and unmixed in your Scriptures; that God
has no further revelation to make?   The answer is:—We
find it convenient to assume all this, and accordingly have
banished Reason from the premises, for she asked troublesome questions.   We condescend to no proof of the facts.
You must take our word for that.   Thus the main doctrines of the theory rest on assumptions; on no-facts.
    This system represents the despair of Man groping after
God.   The religious Element acts, but is crippled by a
philosophy poor and sensual.   Is Man nothing but a combination of five senses, and a thinking machine to grind
up and bolter sensations, and learn of God only by hearsay?   The God of Supernaturalism is a God afar off; its
Religion worn-out and second-hand.   We cannot meet
God face to face.   In one respect it is worse than naturalism; that sets great value on the faculties of Man, which
this depreciates and profanes.   But all systems rest on a
truth, or they could not be; this on a great truth, or it
could not prevail widely.   It admits a qualified immanence
of God in Nature, and declares, also, that mankind is dependent on Him, for religious and moral truth as for all

things else; has a connection with God, who really guides, educates, and blesses the race, for he is transiently present therein. The doctrine of miraculous events, births, persons, deaths, and the like, this is the veil of Poetry drawn over the face of Fact. It has a truth not admitted by Naturalism. As only a few "*thinking*" men even in fancy can be satisfied without a connection with God, so Naturalism is always confined to a few reflective and cultivated persons; while the mass of men believe in the supernatural theory, at least, in the truth it covers up. Its truth is of great moment. Its vice is to make God transiently active in Man, not immanent in him; restrict the divine presence and action to times, places, and persons. It overlooks the fact that if religious truth be necessary for all, then it must either have been provided for and put in the reach of all, or else there is a fault in the divine plan. Then again, if God gives a natural supply for the lower wants, it is probable, to say the least, he will not neglect the higher. Now for the religious consciousness of Man, a knowledge of two great truths is indispensable: namely, a knowledge of the existence of the Infinite God, and of the duty we owe to Him, for a knowledge of these two is implied in all religious teaching and life. Now one of two things must be admitted, and a third is not possible: either Man can discover these two things by the light of Nature, or he cannot. If the latter be the case, then is he the most hopeless of all beings. Revelation of these truths is confined to a few; it is indispensably necessary to all. Accordingly the first hypothesis is generally admitted by the supernaturalists, in New England—though in spite of their philosophy—that these two things can be discovered by the light of Nature. Then if the two main points, the premises which involve the whole of Morals and Religion, lie within the reach of Man's natural powers, how is a miracle, or the tradition of a miracle, necessary to reveal the minor doctrines involved in the universal truth? Does not the faculty to discern the greater include the faculty to discern the less? What covers an acre will cover a yard. Where then is the use of the miraculous interposition?

Neither Naturalism nor Supernaturalism legitimates the fact of Man's religious consciousness. Both fail of satisfy-

ing the natural religious wants of the race.   Each has
merits and vices of its own.   Neither gives for the Soul's
wants a supply analogous to that so bountifully provided
for the wants of the Body, or the Mind.

CHAPTER VIII.

THE NATURAL-RELIGIOUS VIEW, OR SPIRITUALISM.

THIS theory teaches that there is a natural supply for
spiritual as well as for corporeal wants ; that there is a
connection between God and the Soul, as between light
and the eye, sound and the ear, food and the palate, truth
and the intellect, beauty and the imagination ; that as we
follow an instinctive tendency, obey the body's law, get a
natural supply for its wants, attain health and strength, the
body's welfare ; as we keep the law of the mind, and get a
supply for its wants, attain wisdom and skill, the mind's
welfare,—so if, following another instinctive tendency, we
keep the law of the moral and religious faculties, we get a
supply for their wants, moral and religious truth, obtain
peace of conscience and rest for the soul, the highest moral
and religious welfare.   It teaches that the World is not
nearer to our bodies than God to the soul; "for in him we
live and move, and have our being."   As we have bodily
senses to lay hold on Matter and supply bodily wants,
through which we obtain, naturally, all needed material
things ; so we have spiritual faculties to lay hold on God,
and supply spiritual wants ; through them we obtain all
needed spiritual things.   As we observe the conditions of
the Body, we have Nature on our side ; as we observe the
Law of the Soul, we have God on our side.   He imparts
truth to all men who observe these conditions ; we have
direct access to Him, through Reason, Conscience, and the
Religious Faculty, just as we have direct access to Nature,
through the eye, the ear, or the hand.   Through these

channels, and by means of a law, certain, regular, and universal as gravitation, God inspires men, makes revelation of truth, for is not truth as much a phenomenon of God, as motion of Matter? Therefore if God be omnipresent and omniactive, this inspiration is no miracle, but a regular mode of God's action on conscious Spirit, as gravitation on unconscious Matter. It is not a rare condescension of God, but a universal uplifting of Man. To obtain a knowledge of duty, a man is not sent away, outside of himself to ancient documents, for the only rule of faith and practice; the Word is very nigh him, even in his heart, and by this Word he is to try all documents whatever. Inspiration, like God's omnipresence, is not limited to the few writers claimed by the Jews, Christians, or Mahometans, but is coëxtensive with the race. As God fills all Space, so all Spirit; as he influences and constrains unconscious and necessitated Matter, so he inspires and helps free and conscious Man.

This theory does not make God limited, partial, or capricious. It exalts Man. While it honours the excellence of a religious genius, of a Moses or a Jesus, it does not pronounce their character monstrous, as the supernatural, nor fanatical, as the rationalistic theory; but natural, human, and beautiful, revealing the possibility of mankind. Prayer, whether voluntative or spontaneous, a word or a feeling, felt in gratitude or penitence, or joy, or resignation,—is not a soliloquy of the man, not a physiological function, nor an address to a deceased man; but a sally into the infinite spiritual world, whence we bring back light and truth. There are windows towards God, as towards the World. There is no intercessor, angel, mediator between Man and God; for Man can speak and God hear, each for himself. He requires no advocate to plead for men, who need not pray by attorney. Each man stands close to the omnipresent God; may feel his beautiful presence, and have familiar access to the All-Father; get truth at first hand from its Author. Wisdom, Righteousness, and Love, are the Spirit of God in the Soul of Man; wherever these are, and just in proportion to their power, there is inspiration from God. Thus God is not the author of confusion, but Concord; Faith, and Knowledge, and Revelation, and Reason tell the same tale, and so legitimate and confirm one another.[1]

God's action on Matter and on Man is perhaps the same thing to Him, though it appear differently modified to us. But it is plain from the nature of things, that there can be but one kind of Inspiration, as of Truth, Faith, or Love : it is the direct and intuitive perception of some truth, either of thought or of sentiment. There can be but one mode of Inspiration : it is the action of the Highest within the soul, the divine presence imparting light ; this presence as Truth, Justice, Holiness, Love, infusing itself into the soul, giving it new life ; the breathing in of the Deity ; the in-come of God to the Soul, in the form of Truth through the Reason, of Right through the Conscience, of Love and Faith through the Affections and Religious Element. Is Inspiration confined to theological matters alone ? Most surely not. Is Newton less inspired than Simon Peter ?[2]

Now if the above views be true, there seems no ground for supposing, without historical proof, there are different kinds or modes of inspiration in different persons, nations, or ages, in Minos or Moses, in Gentiles or Jews, in the first century or the last. If God be infinitely perfect, He

---

[1] See Jonathan Edwards' view of Inspiration, in his sermon on A divine Light imparted to the Soul, &c. Works, ed. Lond. 1840. Vol. II. p. 12, et seq., and Vol. I. p. cclxix. No. [20].

[2] So long as inspiration is regarded as purely miraculous, good sense will lessen instances of it, as far as possible ; for most thinking men feel more or less repugnance at believing in any violation, on God's part, of regular laws. As spiritual things are commonly less attended to than material, the belief in miraculous inspiration remains longer in religious than secular affairs. A man would be looked on as mad, who should claim miraculous inspiration for Newton, as they have been who denied it in the case of Moses. But no candid man will doubt that, humanly speaking, it was a more difficult thing to write the Principia than the Decalogue. Man must have a nature most sadly anomalous, if, unassisted, he is able to accomplish all the triumphs of modern science, and yet cannot discover the plainest and most important principles of Religion and Morality without a miraculous revelation ; and still more so, if being able to discover, by God's natural aid, these chief and most important principles, he needs a miraculous inspiration to disclose minor details. Science is by no means indispensable, as Religion and Morals. The doctrine of the immortality of the soul, if it is a real advantage, follows unavoidably from the Idea of God. The *Best* Being, he must *will* the best of good things ; the *Wisest*, he must devise plans for that effect ; the *most Powerful*, he must bring it about. None can deny this. Does one ask another " proof of the fact ? " *Is he so very full of faith who cannot trust God, except he have His bond in black and white, given under oath and attested by witnesses !*

does not change; then his modes of action are perfect and unchangeable. The laws of Mind, like those of Matter, remain immutable and not transcended. As God has left no age nor man destitute, by nature, of Reason, Conscience, Affection, Soul, so he leaves none destitute of inspiration. It is, therefore, the light of all our being; the background of all human faculties; the sole means by which we gain a knowledge of what is not seen and felt; the logical condition of all sensual knowledge; our highway to the world of Spirit. Man cannot, more than Matter, exist without God. Inspiration then, like vision, must be everywhere the same thing in kind; however it differs in degree, from race to race, from man to man. The degree of inspiration must depend on two things: first, on the natural ability, the particular intellectual, moral, and religious endowment, or genius, wherewith each man is furnished by God; and next, on the use each man makes of this endowment. In one word, it depends on the man's Quantity of Being, and his Quantity of Obedience. Now as men differ widely in their natural endowments, and much more widely in the use and development thereof, there must of course be various degrees of inspiration, from the lowest sinner up to the highest saint. All men are not by birth capable of the same degree of inspiration; and by culture, and acquired character, they are still less capable of it. A man of noble intellect, of deep, rich, benevolent affections, is by his endowments capable of more than one less gifted. He that perfectly keeps the soul's law, thus fulfilling the conditions of inspiration, has more than he who keeps it imperfectly; the former must receive all his soul can contain at that stage of his growth. Thus it depends on a man's own will, in great measure, to what extent he will be inspired. The man of humble gifts at first, by faithful obedience may attain a greater degree than one of larger outfit, who neglects his talent. The Apostles of the New Testament, and the true Saints of all countries, are proofs of this. Inspiration, then, is the consequence of a faithful use of our faculties. Each man is its subject; God its source; Truth its only test. But as truth appears in various modes to us, higher and lower, and may be superficially divided, according to our faculties, into truths of the

Senses, of the Understanding, of Reason, of Conscience, of the Affections, and the Soul, so the perception of truth in the highest mode, that of Reason, Morals, Philanthropy, Religion, is the highest inspiration.   He, then, that has the most of Wisdom, Goodness, Religion, the most of Truth, in the highest modes, is the most inspired.

Now universal infallible inspiration can of course only be the attendant and result of a perfect fulfilment of all the laws of mind, of the moral, affectional, and religious nature; and as each man's faculties are limited, it is not possible to men.   A foolish man, as such, cannot be inspired to reveal Wisdom; nor a wicked man to reveal Virtue; nor an impious man to reveal Religion.   Unto him that hath, more is given.   The poet reveals Poetry; the artist Art; the philosopher Science; the saint Religion.   The greater, purer, loftier, more complete the character, so is the inspiration; for he that is true to Conscience, faithful to Reason, obedient to Religion, has not only the strength of his own Virtue, Wisdom, and Piety, but the whole strength of Omnipotence on his side; for Goodness, Truth, and Love, as we conceive them, are not one thing in Man, and another in God, but the same thing in each.   Thus Man partakes the Divine Nature, as the Platonists, Christians, and Mystics call it.   By these means the Soul of All flows into the man; what is private, personal, peculiar, ebbs off before that mighty influx from on high.   What is universal, absolute, true, speaks out of his lips, in rude, homely utterance, it may be, or in words that burn and sparkle like the lightning's fiery flash.

This inspiration reveals itself in various forms, modified by the country, character, education, peculiarity of him who receives it, just as water takes the form and the colour of the cup into which it flows, and must needs mingle with the impurities it chances to meet.   Thus Minos and Moses were inspired to make laws; David to pour out his soul in pious strains, deep and sweet as an angel's psaltery; Pindar to celebrate virtuous deeds in high heroic song; John the Baptist to denounce sin; Gerson, and Luther, and Böhme, and Fenelon, and Fox, to do each his peculiar work, and stir the world's heart, deep, very deep.   Plato and Newton, Milton and Isaiah, Leibnitz and Paul, Mozart, Raphael, Phidias, Praxiteles, Orpheus, receive into their various forms, the one spirit from God most high. It appears in action not less than speech. The Spirit inspires Dorcas to make coats and garments for the poor, no less than Paul to preach the Gospel. As that bold man himself has said, " there are diversities of gifts, but the same spirit; diversities of operations, but the same God who worketh all in all."[1] In one man it may appear in the iron hardness of reasoning, which breaks through sophistry, and prejudice, the rubbish and diluvial drift of time. In another it is subdued and softened by the flame of affection; the hard iron of the man is melted and becomes a stream of persuasion, sparkling as it runs.

Inspiration does not destroy the man's freedom; that is left fetterless by obedience. It does not reduce all to one uniform standard, but Habakkuk speaks in his own way, and Hugh de St Victor in his. The man can obey or not obey; can quench the spirit, or feed it as he will. Thus Jonah flees from his duty; Calchas will not tell the truth till out of danger; Peter dissembles and lies. Each of these men had schemes of his own, which he would carry out, God willing or not willing. But when the sincere man receives the truth of God into his soul, knowing it is God's truth, then it takes such a hold of him as nothing else can do. It makes the weak strong; the timid brave; men of slow tongue become full of power and persuasion. There is a new soul in the man, which takes him as it were by the hair of his head, and sets him down where the idea he wishes for demands. It takes the man away from the hall of comfort, the society of his friends; makes him austere and lonely; cruel to himself, if need be; sleepless in his vigilance, unfaltering in his toil; never resting from his work. It takes the rose out of the cheek; turns the man in on himself, and gives him more of truth. Then, in a poetic fancy, the man sees visions; has wondrous revelations; every mountain thunders; God burns in every bush; flames out in the crimson cloud; speaks in the wind; descends with every dove; is All in All. The Soul, deep-wrought in its intense struggle, give outness to its thought, and on the trees and stars, the fields, the floods, the corn ripe for the sickle, on Men and Women it sees its burden writ. The Spirit within constrains the man. It is

[1] 1 Cor. xii. 8, et seq.

like wine that hath no vent. He is full of the God. While
he muses the fire burns; his bosom will scarce hold his
heart. He must speak or he dies, though the earth quake
at his word.[1] Timid flesh may resist, and Moses say, I
am of slow speech. What avails that? The Soul says,
Go, and I will be with thy mouth, to quicken thy tardy
tongue. Shrinking Jeremiah, effeminate and timid, recoils
before the fearful work —"The flesh will quiver when the
pincers tear." He says, I cannot speak. I am a child.
But the great Soul of All flows into him and says, Say
not "I am a child!" for I am with thee. Gird up thy
loins like a man, and speak all that I command thee. Be
not afraid at men's faces, for I will make thee a defenced
city, a column of steel, and walls of brass. Speak, then,
against the whole land of sinners; against the kings thereof, the princes thereof, its people, and its priests. They
may fight against thee, but they shall not prevail; for I
am with thee. Devils tempt the man, with the terror of
defeat and want, with the hopes of selfish ambition. It
avails nothing. A "Get-thee-behind-me, Satan," brings
angels to help. Then are the man's lips touched with a
live coal from the altar of Truth, brought by a Seraph's
hand. He is baptized with the Spirit of fire. His countenance is like lightning. The truth thunders from his
tongue—his words eloquent as Persuasion; no terror is
terrible; no fear formidable. The peaceful is satisfied to
be a man of strife and contention, his hand against every
man, to root up and pluck down and destroy, to build with
the sword in one hand and the trowel in the other. He
came to bring peace, but he must set a fire, and his soul is
straitened till his work be done. Elisha must leave his
oxen in the furrow; Amos desert his summer fruit and his
friend; and Böhme, and Bunyan, and Fox, and a thousand others, stout-hearted and God-inspired, must go forth
of their errand, into the faithless world, to accept the prophet's mission, be stoned, hated, scourged, slain. Resist-
ance is nothing to these men. Over them steel loses its
power, and public opprobrium its shame; deadly things
do not harm them; they count loss gain—shame glory—
death triumph. These are the men who move the world.
They have an eye to see its follies, a heart to weep and

[1] See Lucan IX. 564, et seq.

bleed for its sin. Filled with a Soul wide as yesterday, to-day, and for ever, they pray great prayers for sinful Man. The wild wail of a brother's heart runs through the saddening music of their speech. The destiny of these men is forecast in their birth. They are doomed to fall on evil times and evil tongues, come when they will come. The Priest and the Levite war with the Prophet and do him to death. They brand his name with infamy; cast his un-buried bones into the Gehenna of popular shame; John the Baptist must leave his head in a charger; Socrates die the death; Jesus be nailed to his cross; and Justin, John Huss, and Jerome of Prague, and millions of hearts stout as these and as full of God, must mix their last prayers, their admonition, and farewell blessing, with the crackling snap of faggots, the hiss of quivering flesh, the impotent tears of wife and child, and the mad roar of the exulting crowd. Every path where mortal feet now tread secure, has been beaten out of the hard flint by prophets and holy men, who went before us, with bare and bleeding feet, to smooth the way for our reluctant tread. It is the blood of prophets that softens the Alpine rock. Their bones are scattered in all the high places of mankind. But God lays his burdens on no vulgar men. He never leaves their souls a prey. He paints Elysium on their dungeon wall. In the populous chamber of their heart, the light of Faith shines bright and never dies. For such as are on the side of God there is no cause to fear.

The influence of God in Nature, in its mechanical, vital, or instinctive action, is beautiful. The shapely trees; the leaves that clothe them in loveliness; the corn and the cattle; the dew and the flowers; the bird, the insect, moss and stone, fire and water, and earth and air; the clear blue sky that folds the world in its soft embrace; the light which rides on swift pinions, enchanting all it touches, re-posing harmless on an infant's eyelid, after its long pas-sage from the other side of the universe,—all these are noble and beautiful; they admonish while they delight us, these silent counsellors and sovereign aids. But the in-spiration of God in man, when faithfully obeyed, is nobler and far more beautiful. It is not the passive elegance of unconscious things which we see resulting from Man's voluntary obedience. That might well charm us in Nature; in Man we look for more. Here the beauty is intellectual, the beauty of Thought, which comprehends the world and understands its laws; it is moral, the beauty of Virtue, which overcomes the world and lives by its own laws; it is religious and affectional, the beauty of Holiness and Love, which rises above the world and lives by the law of the Spirit of Life. A single good man, at one with God, makes the morning and evening sun seem little and very low. It is a higher mode of the divine Power that appears in him, self-conscious and self-restrained.

Now this it seems is the only kind of inspiration which is possible. It is coextensive with the faithful use of Man's natural powers. Men may call it miraculous, but nothing is more natural; or they may say, it is entirely human, for it is the result of Man's use of his faculties; but what is more divine than Wisdom, Justice, Benevolence, Piety? Are not these the points in which Man and God conjoin? If He is present and active in spirit—such must be the perfect result of the action. No doubt there is a mystery in it, as in sensation, in all the functions of Man. But what then? As a good man has said, "God worketh with us both to will and to do." Mind, Conscience, the affections, and the Soul mediate between us and God, as the senses between us and matter. Is one more surprising than the other? Is the one to be condemned as spiritual mysticism or Pantheism? Then so is the other as material mysticism or Pantheism. Alas, we know but in part; our knowledge is circumscribed by our ignorance.

Now it is the belief of all primitive nations that God inspires the wise, the good, the holy.[1] Yes, that he works with Man in every noble work. No doubt their poor conceptions of God degraded the doctrine and ascribed to the Deity what came from their disobedience of his law.

The wisest and holiest men have spoken in the name of

---

[1] On this doctrine see Sonntag, Doctrina Inspirationis, &c., 1803, § 1, et seq., and the authors he cites. De Wette, Dogmatik, § 85—96, and § 143—148, gives the Old Testament doctrine of Inspiration. See also Hase, Hutterus redivivus, § 41, Dogmatik, § 8; Bretschneider, Dogmatik, Vol. I. § 14, et seq.; and Baumgarten-Crusius, Dogmengeschichte, Vol. II. p. 775, et seq. Much useful matter has been collected by these writers, and by Münscher, Bauer, Von-Cölln, and Strauss, but a special history of the doctrine is still a desideratum.

God. Minos, Moses, Zoroaster, Confucius, Zaleucus, Numa, Mahomet, profess to have received their doctrine straightway from Him. The sacred persons of all nations, from the Druid to the Pope, refer back to his direct inspiration. From this source the Sibylline oracles, the responses at Delphi, the sacred books of all nations, the Vedas and the Bible, alike claim to proceed. Pagans tell us no man was ever great without a divine afflatus falling upon him.[1] Much falsity was mingled with the true doctrine, for that was imperfectly understood, and violence, and folly, and lies were thus ascribed to God. Still the popular belief shows that the human mind turns naturally in this direction. Each prophet, false or true, in Palestine, Nubia, India, Greece, spoke in the name of God. In this name the apostles of Christ and of Mahomet, the Catholic and the Protestant, went to their work.[2] A good man feels that Justice, Goodness, Truth, are immutable, not dependent on himself; that certain convictions come by a law over which he has no control. There they stand, he cannot alter though he may refuse to obey them. Some have considered themselves bare tools in the hand of God; they did and said they knew not what, thus charging their follies and sins on God most high. Others, going to a greater degree of insanity, have confounded God with themselves, declaring that they were God. But even if likeness were perfect, it is not identity. Yet a ray from the primal light falls on Man. No doubt there have been men of a high degree of inspiration, in all countries; the founders of the various religions of the world. But they have been limited in their gifts, and their use of them. The doctrine they taught had somewhat national, temporal,

---

[1] See the opinions of the ancients in the classic passages, Cicero de Nat. Deorum, II. 66; Orat. pro Arch. c. 8; Xenophon Memorab. I. 1; Seneca, Ep. XLI. See many passages collected in Sonntag. See also Barclay's Apology for the Quakers, Prop. I.—III. XI.; Sewell's History of the Quakers, B. IX.—XII., and p. 693; and George Fox's Journal, passim.

[2] The history of the formation of the ecclesiastical doctrine of inspiration, which is the Supernatural View, is curious. It did not assume its most exclusive shape in the early teachers. In John of Damascus it appears in its vigour. In Abelard and Peter Lombard, it is more mild and liberal. Since the Reformation, it has been violently attacked. Luther himself is fluctuating in his opinions. As men's eyes opened they would separate falsehood from truth. The writings of the English deists had a great influence in this matter. See Walch's Religions-Streitigkeiten, Vol. V. ch. vii. Strauss also, Vol. I. § 14, et seq., gives a brief and compendious account of attacks on this doctrine.

even personal, in it, and so was not the Absolute Religion. No man is so great as human Nature, nor can one finite being feed for ever all his brethren. So their doctrines were limited in extent and duration.

Now this inspiration is limited to no sect, age, or nation. It is wide as the world, and common as God. It is not given to a few men, in the infancy of mankind, to monopolize inspiration and bar God out of the soul. You and I are not born in the dotage and decay of the world. The stars are beautiful as in their prime; "the most ancient Heavens are fresh and strong;" the bird merry as ever at its clear heart. God is still everywhere in nature, at the line, the pole, in a mountain or a moss. Wherever a heart beats with love, where Faith and Reason utter their oracles, there also is God, as formerly in the heart of seers and prophets. Neither Gerizim nor Jerusalem, nor the soil that Jesus blessed, so holy as the good man's heart; nothing so full of God. This inspiration is not given to the learned alone, not to the great and wise, but to every faithful child of God. The world is close to the body; God closer to the soul, not only without but within, for the all-pervading current flows into each. The clear sky bends over each man, little or great; let him uncover his head, there is nothing between him and infinite space. So the ocean of God encircles all men; uncover the soul of its sensuality, selfishness, sin, there is nothing between it and God, who flows into the man, as light into the air. Certain as the open eye drinks in the light, do the pure in heart see God, and he that lives truly feels him as a presence not to be put by.[1]

But this is a doctrine of experience as much as of abstract reasoning. Every man who has ever prayed—prayed with the mind, prayed with the heart greatly and strong, knows the truth of this doctrine, welcomed by pious souls. There are hours, and they come to all men, when the hand of destiny seems heavy upon us; when the thought of time misspent; the pang of affection misplaced or ill-requited; the experience of man's worse nature and the sense of our own degradation, come over us. In the

---

[1] Such as like to settle questions by *authority*, will see that this is the doctrine of the more spiritual writers of the Old and New Testaments, especially of John and Paul. It seems to me this was the doctrine of Jesus himself.

outward and inward trials, we know not which way to
turn. The heart faints and is ready to perish. Then in
the deep silence of the soul, when the man turns inward
to God, light, comfort, peace dawn on him. His troubles
—they are but a dew-drop on his sandal. His enmities
or jealousies, hopes, fears, honours, disgraces, all the un-
deserved mishaps of life, are lost to the view; diminished,
and then hid in the mists of the valley he has left behind
and below him. Resolution comes over him with its
vigorous wing; Truth is clear as noon; the soul in faith
rushes to its God. The mystery is at an end.

It is no vulgar superstition to say men are inspired in
such times. They are the seed-time of life. Then we live
whole years through in a few moments, and afterwards, as
we journey on in life, cold, and dusty, and travel-worn,
and faint, we look to that moment as a point of light; the
remembrance of it comes over us like the music of our
home heard in a distant land. Like Elisha in the fable,
we go long years in the strength thereof. It travels with
us, a great wakening light; a pillar of fire in the darkness,
to guide us through the lonely pilgrimage of life. These
hours of Inspiration, like the flower of the aloe-tree, may
be rare, but are yet the celestial blossoming of Man; the
result of the past, the prophecy of the future. They are
not numerous to any man. Happy is he that has ten such
in a year, yes, in a lifetime.

Now to many men, who have but once felt this—when
Heaven lay about them, in their infancy, before the world
was too much with them, and they laid waste their powers,
getting and spending,—when they look back upon it,
across the dreary gulf, where Honour, Virtue, Religion
have made shipwreck and perished with their youth, it
seems visionary, a shadow, dream-like, unreal. They count
it a phantom of their inexperience; the vision of a child's
fancy, raw and unused to the world. Now they are wiser.
They cease to believe in inspiration. They can only credit
the saying of the priests, that long ago there were inspired men; but none now; that you and I must bow our
faces to the dust, groping like the Blind-worm and the
Beetle; not turn our eyes to the broad, free Heaven; that
we cannot walk by the great central and celestial light
which God made to guide all who come into the world, but
only by the farthing-candle of tradition, poor and flicker-

ing light which we get of the priest, which casts strange
and fearful shadows around us as we walk, that "leads to
bewilder and dazzles to blind." Alas for us if this be all !

But can it be so ? Has Infinity laid aside its Omnipresence, retreating to some little corner of space ? No. The
grass grows as green ; the birds chirp as gaily ; the sun
shines as warm ; the moon and the stars walk in their
pure beauty, sublime as before ; morning and evening
have lost none of their loveliness ; not a jewel has fallen
from the diadem of night. God is still there ; ever present
in Matter, else it were not ; else the serpent of Fate would
coil him about the All of things ; would crush it in his remorseless grasp, and the hour of ruin strike creation's knell.

Can it be then, as so many tell us, that God, transcending Time and Space, immanent in Matter, has forsaken
Man ; retreated from the Shekinah in the Holy of Holies,
to the court of the Gentiles ; that now he will stretch forth
no aid, but leave his tottering child to wander on, amid
the palpable obscure, eyeless and fatherless, without a
path, with no guide but his feeble brother's words and
works ; groping after God if haply he may find him ; and
learning, at last, that he is but a God afar off, to be approached only by mediators and attorneys, not face to face
as before ? Can it be that Thought shall fly through the
Heaven, his pinion glittering in the ray of every star,
burnished by a million suns, and then come drooping back,
with ruffled plume and flagging wing, and eye which once
looked undazzled on the sun, now spiritless and cold—come
back to tell us God is no Father ; that he veils his face and
will not look upon his child ; his erring child ! No more
can this be true. Conscience is still God-with-us ; a
Prayer is deep as ever of old ; Reason as true ; Religion as
blest. Faith still remains the substance of things hoped
for, the evidence of things not seen. Love is yet mighty
to cast out fear. The Soul still searches the deeps of
God ; the pure in heart see him. The substance of the
Infinite is not yet exhausted, nor the well of Life drunk
dry. The Father is near us as ever, else Reason were a
traitor, Morality a hollow form, Religion a mockery, and
Love a hideous lie. Now, as in the days of Adam, Moses,
Jesus, he that is faithful to Reason, Conscience, Heart and
Soul, will, through them, receive inspiration to guide him
through all his pilgrimage.

BOOK III.

" Where there is a great deal of smoke and no clear flame, it argueth much moisture in the matter, and yet it witnesseth certainly that there is fire there ; and therefore dubious questioning is a much better evidence than that senseless deadness which most men take for believing. Men that know nothing in sciences have no doubts."— LEIGHTON, cited by COLERIDGE, *Aids to Reflection*, American edition, 1829, p. 64.

" He who begins by loving Christianity better than Truth will proceed by loving his own Sect or Church better than Christianity, and end in loving himself better than all."—COLERIDGE, *ubi sup.* p. 64, 65.

" While everybody wishes to believe rather than examine and decide, a just judgment is never passed upon a matter of the greatest importance ; our opinion thereof is taken on trust. The error of our fathers which has fallen into our hands whirls us round and drives us headlong. We are ruined by the example of others. We shall be healed if we separate from the rabble. Now the people, in hostility with Reason, stand up as the defence of what is their own mischief."—SENECA, *De Vita beata*, Ch. I., a free translation.

BOOK III.

CHAPTER I.

STATEMENT OF THE QUESTION AND THE METHOD OF INQUIRY.

It was said before, that Religion, like Love, is always
the same thing in kind, though both are necessarily modified by other emotions combining therewith, and by the
conception of the object to which the emotion is directed.
Thus Love is modified as it chances to coexist with weakness or strength, folly or wisdom, selfishness or morality,
—qualities in the Subject who loves. By these qualities
the degree of Love is determined. It is modified also by
the qualities of the Object; as love is directed towards a
child, a wife, or a friend. Hence come the different mo-
difications of Religion as it coexists with faith or fear,
wisdom or ignorance, love or hate in the worshipping subject; and again as the object of worship is conceived to be
one being, or many beings, or all being; as it is conceived
of as the absolutely Perfect, or represented as finite, cruel,
capricious, and unlovely. The only perfect form of Religion is produced by all the powers of a man's nature, acting harmoniously together. All manifestations of Religion
proceed from the religious element in Man, and are, more
or less, imperfect representations of that element, as its
action is more or less impeded or promoted by various
causes.

If this be so, it follows that the religious Element or faculty in Man bears the same relation to each and all particular forms and teachers of Religion, that Reason bears to each and all particular systems or teachers of Philosophy. That is, as no one teacher or system of Philosophy, nor all teachers and systems taken together, have exhausted Reason, which is the groundwork and standard-measure of them all, and is represented more or less partially in each of them, and therefore as new teachers and new systems of Philosophy are always possible and necessary until a system is discovered which embraces all the facts of Science, sets forth and legitimates all the laws of Nature, and thus represents the Absolute Science, which is implied in the Facts of Nature, or the Ideas of God ; so no one teacher or form of Religion, nor all teachers and forms put together, have exhausted the religious Faculty, which is the groundwork and standard-measure of them all, and is represented more or less partially in each, and so new teachers and new forms of Religion are always possible and necessary, until a form is discovered, which embraces all the facts of Man's moral and religious nature, sets forth and legitimates all the laws thereof, and thus represents the Absolute Religion, as it is implied in the Facts of Man's nature, or the Ideas of God. As no system or teacher of Philosophy is greater than Reason, and competent to give laws to Nature, but at the utmost is only coördinate with Reason, and competent to discover and announce the laws of Nature previously existing ; so no form or teacher of Religion can be greater than the religious Element, and competent to give laws to Man, but at the utmost is only coördinate with the religious Element, and competent to discover and announce the laws of Man previously existing. In one word, Absolute Science answers exactly to Reason, and is what Reason demands ; Absolute Religion answers exactly to the religious Element, and is what the religious Element demands. Therefore until Philosophy and Religion attain the Absolute, each form or teacher of either is subject to be modified or supplanted by any man who has a truth not embraced by the Philosophy or Religion at that time extant. However, there are certain primary truths of Science and Religion, which alone render the two possible, and which are possessed with more or less of a distinct understanding by all teachers of the two, and attain greater prominence with some. Though a system may have many faults accidentally connected with it, though others may point out the faults and develope the system still further, yet the first principles remain. Thus in Science the maxims of Geometry, in Morals the first truths thereof, must reappear in all the systems.

Now to make a special application of these general remarks: Christianity can be no greater than the Religious Faculty, though it may be less; as the water can of itself rise no higher in the pipe than in the fountain, though if the pipe be defective it may fail of its former height. Religion is the universal term; Absolute Religion and Morality its highest expression; Christianity is a particular form under this universal term; one form of religion among many others. It is either Absolute Religion and Morality, or it is less; greater it cannot be, as there is no greater. Christianity then is a form of Religion. As it is actual, it must have been revealed; if it is true, it must be natural. It is therefore to be examined and judged of as other forms of Religion, by Reason and the religious Element. It is true or false; perfect or imperfect.

The question then reduces itself to this. Is Christianity the Absolute Religion? To answer this question we must know, first, what Christianity is; secondly, what Absolute Religion is. If Christianity is not the Absolute, we must of course look for a more perfect manifestation of Religion, just as we look for improvements in Science till Philosophy becomes absolute. But if Christianity be this, or involve it, and nothing contradicts or impedes this, then we can expect nothing higher in Religion, for there is no higher; but have only to understand this, and develope its principles; applying it to life, in order to attain perfect religious welfare.

To ascertain what is Absolute Religion, is no difficult matter; for Religion is not an external thing, like Astronomy, to be learned by long observation, and the perfection of scientific instruments and algebraic processes; but something above all, inward and natural to Man. As it was said before, Absolute Religion is perfect obedience to the Law of God; the service of God by the normal use, development, and discipline of every limb of the body, every faculty of the spirit; perfect Love towards God and Man, exhibited in a life allowing and demanding a harmonious action of all Man's faculties, so far as they act at all.

But to answer the historical question, Did Jesus of Nazareth teach Absolute Religion? is a matter vastly more difficult, which it requires learning, critical skill, and no little painstaking to make out. To answer the first question, What is Christianity? is a very difficult thing. No two men seem agreed about it; the wickedest of wars have been fought to settle it. To answer the query, are we to take what is popularly called Christianity? No Protestant thinks the Christianity of the Catholic Church is Absolute Religion; nor will the Catholic think better of the Protestant faith. A pious man, free from bigotry, and capable of judging, would surely make very short work of the question, and decide that Christianity, as popularly taught by both these churches, taken together, is not Absolute Religion.

But we must look deeper than Protestantism and Popery. We must distinguish Christianity from the popular Conceptions of Christianity; from its Proof and its Form. To do this, we must go back, historically, to the fountain-head, the words of Jesus. We must then take these words in the abstract, separate from any church; apart from all authority, real or pretended; without respect of any application thereof to life, that was made by its founder or others. If all churches have believed it, if miracles have been wrought in its favour, if its application have been good in this or that case, it does not follow that Christianity is absolute and final. The Church has been notoriously mistaken on many points. Miracles are claimed for Judaism, Mahometanism, and Idolatry; each heresy is thought by its followers to work well. We must look away from all these considerations. If Jesus of Nazareth lived out his idea, and was the greatest of saints, it does not follow that his Idea was absolute, and therefore final. If he did not perfectly live it out, the reverse does not follow. The good life of a teacher proves nothing of any speculative doctrine he entertains, either in morals or mathematics. A man would be thought insane who should say Euclid's demonstration of the forty-seventh problem was true, because Euclid lived a good life, and raised men from the dead; or that it was false, because he lived a bad life, and murdered his mother. If Christianity be the Absolute, it is independent of all circumstances; eternally true, as much before its declaration as after it is brought to light and applied to life.[1] Before its revelation it was active, but unknown; afterwards known to be active. To illustrate this point: the three angles of a triangle are equal to two right angles. This is eternally true; and applies to all triangles that were, are, or are to be conceived of. It was just as true before any one discovered and declared it, as afterwards. Its truth depends not on the fact that Thales or Stilpo demonstrates the theorem, nor on the authority of him who asserts it. Its truth exists in the very nature of things, or, to use other words, in the Ideas of God. It was just the same before creation as afterwards. Other things remaining the same, even Omnipotence cannot make these three angles to be more or less than two right angles, for Infinite power of course excludes contradictions.

Now here are two things: first, Religion as it exists in the facts of man's nature, and secondly, Religion as taught by Jesus of Nazareth. The first must be eternally true. But it follows from no premise that the second is eternally true. He may have taught Absolute Religion, or an imperfect form; he may have omitted what was essential, or have added what was national, temporal, personal. In either case Christianity is not the Absolute Religion. But if it have none of these faults, and really conforms with this ideal standard, or involves this, and if nothing therein contradicts it, then Christianity is the Absolute Religion; eternally true, before revelation, after revelation; the Law God made for Man, and wrote in his nature.

Then again if the character of Jesus was not a perfect manifestation of this perfect Religion which he taught or implied; if his application of it to life, was limited by his position, his youth, his indiscretion, fanaticism, prejudice, ignorance, selfishness, as some have contended, it does not make the Religion he taught any the less perfect in itself; if true at all it is eternally true. If Christianity be true at all, it would be just as true if Herod or Catiline had

---

[1] See this point touched in a pamphlet entitled "The Previous Question between Mr. Andrews Norton and his Alumni, moved and handled, by Levi Blodgett." Boston, 1840.

taught it.   Therefore if the intellectual character of Jesus had never so many defects, if he entertained false notions about himself, his office, ministry, destination; respecting ancient history and Jewish literature; the existence and agency of devils, and in general, respecting things past, present, and to come; if he entertained the absurdest notions at the same time with his pure doctrine; nay, if he had never so many moral deficiencies, if he denounced his enemies, and was frighted at danger, and fled away from death, or had even recanted his most vigorous statements, still his religious doctrine remains unaffected by all of these circumstances.   To make this point clear by recurring to a former illustration, a philosopher may show that the three angles of a triangle are equal to two right angles, yet lead an immoral life, believe in witches, devils, the philosopher's stone, and imputed righteousness.   His absurd belief and wicked life do not affect the truth of his theorem.

Now then to determine what Christianity is, we must remove all those extraneous matters relating to the person, character, and authority of him who first taught it; we must separate it from all applications thereof which have been made to life; must view it by itself, as doctrine, as life; and measure it by this ideal standard of Absolute Religion.   After we have determined this question, we may then judge of the applications of Christianity to life; of the character of its Revealer, and try both by the standard he offers.

<hr>

CHAPTER II.

REMOVAL OF SOME DIFFICULTIES.   CHARACTER OF THE CHRISTIAN RECORDS.

THE method of acquiring a knowledge of Absolute Religion is plain and easy, but to get a knowledge of the doctrine taught by any teacher of ancient times is more difficult.   This, however, may be said in general, that there are three sources of knowledge accessible to Men, two of these are direct, and one indirect. First, Perception through the senses ; by this we only get an acquaintance with material things and their properties. Second, Intuition through Intellect, Conscience, the Religious Faculty, by which we get an acquaintance with spiritual things, which are not objects of sense. Third, Reflection, a mental process, by which we unfold what is contained or implied or suggested in perceptions or intuitions. Then as a secondary, but not ultimate source, there is Testimony, by which we learn what others have found out through perception, intuition, or reflection. Now thoughts or objects of thought may be classified in reference to their sources. The truths of Absolute Religion are not matters of Sense, it is plain. If objects of Reflection or Intuition, they must be obvious to all who have the intuitive or reflective faculty, and will use it. They therefore are matters of direct personal experience ; not so a knowledge of any given historical form of Religion. As it has been before said, the great truths of Religion are matters of spontaneous Intuition, and then of voluntary Reflection, God helping the faithful, who use their faculties justly. Therefore, theoretically, each may depend on his own intuitions and reflections. The aid, the counsel, the example of good men help us to the truth. The wise and the pious are the educators whom God appoints for the race. By their superior gift, they help feebler men to understand, what else the latter might never have reached. The same rule holds good in both Philosophy and Religion ; the weak need the help of the strong ; youth of experience ; the faithless of the faithful. Even the experience of wicked men is an element of human progression, a warning light. The works and words of the saint help the sinner to the source of truth. This is the office of prophets and apostles.

In historical questions, respecting events that took place out of the sphere of our observation, we must depend on the testimony of others who report what they have seen and heard, felt or thought. To determine what Jesus taught, we must depend on the testimony of the Evangelists, who profess to relate his works and words, and the Apostles, who reduced his thought to organization and applied it to life. To speak of the four Evangelists—

admitting, for the sake of the argument, we have their evidence, and the books in our hands come really from Matthew, Mark, Luke, and John, and that they bore the relation to Jesus which they claim ; the question comes :— Are they competent to testify in the case ? Can we trust them to give us the whole truth and nothing but the truth ? Admitting they were honest, yet if they were but men, there must be limitations to the accuracy of their testimony. They must omit many things that Jesus said and did, perhaps both actions and words important in estimating his doctrines. They can express only so much of their teacher's opinions as they know ; to do this they might perhaps modify, at least colour, the doctrine in their own mind. They might sometimes misunderstand what they heard ; mistake a general for a particular statement, and the reverse ; a new doctrine of the teacher might accidentally coincide in part with an old doctrine, and he be supposed to teach what he did not teach ; a parable or an action might be misunderstood ; a quotation misapplied or forgotten, and another put in its place ; a general prediction, wish, or hope referred to a specific time, or event, when it had no such reference. He may have merely allowed things which he was afterwards supposed to have commanded. The writers might unconsciously exaggerate or diminish the fact ; they might get intelligence at second-hand, from hearsay, and popular rumour. Their national, sectarian, personal prejudices must colour their narrative. They might confound their own notions with his, and represent them as teaching what he did not teach. They might not separate fact from fancy. Their love of the marvellous might lead them astray. If they believed in miracles they would easily incline to ascribe prodigious things to their teacher. Had they a faith in ghosts and devils, they would naturally interpret his words in favour of their own notions, rather than in opposition thereto. If the writers were ignorant men ; if they wrote in one language and he spoke in another ; yet more, if they wrote at some distance of time from the events, and were not skilled in sifting rumours and separating fact from fiction, the difficulty becomes still greater.

These defects are common, more or less, to all historical testimony. In the case of the Evangelists, they constitute a very serious difficulty. We know the character of the writers only from themselves; they relate much from hearsay; they continually mingle their own personal prejudices in their work; their testimony was not reduced to writing, so far as we know, till long after the event; we see that they were often mistaken, and did not always understand the words or actions of their teacher; that they contradict one another, and even themselves; that they mingle with their story puerile notions and tales which it is charitable to call absurd; that they do not write for a purely historical purpose, relating facts as they were, but with a doctrinal or controversial aim. Such testimony could not be received if found in Valerius Maximus and Livy, or offered in a court of justice when only a few dollars were at stake, without great caution.

Now the difficulty in this case is enormous. It has been felt from an early age. To get rid of the evil, it has been taught, and even believed, that the Evangelists and Apostles were miraculously inspired to such a degree that they could commit no mistake of any kind in this matter, and had none of the defects above hinted at. The assumption is purely gratuitous: there is not a fact on which to base it. The writers themselves never claim it. From the doctrine of inspiration as before laid down, it appears such infallibility is not possible; and from an examination of the facts of the case, it appears it was not actual: the Evangelists differ widely from the Apostles; the Synoptics [1] give us in Jesus a very different being from the Christ whom John describes, and all four make such contradictory statements on some points, as to show they were by no means infallibly inspired, for in that case not only the smallest contradiction would have been impossible, but, without concert, they must all have written exactly the same thing, yet John omits the most surprising facts, the Synoptics the most surprising doctrines.

What has been said is sufficient to show that we must proceed with great caution in accepting the statements of the Gospels. The most careless observer discovers inconsistencies, absurd narrations; finds actions attributed to Jesus, and words put in his mouth, which are directly at variance with his great principles, and the general tone

[1] Matthew, Mark, and Luke.

of his character.   Still there must have been a foundation
of fact for such a superstructure; a great spirit to have
commenced such a movement as the Christian; a great
doctrine to have accomplished this, the most profound and
wondrous revolution in human affairs.   We must conclude
that these writers would describe the main features of his
life, and set down the great principles of his doctrine,
its most salient points, and his most memorable sayings,
such as were poured out in the highest moments of inspiration.   If the teacher were true, these sayings would
involve all the rest of his doctrine, which any man of simple character, religious heart, and mind free from prejudice,
could unfold and develope still further.   The condition and
nature of the Christian records will not allow us to go
further than this, and be curious in particulars.   Their
legendary and mythical character does not warrant full confidence in their narrative.   There are certain main features
of doctrine in which the Evangelists and the Apostles all
agree, though they differ in most other points.[1]

[1] The character of the record is such that I see not how any stress can be laid
on each particular action attributed to Jesus.   That *he lived a divine life, suffered a violent death, taught and lived a most true and beautiful religion*, this
seems the great fact about which a mass of truth and error has been collected.
That he should gather disciples, be opposed by the Priests and Pharisees, have
controversies with them—this lay in the nature of things.   His loftiest sayings
seem to me the most likely to be genuine.   The great stress laid on the *Person
of Jesus* by his followers, shows what the person must have been.   They put the
Person before the thing, the fact above the Idea.   But it is not about vulgar
men that such mythical stories are told.   See Paulus, Leben Jesu, 1828;
Furness, Jesus and his Biographers; Strauss, Leben Jesu, 4th ed. 1840;
English Tr. of Strauss, 1846; Hase, Leben Jesu, 3d ed. 1840; Theile, Zur
Biographie Jesu, 1837; Weisse, Evangelische Geschichte, 1838; Gfrörer,
Urchristenthum, &c., 1836; Hennel, Inquiry concerning the Origin of Chris-
tianity, Lond. 1838; Harwood, German Anti-supernaturalism, Lond. 1840.
See the voluminous replies to Strauss by Tholuck, Neander, Ebrard, Lange,
Harless, &c. &c.   See the valuable paper of Dr Kling on recent Apologetic
Literature of the N. T. in Stud. und Krit. for Oct. 1846, p. 953, et seq.   Norton, ubi sup. Vol. II. p. cliv., considers it an "*unquestionable fact, that the
words of our Saviour are not always reported with perfect correctness.*"   See too
p. clxii. cxciii., and Vol. I. p. lix. lxi. et seq.
    See the recent works of Ewald, F. C. Baur, Köstlin, Schwegler, Zeller, Hil-
genfeld, Anger, Lekebusch, Luthardt, Meyer, Lechler, Hase, Ritschl, Volckmar,
and Norton, on matters pertaining to this subject.   Zeller's Theologische
Jahrbücher (Tüb. 1842, et seq.), and Ewald's Jahrbücher der Biblischen
Wissenschaft (Gött. 1849, et seq.), abound in valuable materials.   The new
edition of the Clementine Homilies, (Dressell, Gött. 1853), containing matter
not published before, and the various books of Bunsen, Baur, Petermann,
Cureton, and others, relating to the Ignatian writings, and the work ascribed to
Hippolytus, with the controversial writings thereon, all throw light on the sub-
jects of this chapter.

CHAPTER III.

THE RELIGIOUS AND THEOLOGICAL DOCTRINES OF JESUS.

IT is quite plain to all impartial students, that Jesus of Nazareth did not teach that complicated system of theological doctrines now called "Christianity:" that is the growth of the ages after him. But yet it is not easy, nor perhaps possible, to determine what doctrines he taught on all important matters. For when we turn away from the sects of the Christian Church, we find it difficult to obtain the exact words of Jesus himself.

There are two collections of ancient documents which relate to his life and teachings,—the Canonical, and the Apocryphal Gospels. The two agree in their common reverence for Jesus, and their mythological treatment of his life, differing only in degree, not kind. Neither collection consists of simple historical documents. The Apocryphal Gospels are of small value for our present purpose, though highly important monuments of the age when such weeds grew out of the soil deeply ploughed by Revolution: they are a wild growth of fancy and religious zeal, yet bear doubtless some historic flowers.[1]

Of the Canonical Gospels, after impartial study, we must reject the fourth, as of scarcely any historical value. It appears to be written more than a hundred years after the birth of Jesus, by an unknown author, who had a controversial and dogmatic purpose in view, not writing to report facts as they were; so he invents actions and doc-

[1] See them in the collections of Fabricius, Codex Apocryphus, N. T. 3 vols. 8vo, Hamb. 1719; Thilo, Codex Apoc. N. T. Vol. I., Lips. 1832; Tischendorf, De Evang. Apoc. Origine et Usu, Hag. Com. 1851; Evang. Apoc., Lips. 1853; Acta Apostol. Apoc., ib. 1851. See also Hoffman, Das Leben Jesu nach den Apocryphen, Leip. 1851. And see who will, Gesch. des Rabbi Jeschua Ben Josef hanootsri, Altona, 1853. See Fabricius, Codex Pseudepig. V. T. 2 vols. 8vo, Hamb. 1724.

trines to suit his aim, and ascribes them to Jesus with no authority for so doing. Yet this Gospel, ascribed to John, one of the Sons of Thunder who appears in actual history, is full of deep religious feeling and thought,—in this its value consists, not at all in its report of matters-of-fact.

We come to the Synoptics; it is by no means clear when they were written, by whom, or with what documentary materials of history: most conflicting results are rested in by different scholars. Fact and fiction are mingled together in all these three Gospels as in the Apocryphal. Calling them by the names of their alleged Authors, Matthew, Mark, Luke, the first seems to be the oldest of all; Luke appears to come next in order; while Mark mediates between the two. But some critics place Mark before Luke in time.

These three follow the same general tradition respecting the life, actions, and doctrines of Jesus, wherein they differ widely and irreconcilably from John. But the individual differences between the accounts of Matthew and Luke are equally remarkable and irreconcilable. In Matthew Jesus forbids his disciples to visit the Gentiles or the Samaritans, while in Luke he does miracles in Samaria; and the model of Christian excellence was found in that despised land. Luke relates the story of the Good Samaritan, and the Prodigal Son,—both probably founded on facts well known at the time,—which Matthew fails to report, and which Mark also neglects to copy into his compromising Gospel. If these two grand lessons of Religion came from Jesus, as there seems no reason to doubt, then what can be said for the historic fairness, or the competence, of the two biographers who omit such important facts? Either that they were grossly ignorant of his doctrines, or else culpably unjust. If Luke invented these noble passages, then the blame rests on him for violating the truth of history by putting their beauty and sublimity upon one who had no claim thereto.

These facts show the difficulty of reconstructing the doctrines of Jesus: for if one Gospel be taken as the historic standard, then much of the others must be thrown away. The results attained will depend on the subjective peculiarities of the inquirer, and so have the uncertainty of mere opinion, not the stability of historic knowledge.

Even Matthew presents us with passages so inconsistent that the fragmentary character of this old Gospel becomes clear to the careful scholar.[1]

Jesus, a young man full of genius for Religion, seems to have begun his public career with the narrow aim of reforming Judaism. He would put all human Piety and Morality into the venerable forms of Jewish tradition. He came not to destroy but to fulfil the Mosaic Law; that was eternal;—his followers were to observe and teach all the customs of the Scribes and Pharisees; the sick man on recovery must offer the Levitical sacrifice. Like John the Baptist, he preaches the coming of the Messiah, and the Kingdom of Heaven. He would not labour for Mankind, but only for the children of Israel—for it is not meet to give the dogs the children's bread. But as he went on he found his new wine of Piety and Humanity burst the old wine-skins of Judaism; the old garments which Scribes and Pharisees had inherited from dead prophets could not be patched with new Philanthropy, and the nation be thereby clothed withal. He gradually breaks with Judaism, neglects the ceremonial fast, violates the Sabbath, speaks evil of the clerical dignities—they are covered pits in the highway, whereinto men fall and perish. He claims himself to be the Messiah; John the Baptist was the Elias who was to come and make ready. He had political plans that lie there indistinctly seen through the mythic cloud which wraps the whole. He reaches beyond Judea to Samaria at least, perhaps to other nations, and developes his religious scheme more freely than at first.

Religion is no longer fettered by conventional restraint; it is Love to God, Love to man: on this hang all the Law and the Prophets. There must be no revenge, but continual forgiveness, seventy times seven. In the next stage of life a man's eternal condition depends wholly on his natural morality and humanity in this.[2] His commands and requisitions related to moral conduct, not belief or liturgical ceremonies; God preferring goodness to sacramental forms.[3] He puts the substance of religion before its acci-

---

[1] Hilgenfeld tries to make out *two* main documents which form the bulk of this Gospel, p. 106, et seq.
[2] Matt. xxii. 34—40, xxv. 14—30, 34—46, et al. and parallels.
[3] Matt. ix. 13, xxiii. 23, et passim.

dents, and utters magnificent beatitudes of Piety and Humanity.

But he does not appear to have been conscious of the Infinite Perfection of God, for though he calls Him our Father, and insists on Absolute Love for God, which certainly seems to imply a Feeling of his Perfection, yet he considers God so imperfect as to damn the majority of men to eternal torment.[1] Beside God he places a Devil absolutely evil, the adversary of God and enemy of man. Hell is eternal, and the wide road thereto is travelled well.

He claimed to be the Messiah spoken of by the writers of the Old Testament, John the Baptist, preparing the way for him, was equal to the greatest of men, but the least in the Kingdom of Heaven was greater than John. Men must believe that he is the Messiah, and confess him before men, or suffer future torment; in the day of judgment the cities which rejected his claim would fare worse than Sodom and Gomorrah, while men who believed and followed him would have immense power and glory.[2] A great crisis, or revolution, is soon to take place, and the Son of Man is to establish the Kingdom of Heaven; the time is near but yet still uncertain; he himself knows not the day and hour.[3] But he is already highly exalted, greater than the Sabbath and the Temple, all things are given to him by the Father, whom he alone knows, and by whom alone he is directly known.[4]

In this new state of things all temporal and material cares were to cease, so he bids men not lay up treasures on earth, but only in Heaven; to take no thought for life, what they should eat, or drink, or wherewithal be clad; for if they seek first the Kingdom of God and its righteousness all these things will be added, and they be fed like the wild birds, and clothed as the lilies are. If God care for grass and sparrows so will he much more for them, and give good things to such as ask him.[5] If brought to trial before magistrates for attempting to establish this Kingdom, they must take no thought for defence, for it

[1] Matt. xxv. 46, vii. 13, 14, xiii. 37—42, 49, 50, et al.
[2] Matt. x. 32—36, 37—39, xi. 20—24, xvi. 14—20, 24—28, xix. 27—30, et al. parallels.
[3] Matt. x. 5—15, 23—34, xxiv. et al.
[4] Matt. xii. 1—8, xi. 25—27, et al. parallels.
[5] Matt. vi. 19—21, 24—34, vii. 7—11, xviii. 18, 19, xix. 21—24.

will be given them at the moment what they shall say; it is not they but God who speaks, only through them.

Yet spite of these obvious defects in his scheme of doctrine, which ought not to astonish us or to be denied, there is such a deep, fresh, manly piety in his teachings, such love for man under all circumstances, poor, oppressed, despised, and sinful, as we find nowhere else in the whole compass of antiquity. God is a Father even to the Prodigal, goes out after him, falls on his neck with welcoming delight that the lost is found, and the dead come back alive once more. Men are to be brothers, each neighbour to all mankind: the greatest is to serve the least; even enemies must be forgiven seventy times seven, and prayed for spite of their active cursing. According to one biographer, on the cross he prayed " Father, forgive them, for they know not what they do."

But this synoptical doctrine alone was felt to be inadequate to the wants of Man; so many other gospels were written, which were variously received and found acceptance with the great writers of the Christian Church till the third and fourth century.[1] The fourth canonical Gospel contains much which is fair and good but utterly foreign to the other three; yet while free from Jewish limitation other new restrictions are therein put on the free development of Religion: men must believe that Jesus is the Messiah and the Logos. No doubt the teaching of Jesus in the Synoptics was thought too external and exclusively practical by some, and the fourth Gospel, with divers others, was written to supply a conscious want. The Epistles of Paul betray the same thing.

To sum up the main points of the matter more briefly; in an age of gross wickedness, among a people arrogant, and proud of their descent from Abraham—a mythological character of some excellence; wedded to the ritual Law, which they professed to have received, by miracle from God, through Moses—another and greater mythological hero—in a nation of Monotheists, haughty yet cunning,

---

[1] See how they were used by Tatian, whose *Diatessaron* was a *Diapente*, Justin Martyr, Ignatius, the Clements of Rome and Alexandria, Origen, &c. The lost work of Papias would doubtless settle many curious questions. See Credner's Beiträge, and Ewald in his Jahrbücher, B. V. p. 62, et seq.

morose, jealous, vindictive, loving the little corner of space called Judea above all the rest of the world; fancying themselves the "chosen people" and special favourites of God; in the midst of a nation wedded to their forms, sunk in ignorance, precipitated into sin, and, still more, expecting a Deliverer, who would repel their political foes, reunite the scattered children of Jacob, and restore them to power, conquer all nations, reëstablish the formal service of the Temple in all its magnificent pomp, and exalt Jerusalem above all the cities of the earth for ever,—amid all this, and the opposition it raised to a spiritual man, Jesus fell back on the moral and religious Sentiment in Man; uttered manifold Oracles of Humanity, as the Infinite spoke in his noble soul; stirred men to deep emotions; laid down some principles of conduct wide as the Soul of man and true as eternal God; taught a form of Religion,—Piety and Morality,—far before anything known then to the world of men; but yet mistook himself for that miraculous and impossible deliverer of his nation whom the people waited for in vain.

In an age full of vengeance he makes love the pivotal Principle which all things must turn upon. Take one example as it stands in the Synoptics. A man asks what he shall do to fulfil the idea of Man, and have "eternal life?" He bids him keep the moral law, written eternally in the nature of man; specifies some of its plainest prohibitions, and adds, Love your neighbour as yourself. When asked the greatest commandment of the Law, he thus sums up all the Law and the Prophets also: "Thou shalt love the Lord thy God with all thy heart, and with all thy soul, and with all thy mind. Thou shalt love thy neighbour as thyself." Here is the sum of religious doctrine. He gives the highest aim for man: Be perfect as God. He declares the blessedness, present and eternal, of such as do the Will of God. The Spirit of God shall be in them, revealing Truth; the Kingdom of God shall be theirs.

He gives no extended form of his views in Theology, Anthropology, Politics, or Philosophy. But the great truth of God's goodness, and man's spiritual nature, are implied in all his teachings. He says little of the Immortality of the Soul; much less than some "Heathens" before him;

but it is everywhere implied. As the doctrine was familiar, he dwells little upon it.

It is vain to deny, or attempt to conceal, the errors in his doctrine,—a revengeful God, a Devil absolutely evil, an eternal Hell, a speedy end of the world; but the actual superiority of the mode of Religion he taught, its sublime faith in God, its profound Humanity, seem also as clear as the noonday sun.

Such, then, is the religious doctrine of Jesus. It was always taught with direct application to life; not as Science, but as daily Duty. Love of God was no abstraction. It implied love of Wisdom, Justice, Purity, Goodness, Holiness, Charity. To love these is to love God; to *love* them is to *live* them. It implies abhorrence of evil for its own sake; a desire and effort to be perfect as God, to tolerate no wrong action, wrong thought, or wrong feeling; to make the heart right, the head right, the hand right; to serve God, not with the lips alone, but the life, not only in Jerusalem and Gerizim, but everywhere; not by tithing mint, anise, and cumin, but by judgment, mercy, and faith; not by saying " Lord, Lord," " Save us, good Lord," but by doing the Father's will. It implies a Faith that is stronger than Fear, prevails over every sorrow, grief, disappointment, and asks only this—Thy will be done; a Love which is strongest in times of trouble, which never fails when mere human affection goes stooping and feeble, weeping its tears of blood; a Love which annihilates temptation, and in the hour of mortal agony brings as it were an angel from the sky; an absolute Trust in God, a brave unconcern for the morrow, so long as the day's duties are faithfully done. It is a love of Goodness and Religion for their own sake, not for the bribe of Heaven, or the dread of Hell. It implies a reunion of Man and God, till we think God's thought, and will God's will, and so have God abiding in us, and become one with Him.

The other doctrine, Love of Man, is Love of all as yourself, not because they have no faults, but in spite thereof. To feel no enmity towards enemies; to labour for them with love; pray for them with pitying affection, remembering the less they deserve, the more they need; this was the doctrine of Love. It demands that the rich, the

wise, the holy, help the poor, the foolish, the sinful; that
the strong bear the burdens of the weak, not bind them
on anew.   It tells a man that his excellence and ability
are not for himself alone, but for all mankind, of which he
is but one, beginning first with the nearest of the needy.
It makes the strong the guardians, not the tyrants, of the
weak.   It said: Go to the publicans and sinners, and call
them to repentance; go to men trodden down by the hoof
of the oppressor, rebuke him lovingly, but snatch the
spoil from his bloody teeth; go to men sick with desolation, covered all over with the leprosy of sin, bowed together and squalid with their inveterate disease, bid them
live and sin no more.   It despairs of no man; sees the
soul of goodness in things evil; knows the soul in its intimate recess never consents to sin, nor loves the Hateful.
It would improve men's circumstances to mend their
heart; their heart to mend their circumstances.   It does
not say alone, with piteous whine—God save the wicked
and the weak, but puts its own shoulder to the work;
divides its raiment and shares its loaf.

To say all, in brief, these two cardinal doctrines demanded a DIVINE LIFE, where every action of the hand, the
head, the heart, is in obedience to the Law of the Soul; in
harmony with the All-perfect.   This was Christ's notion
of worship.   It asked for nothing ritual, formal; laid no
stress on special days, forms, rites, creeds.   Its rite, its
creed, its substance, and its form, are all contained in that
one command, LOVE MAN AS YOURSELF; GOD ABOVE ALL.
None can say, or need suppose, that Jesus consciously intended all the consequences which we see resulting from
these principles, or that he even foresaw the effects thereof, more than Monk Schwarz expected the results of his
invention.

Thus far the application was universal as the doctrine.
But he taught something which is ritual. *Baptism and the
Supper.*   The first was a common rite at the time, used
even by the "heathens."   In a nation dwelling in a warm
climate, and so fond of symbols as the Jews, it was a natural expression of the convert's change of life.   Sensual
men must interpret their Religion to the senses, as the
Hollanders have their Bible in Dutch.   It seems to have

been an accommodation to the wants of the times, as he spoke the popular language. Did he lay any stress on this watery dispensation; count it valuable of itself? Then we must drop a tear for the weakness; for no outward act can change the heart, and God is not to be mocked, pleased, or served with a form. Is there any reason to suppose he ever designed it to be permanent? It is indeed said that he bade the disciples teach all nations, "baptizing them in the name of the Father, and of the Son, and the Holy Ghost." [1] But since the Apostles never mention the command, nor the form, since it is opposite to the general spirit of his precepts, it must be put with the many other things which are to be examined with much care before they are referred to him. But if it came from him, we can only say, There is no perfect Guide but the Father.

The second form,—was it of more account than the first? Who shall tell us the "Lord's Supper" was designed to be permanent more than washing the feet, if that be a fact, which the Pope likewise imitates? Did he place any value on the dispensation of wine; design it to extend beyond the company then present? If we may trust the account, he asks his friends, at supper, to remember him, when they break bread. It was simple, natural, affectionate, beautiful. Was this a foundation of a form; to last for ever; a form valuable in itself; essential to man's spiritual welfare; a form pleasing to Him who is All in All? To say Jesus laid any stress on it as a valuable and perpetual rite is, to go beyond what is written. It needs no reply. The thing may be useful, beautiful, comforting to a million souls; truly it has been so. In Christianity there is milk for babes and meat for men, that the truth may be given as they can receive it. Let each be fed with the Father's bounty. [2]

---

[1] Math. xxviii. 19, and the parallels.
[2] In the first edition I inserted here these lines :—

> "Behold the child, by nature's kindly law,
> Pleased with a rattle, tickled with a straw;
> Some livelier plaything gives his youth delight,
> A little louder, but as empty quite."

The thought I wished to express was this: The two ordinances, in comparison with a religious life and character, are no more than the rattles and straws of a child, compared with the attainments of an accomplished man; it is a beautiful feature of God's Providence, that things in themselves of no value, can yet serve

CHAPTER IV. ·

THE AUTHORITY OF JESUS, ITS REAL AND PRETENDED SOURCE.

On what authority did Jesus teach? On that of the most high God, as he expressly states, and often. But to have the authority of God, is not that miraculous? How can man have God's authority in the natural way? Let us look at the matter.

I. *The only Authority of a Doctrine is its Truth.*

Truth is the relation of things as they are; falsehood, as they are not. No doctrine can have a higher condemnation than to be convicted of falsehood; none a higher authority than to be proved true. God is the author of things as they are; therefore of this relation, and therefore of Truth. He that delivers the Truth then has so far the authority of Truth's God. Then it will be asked, How do we know Christianity is true, or that it is our duty to love Man and God? Now when it is asked, How do I know that I exist; that doubting is doubting; that half is less than the whole; that it is impossible for the same thing to be and not to be? the questioner is set down as a strange man. But it has somehow come to pass, that he is reckoned a very acute and Christian person, who doubts moral and religious axioms, and asks, How do I know that Right is right, and Wrong wrong, and Goodness good? Alas, there are men among the Christians who place virtue and religion on a lower ground than Aristippus and Democritus,

so important a purpose as the intellectual, moral, and religious development of a man. The words were understood in a very different sense—sometimes even by my Friends. I omitted them in the English edition—for the publisher at first designed to have no notes in that, and I did not wish to reprint, without explanation, what had been so much misunderstood before.

men branded as Heathens and Atheists. Let us know what we are about.

It was said above,[1] there are, practically, four sources of knowledge—direct and indirect, primary and secondary,—namely, Perception for sensible things; Intuition for spiritual things; Reflection for logical things; and Testimony for historical things. If the doctrines of Christianity are eternal truths, they are not sensible things, not historical things, and of course do not depend on sensual perception, nor historical testimony, but can be presented directly to the consciousness of men at one age as well as another, and thus if they are matters of reflection, may be made plain to all who have the reflective faculty and will use it; if they are matters of intuition, to all who have the intuitive faculty, and will let it act. Now the duty we owe to Man, that of loving him as ourselves; the duty we owe to God, that of loving him above all, is a matter of intuition; it proceeds from the very nature of Man, and is inseparable from that nature; we recognize the truth of the precept as soon as it is stated, and see the truth of it as soon as the unprejudiced mind looks that way. It is no less a matter of reflection likewise. He that reflects on the Idea of God as given by intuition, on his own nature as he learns it from his mental operations, sees that this twofold duty flows logically from these premises. The truth of these doctrines, then, may be known by both intuition and reflection. He that teaches a doctrine eternally true, does not set forth a private and peculiar thing resting on private authority and historical evidence, but an everlasting reality, which rests on the ground of all truth, the public and eternal authority of unchanging God. A false doctrine is not of God. It has no background of Godhead. It rests on the authority of Simon Peter or Simon Magus; of him that sets it forth. It is his private, personal property. When the Devil speaks a lie, he speaketh of his own; but when a Son of God speaks the truth, he speaks not his own word but the Father's. Must a man indorse God's word to make it current?

Again, if the truth of any doctrines rest on the personal authority of Jesus, it was not a duty to observe them before he spoke; for he, being the cause, or indispensable

[1] Book III. ch. ii.

occasion of the duty, to make the effect precede the cause is an absurdity too great for modern divines. Besides, if it depends on Jesus, it is not eternally true; a religious doctrine that was not true and binding yesterday, may become a lie again by to-morrow; if not eternally true, it is no truth at all. Absolute truth is the same always and everywhere. Personal authority adds nothing to a mathematical demonstration; can it more to a moral intuition? Can authority alter the relation of things? A voice speaking from Heaven, and working more wonders than Æsop and the Saints, or Moses and the Sibyl, relate, cannot make it our duty to hate God, or Man; no such voice can add any new obligation to the law God wrote in us.

When it is said the doctrines of Religion, like the truth of Science, rest on their own authority, or that of unchanging God, they are then seen to stand on the highest and safest ground that is possible—the ground of absolute truth. Then if all the Evangelists and Apostles were liars; if Jesus were mistaken in a thousand things; if he were a hypocrite; yes, if he never lived, but the New Testament were a sheer forgery from end to end, these doctrines are just the same, absolute truth.

But, on the other hand, if these depend on the infallible authority of Jesus, then if he were mistaken in any one point his authority is gone in all; if the Evangelists were mistaken in any one point, we can never be certain we have the words of Jesus in a particular case, and then where is "historical Christianity?"

Now it is a most notorious fact, that the Apostles and Evangelists were greatly mistaken in some points. It is easy to show, if we have the exact words of Jesus, that he also was mistaken in some points of the greatest magnitude—in the character of God, the existence of the Devil, the eternal damnation of men, in the interpretation of the Old Testament, in the doctrine of demons, in the celebrated prediction of his second coming and the end of the world, within a few years. If Religion or Christianity rest on his authority, and that alone, it falls when the foundation falls, and that stands at the mercy of a schoolboy. If he is not faithful in the unrighteous mammon, who shall commit to him the true riches?

II. *Of the Authority derived from the alleged Miracles of Jesus.*

Of late years it has been unpopular with theological writers to rest the authority of Christianity on its truth, and not its truth on its authority. It must be confessed there is some inconvenience in the case, for if this method of trusting Truth alone and not Authority be followed, by and by some things which have much Authority and no Truth to support them, may come to the ground. The same thing took place in the middle ages, when Abelard looked into Theology, explaining and defending some of the doctrines of the Church by Reason. The Church said, If you commend the Reasonable as such, you must condemn the Not-Reasonable, and then where are we? A significant question truly. So the Church "cried out upon him" as a heretic, because he trusted Reason more than a blind belief in the traditions of men, which the Church has long had the impudence to call "Faith in God." It is often said, in our times, that Christianity rests on miracles; that the authority of the miracle-worker authenticates his doctrine; if a teacher can raise the dead, he must have a commission from God to teach true doctrine; his word is the standard of truth. Here the fact and the value of miracles are both assumed outright.

Now if it could be shown that Christianity rested on Miracles, or had more or less connection with them, it yet proves nothing peculiar in the case, for other forms of Religions, fetichistic, polytheistic, and monotheistic, appeal to the same authority. If a nation is rude and superstitious, the claim to miracles is the more common; their authority the greater.[1] To take the popular notion, the

---

[1] See a curious story respecting an Eastern Calif and his decision between the conflicting claims of the Christians and Mahometans, in Marco Polo, ed. Marsden, Book I. ch. viii. p. 67—69. See also Book II. ch. ii. p. 275, et seq.; Book III. ch. xx. § 4, p. 648, et seq. See the numerous miracles collected by Valerius Maximus in his treatise, De Prodigiis, Opp. ed. Hase, Vol. I. Lib. i. ch. vi.; De Somniis, ch. vii.; De Miraculis, ch. viii.: Julius Obsequens, Prodigiorum, Liber imperfectus: Jo. Laurenti Lydi, De Ostentis, Fragmenta, passim, ad calc. Opp. Val. Max. See the Incarnation and Ascension of Budha, in Upham, The Mahávansi, the Raja Ratnacari, and the Rajavali, Lond. 1833, Vol. I. p. 1, et seq.; for miracles and marvels, passim. See Spencer's Discourse concerning Prodigies, Lond. 1665. But see Trenck, Notes on the Miracles, &c., N. Y. 1850, p. 25, et seq., p. 75, et seq.

Jewish Religion began in miracles, was continued, and will end in miracles. The Mahometan tells us the Koran is a miracle; its author had miraculous inspiration, visions, and revelations. The writings of the Greeks, the Romans, the Scandinavians and the Hindoos, the Chinese and Persians, are full of miracles. In Fetichism all is miracle, and its authority, therefore, the best in the world. The Catholic Church and the Latter-day-Saints still claim the power of working them, and, therefore, of authenticating whatever they will, if a miracle have the alleged virtue.

Now in resting Christianity on this basis we must do one of two things: either, first, we must admit that Christianity rests on the same foundation with the lowest Fetichism, but has less divine authority than that, for if miracles constitute the authority, then that is the best form of Religion which counts the most miracles; or, secondly, we must deny the reality of all miracles except the Christian, in order to give exclusive sway to Christianity. But the devotees of each other form will retort the denial, and claim exclusive credence for their favourite wonders. The serious inquirer will ask, If such be the Evidence, what is Truth, and how shall I get at it? And if he does not stop for a time in scepticism, at best in indifference, why he is a very rare man. In this state of the case theologians have felt bound, in logic, either to prove the superiority of Christian miracles, or to deny all other miracles. The first method is not possible, the Hindoo Priest surpasses the Christian in the number and magnitude and antiquity of his miracles. The second, therefore, is the only method left. Accordingly, most ingenious attempts have been made to devise some test which will spare the Christian and condemn all other miracles. The Protestant saves only those mentioned in the Bible; the Catholic, more consistently, thinks the faculty immanent in the Church, and claims miracles down to the present day. But all these attempts to establish a suitable criterion have been fruitless, and even worse, often exposing more than the folly of their authors.[1] However, they who

[1] See Douglas's Criterion, or Miracles Examined, Lond. 1754, and Leslie's Short Method with the Deists. See an ingenious illustration of the folly of one of Leslie's canons in Palfrey, Academical Lectures, &c. Vol. II. p. 150, note 11. See Fehmelius De Criteriis Errorum circa Religionem communibus, Lips. 1713, 1 Vol. 4to.

argue from the miracles alone, assume two things; first, that miracles prove the divinity of a doctrine; secondly, that they were wrought in connection with the Christian doctrine. If one ask proof of these significant premises, it is not easy to come by. This subject of miracles demands a careful attention. Here are two questions to be asked. First, Are miracles possible? Second, Did they actually occur in the case of Christianity?

I. *Are Miracles possible?*

The answer depends on the definition of the term. The point we are to reason from is the idea of God, who must be the cause of the miracle. Now a miracle is one of three things :—

1. It is a transgression of all law which God has made; or,

2. A transgression of all known laws, but obedience to a law which we may yet discover; or,

3. A transgression of all law known or knowable by man, but yet in conformity with some law out of our reach.

1. To take the first definition. A miracle is not possible, as it involves a contradiction. The infinite God must have made the most perfect laws possible in the nature of things; it is absurd and self-contradictory to suppose the reverse. But if his laws are perfect and the nature of things unchangeable, why should he alter these laws? The change can only be for the worse. To suppose he does this is to accuse God of caprice. If he be the ultimate cause of the phenomena and laws of the universe, to suppose in a given case he changes these phenomena and laws, is either to make God fickle and therefore not worthy to be relied on; or else inferior to Nature, of which he is yet the cause.

2. To take the second definition. It is no miracle at all, but simply an act, which at first we cannot understand and refer to the process of its causation. The most common events, such as growth, vitality, sensation, affection, thought, are miracles. Besides, the miracle is of a most fluctuating character. The miracle-worker of to-day is a matter-of-fact juggler to-morrow. The explosion of gun-

powder, the production of magnified images of any object, the phenomena of mineral and animal magnetism, are miracles in one age, but common things in the next. Such wonders prove only the skill of the performer. Science each year adds new wonders to our store. The master of a locomotive steam-engine would have been thought greater than Jupiter Tonans or the Elohim thirty centuries ago.

3. To take the third hypothesis. There is no antecedent objection, nor metaphysical impossibility in the case. Finite Man not only does not, but cannot understand all the modes of God's action; all the laws of His Being. There may be higher beings, to whom God reveals· himself in modes that we can never know, for we cannot tell the secrets of God, nor determine à priori the modes of his manifestation. In this sense a miracle is possible. The world is a perpetual miracle of this sort. Nature is the Art of God; can we fully comprehend it? Life, Being, Creation, Duration, do we understand these actual things? How then can we say to the Infinite, Hitherto shalt thou come, but no further; there are no more ways wherein thy Being acts?[1] Man is not the measure of God. Let us use the word in this latter sense.

II. *Did Miracles occur in the case of Jesus?*

This question is purely historical; to be answered, like all other historical questions, by competent testimony. Have we testimony adequate to prove the fact?

[1] See Babbage, Ninth Bridgewater Treatise, Phila. 1841, p. vii. xxvi. and Sir John Herschel's Letter to Mr Lyell therein, p. 212; Vestiges of Nat. Hist. of Creation, p. 145, et seq. Pascal has some remarkable speculations on Miracles; Pensées, P. II. Art. 16, ed. Paris, 1839, p. 323, et seq. He defines a miracle as *an effect which exceeds the natural force of the means employed to bring it about*. The non-miracle is an effect which does not exceed the force, p. 342. He adds, they who effect cures by the invocation of the Devil, work no miracle, for *that does not exceed the Devil's natural power! A fortiori*, it is impossible for God to work a miracle. Leibnitz has some strange remarks on this subject scattered about in his disorderly writings. See what he says in reply to M. Bayle, Théodicée, Pt. III. § 248-9. See too p. 776, ed. Erdmann. See the acute remarks of Thomas Aquinas, Summa Theologiæ, Pt. I. qu. 101, et seq. See Theol. Quartal Schrift (Tübig.) for 1845, p. 265, et seq.; C. F. Ammon, Nova Opuscula theologica, Gött. 1803, p. 157, et seq. See Gazzaniga, Praelectiones theologicæ, &c., Venet. 1803, 9 vols. 4to., Vol. I. Diss. ii. c. 7, p. 71, et seq.

Antecedent to all experience one empirical thing is probable as another. To the first man, with no experience, birth from one parent is no more surprising than birth from two; to feed five men with five ship-loads of corn, or five thousand with five loaves; the reproduction of an arm, or a finger nail; the awakening from a four days' death, or a four hours' sleep; to change water into wine, or mineral coal into burning gas; the descent into the sea, or the ascent into the sky; the prediction of a future or the memory of a past event;—all are alike, one as credible as the other. But to take our past experience of the nature of things, the case wears a different aspect. We demand more evidence for a strange than a common thing. From the very constitution of the mind a prudent man supposes that the Laws of Nature continue; that the same cause produces always the same effects, if the circumstances remain the same. If it were related to us, by four strangers who had crossed the ocean in the same vessel, that a man, now in London, cured diseases, opened the blind eyes, restored the wasted limb, and raised men from the dead, all by a mere word; that he himself was born miraculously, and attended by miracles all his life,— who would believe the story? We should be justified in demanding a large amount of the most unimpeachable evidence. This opinion is confirmed by the doubt of scientific men in respect of "animal magnetism" and "spiritualism"—where no law is violated, but a faculty hitherto little noticed is disclosed.

Now if we look after the facts of the case, we find the evidence for the Christian miracles is very scanty in extent, and very uncertain in character. We must depend on the testimony of the epistolary and the historical books of the New Testament. It is a notorious fact that the genuine Epistles, the earliest Christian documents, make no mention of any miracles performed by Jesus; and when we consider the character of Paul, his strong love of the marvellous, the manner in which he dwells on the appearance of Jesus to him after death, it seems surprising, if he believed the other miracles, that he does not allude to them. To examine the testimony of the Gospels; two profess to contain the evidence of eye-witnesses. But we are not certain these books came in their present shape

from John and Matthew; it is certain they were not written till long after the events related. The Gospel ascribed
to John is of small historical value if of any at all. But
still more, each of them relates what the writers could
not have been witness to; so we have nothing but
hearsay and conjecture. Besides, these authors shared
the common prejudice of their times, and disagree one
with the other. The Gospels of Mark and Luke—who
were not eye-witnesses—in some points corroborate the
testimony of John and Matthew; in others add nothing; in yet others they contradict each other as well
as John and Matthew. But there are still other accounts
—the Apocryphal Gospels—some of them perhaps older
than the Gospel of Matthew, certainly older than John,
and these make the case worse by disclosing the fondness
for miracles that marked the Christians of that early
period.[1] Taking all these things into consideration, and
remembering that in many particulars the three first Gospels are but one witness, adding the current belief of the
times in favour of miracles, the evidence to prove their
historical reality is almost nothing, admitting we have the
genuine books of the disciples; it at least is such evidence
as would not be considered of much value in a court of
justice. However, the absence of testimony does not
prove that miracles were not performed, for a universal
negative of this character cannot be proved.[2]

If one were to look carefully at the evidence in favour
of the Christian miracles, and proceed with the caution
of a true inquirer, he must come to the conclusion, I
think, that they cannot be admitted as facts. The Resurrection—a miracle alleged to be wrought upon Jesus,

[1] See these Apocryphal Works referred to in note on p. 163. Also Jones,
Method of settling the canonical Authority of the N. T., Oxford, 1797, 3 vols.;
The Apoc. N. T., Boston, 1832; Wake, Epistles of the Apostolic Fathers,
&c., Oxford, 1840. See Mosheim's Dissertation on the causes which led to the
composition of supposititious works among the early Christians, in his Diss. ad
H. E. pertinentes, Alt. 1743, Vol. I. p. 221, et seq. Mr Norton, ubi sup., Vol.
III. Ch. xi., treats of the subject but not with his usual learning.

[2] See some just remarks in Hennel, ubi sup., Ch. VIII.; Strauss, Leben Jesu.
§ 1—15, § 90—103, 132—139; Glaubenslehre, § 17, and on the other hand
Neander and Tholuck. See De Wette, Wesen des Glaubens, § 60; Flügge,
Gesch. theol. Wissenschaften, Halle, 1796, Vol. I. p. 97, et seq. For the
value early set on miraculous evidence, see the Treatise of Theophilus, (Bp of
Antioch, in the 2d cent.,) address to Autolycus, Lib. I. C. 13, et al; Treack,
ubi sup.

not by him,—has more evidence, though of the same inferior kind, than any other, for it is attested by the Epistles, as well as the Gospels, and was one corner-stone of the Christian church. But here, is the testimony sufficient to show that a man thoroughly dead as Abraham and Isaac were, came back to life; passed through closed doors, and ascended into the sky? I cannot speak for others—but most certainly I cannot believe such monstrous facts on such evidence.[1]

There is far more testimony to prove the fact of miracles, witchcraft, and diabolical possessions in times comparatively modern, than to prove the Christian miracles. It is well known, that the most credible writers among the early Christians, Irenæus, Origen, Tertullian, Cyprian, Augustine, Chrysostom, Jerome, Theodoret, and others, believed that the miraculous power continued in great vigour in their time.[2] But to come down still later, the case of St Bernard of Clairvaux is more to the point. He lived in the eleventh and twelfth centuries. His life has been written in part by William, Abbot of St Thierry, Ernald, Abbot of Bonnevaux, and Geoffrey, Abbot of Igny, " all eye-witnesses of the saint's actions." Another life was written by Alanus, Bishop of Auxerre, and still another by John the Hermit, not long after the death of Bernard, both his contemporaries. Besides, there are three books on his miracles, one by Philip of Clairvaux, another by the

---

[1] But see Furness, ubi sup. ch. VII. VIII. XIII. See the candid remarks of De Wette, ubi sup. § 61. He admits the difficulties of the case, and only saves the general fact of the resurrection, by rejecting the authenticity of the 4th and part of the 3d Gospel (p. 315, et seq.), for he thinks the details of their accounts are inadmissible.

[2] On this subject of the miraculous power in the early church, see the celebrated treatise of Middleton, A Free Inquiry into the Miraculous Powers in the Christian Church, &c., Lond. 1749, in his Works, Lond. 1752, Vol. I. See Mosheim's Eccles. Hist. Pt. I. ch. i. § 8, and Murdock's note. The testimony of Chrysostom is fluctuating. See Middleton, Vol. I. p. 105, et seq. See Newman's defence of the Cath. miracles in the dissertation prefixed to Vol. I. of the Tr. of Fleury's History of the Church; Conrad Lycosthenes, Prodigiorum ac Ostentorum Chronicon, Basil, 1557, 1 Vol. Fol. ; The treatise of St Ephraim of Cherson on the miracle wrought by Clement, at the end of Cotelerius, Pat. Apost., Ant. 1698, Vol. I. p. 811, et seq. The story of Simon Magus shows the credulity of the early Church. See it in Hegesippus, Lib. III. C. ii. See too Leo, Ep. ad Constant. Imp.; Augustinus, Ep. 86, and Const. Apost. VI. 9; Bernino, Istoria, de tuttel, Heresie, Venet. 1711, 4 vols. 4to, Sec. I. Ch. i. See the curious Miracles related by Victor Vitensis and Aeneas Gazaeus, in Gibbon, Hist. ch. XXXVII.

monks of that place, and a third by the above-mentioned
Geoffrey. He cured the deaf, the dumb, the lame, the
blind, men possessed with devils, in many cases before
multitudes of people : he wrought thirty-six miracles in a
single day, says one of these historians ; converted men
and women that could not understand the language he
spoke in. His wonders are set down by the eye-witnesses
themselves, men known to us by the testimony of others.[1]
I do not hesitate in saying that there is far more evidence
to support the miracles of St Bernard than those mentioned
in the New Testament.[2]

But we are to accept such testimony with great caution.
The tendency of men to believe the thing happens which
they expect to happen ; the tendency of rumour to exaggerate a real occurrence into a surprising or miraculous
affair, is well known. A century and a half have not gone
by since witches were tried by a special court in Massa-

[1] See these books in Mabillon's edition of Bernard, Paris, 1721, Vol. II. p.
1071, et seq. See Fleury, Histoire Ecclesiastique, Liv. LXVI. et seq., and
especially LXIX. ch. xvii., ed. Nismes, 1779, Vol. X. p. 147, et seq., where
is a summary of some of his most important miracles. See likewise Les Vies
des Saints, Paris, 1701, Vol. II. p. 288—326 ; Butler's Lives of the Saints,
Lond. 1815, Vol. VIII. p. 227—274 ; Milner's History of the Church of Christ,
&c., Vol. III., Christian Examiner for March, 1841, Art. I.   At the recent
exhibition of " the holy Robe of Jesus " at Tréves, *no less than eleven miraculous cures were effected*, so it is said.   Miracula Stultis ! See Marx, History of
the Holy Robe of J. C., with an account of the miraculous cures performed by
the said Robe from 18th August to 6th October, 1844, Phil. 1845. Numerous
Bishops attended the exhibition, and more than 1,100,000 persons, says the
book. See p. 97, et seq. See too John Ronge, the Holy Coat of Tréves and the
new German Catholic Church, New York, 1845. See an account of the miracle wrought by Vespasian, in Tacitus, Hist. Lib. IV. C. 81, Opp. ed. Paris,
1819, III. p. 490, et seq.   See several similar wonders in Ammon, ubi sup. p.
165, et seq.
[2] Bernino, ubi sup. Vol. I. p. 204, gives a very dramatic account of a scene
between St Macarius and a Heretic, in which, to prove the truth of the catholic doctrine, the saint raises from the dead a monk who had been buried about
a month ! For other confirmatory miracles, see Bernino, passim.   It is well
known that Petrarch, in the 14th century, believed the miracles of Pope Urban
his own contemporary ; and de Sade his biographer, writing in 1767, will have
us believe that the Pope actually performed 80 miracles, besides raising two
girls from the dead in the city of Avignon.   Junker, in his Ehrengedächtnitz
Lutheri, (p. 276—289, ed. 1707,) says that a portrait of Luther at Ober-
Rossla in Weimar, at three different times, was covered with a profuse sweat
while the preacher was speaking of the sad state of the schools and churches.
See Reformation Almanach für 1817, p. xxvi. See the story of Spiridion,
and his numerous miracles, in Sozomen, Hist. Eccles. Lib. I. C. xi., ed. Par.
1544, p. 14, et seq. See Wright's Essay on the Lit. and Superstitions of England in the Middle Ages, Lond. 1846, Vol. II. Essay x. xii.

—

chusetts; convicted by a jury of twelve good men and true; preached against by the clergy, and executed by the common hangman. Any one who looks carefully and without prejudice into the matter sees, I think, more evidence for the reality of those "wonders of the invisible world" than for the Christian miracles. Here is the testimony of scholars, clergymen, witnesses examined under oath, jurymen, and judges; the confession of honest men, of persons whose character is well known at the present day, to prove the reality of witchcraft and the actual occurrence of miraculous facts; of the interference of powers more than human in the affairs of the world.[1] The appearance of spectres and ghosts, of the Devil as "a little black man;" the power of witches to ride through the air, overturn a ship, raise storms, and torture men at a distance, is attested by a cloud of witnesses, perfectly overshadowing to a man of easy faith.[2] In the celebrated case

[1] See, who will, Cotton Mather's Wonders of the Invisible World, Boston, 1693; Increase Mather's Cases of Conscience, &c., and the learned authors in Diabology therein cited. See also Hale's Modest Inquiry into the Nature of Witchcraft, &c., Boston, 1702; Calef, More Wonders from the Invisible World, London, 1700; Upham's Lectures on Witchcraft, &c.; Stone's History of Beverley, Boston, 1843, p. 213, et seq.; Mather's Magnalia, passim; Chandler's Criminal Trials, p. 65, et seq.; Bancroft, ubi sup. ch. XIX. See many curious particulars in Hutchinson's Essay concerning Witchcraft, &c., second edition, London, 1720. See Remigius, Demonolatriæ, Libri III., Col. 1576, 1 vol. 12mo. I have not seen the book, but it is said to contain matter derived from the cases of about 900 persons executed for witchcraft in 15 years at Lorraine. See a contemporary Narrative of the Proceedings against Dame Alice Kyteler, prosecuted for sorcery in 1324 by the Bp of Ossory, Lond. 1843, 1 vol. 4to, Introduction. See Account of the Trial, Confession, &c., of Six Witches at Maidstone, &c., 1652, and the Trial of Three Witches, &c., 1645, Lond. 1837. In the 13th century the Cath. Church declared a disbelief of witchcraft to be Heresy. See, who will, the Bulls of the Popes relative to this from Greg. IX. down to the famous Bull of Innoc. VIII. (1484), Summis desiderantes. The celebrated work of Sprenger and Kramer, Malleus Malleficarum (1484 at Saesse), may be consulted by the curious. In 1487 this infamous work was approved by the theological faculty at Cologne, and acquired a great reputation in the church. It is remarkable that in 1650, when two Jesuits in Germany wrote against trials for witchcraft, the most famous Protestant divines—as Pott at Jena and Carpzov at Leipsic—defended the prosecution, and wished men punished for disbelieving in witchcraft. See Gazzaniga, ubi sup. Vol. IV. Diss. I. C. 20, p. 44, et seq.

[2] Henry More has made a pretty collection of cases out of authors now forgotten, in Antidote against Atheism, Book III. ch. i.—xiv., Appendix, ch. xii. xiii.; Immortalitas Animæ, Lib. II. ch. xv.—xvii.; Lib. III. ch. iv. See his Enchiridion Metaphysicum, Pars I ch. xxvi. W. G. Solden has written a Geschichte der Hexen-Processe, &c., Stuttgart, 1843. See too Hauber's Zauberbibliothek, 3 vols. 8vo; Horst, Zauberbibliothek, 6 vols. 8vo; and Grässe, Bibliotheca Magica, &c., Leip. 1843.

of Richard Dugdale, the "Surey Demoniack," or "Surey Impostor,"[1]—which occurred in the latter part of the seventeenth century, in England, and was a most notorious affair,—we have the testimony of nine dissenting clergymen, to prove his diabolical miracles, all of them familiar with the "Demoniack;" and also the depositions of many "credible persons," sworn to before two magistrates, to confirm the wonder. Yet it turned out at last that there was no miracle in the case.[2] It it needless to mention the "miracles" wrought at the tomb of the Abbé de Paris, during the last century,[3] or, in our own time, those of father Matthews in Ireland, and the Mormonites in New England. A miracle is never looked for but it comes.[4]

[1] "The Surey Demoniack, or an Account of Satan's Strange and Dreadful Actings in and about the Body of Richard Dugdale," &c. &c., London, 1697.

[2] See Taylor's "The Devil turned Casuist," &c., London, 1697; "Lancashire Levite Rebuked," 1698; and "The Surey Impostor." The latter I copy from citations in "A Vindication of the Surey Demoniack," &c., London, 1698. Such as wish to see melancholy specimens of human folly may consult also Barrows, "The Lord's Arm stretched out," &c. &c., London, 1664; "The Second Part of the Boy of Bilson," &c. &c., London, 1698; "A Relation of the Diabolical Practices of above twenty Witches of Renfreu, &c., contained in their Tryals, &c., and for which several of them have been executed the present Year," 1697, London, 1697; "Sadducismus Debellatus, Narrative of the Sorceries and Witchcrafts of the Devil upon Mrs Christian Shaw, &c., of Renfreu," &c., London, 1698. See Glanvill, a Blow at Modern Sadducism, in some considerations about Witchcraft, &c. &c., 4th ed., London, 1668; Essays, &c., London, 1676, Essay VI. Against Modern Sadducism in the matter of Witches and Apparitions; Sadducismus triumphatus, or Evidence concerning Witches and Apparitions, &c. &c., 4th ed. London, 1726. Yet the Author was a highly intelligent man, who appreciated Bacon and applauded Descartes, and contended for free inquiry and against Superstition and Fanaticism, with wit and argument (see Essay VII.). Howell estimates that thirty thousand suffered death for Witchcraft, in England, during one hundred and fifty years. State Trials, Vol. II. p. 1051, as cited by Chandler, ubi sup. p. 69.

[3] See the celebrated work of M. de Montgéron, La Vérité des Miracles de M. de Paris, demontrée, &c., Utrecht, 1737, 1 vol. 4to. The Author was a *Conseiller au Parlement*, and himself converted by these miracles. See too the *Avertissement* of this ed., and the "consequens qu'on doit tirer des Miracles, &c.," with the remarkable "Piéces justificatives," at the end of the volume. See Mosheim Dissert. on this subject, ubi sup. Vol. II. p. 309, et seq. It is instructive to find Irenæus (II. 57) declaring that the *true disciples of Christ could work miracles in his time*, and that the Dead *were raised and remained alive some years*. Eusebius, H. E. IV. 3, cites Quadratus, who lived half a century before Irenæus, to prove that men miraculously raised from the dead lived a considerable time, ed. Heinichen, Vol. I. p. 292. See the curious papers on *Folk-Lore*, in the Athenæum (London) for 1846.

[4] Well says Livy, XXIV. 10, Quæ [Miracula] quo magis credebant simplices et religiosi homines, eo plura nunciabantur! See the remarkable literature

No man can say there was not something at the bottom of the Christian "miracles," and of witchcrafts and possessions; I doubt not something not yet fully understood; but to suppose, on such evidence, that God departed from the usual law of the world, in these cases, is not very rational, to say the least; to make such a belief essential to Christianity is without warrant in the words of Christ.

But now admitting in argument that Jesus wrought all the miracles alleged; that his birth and resurrection were both miraculous; that he was the only person endowed with such miraculous power—it does not thence follow that he would teach true doctrine. Must a revealer of transient miracles to the sense necessarily be a revealer of eternal truth to the soul? It follows no more than the reverse. But admit it in argument. Then he must never be mistaken in the smallest particular. But this is contrary to fact; for if we may trust the record, he taught that he should appear again after his alleged ascension, and the world would end in that age.

·Practically speaking, a miracle is a most dubious thing; in this case its proof the most uncertain. But on the supposition that our conviction of the truth of Religion must rest wholly or mainly on the fact, that Jesus wrought the alleged miracles, then is Religion itself a most uncertain thing, and we in this age can never be sure thereof, though our soul testify to its truth, as the old Jews, who rejected him, and yet had their senses to testify to the miracles. If the proof of Religion be the sensations of the evangelists, then we can be no more certain of its truth than of the fact that Jesus had no human father!

But this question of miracles, whether true or false, is of no religious significance. When Mr Locke said the doctrine proved the miracles, not the miracles the doctrine, he silently admitted their worthlessness. They can be useful only to such as deny our internal power of discerning truth.[1] Now the doctrine of Religion is eternally

connected with what is called "Spiritualism," already so copious, especially the works of Edmunds, Rogers, Ballou, Bell, and Hare. The writings of A. J. Davis seem to be one of the most remarkable literary phenomena in the world, but it would be absurd to call them miraculous.

[1] "Let us see how far inspiration can enforce on the mind any opinion concerning God or his worship, when accompanied with a power to do a miracle, and here too, I say, the last determination must be that of reason. 1. Because

true.   It requires only to be understood to be accepted.
It is a matter of direct and positive knowledge, dependent
on no outside authority, while the Christian miracles are,
at best, but a matter of testimony, and therefore of
secondary and indirect knowledge.   The thing to be
proved is notoriously true; the alleged means of proof
notoriously uncertain.   Is it not better, then, to proceed
to Religion at once? for when this is admitted to be as
true as the demonstrations and axioms of science, as much
a matter of certainty as the consciousness of our existence,
then miracles are of no value.   They may be interesting to
the historian, the antiquary, or physiologist, not to us as
religious men.   They now hang as a mill-stone about the
neck of many a pious man, who can believe in Religion,
but not in the transformation of water to wine, or the resurrection of a body.

reason must be the judge what is a miracle, and what is not, which—not knowing how far the power of natural causes do extend themselves, and what strange
effects they may produce—is very hard to determine.   2. *It will always be as
great a miracle that God should alter the course of natural things,* as overturn
the principles of knowledge and understanding in a man, by setting up anything
to be received by him as a truth which his reason cannot assent to, *as the miracle
itself;* and *so at best it will be but one miracle against another, and the greater
still on reason's side;* it being harder to believe God should alter and put out of
its ordinary course some phenomenon of the great world for once, and make
things act contrary to their ordinary rule, purposely, that the mind of man might
do so always afterwards, than that this is some fallacy or natural effect, of which
he knows not the cause, let it look never so strange. . . .   I do not hereby deny
in the least, that God can do, or hath done, miracles for the confirmation of
truth; but I only say that we cannot think he should do them to enforce doctrines or notions of himself or any worship of him not conformable to reason,
or that we can receive such for truth for the miracle's sake; and even in those
books which have the greatest proof of revelation from God, and the attestation
of miracles to confirm their being so, *the miracles are to be judged by the doctrine,
and not the doctrine by the miracle.*"   King's Life of Locke, Vol. I. p. 231, et
seq.   See the remarks of Calvin, Institutes, Dedication to Francis I., Allen's
Tr., Lond. 1838, Vol. I. p. xix.   Gerhard, in his Common Places, says,
" Miracles prove nothing, unless they have a doctrinal Truth connected with
them."

CHAPTER V.

THE ESSENTIAL EXCELLENCE OF THE CHRISTIAN RELIGION.

LET us call the religious teachings of Jesus Christianity; it agrees generically with all other forms in this, that it is a Religion. Its peculiarity is not in its doctrine of one Infinite God, of the Immortality of Man, nor of future Retribution. It is not in particular rules of Morality, for precepts as true and beautiful may be found in Heathen writers, who give us the same view of Man's nature, duty, and destination. The great doctrines of Christianity were known long before Jesus, for God did not leave man four thousand years unable to find out his plainest duty. There is no precept of Jesus, no real duty commanded, no promise offered, no sanction held out, which cannot be paralleled by similar precepts in writers before him. The pure in heart saw God before as well as after him. Every imperfect form of Religion was, more or less, an anticipation of Christianity. So far as a man has real Religion, so far he has what is true in Christianity.[1] By its light Zoroaster, Confucius, Pythagoras, Socrates, with many millions of holy men, walked in the early times of the world. By this they were cheered when their souls were bowed down, and they knew not which way to turn. They and their kindred, like Moses, were schoolmasters to prepare the world for Christianity; shadows of good things to come; the dayspring from on high; the Bethlehem star announcing

---

[1] See Tindal, Christianity as Old as the Creation, &c. See Lactantius, Hist. Div. Lib. VII. C. 7, Nos. 4 and 7, who admits that all the doctrines of Christianity were taught before, but not collected into one mass. See Clem. Alex. Strom. I. 13, p. 349. Dr Reginald Peacock, writing in the 15th century against the Lollards, says that Christianity added nothing at all (except *the Sacraments*) *to the moral law, for all of that was primarily established, not on the Scriptures but on natural reason;* and adds that *natural Law must be obeyed, even if Christ and the apostles had taught what was opposed thereto.* Wharton in Appendix to Cave, Historia literaria, &c., Lond. 1698, Vol. I. p. 136.

the Perfect Religion which is to follow. Modern Christians
love to deny that there are points of agreement between
Christianity and its predecessors. The early apologists
took just the opposite course.

1. The religious teachings of Jesus have this chief
excellence, they allow men to advance indefinitely beyond
him. He does not foreclose human consciousness against
the income of new truth, nor make any one fact of human
history a bar to the development of human nature. I do
not find that he taught his doctrines either as a Finality,
or as one of many steps in the progressive Development
of mankind : he gives no opinion. The author of the
fourth Gospel makes him tell his disciples that he had
other things to make known ; that the Comforter would
teach them all things, and they should do greater works
than he. Paul, professing to receive new revelation from
the immortal Jesus, revolutionizes the doctrines of the historical person ; and notwithstanding the profession of
"following Jesus" as the sole authority, the Christian
Church has built up a " Scheme of Divinity" and a " Plan
of Salvation " as much at variance with the recorded words
of Jesus in the Synoptics, as repugnant to common sense.
No sect has practically taken the words of Jesus for a
finality, though each counts its own doctrine as the last
word of God.

Judaism and Mahometanism each sets out from the
alleged words of one man, which are made the only measure of Truth for the whole human race. There can be no
progress. The devotee of Judaism or Mahometanism must
logically believe his form of Religion perpetual : so if a
man teach what is hostile to it, he must be put to death,
though his doctrine be true.

Whatever is consistent with Reason, Conscience, and
the Religious Faculty, is consistent with the Christianity
of Jesus, all else is hostile ; whoever obeys these three
oracles is essentially a Christian, though he lived ten thousand years before Jesus, or living now, does not own his
name. Let men improve in Reason, Conscience, Heart,
and Soul, in what most becomes a man—they outgrow each
form of worship ; they pass by all that rests on historical
things, signs, wonders, miracles, all that does not rest on

the eternal God, ever acting in Man ; yet they are not the further from this Christianity, but all the nearer by the change. These things are left behind, as the traveller leaves the mire and stones of the road he travels, and shakes off the dust of his garments as he approaches some queenly city, throned amid the hills, and looks back with sorrow on the crooked way he has traversed, where others still drag their slow and lingering length along. Men must come to such Christianity when they come to real manly excellence. This proposes no partial end, but an absolute Object—the perfection of Man, or oneness with God. Therefore it leaves men perfect freedom ; the liberty that comes of obedience to the Law of the Spirit of Life. Other forms of worship, ancient and modern, confine men in a dungeon ; make them think the same thought, and speak the same word, and worship in the same way ; Jesus would leave them the range of the world, scope and verge enough. Where the Spirit of the Lord is, there is Liberty ; the liberty of perfect obedience ; the largest liberty of the sons of God. Reason and Love are hostile to every limited form of religion, which says, Believe, Believe ; they welcome that Religion of Jesus which says, Be perfect as God.

2. A second excellence is this : It is not a System of theological or moral Doctrines, but a Method of Religion and Life. It lays down no positive creed to be believed in ; commands no ceremonial action to be done ; it would make the man perfectly obedient to God, leaving his thoughts and actions for Reason and Conscience to govern. It widens the sphere of thought and life : it reaffirms some of the great religious truths implied in Man's nature ; shows their practical application and its result. A religious system, with its forms, and its ritual, lops off the sacred peculiarities of Individual Character ; chains Reason and fetters the Will ; seeks to unite men in arbitrary creeds and forms—where the union can be but superficial and worthless—and it lays stress on externals. This Christianity insists on rightness before God ; ties no man down to worship in this mountain, nor yet in Jerusalem ; on the first day of the week, or the last day ; in the church or the fields ; socially or in private ; with a creed, ritual, priest, symbol, spoken prayer, or without these. It

breaks every yoke, seen or invisible; bids men worship
in love. It does not ask man to call himself a Christian,
or his Religion Christianity. It bids him be perfect;
never says to Reason, Thus far and no further; forbids no
freedom of inquiry, nor wide reach of thought; fears nothing from the Truth, or for it. It never encourages that
cowardice of soul which dares not think, nor look facts in
the face, but sneaks behind altars, texts, traditions, because they are of the fathers; that cowardice which
counts a mistake of the apostles better than truth in you
and me, and which reads both Piety and Common Sense
out of its church because they will not bow the knee nor
say the creed. Christianity asks no man to believe the Old
Testament, or the New Testament, the divine infallibility of
Moses or Jesus, but to prove all things; hold fast what
is good; do the will of the Father; love Man and God.

The method of such Christianity is a very plain one.
Obedience, not to that old teacher, or this new one; but
to God, who filleth all in all, to His Law written on the
tablets of the heart. It exhorts men to a divine life, not
as something foreign but as something native and welcome to Man. It is the life of many Systems of Religion,
Theology, and practical Morality, as the ocean has many
waves and bubbles; but these are not Christianity more
than a wreath of foam is the Atlantic.

3. It differs from others in its eminently practical
character. It counts a manly life better than saying
"Lord, Lord;" puts mercy before sacrifice, and pro-
nounces a gift to man better than a gift to God. It
dwells much on the brotherhood of men; annihilates national and family distinctions; all are sons of God, and
brothers; Man is to love his brother as himself, and bless
him, and thus serve God. It values Man above all things.
Is he poor, weak, ignorant, sinful, it does not scorn him,
but labours all the more to relieve the fallen. It sees the
"archangel ruined" in the sickly servant of Sin. It looks
on the immortal nature of Man, and all little distinctions
vanish. It bids each man labour for his brother, and never
give over till Ignorance, Want, and Sin are banished from
the earth; to count a brother's sufferings, sorrows, wrongs,
as our sufferings, sorrows, and wrongs, and redress them.
It says, Carry the Truth to all. Before Jesus, the Greek,

the Roman, and the Jew, went to other lands to learn their
arts, customs, and laws, study their religion. Jesus sent his
disciples to teach and serve; only Budha and his followers
had done it before.

This Christianity allows no man to sever himself from
the race, making this world an Inn for him to take his
ease. It does nothing for God's sake, each good act for
its own sake; sends the devotee from his prayers to make
peace with his brother; does not rob a man's father to
enrich God; nor fancy He needs anything, sacrifice, creeds,
fasts, or prayers. It makes worship consist in being good,
and doing good; faith within and works without; the test
of greatness the amount of good done. Thus it is not a
Religion of temples, days, ceremonies, but of the street,
the fire-side, the field-side. Its temple is all space; its
worship in spirit and truth; its ceremony a good life,
blameless and beautiful; its priest the Spirit of God in the
soul; its altar a heart undefiled. It places duty above cant.
It promises, as the result of obedience—oneness with God,
and inspiration from Him. It offers no substitute for this,
for nothing can do the work of Goodness and Piety but
Goodness and Piety. It offers no magic to wipe sin out of
the soul, and insure the rewards of Religion without sharing
its fatigues; knows nothing of vicarious goodness. Its
Heaven is doing God's will now and for ever; thus it makes
no antithesis between this and the next life. It puts nothing between men and God; makes Jesus our friend, not
master; a teacher who blesses, not a tyrant who commands us; a brother who pleads with us, not an Attorney
who pleads with God, still less a sacrifice for sins he never
committed, and therefore could not expiate.

These are not the peculiarities oftenest insisted on, and
taught as Christianity; it is not the mystery, the miraculous birth, the incarnation, the God-man, the miracles, the
fulfilment of prophecy, the transfiguration, the atonement, the resurrection, the angels, the ascension, the " five
points; "—other religions have enough such things, Jesus
had but little.

Notwithstanding the anticipation of the doctrines of Jesus centuries before him,—Christianity was a new thing;
new in its Spirit, proved new by the Life it wakened in

the world.   Alas, such is not the Christianity of the
Churches at this day, nor at any day since the crucifixion ;
but is it not the Christianity of Christ, the one only Religion, everlasting, ever blest ? [1]

CHAPTER VI.

THE MORAL AND RELIGIOUS CHARACTER OF JESUS OF NAZARETH.

REVERENCE and Tradition have woven about Jesus such a
shining veil, that with the imperfect and doubtful materials in our hands, it is not easy to determine in detail and
with minuteness the character that moved and lived
among his fellow-men, and commenced what may be called
the Christian movement.   The difficulty is twofold : to
avoid traditional prejudice, and to get at the facts.   Perhaps it is impossible to separate the pure fact from the
legendary and mythological drapery that surrounds it.
Besides, the Gospels pretend to cover but a few months of
his active life.   Still some conclusion may be reached.
From Christianity we have separated the life and character
of Jesus, that we might try the doctrine by Absolute Religion ; it now remains to examine the life of the man by
the standard himself has given.

I. *The Negative Side, or the Limitations of Jesus.*

It is apparent that Jesus shared the erroneous notions
of the times respecting devils, possessions, and demonol-
ogy in general ; respecting the character of God, and the
eternal punishment he prepares for the Devil and his
angels, and for a large part of mankind.   If we may credit

[1] See the Critical and Miscellaneous Writings of Theodore Parker, Boston,
1843, Art. I. and X. ; Sermons of Theism, Serm. III.—VI. Also, Relation between the Ecclesiastical Institutions and the Religious Consciousness of the
American People ; and Function of a Teacher of Religion.

the most trustworthy of the Gospels, he was profoundly in error on these important points, whereon absurd doctrines have still a most pernicious influence in Christendom. But it would be too much to expect a man "about thirty years of age" in Palestine, in the first century, to have outgrown what is still the doctrine of learned ministers all over the Christian world.

He was mistaken in his interpretation of the Old Testament, if we may take the word of the Gospels. But if he supposed that the writers of the Pentateuch, the Psalms, and the Prophecies, spoke of him, if he applied their poetic figures to himself, it is yet but a trifling mistake, affecting a man's head, not his heart. It is no more necessary for Jesus than for Luther to understand all ancient literature, and be familiar with criticism and antiquities; though with men who think Religion rests on his infallibility, it must be indeed a very hard case for their belief in Christianity.

Sometimes he is said to be an enthusiast,[1] who hoped to found a visible kingdom in Judea, by miraculous aid— as the prophets had distinctly foretold their "Messiah" should do, that he should be a King on earth, and his disciples also, not forgetting Judas, should sit on twelve thrones and judge the restored tribes; that he should return in the clouds. Certainly a strong case, very strong, may be made out from the Synoptics to favour this charge. But what then? Even if the fact be admitted, as I think it must be, it does not militate with his morality and religion. How many a saint has been mistaken in such matters! His honesty, zeal, self-sacrifice, heavenly purity still shine out in the whole course of his life.[2]

Another charge, sometimes brought against him, and the only one at all affecting his moral and religious character, is this; that he denounces his opponents in no measured terms; calls the Pharisees "hypocrites" and "children of the devil." We cannot tell how far the his-

---

[1] See in Eusebius, Dem. Ev. Lib. III. C. 3, the noble passage defending him from the charge, often brought of old time—of seducing the people.

[2] On this point see, who will, the charges against Jesus in the Wolfenbüttel, Fragmente; in the Writings of Wünsch, Bahrdt, Paalzow, and Salvador. See also Hennel, ubi sup. Ch. XVI.; and, on the other hand, Reinhard's Plan of the Founder of Christianity, Andover, 1831, and Furness, ubi sup. passim, and Ullmann, Sündlosigkeit Jesu.

torians have added to the fierceness of this invective, but the general fact must probably remain, that he did not use courteous speech. We must judge a man by his highest moment. His denunciation of sleek, hollow Pharisees, say some, is certainly lower than the prayer, "Father, forgive them;" not consistent with the highest thought of humanity. But if such would consider the youth of the man, it were a very venial error—to make the worst of it. The case called for vigorous treatment. Shall a man say, "Peace, peace," when there is no peace? Sharp remedies are for inveterate and critical disease. It is not with honeyed words, neither then nor now, that great sins are to be exposed. It is a pusillanimous and most mean-spirited wisdom that demands a religious man to prophesy smooth things, lest Indolence be rudely startled from his sleep, and the delicate nerves of Sin, grown hoary and voluptuous in his hypocrisy, be smartly twitched. It seems unmanly and absurd to say a man filled with divine ideas should have no indignation at the world's wrong. Rather let it be said, No man's indignation should be like his, so deep, so uncompromising, but so holy and full of love. Let it be indignation; not personal spleen; call sin sin, sinners by their right name.

Yet in this general and righteous, though to some it might seem too vehement, indignation against men when he speaks of them as a class and representatives of an idea, there is no lack of charity, none of love, when he speaks with an individual. He does not speak harshly to that young man who went away sorrowful, his great possessions on the one hand and the Kingdom of Heaven on the other; does not call Judas a traitor, and Simon Peter a false liar as he was; says only to James and John—ambitious youths—They know not what they ask; never addresses scornful talk to a Pharisee, or long-robed doctor of the law, Herodians or Scribes, spite of their wide phylacteries, their love of uppermost seats, their devouring of widows' houses in private, their prayers and alms to be seen of men. He only states the fact, but plainly and strongly, to their very face. Even for these men his soul is full of affection. He could honour an Herodian; pray for a Scribe; love even a Pharisee. It was not hatred, personal indignation, but love of men, which lit that burning zeal, and denounced such as sat in Moses' seat, boasting themselves children of Abraham, when they were children of the Devil, and did his works daily—dutiful children of the father of lies. How he wailed like a child for the mother that bore him : " Oh Jerusalem, Jerusalem, thou that killest the prophets and stonest them that are sent unto thee ! ' How he prayed like a mother for her desperate son, " Father, forgive them, for they know not what they do." Are these the words of one that could hate even the wickedest of the deceitful ? Who then can love his fellow-men ?

II. *The Positive Side, or the Excellences of Jesus.*

In estimating the character of Jesus it must be remembered that he died at an age when a man has not reached his fullest vigour. The great works of creative intellect ; the maturest products of Man ; all the deep and settled plans of reforming the world, come from a period, when experience gives a wider field as the basis of hope. Socrates was but an embryo sage till long after the age of Jesus. Poems and Philosophies that live, come at a later date. Now here we see a young man, but little more than thirty years old, with no advantage of position ; the son and companion of rude people ; born in a town whose inhabitants were wicked to a proverb ; of a nation above all others distinguished for their superstition, for national pride, exaltation of 'themselves and contempt for all others ; in an age of singular corruption, when the substance of religion had faded out from the mind of its anointed ministers, and sin had spread wide among a people turbulent, oppressed, and downtrodden ; a man ridiculed for his lack of knowledge, in this nation of forms, of hypocritical priests and corrupt people, falls back on simple Morality, simple Religion, unites in himself the sublimest precepts and divinest practices, thus more than realizing the dream of prophets and sages ; rises freq from so many prejudices of his age, nation, or sect ; gives free range to the spirit of God in his breast ; sets aside the Law, sacred and time-honoured as it was, its forms, its sacrifice, its temple and its priests ; puts away the Doctors of the law, subtle, learned, irrefragable, and pours out doctrines, beautiful as the light, sublime as Heaven, and true as God.

13*

The Philosophers, the Poets, the Prophets, the Rabbis,—
he rises above them all.   Yet Nazareth was no Athens,
where Philosophy breathed in the circumambient air ; it
had neither Porch nor Lyceum, not even a school of the
Prophets.   Doubtless he had his errors, his follies, faults,
and sins even ; it is idle and absurd to deny it.   But there
was a divine manhood in the heart of this youth.   Old
teachers, past times, the dead letter of forms a century deceased, enslaved his fellow-men, the great, the wise ; what
were they to him ?   Let the dead bury their dead.   Men
had reverence for institutions so old, so deep-rooted, so
venerably bearded with the moss of age.   Should not he,
at least, with that sweet conservatism of a pious heart,
sacrifice a little to human weakness, and put his zeal, faith,
piety, into the old religious form, sanctified by his early
recollections, the tender prayer of his mother, and a long
line of saints ?   New wine must be put into new bottles,
says the young man, triumphing over a sentiment, natural
and beautiful in its seeming ; triumphant where strife is
most perilous, victory rarest and most difficult.   The
Priest said, Keep the Law and reverence the Prophets.
Jesus sums up the excellence of both, Love man and love
God, leaving the chaff of Moses, and the husk of Ezekiel,
with their " Thus-saith-the-Lord," to go to their own
place, where the wind might carry them.

He looked around him and saw the wicked, men who
had served in the tenth legion of sin, pierced with the
lances and torn with the shot ; men scarred and seamed
all over with wounds dishonourably got in that service ;
men squalid with this hideous disease, their moral sense
blinded, their nature perverse, themselves fallen from the
estate of Godliness for which they were made, and unable,
so they fancied, to lift themselves up ; men who called
good evil, and evil good,—he bade them rise up and walk,
waiting no longer for a fancied redeemer that would never
come.   He told them they also were men ; children of
God, and heirs of Heaven, would they but obey.   So corrupt were they, there was no open vision for them : the
voice of God was a forgotten sound in their bosoms.   To
them he said, I am the good Shepherd ; follow me.   At
the sight of their penitence he says, Thy sins are forgiven
thee : go, and sin no more.   Is not penitence itself the

forgiveness of sins, the dawn of reconciliation with God ? He showed men their sin, the disease of the soul living false to its law ; told them their salvation ; bade them obey and be blessed.

He saw the oppressor, with his yoke and heavy burden for Man's neck ; the iron that enters the soul ; men who were the corrupters, the bane, the ruin of the land ; base men with an honourable front ; low men, crawling, as worms, their loathsome track in high places ; deceitful hucksters of salvation, making God's house of prayer a den of thieves, fair as marble without, but all rottenness within. What wonder if Love, though the fairest of God's daughters, at sight of such baseness pours out the burning indignation of a man stung with the tyranny of the strong, ashamed at the patience of mankind ; the word of a man fearless of all but to be false when Truth and Duty bid him speak ? To call the Whelp of Sin a devil's child —is that a crime ? Doubtless it is, in men stirred by passion ; not in a soul filled to the brim and overflowing with love.

He looks on the nation, the children of pious Abraham ; men for whom Moses made laws, and Samuel held the sceptre, and David prayed, and prophets admonished in vain, pouring out their blood as water ; men for whom psalmist and priest and seer and kings had prayed and wept in vain,—well might he cry, " Oh Jerusalem, Jerusalem." Few heard his cries. That mightiest heart that ever beat, stirred by the Spirit of God, how it wrought in his bosom ! What words of rebuke, of comfort, counsel, admonition, promise, hope, did he pour out ; words that stir the soul as summer dews call up the faint and sickly grass ! What profound instruction in his proverbs and discourses ; what wisdom in his homely sayings, so rich with Jewish life ; what deep divinity of soul in his prayers, his action, sympathy, resignation ! Persecution comes ; he bears it : contempt ; it is nothing to him. Persecuted in one city, he flees into another. Scribes and Pharisees say, He speaketh against Moses ; he replies, The Kingdom of Heaven is at hand. They look back to the past, and say, We have Abraham to our father ; he looks to the Comforter, and says, Call no man your Father on Earth. They say, He eats bread with unwashed hands, plucks corn and relieves disease on the holy Sabbath day, when even God rested from his labours ; he says, Worship the Father in spirit and in truth.   They look out to their Law, its Festivals, its Levites, its Chief Priests, the Ancient and Honourable of the earth, the Temple and the Tithe ; he looks in to the Soul, Purity, Peace, Mercy, Goodness, Love, Religion. The extremes meet often in this world. Comedy and Tragedy jostle each other in every dirty lane.   But here it was the Flesh and the Devil on one side, and the Holy Spirit on the other.

CHAPTER VII.

MISTAKES ABOUT JESUS——HIS RECEPTION AND INFLUENCE.

WE often err in our estimate of this man.   The image comes to us, not of that lowly one ; the carpenter of Nazareth ; the companion of the rudest men ; hard-handed and poorly clad ; not having where to lay his head ; "who would gladly have stayed his morning appetite on wild figs, between Bethany and Jerusalem ; " hunted by his enemies ; stoned out of a city, and fleeing for his life. We take the fancy of poets and painters ; a man clothed in purple and fine linen, obsequiously attended by polished disciples, who watched every movement of his lips, impatient for the oracle to speak.   We conceive of a man who was never in sin, in error, or even in fear or doubt ; whose course was all marked out before him, so that he could not miss the way. But such it was not, if the writers tell truly ; nay, such it could not be.   Did he say, I came to fulfil the Law and the Prophets, and it is easier for Heaven and Earth to pass than for one jot or tittle of the Law to fail ? Then he must have doubted, and thought often and with a throbbing heart, before he could say, I am not come to bring peace, but a sword ; to light a fire, and would God it were kindled : many times before the fulness of peace dwelt in him, and he could say, The hour cometh and now is, when the true worshipper shall worship in spirit and in truth !

We do not conceive of that sickness of soul, which must have come at the coldness of the wise men, the heartlessness of the worldly, at the stupidity and selfishness of the disciples. We do not think how that heart, so sensitive, so great, so finely tuned, and delicately touched, must have been pained to feel there was no other heart to give an answering beat. We know not the long and bitter agony which went before the triumph-cry of faith, I am not alone, for the Father is with me ; we do not heed that faintness of soul which comes of hope deferred, of aspirations all unshared by men, a bitter mockery the only human reply, the oft-repeated echo to his prayer of faith. We find it difficult to keep unstained our decent robe of goodness when we herd only with the good and shun the kennel where Sin and Misery, parent and child, are huddled with their rags ; we do not appreciate that strong and healthy pureness of soul which dwelt daily with iniquity, sat at meat with publicans and sinners, and yet with such cleanness of life as made even Sin ashamed of its ugliness, but hopeful to amend. Rarely, almost never, do we see the vast divinity within that soul, which, new though it was in the flesh, at one step goes before the world whole thousands of years ; judges the race ; decides for us questions we dare not agitate as yet, and breathes the very breath of heavenly love. The Christian world, aghast at this venerable beauty in the flesh ; transfixed with wonder as such a spirit rises in his heavenly flight, veils its face and says, It is a God ; such thoughts are not for men ; the life betrays the Deity. And is it not the Divine which the flesh enshrouds ; to speak in figures, the brightness of His glory, the express image of His person ; the clear resemblance of the All-beautiful ; the likeness of God in which Man is made ? But alas for us, we read our lesson backward ; make a God of our brother, who should be our Servant and Helper. So the new-fledged eaglets may see the parent bird, slow rising at first with laborious efforts, then cleaving the air with sharp and steady wing, and soaring through the clouds, with eye undazzled, to meet the sun ; they may say, We can only pray to the strong pinion. But anon, their wings shall grow, and flutter impatient for congenial skies, and their parent's example guide them on. But men are still so sunk in sloth, so blind and deaf with sensuality and sin, they will not see the greatness of Man in him, who, falling back on the inspiration God normally imparts, asks no aid of mortal men, but stands alone, serene in awful loveliness, not fearing the roar of the street, the hiss of the temple, the contempt of his townsmen, the coldness of this disciple, the treachery of that; who still bore up, had freest communion when all alone; was deserted, never forsaken; betrayed, but still safe; crucified, but all the more triumphant. This was the victory of the Soul; a Man of the highest type. Blessed be God that so much manliness has been lived out, and stands there yet, a lasting monument to mark how high the tides of divine life have risen in the human world. It bids us take courage, and be glad, for what Man has done, he may do; yea more.

> " Jesus, there is no dearer name than thine,
> Which Time has blazoned on his mighty scroll;
> No wreaths nor garlands ever did entwine
> So fair a temple of so vast a soul.
> There every Virtue set his triumph-seal;
> Wisdom conjoined with Strength and radiant Grace,
> In a sweet copy Heaven to reveal,
> And stamp Perfection on a mortal face;
> Once on the earth wert thou, before men's eyes,
> That did not half thy beauteous brightness see;
> E'en as the Emmet does not read the skies,
> Nor our weak orbs look through immensity.
> Once on the earth wert thou, a living Shrine,
> Wherein conjoining dwelt, the Good, the Lovely, the Divine."

Here was the greatest soul of the sons of men; a man of genius for Religion; one before whom the majestic mind of Grecian sages and of Hebrew seers must veil its face. Try him as we try other teachers. They deliver their word, find a few waiting for the consolation, who accept the new tidings, follow the new method, and soon go beyond their teacher, though less mighty minds than he. Such is the case with each founder of a school in Philosophy, each sect in Religion. Though humble men, we see what Socrates and Luther never saw. But eighteen centuries have past since the tide of humanity rose so high in Jesus; what man, what sect, what church has mastered his noblest thought; comprehended his method, and fully applied it to life! Let the world answer in its cry of anguish. Men have parted his raiment among them; cast lots for his seamless coat; but that spirit which toiled so manfully in a world of sin and death; which did and suffered, and overcame the world,—is that found, possessed, understood? Nay, is it sought for and recommended by any of our churches?

But no excellence of aim, no sublimity of achievement, could screen him from distress and suffering. The fate of all Saviours was his—despised and rejected of men. His father's children " did not believe in him;" his townsmen " were offended at him," and said, " Whence hath he this wisdom? Is not this the son of Joseph the carpenter?" Those learned scribes who came all the way from Jerusalem to entangle him in his talk, could see only this, " He hath Beelzebub." " Art thou greater than our father Jacob?" a conservative might ask. Some said, " He is a good man." " Ay," said others, but " He speaketh against the temple." The sharp-eyed Pharisees saw nothing marvellous in the case. Why not? They were looking for signs and wonders in the heavens; not Sermons on the Mount, and a " Woe-unto-you, Scribes and Pharisees, Hypocrites;" they looked for the Son of David, a king, to rule over men's bodies, not the son of a peasant-girl, born in a stable, the companion of fishermen, the friend of publicans and sinners, who spoke to the outcast, brought in the lost sheep, and so ruled in the soul, his kingdom not of this world. They said, " He is a Galilean, and of course no prophet." If he called men away from the senses to the soul, they said, " He is beside himself." " Have any of the Rulers or the Pharisees believed on him?" asked some one who thought the answer would settle the matter. When he said, If a man live by God's law, " he shall never see death," they exclaimed, those precious shepherds of the people, " Now we know thou hast a devil, and art mad. Abraham is dead, and the prophets! Art thou greater than our father ABRAHAM? Who are you, sir?" What a faithful report would Scribes and Pharisees and Doctors of the Law have made of the Sermon on the Mount; what omissions and redundances

would they not have found in it; what blasphemy against
Moses and the Law, and the Ark of the Covenant, and the
Urim and the Thummim, and the Meat-offering and the
New-moons; what neglect to mention the phylacteries,
and the shew-bread and the Levite, and the priest and the
tithes, and the other great "essentials of Religion;" what
"infidelity" must these pious souls have detected! How
must they have classed him with Korah, Dathan, and
Abiram, the mythological "Tom Paines" of old time;
with the men of Sodom and Gomorrah! The popular
praise of the young Nazarene, with his divine life and lip
of fire; the popular shout, "Hosannah to the Son of
David," was no doubt " a stench in the nostrils of the righteous." "When the Son of Man cometh, shall he find
faith on the earth?" Find Faith? He comes to bring it.
It is only by crucified redeemers that the world is " saved."
Prophets are doomed to be stoned; apostles to be sawn
asunder. The world knoweth its own and loveth them.
Even so let it be; the stoned prophet is not without his
reward. The balance of God is even.

Yet there were men who heard the new word. Truth
never yet fell dead in the streets; it has such affinity with
the Soul of Man, the seed, however broadcast, will catch
somewhere, and produce its hundred-fold. Some kept his
sayings and pondered them in their heart. Others heard
him gladly. Did priests and Levites stop their ears?
Publicans and harlots went into the kingdom of God before them. Those blessed women, whose hearts God has
sown deepest with the orient pearl of faith; they who
ministered to him in his wants, washed his feet with tears
of penitence, and wiped them with the hairs of their head,
was it in vain he spoke to them? Alas for the anointed
priest, the child of Levi, the son of Aaron, men who shut
up inspiration in old books, and believed God was asleep.
They stumbled in darkness, and fell into the ditch. But
doubtless there was many a tear-stained face that bright-
ened like fires new stirred as Truth spoke out of Jesus'
lips. His words swayed the multitude as pendant vines
swing in the summer wind; as the spirit of God moved on
the waters of chaos, and said, "Let there be light," and
there was light. No doubt many a rude fisherman of
Gennesareth heard his words with a heart bounding and

scarce able to keep in his bosom, went home a new man, with a legion of angels in his breast, and from that day lived a life divine and beautiful. No doubt, on the other hand, Rabbi Kozeb Ben Shatan, when he heard of this eloquent Nazarene, and his Sermon on the Mount, said to his disciples in private at Jerusalem, This new doctrine will not injure us, prudent and educated men; we know that men may worship as well out of the temple as in it; a burnt-offering is nothing; the ritual of no value; the Sabbath like any other day; the Law faulty in many things, offensive in some, and no more from God than other laws equally good. We know that the priesthood is a human affair, originated and managed like other human affairs. We may confess all this to ourselves, but what is the use of telling of it? The people wish to be deceived; let them. The Pharisee will behave wisely like a Pharisee—for he sees the eternal fitness of things—even if these doctrines should be proclaimed. But this people, who know not the law, what will become of them? Simon Peter, James and John, those poor unlettered fishermen, on the lake of Galilee, to whom we gave a farthing and the priestly blessing in our summer excursion, what will become of them when told that every word of the Law did not come straight out of the mouth of Jehovah, and the ritual is nothing! They will go over to the Flesh and the Devil, and be lost. It is true, that the Law and the Prophets are well summed up in one word, Love God and Man. But never let us sanction the saying; it would ruin the seed of Abraham, keep back the kingdom of God, and destroy our usefulness."[1]

Thus went it at Jerusalem. The new word was "Blasphemy," the new prophet an "Infidel," "beside himself," had "a devil." But at Galilee, things took a shape somewhat different; one which blind guides could not foresee. The common people, not knowing the Law, counted him a prophet come up from the dead, and heard him gladly. Yes, thousands of men, and women also, with hearts in their bosoms, gathered in the field and pressed about him in the city and the desert place, forgetful of hunger and thirst, and were fed to the full with his words, so deep a child could understand them; James and John leave all to

[1] Parker, Miscellanics, Art. VII.; and Speeches, Vol. I. Art. I.

follow him who has the word of eternal life; and when that young carpenter asks Peter, Whom sayest thou that I am? it had been revealed to that poor unlettered fisherman, not by flesh and blood, but by the word of the Lord, and he can say, Thou art the Christ, the Son of the living God. The Pharisee went his way, and preached a doctrine that he knew was false; the fisherman also went his way, but which to the Flesh and the Devil?[1]

We cannot tell, no man can tell the feelings which the large free doctrines of such humane Religion awakened when heard for the first time. There must have been many a Simeon waiting for the consolation; many a Mary longing for the better part; many a soul in cabins and cottages and stately dwellings, that caught glimpses of the same truth as God's light shone through some crevice which Piety made in that wall Prejudice and Superstition had built up betwixt Man and God; men who scarce dared to trust that revelation—"too good to be true"—such was their awe of Moses, their reverence for the priest. To them the word of Jesus must have sounded divine; like the music of their home sung out in the sky, and heard in a distant land, beguiling toil of its weariness, pain of its sting, affliction of despair. There must have been men, sick of forms which had lost their meaning; pained with the open secret of sacerdotal hypocrisy; hungering and thirsting after the truth, yet whom Error, and Prejudice, and Priestcraft had blinded so that they dared not think as men, nor look on the sunlight God shed upon the mind.

But see what a work it has wrought. Men could not hold the word in their bosoms; it would not be still. No doubt they sought—those rude disciples—after their teacher's death, to quiet the matter and say nothing about it; they had nerves which quivered at the touch of steel; wives and children whom it was hard to leave behind, to the world's uncertain sympathy; respectable friends, it may be, who said, The old Law did very well; let well enough alone; the people must be deceived a little; the world can never be much mended! No doubt the Truth stood on one side, and Ease on the other; it has often been so.

[1] Parker, Miscellanies, Art. XI.

Perhaps the disciples went to the old synagogue more sedulous than before ; paid tithes ; kept the new-moons ; were sprinkled with the blood of the sacrifice ; made low bows to the Levite ; sought his savoury conversation, and kept the rules which a priest gave George Fox. But it would not do. There was too much truth to be hid. Even selfish Simon Peter has a cloven tongue of fire in his mouth, and he and the disciples go to their work, the new word swelling in their labouring heart.[1]

Then came the strangest contest the world ever saw. On the one side was all the strength of the world—the JEWS with their Records, from the hand of Moses, David, and Esaias ; "supernatural records," that go back to the birth of time ; their Law derived from Jehovah, attested by miracles, upheld by prophets, defended by priests, children of Levi, sons of Aaron, the Law which was to last for ever; the Temple, forty and seven years in being built, its splendid ceremonies, its beautiful gate and golden porch ; there was the wealth of the powerful ; the pride, the self-interest, the prejudice of the priestly class ; the indifference of the worldly ; the hatred of the wicked ; the scorn of the learned ; the contempt of the great. On the same side were the GREEKS, with their Chaos of Religion, full of mingled beauty and ugliness, virtue and vice, piety and lust, still more confounded by the deep mysteries of the priest, the cunning speculations of the sophist, the awful sublimity of the sage, by the sweet music of the philosopher, and moralist and poet, who spoke and sung of man and God in strains so sweet and touching ; there were rites in public ; solemn and pompous ceremonies, processions, festivals, temples, games, to captivate that wondrous people ; there were secret mysteries, to charm the curious and attract the thoughtful ; Greece, with her Arts, her Science, her Heroes and her Gods, her Muse voluptuous and sweet. There too was ROME, the Queen of nations, and Conqueror of the world, who sat on her seven-hilled throne, and cast her net eastward and southward and northward and westward, over tower and city and realm and empire, and drew them to herself a giant's spoil ; with a form of Religion haughty and insolent, that

[1] See Sermon of the Relation of Jesus to his Age and the Ages, by Theodore Parker, in Speeches, Vol. I. Art. I.

looked down on the divinities of Greece and Egypt, of
" Ormus and the Ind," and gave them a shelter in her capa-
cious robe : Rome, with her practised skill ; Rome, with
her eloquence ; Rome, with her pride ; Rome, with her
arms, hot from her conquest of a thousand kings. On the
same side were all the institutions of all the world ; its
fables, wealth, armies, pride, its folly, and its sin.

On the other hand, were a few Jewish fishermen, un-
taught, rude, and vulgar ; not free from gross errors ; despised at home, and not known abroad ; collected together
in the name of an enthusiastic young carpenter, who died
on the gallows fancying himself the Messiah and that the
world would perish soon—and whom they declared to be
risen from the dead ; men with no ritual, no learning, no
books, no brass in their purse, no philosophy in their
mind, no eloquence on their tongue. A Roman Sceptic
might tell how soon these fanatics would fall out, and destroy themselves, after serving as a terror to the maids
and a sport to the boys of a Jewish hamlet, and so that
" detestable superstition " come to an end ! A priest of
Jerusalem, with his oracular gossip, could tell how long
the Sanhedrim would suffer them to go at large, in the
name of " that deceiver," whose body " they stole away
by night ! " Alas for what man calls great ; the pride of
prejudice ; the boast of power. The fishermen of Galilee
have a truth the world has not, so they are stronger than
the world. Ten weak men may chain down a giant ; but
no combination of errors can make a Truth or put it
down ; no army of the ignorant equals one man who has
the Word of Life. Besides, all the old Truth in Judea,
Greece, Rome, was an auxiliary to favour the new Truth.

: The first preachers of Christianity had false notions on
many points ; they were full of Jewish fables and techni-
calities ; thought the world would soon end, and Jesus
come back " with power and great glory." Peter would
now and then lie to serve his turn ; Paul was passionate,
often one-sided, dogmatic, and mistaken ; Barnabas and
Mark could not agree. There was something of furious
enthusiasm in all these come-outers. James thunders like
a " Fanatic " or " Radical " at the rich man, not without
cause ; they soon had divisions and persecutions among
themselves, foes in the new household of Christianity.

But, spite of the follies or limitations of these earnest and manly Jews, a religious fire burned in their hearts; the Word of God grew and prevailed. The new doctrine passes from its low beginnings on the Galilean lake, step by step, through Jerusalem, Ephesus, Antioch, Alexandria, Corinth, Rome, till it ascends the throne of the world, and kings and empires lie prostrate at its feet.[1] But alas, as it spreads it is corrupted also. Judaism, Paganism, Idolatry, mingle their feculent scum with the living stream, and trouble still more and further the water of Life.

Christianity came to the world in the darkness of the nations; they had outgrown their old form, and looked for a new. They stood in the shadow of darkness, fearing to go back, not daring to look forward; they groped after God. The Piety and Morality which Jesus taught and lived came to the Nations as a beam of light shot into chaos; a strain of sweet music,—so silvery and soft we know not we are listening,—to him who wanders on amid the uncertain gloom, and charms him to the Light, to the River of God and the Tree of Life. It was the fulfilment of the prophecy of holy hearts, human Religion, human Morality, and above all things revealing the Greatness of Man.

It is sometimes feared that Christianity is in danger; that its days are numbered.[2] Of the Christianity of the Churches, no doubt it is true. That child of many fathers cannot die too soon. It cumbers the ground. The errors which Jesus taught will also fall and die. But Absolute Religion, Absolute Morality, cannot perish; never till Love, Goodness, Devotion, Faith, Reason, fail from the heart of man; never till God melts away and vanishes, and nothing takes the place of the All-in-All. Religion can no more be separated from the race than thought and feeling; nor Absolute Religion die out more than wisdom perish from among men. Man's words, thoughts, churches, fail and pass off like clouds from the sky that leave no track behind. But God's Word can

---

[1] Parker, Miscellanies, Art. I. and XI.
[2] See Comte and Leroux, ubi sup. passim, and de Potter, Hist. Philosophique politique et critique du Christianisme; Bruxelles, 1838, Vol. I. Introd. § 1.

never change. It shines perennial like the stars. Its testimony is in man's heart. None can outgrow it; none destroy. For eighteen hundred years, this Christianity of Christ has been in the world, to warn and encourage. Violence and Cunning, allies of Sin, have opposed. Every weapon Learning could snatch from the arsenals of the past, or Science devise anew, or Pride, and Cruelty, and Wit invent, has been used by mistaken men to destroy this fabric. Not a stone has fallen from the heavenly arch of real Religion; not a loophole been found where a shot could enter. But alas, vain doctrines, follies, absurdities, without count, have been piled against the temple of God, marring its beauteous shape. That Religion continues to live, spite of the traditions, fables, doctrines wrapped about it—is proof enough of its truth. Reason never warred against love of God and Man, never with the absolute Religion, but always with that of the Churches.[1] There is much destructive work still to be done, which scoffers will attempt, if wise religious men withhold the medicative hand.

Can Man destroy Absolute Religion? He cannot with all the arts and armies of the world destroy the pigment that colours an emmet's eye. He may obscure the Truth to his own mind. But it shines for ever unchanged. So boys of a summer's day throw dust above their heads, to blind the sun; they only hide it from their blinded eyes.[2]

---

[1] Even M. de Potter was only against Christianity "hierarchically organized." "Jesus and his principles of social equality, of universal brotherhood, are to him the meek, sublime manifestation of the moral man," ubi sup., Vol. I. p. ii.

[2] Parker, ubi sup., Art. VI., Of the Transient and Permanent in Christianity   See also Speeches and Occasional Sermons, Vol. I. Art. i. ii. xii.; Sermons of Theism, &c., Serm. III—VI.

BOOK IV.

"No man would be so ridiculous as (since Columbus discovered the new world of America, as big as the old, since the enlarged knowledge of the North of Europe, the South and East of Asia and Africa, besides the new divisions, names, and inhabitants of the old parts,) to forbid the reading of any more Geography than is found in Strabo, or Mela; or, since the Portuguese have sailed to the Indias by the Cape of Good Hope, to admit of no other Indian commodities than what are brought on Camels to Aleppo; or if posterity shall find out the North-east or North-west way to Cathajo and China, or shall cut the Isthmus between the Red Sea and the Mediterranean, will it be unlawful to use the advantage of such noble achievements? If any man love *acorns* since *corn* is invented, let him eat *acorns*; but it is very unreasonable he should forbid others the use of *wheat*. Whatever is *solid* in the writings of Aristotle, these new philosophers will readily embrace; and they that are most accused for affecting the *new*, doubt not but they can give as good an account of the *old philosophy* as their most violent accusers, and are probably as much conversant in Aristotle's writings, though they do not much value these small wares that are usually retailed by the generality of his interpreters." *A brief Account of the new sect of Latitudemen*, by G. B. Oxford, 1662, p. 13, 14.

BOOK IV.

CHAPTER I.

POSITION OF THE BIBLE——CLAIMS MADE FOR IT——STATEMENT
OF THE QUESTION.

VIEW it in what light we may, the Bible is a very surprising phenomenon. In all Christian lands, this collection of books is separated from every other, and called
sacred ; others are profane. Science may differ from them,
not from this. It is deemed a condescension on the part
of its friends, to show its agreement with Reason. How
much has been written by condescending theologians to
show the Bible was not inconsistent with the demonstrations of Newton! Should a man attempt to reëstablish
the cosmogonies of Hesiod and Sanchoniathon, to allego-
rize the poems of Anacreon and Theocritus as divines
mystify the Scripture, it would be said he wasted his oil,
and truly.[1]

This collection of books has taken such a hold on the
world as no other. The literature of Greece, which goes
up like incense from that land of temples and heroic deeds,
has not half the influence of this book from a nation alike
despised in ancient and modern times. It is read of a Sunday in all the thirty thousand pulpits of our land. In all

---

[1] See the recent literature relating to a Plurality of Worlds for another illustration.

14 *

the temples of Christendom is its voice lifted up, week by week. The sun never sets on its gleaming page. It goes equally to the cottage of the plain man and the palace of the king. It is woven into the literature of the scholar, and colours the talk of the street. The bark of the merchant cannot sail the sea without it; no ship of war goes to the conflict but the Bible is there! It enters men's closets; mingles in all the grief and cheerfulness of life. The affianced maiden prays God in Scripture for strength in her new duties; men are married by Scripture. The Bible attends them in their sickness; when the fever of the world is on them, the aching head finds a softer pillow if such leaves lie underneath. The mariner, escaping from shipwreck, clutches this first of his treasures, and keeps it sacred to God. It goes with the peddler, in his crowded pack; cheer him at eventide, when he sits down dusty and fatigued; brightens the freshness of his morning face. It blesses us when we are born; gives names to half Christendom; rejoices with us; has sympathy for our mourning; tempers our grief to finer issues. It is the better part of our sermons. It lifts man above himself; our best of uttered prayers are in its storied speech, wherewith our fathers and the patriarchs prayed. The timid man, about awaking from this dream of life, looks through the glass of Scripture and his eye grows bright; he does not fear to stand alone, to tread the way unknown and distant, to take the death-angel by the hand and bid farewell to wife, and babes, and home. Men rest on this their dearest hopes. It tells them of God, and of his blessed Son; of earthly duties and of heavenly rest. Foolish men find it the source of Plato's wisdom, and the science of Newton, and the art of Raphael; wicked men use it to rivet the fetters on the slave. Men who believe nothing else that is spiritual, believe the Bible all through; without this they would not confess, say they, even that there was a God.

Now for such effects there must be an adequate cause. That nothing comes of nothing is true all the world over. It is no light thing to hold, with an electric chain, a thousand hearts though but an hour, beating and bounding with such fiery speed. What is it then to hold the Christian world, and that for centuries? Are men fed with chaff and husks? The authors we reckon great, whose word is in the newspaper and the market-place, whose articulate breath now sways the nation's mind, will soon pass away, giving place to other great men of a season, who in their turn shall follow them to eminence, and then oblivion. Some thousand "famous writers" come up in this century, to be forgotten in the next. But the silver cord of the Bible is not loosed, nor its golden bowl broken, as Time chronicles his tens of centuries passed by. Has the human race gone mad? Time sits as a refiner of metal; the dross is piled in forgotten heaps, but the pure gold is reserved for use, passes into the ages, and is current a thousand years hence as well as to-day. It is only real merit that can long pass for such. Tinsel will rust in the storms of life. False weights are soon detected there. It is only a heart that can speak, deep and true, to a heart; a mind to a mind; a soul to a soul; wisdom to the wise, and religion to the pious. There must then be in the Bible, mind, conscience, heart and soul, wisdom and religion. Were it otherwise how could millions find it their lawgiver, friend, and prophet? Some of the greatest of human institutions seem built on the Bible; such things will not stand on heaps of chaff, but mountains of rocks.

What is the secret cause of this wide and deep influence? It must be found in the Bible itself, and must be adequate to the effect. To answer the question we must examine the Bible, and see whence it comes, what it contains, and by what authority it holds its place. If we look superficially, it is a collection of books in human language; from different authors and times; we refer it to a place amongst other books, and proceed to examine it as the works of Homer and Xenophon. But the popular opinion bids us beware, for we tread on holy ground. The opinion commonly expressed by the Protestant churches is this: The Bible is a miraculous collection of miraculous books; every word it contains was written by a miraculous inspiration from God, which was so full, complete, and infallible, that the authors delivered the truth and nothing but the truth; that the Bible contains no false statement of doctrine or fact, but sets forth all religious and moral truth which man needs, or which it is possible for him to receive in,

and no particle of error :—therefore that the Bible is the
only authoritative rule of religious faith and practice.[1] To
doubt this is reckoned a dangerous error, if not an unpar-
donable sin. This is the supernatural view. Some scholars
slyly reject the divine authority of the Old Testament.
Others reject it openly, but cling strongly as ever to the
New. Some make a distinction between the genuine and
the spurious books of the New Testament; thus there is a
difference in the less or more of an inspired and miraculous
canon. The modern Unitarians have perhaps reduced the
Scripture to its lowest terms. But Protestants, in general,
in America, agree that in the whole or in part the Bible is
an infallible and exclusive standard of religious and moral
truth. The Bible is master to the Soul; superior to Intellect; truer than Conscience; greater and more trustworthy than the Affections and the Soul.

Accordingly, with strict logical consistency, a peculiar
method is used both in the criticism and interpretation of
the Bible; such as men apply to no other ancient documents. A deference is paid to it wholly independent of its
intrinsic merit. It is presupposed that each book within
the lids of the Bible has an absolute right to be there, and
each sentence or word therein is infallibly true.[2] Reason
has nothing to do in the premises, but accept the written
statement of "the Word;" the duty of belief is just the

---

[1] It is scarce necessary to cite authorities to prove this statement, as it is a
notorious fact. But see the most obvious sources, Westminster Catechism,
Quest. 2; Calvin's Institutes, Book I. ch. vi.—ix.; Knapp, ubi sup., § 1—13,
especially Vol. I. p. 130, et seq. See also Gaussen's Theopneusty, or the plenary
Inspiration of the Holy Scriptures, translated by E. N. Kirk, New York, 1842.
The latter maintains that "all the written Word is inspired of God even to a
single iota or tittle," p. 333, and passim. See Musculus, Loci communes, ed.
1564, p. 178. But see also Faustus Socinus, De Auctoritate Sac. Scrip. in
Bibliotheca Fratrr. Polon. Vol. I.; Limborch, Theol. Lib. I.; Episcopius, In-
stit. P. IV.

[2] The writings of most of the early Unitarians are exceptions to this general
rule. They attempted to separate the spurious from the genuine. See earlier
numbers of the Christian Examiner, passim; Norton, Statement of Reasons,
&c., p. 136, et seq.; Evidences of the Genuineness of the Gospels, Vol. I. p.
liii. et seq. See especially p. lxi. Vol. II. p. cliv., clxii., cxciii., and the whole
of the additional note on the O. T., p. xlviii., et seq.; Internal Evidences, &c.
(1855), p. 13; and Translation of the Gospels (1855), Vol. II. note E. See
also Stuart, Critical History and Defence of the O. T. Canon, Andover, 1845.
Dr. Palfrey, ubi sup., denies the miraculous inspiration of all the Old Testament,
except the last four books of Moses, and there diminishes its intensity.

same whether the Word contradicts Reason and Conscience, or agrees with them.[1]

This opinion about the Bible is true, or not true. If true it is capable of proof, at least of being shown to be probable. Now there are but four possible ways of establishing the fact, namely :—

1. By the authority of Churches, having either a miraculous inspiration, or a miraculous tradition, to prove the alleged infallibility of the Bible. But the Churches are not agreed on this point. The Roman Church very stoutly denies the fact, and besides, the Protestants deny the authority of the Roman Church.

2. By the direct testimony of God in our Consciousness assuring us of the miraculous infallibility of the Bible. This would be at the best one miracle to prove another, which is not logical. The proof is only subjective, and is as valuable to prove the divinity of the Koran, the Shaster, and the Book of Mormon, as that of the Jewish and Christian Scriptures. It is the argument of the superstitious and enthusiastical.

3. By the fact that the Bible claims this divine infallibility. This is reasoning in a circle, though it is the method commonly relied on by Christians. It will prove as well the divinity of any impostor who claims it.[2]

4. By an examination of the contents of the Bible, and the external history of its origin. To proceed in this way, we must ask, Are all its statements infallibly true? But to ask this question presupposes the standard-measure is in ourselves, not in the Bible ; so at the utmost the Book can be no more infallible, and have no more authority, than Reason and the Moral Sense by which we try it. A single mistake condemns its infallibility, and of course its divinity. But the case is still worse. After the truth of a book is made out, before a work in human language, like other books, can be referred to God as its author, one of two things must be shown : either That its contents could not

---

[1] See Gaussen, ubi sup. ; Horne, Introduction to the Holy Scriptures, Philad. 1840, Vol. I. p. 1—187.

[2] See this claim made in the Koran, Sales's translation, London, new edition, p. 162, et seq., 206, 372, 400, 152, &c., 219, 127, et al., and the Book of Mormon, (Nauvoo, 1840,) passim.

have come from man, and then it follows by implication
that they came from God; or That at a certain time and
place, God did miraculously reveal the contents of the
book.

Now it is a notorious fact, first, that it has not been and
cannot be proved, that every statement in the Bible is
true; or, secondly, that its contents, such as they are,
could not have proceeded from man, under the ordinary
influence of God; or, finally, that any one book or word
of the Bible was miraculously revealed to man. In the absence of proof for any one of these three points, it has been
found a more convenient way to assume the truth of them
all, and avoid troublesome questions.[1]

Laying aside all prejudices, if we look into the Bible in
a general way, as into other books, we find facts which
force the conclusion upon us, that the Bible is a human
work, as much as the Principia of Newton or Descartes,
or the Vedas and Koran. Some things are beautiful and
true, but others no man, in his reason, can accept. Here
are the works of various writers, from the eleventh century
before to the second century after Christ, thrown ca-
priciously together, and united by no common tie but the
lids of the bookbinder. Here are two forms of Religion,
which differ widely, set forth and enforced by miracles;
the one ritual and formal, the other actual and spiritual;
the one the religion of Fear, the other of Love; one final,
and resting entirely on the special revelation made to
Moses, the other progressive, based on the universal revelation of God, who enlightens all that come into the world;
one offers only earthly recompense, the other makes immortality a motive to a divine life; one compels men, the
other invites them. One half the Bible repeals the other
half. The Gospel annihilates the Law; the Apostles take
the place of the Prophets, and go higher up. If Christianity and Judaism be not the same thing, there must be
hostility between the Old Testament and the New Testament, for the Jewish form claims to be eternal. To an
unprejudiced man this hostility is very obvious. It may
indeed be said Christianity came not to destroy the Law

---

[1] See some pertinent remarks in J. H. Thom's Life of Joseph Blanco White,
London, 1845, Vol. I. p. 275, et seq., Vol. II. p. 18, et seq., and the remarks
of Mr Norton, p. 250, et seq.; De Wette, Wesen, § 6.

and the Prophets, but to fulfil them, and the answer is plain, their historic fulfilment was their destruction.

If we look at the Bible as a whole, we find numerous contradictions; conflicting Histories which no skill can reconcile with themselves or with facts; Poems which the Christians have agreed to take as histories, but which lead only to confusion on that hypothesis; Prophecies that have never been fulfilled, and from the nature of things never can be.[1] We find stories of miracles which could not have happened; accounts which represent the laws of nature completely transformed, as in fairy-land, to trust the tales of the old romancers; stories that make God a man of war, cruel, capricious, revengeful, hateful, and not to be trusted. We find amatory songs, selfish proverbs, sceptical discourses, and the most awful imprecations human fancy ever clothed in speech. Connected with these are lofty thoughts of Nature, Man, and God; devotion touching and beautiful, and a most reverent faith. Here are works whose authors are known; others, of which the author, age, and country are alike forgotten. Genuine and spurious works, religious and not religious, are strangely mixed. But the subject demands a more minute and detailed examination in each of its main parts.

[1] It is instructive to see that the Greeks sometimes regarded the writings of Homer with the same superstitious veneration which is often paid to the Bible. They found therein the Neptunian and Vulcanian theory; the sphericity of the earth; the doctrines of Democritus, Heraclitus, and of Socrates and Plato in their turn. See Heraclides Ponticus, Alleg. Hom. in Gale, ubi sup. p. 436, et seq., 488, et seq. Pausanias, IX. 41, p. 452, ed. Schubert, seriously urges the question whether any works from the Shop of Vulcan were then in existence. According to Aristotle, (de Part. Animal. III. 10, p. 87, ed. Bekker,) some concluded in his time that the human head could speak when separated from the body—and that on the authority of Homer, "*And while he speaks his head was mingled with the dust.*" Ilias X. 427. Some quoted Homer to show that Horses had spoken—as some divines quote Moses to prove the same of the Ass.

CHAPTER II.

AN EXAMINATION OF THE CLAIMS OF THE OLD TESTAMENT TO
BE A DIVINE, MIRACULOUS, OR INFALLIBLE COMPOSITION.

It is not possible to prove directly the divine and miraculous character of the Old Testament by showing that God miraculously revealed it to the writers thereof, for we do not know who were the writers of the greater part of the books; and when the authors are known, it is only by their own testimony, which we have no right to assume to be infallible. We have not the faintest direct evidence to show there was anything miraculous in their composition. The indirect evidence may be reduced to two branches :—first that which shows that all the statements of the Old Testament are true, and second that which shows it contains statements of things above human apprehension. From the nature of the case, the former proposition cannot be proved, since many things treated of in the Bible are known to us by that book alone. To say they are true, is to assume the fact at issue. Besides, a true statement is not necessarily miraculous; if it were, the multiplication table of Pythagoras would be a divine and miraculous composition. The latter proposition has also its difficulty. How do we know its statements are above human apprehension? But suppose they are, how do we know they are true? These difficulties are insuperable. To assume the divinity of the Old Testament is quite as absurd as to assume the same for the next book that shall be printed; to declare it miraculous on account of the beautiful piety in some parts of it is as foolish as to make the same claim for the Geometry of Euclid and the Poems of Homer, on account of their great excellence; to admit this claim because made by some of the Jews, is no more wise than to admit the claims of the Zoroastrian records and the Sibylline oracles, and the religious books of all nations; then, among so many, one is of no value, for the very excellence of a miraculous work is thought to consist in the fact of its being the only miraculous work.

To leave these assumptions and come to facts, this general thesis may be laid down, and maintained: Every book of the Old Testament bears distinct marks of its human origin; some of human folly and sin; all of human weakness and imperfection. If this thesis be true, the Bible is not the direct work of God; not the master of the Mind and Conscience, Heart and Soul of man. To prove this proposition it is necessary to go into some details. The Hebrews divided their scriptures into the Law, the Prophets, and the Writings, to each of which they assigned a peculiar degree of inspiration. The Law was infallibly inspired, God speaking with Moses face to face; the Prophets less perfectly, God addressing them by visions and dreams; the Writings still more feebly, God communicating to their authors by figures and enigmas.[1] This ancient division may well enough be followed in this discussion.

I. *Of the Law.*

This comprises the first five books of the Bible. They are commonly ascribed to Moses; but there is no proof that he wrote a word of them. Only the Decalogue, in a compendious form, and perhaps a few fragments, can be referred to him with much probability. From the use of peculiar words, from local allusions, and other incidental signs, it is plain here are fragments from several different writers, who lived no one knows when or where, their names perfectly unknown to us. They all bear marks of an age much later than that of Moses, as any one familiar with ancient history, and free from prejudice, may see on examination.[2]

But if they were written by Moses, we are not, on the bare word of a writer, to admit the miraculous infallibility

[1] See Philo, De Monarch. I. p. 820; De Vita Mosis, III. p. 681, II. p. 666, et seq.; Josephus, Cont. Apion, I. 8.

[2] The proofs of this assertion cannot be adduced in a brief discourse like the present; see thereon de Wette, Introduction to the O. T., tr. by Theo. Parker, Vol. II. § 138, et seq.

of his statements.   Besides, the character of the books is such that a very high place is not to be assigned them among human compositions, measured by the standard of the present day.   The first chapter of Genesis, if taken as a history, in the unavoidable sense of its terms, is at variance with facts.   It relates that God created the sun, moon, stars, and earth, and gave the latter its plants, animals, and men, in six days; while science proves that many thousands, if not millions of years must have passed between the creation of the first plants, and man, the crown of creation; that the surface of the earth gradually received its present form, one race of plants after the other sprang up, animals succeeded animals, the simpler first, then the more complex, and at last came man.   This chapter tells of an ocean of water above our heads, separated from us by a solid expanse, in which the greater and lesser lights are fixed; that there was evening and morning before there was a sun to cause the difference between day and night; that the sun and stars were created after the earth, for the earth's convenience; and that God ceased his action, and rested on the seventh day and refreshed himself. Here the Bible is at variance with science, which is Nature stated in exact language.   Few men will say directly what the schoolmen said to Galileo, "If Nature is opposed to the Bible then Nature is mistaken, for the Bible is certainly right;" but the popular view of the Bible logically makes that assertion.   Truth and the book of Genesis cannot be reconciled, except on the hypothesis that the Bible means anything it can be made to mean,[1] but then it means nothing.

A similar decision must be pronounced upon many accounts in the Law,—on the creation of woman; the

---

[1] See Augustine, Confessiones, Lib. XII. C. 18, et al. See in Whewell's Philosophy of the Inductive Sciences, Lond. 1840, Vol. II. p. 137, et seq., the remarkable chapter on "the Relation of Tradition to Palæontology." He thinks the interpretation of the Scriptures ought to change to suit the advance of physical science; and quotes, approvingly, the celebrated expression of Bellarmine: "When a demonstration shall be found to establish the Earth's motion, it will be proper to interpret the Sacred Scriptures otherwise than they have hitherto been interpreted in those passages where mention is made of the stability of the Earth and movement of the Heavens." Thus he makes the interpretation of the Bible purely arbitrary: you can interpret *into* it, or *out of* it, what you will. If you may so deal with the Bible why not with Homer, Plato, Milton, and Hobbes? In fact, the sound interpretation of the Bible is no more arbitrary than that of Lyttleton's Tenures, and that of Nature itself.

story of the garden, the temptation and fall of man; the
appearances of God in human shape, eating and drinking
with his favourite, and making covenants; the story of the
flood and the ark; the miraculous birth of Isaac; the promise to the patriarchs; the great age of mankind; the
tower of Babel and confusion of tongues; the sacrifice of
Isaac; the history of Joseph; of Moses; the ten plagues
miraculously sent; the wonderful passage of the Red Sea;
the support of the Hebrews in the wilderness on manna;
the miraculous supply of food, water, and clothing, and
the delivery of the Law at Mount Sinai.[1] On these it is
needless to dwell. But there is one account in the Law too
significant to be passed over. It is briefly this.[2] As the
Jews approached the land of Canaan, Moses sent twelve
men, " heads of the children of Israel," to examine the
land, and report to the people. They spent a long time in
their tour, reported that the land was fertile, exhibited
specimens of its productions, but added, it was full of
warlike nations. The Jews were afraid to invade it;
" They wept all night and said, Would God we had
died in the land of Egypt." They rebelled, and wished
to choose a leader and return. Moses and Aaron, and
Caleb and Joshua—two of the twelve messengers—
urge them to battle, and say, " Jehovah is with us." The
people refuse, and would stone them. Then the glory of
Jehovah appeared before the face of the people, and God
says to Moses, " How long will this people provoke
me ? . . . I will smite them with the pestilence and disin-
herit them, and make of thee a greater nation and mightier
than they." But Moses, more merciful than his God,
attempts to appease the Deity, and that by an appeal to
his vanity; And Moses said unto Jehovah, Then the Egyptians shall hear of it, and they will tell it to the inhabitants
of this land. . . . Now if thou shalt kill all this people as
one man, then the nations will speak, saying, Because
Jehovah was not able to bring this people into the land he
sware unto them, therefore he hath slain them." Then
he proceeds to soothe his Deity; " Pardon the iniquity of
this people;" " Jehovah is long-suffering and of great

[1] See Geddes, Critical Remarks on the Hebrew Scriptures, Lond. 1800;
Holy Bible, &c., &c. See some valuable remarks in Palfrey, ubi sup. Vol. II.
p. 133; Norton, Vol. II. Note D. [2] Numbers xiv.

mercy, forgiving iniquity and transgression, but by no means clearing the guilty." Jehovah consents, but adds, "As truly as I live, all the earth shall be filled with the glory of Jehovah," but "because all these men . . . have tempted me now these ten times, . . . surely they shall not see the land which I sware unto their fathers, . . . your carcasses shall fall in this wilderness, . . . in this wilderness they shall be consumed, and there they shall die."

If an unprejudiced Christian were to read this for the first time in a heathen writer, and it was related of Kronos or Moloch, he would say, What foul ideas those heathens had of God; thank Heaven we are Christians, and cannot believe in a deity so terrible. It is true there are now pious men, who believe the story to the letter, profess to find comfort therein, and count it part of their Christianity to believe it. But is God angry with men; passionate, revengeful; offended because they will not war, and butcher the innocent? Would he violate his perfect law and by a miracle destroy a whole nation, millions of men, women, and children, because they fall into a natural fit of despair, and refuse to trust ten witnesses rather than two witnesses? Does God require man's words to restrain his rage, violence, and a degree of fury which Nero and Caracalla, butchers of Men though they were, would have shuddered to think of? Is He to be teased and coaxed from murder? Are we called on to believe this in the name of Christianity? Then perish Christianity from the face of earth, and let Man learn of his Religion and his God from the stars and the violet, the lion and the lamb. View this as the savage story of some oriental who attributed a bloodthirsty character to his God, and made a Deity in his own image, and it is a striking remnant of barbarism that has passed away, not destitute of dramatic interest; not without its melancholy moral. There are some things which may be true, but must be rejected for lack of evidence to prove them true; but this story no amount of evidence could make credible.

Throughout the whole of the Law, fact and fiction, history and mythology, are so intimately blended, that it seems impossible to tell where one begins and the other ends. The laws are not perfect; they contain a mingling of good and bad, wise and absurd, and if men will maintain that God is their author, we must still apply to them the words which Ezekiel puts in his mouth :[1] "I gave them statutes that were not good, and judgments whereby they should not live ;" or say with Jeremiah, "-I spake not unto your fathers in the day that I brought them up out of Egypt, concerning burnt-offerings, or sacrifices."

II. *Of the Prophets.*

The Hebrews divide the prophets into the earlier and the later : the first including the four historical works of Joshua, Judges, Samuel, and the Kings ; the second, the prophets properly so called, with the exception of Daniel, the three major, the twelve minor prophets.

1. *Of the Early Prophets.*

No one knows the date or the author of any one of these books ; they all contain historical matter of doubtful character, such as the miraculous passage of the Jordan ; the destruction of Jericho ; the standing still of the sun and moon at the command of Joshua ; the story of Samson ; the destruction of the Benjamites ; the birth and calling of Samuel ; the wonders wrought by the Ark ; the story of Saul, David, and Goliah, the miraculous pestilence, of Solomon, Elijah, Elisha, and others. Of all these, perhaps the story of Samson is the most strikingly absurd,—a man of miraculous birth and miraculous strength, whose ability lay in his long hair, and which went from him when his locks were shorn off. When we read in Hesiod and elsewhere, the birth and exploits of Hercules,—who bears a resemblance to Samson in some respects, though vastly his superior on the whole—we refer the tale to human fancy in a low stage of civilization ; a mind free from prejudice will do the same with the story of Samson.[2] No one can reasonably contend that it requires a mind miraculously enlightened to produce such books as these of the early prophets. They belong to the

---

[1] Ezekiel, ch. xx. 25 ; Jer. vii. 22.
[2] See Palfrey, ubi sup., Vol. II. p. 194, et seq., and on these books in general, p. 134—300 ; Horne, ubi sup., Vol. II. p. 216, et seq.

fabulous period of Jewish history. Mythology, poetry, fact, and fiction, are strangely woven together. The authors, whoever they were, claim no inspiration. However, as a general rule, they contain less to offend a religious mind than the books of the Law.

2. *The Prophets, properly so called.*

It may be said of these writings, in general, that they contain nothing above the reach of human faculties. Here are noble and spirit-stirring appeals to men's conscience, patriotism, honour, and religion ; beautiful poetic descriptions, odes, hymns, expressions of faith, almost beyond praise. But the mark of human infirmity is on them all, and proofs or signs of miraculous inspiration are not found in them. In the minor prophets, there is nothing worthy of special notice in this place, unless it be the story of Jonah, which is unique in the ancient Hebrew literature, and tells its own tale.[1] These books do not require a detailed examination.[2] The greater prophets, Isaiah, Jeremiah, and Ezekiel, are more important, and require a more minute notice. In these, as well as in other prophetical books, and the Law, claim is apparently made to miraculous inspiration. "Thus saith Jehovah," is the authority to which the prophet appeals ; "Jehovah said unto me," "The command of Jehovah came unto me," "I saw in a vision," "The spirit of Jehovah came upon me." These and similar expressions occur often in the prophets. But do these phrases denote a claim to miraculous inspiration as we understand it ? We limit miraculous inspiration to a few cases, where something is to be done above human ability. Not so the Hebrews ; they did not make a sharp distinction between the miraculous and the common. All religious and moral power was regarded as the direct gift of God ; an outpouring of his spirit. God teaches David to fight ; commands Gideon to select his soldiers, to arise

---

[1] Pausanias says he saw a dolphin carry a boy on his back as a recompense for being healed of a wound by the boy ! Lib. III., C. 25, p. 573. A man who should believe such a story on such evidence would be thought not a little credulous by the men who declare it dangerous to doubt the stories in Jonah and Daniel. See too Pausanias, Lib. I. C. 44, § 8, and X. C. 13, § 10.

[2] For this, see De Wette, Introd. Vol. II., and Palfrey, ubi sup., Vol. II. p. 362, et seq.

in the night and attack the foe. The Lord set his enemies to fight amongst themselves. He teaches Bezaleel and Aholiab. They, and all the ingenious mechanics, are filled with "the spirit of God." The same "spirit of the Lord" enables Samson to kill a lion, and many men. These instances show with what latitude the phrase is used, and how loose were the notions of inspiration.[1] The Greeks also referred their works to the aid of Phœbus, Pallas, Vulcan, or Olympian Jove, in the same way.

It has never been rendered probable that the phrase, Thus saith the Lord, and its kindred terms, were understood by the prophets or their hearers to denote any miraculous agency in the case. They employ language with the greatest freedom. Thus a writer says, "I saw Jehovah sitting upon a throne, high and lifted up, and his train filled the temple; above it stood the seraphim." No thinking man would suppose the prophet designed to assert a fact, or that his countrymen understood him to do so. Certainly it is insulting to suppose a philosophic man would believe God sat on a throne, with a troop of courtiers around him, like a Persian king. When a prophet says Jehovah appeared to him in a dream, he can only mean, either he dreamed Jehovah appeared, which is somewhat different, or that he chose this symbolical way of stating his opinion. Thus a Grecian prophet might say, "The muse came down from high Olympus' shaggy top, and whispered unto me, her favourite son."[2] Not stating a fact, he would give an outness to what passed in his mind. However, if these writers claimed miraculous inspiration ever so strongly, we are not to grant it unless they abide the test mentioned above.

If they utter predictions—which they rarely attempt— we are not to assume their fulfilment, and then conclude the prophet was miraculously inspired, common as the method is. But what is the value of the claim made for them? Has any one of them ever uttered a distinct, definite, and unambiguous prediction of any future event that has since taken place, which a man without a miracle

---

[1] See Glassius, Philologia sacra, ed. Dathe, Vol. II. p. 815, et seq.; Bauer, Theologie des A. T., § 51—54, et al.
[2] See Cicero, De Nat. Deorum, Lib. I. ch. i. and ii.; Ovid, Metamorph. Lib. II. 640, et seq.

could not equally well predict ?   It has never been shown.
Most of the prophetic writings relate to the past and the
present ; to the political, civil, and moral condition of the
people, at the time ; they exhort backsliding Israel to forsake his idols, return to Jehovah, live wisely and well.
They state the result of obedience or of disobeying, for individuals and the nation.   It is rare they predict distinctly
and definitely any specific event ; sometimes they foretell,
in the most general terms, good or ill fortune, the destruction of a city, the defeat of an army, the downfal of a
king.   But in case the prediction came to pass, who shall
tell us, at this distance of time, that it was not either a
lucky hit, or the result of sagacious insight ?   Certainly
the supposition is against a miracle. The Tripod of Delphi
delivered some oracles that were extraordinarily felicitous ;
Seneca made a very clear prediction of the discovery of
America, and Lactantius of the rise and downfal of Napoleon, and Lotichius of the capture of Magdeburg.   Does
the fulfilment prove the miraculous inspiration of the
oracle in these cases ? [1]

But to recur to the other test, there are statements in
the prophets which are not true ; predictions that did not
come to pass.   Under this rubric may be placed three of
the most celebrated oracles in the Old Testament.

1. *Jeremiah's Prediction of the Seventy Years of Exile.*

It was an easy thing in Jeremiah's position to see that
the little nation of Judea could not hold out against the
Babylonian forces, and therefore must experience the common fate of nations they conquered, and be carried into
exile.[2]   But would the Lord forsake his people ; the seed
of Abraham ?   A pious Jew could not believe it.   It was
unavoidable, with the common opinion of his countrymen,
that he should expect their subsequent restoration.   But
why predict an exile of just seventy years, unless miraculously directed ? [3]   He may have used that term for an indefinite period ; a common practice.   In that case there is

---

[1] See De Wette, ubi sup., Vol. II. § 201, et seq.
[2] On this custom of the Chaldees, see Heeren, Ideen, Vol. I. ; Gesenius On
Isa. xxxvi. 16.
[3] Jer. xxv.

no miracle. But on the other hand, if he predicted an exile of just seventy years, the oracle was a failure. The people were not carried into captivity all at once. From which of the two or three times of deportation shall we set out? The books of Kings and Chronicles differ some-what.[1] But to take the chronology of Jeremiah himself, if the passage be genuine;[2] the deportation began in the seventh year of Nebuchadnezzar, 599 before Christ; it was continued in the year 588, and concluded in 583. The exile ended in the year 536. The longest period that can be made out extends to but sixty-three, and the shortest to but forty-seven years. To make out the seventy years we must date arbitrarily from the year 606.

2. *Ezekiel's Oracle against Tyre.*

This prophet predicts that Nebuchadnezzar shall destroy Tyre.[3] The prediction is clear and distinct; the destruction is to be complete and total. " With the hoofs of his horses shall he tread down all thy streets; he shall slay thy people by the sword, and thy strong garrison shall go down to the ground. . . . I will make thee like the top of a rock; thou shalt be to spread nets upon; thou shalt be built up no more." But it was not so. Nebuchadnezzar was obliged to raise the siege after investing the city for thirteen years, and go and fight the Egyptians. Then six-teen years after the first oracle, Ezekiel takes back his own words: " The word of the Lord came unto me, saying, Son of man, Nebuchadnezzar . . . caused his army to serve a great service against Tyrus; every head was made bald," with the chafing of the helmet, " every shoulder was peeled," with the pressure of burdens; " yet he had no wages, nor his army from Tyrus. . . .Therefore, behold, I will give the land of Egypt unto Nebuchadnezzar."[4]

These things speak for themselves, and show the nature of the prophetic discourses, that they were moral ad-dresses, or poetical odes. Ezekiel's celebrated prediction

---

[1] See 2 Kings xxiv. xxv.; 2 Chron. xxxvi.
[2] Jer. lii. 28—30; but see verses 4—15. See the forced combinations in Jahn's Hebrew Commonwealth, Ch. V. § 43.
[3] xxvi. 1, et seq.
[4] xxix. 17, et seq. See Isaiah xxiii., and Gesenius's remarks, in his Commentar., Vol. i. p. 711, et seq.; Rosenmüller, Alterth. Vol. II. pt. i. p. 34.

of an impossible city,[1] is a standing monument of the prophetic character, and of the lasting folly of interpreters. It were easy to collect other instances of palpable mistake.[2]

3. *The alleged Predictions of Jesus as the Messiah.*

The Messianic prophecies are the most famous of all. It is commonly pretended that there are in the Old Testament clear and distinct predictions of Jesus of Nazareth. But I do not hesitate to say, it has never been shown that there is, in the whole of the Old Testament, one single sentence that in the plain and natural sense of the words foretells the birth, life, or death of Jesus of Nazareth.   If the Scripture have seventy-two senses, as one of the Rabbins declares, or if it foretell whatever comes to pass, as Augustine has said, and means all it can be made to mean, as many moderns seem to think, why predictions and types of Jesus may be found in the first chapter of Genesis, in Noah and Abraham and Samson, as well as in Virgil's fourth Eclogue, the Odes of Horace, and the story of the Trihemerine Hercules.

The Messianic expectations and prophecies seem to have originated in this way : After the happy and successful period of David and Solomon, the kingdom was divided into Judah and Israel, the two tribes and the ten, the national prosperity declined.   Pious men hoped for better times ; they naturally connected these hopes with a personal deliverer ; a descendant of David, their most popular king.   The deliverer would unite the two kingdoms under the old form.   A poetic fancy endowed him with wonderful powers ; made him a model of goodness.   Different poets arrayed their expected hero in imaginary drapery to suit their own conceptions.   Malachi gives him a forerunner.   The Jews were the devoutest of nations ; the popular deliverer must be a religious man.   They were full of pious faith ; so the darker the present, the brighter shone the Pharos of Hope in the future.   Sometimes this de-

---

[1] Ch. xl.—xlviii.
[2] On the Prophecies in general, see the Essay of Prof. Stuart, in Bib. Rep., Vol. II. p. 217, et seq. ; of Hengstenberg, ibid. p. 139, et seq ; Noyes in Christian Examiner, Vol. XVI. p. 321, et seq.   See also the able Essay of Knobel, Prophetismus der Hebräer, Vol. I. Einleit.

liverer was called the Messiah; this term is not common in the Old Testament, however, but is sometimes applied to Cyrus by the Pseudo-Isaiah.[1]

These hopes and predictions of a deliverer involved several important things : A reunion of the divided tribes; a return of the exiles; the triumph and extension of the kingdom of Israel, its eternal duration and perfect happiness; idolatry was to be rooted out; the nations improved in morals and religion; Truth and Righteousness were to reign; Jehovah to be reconciled with his people; all of them were to be taught of God; other nations were to come up to Jerusalem, and be blessed. But the Mosaic Law was to be eternal; the old ritual to last for ever; Jerusalem to be the capital of the Messianic kingdom, and the Jewish nation to be reëstablished in greater pomp than in the times of David. Are these predictions of Jesus of Nazareth? He was not the Messiah of Jewish expectation and of the prophets' foretelling. The furthest from it possible. The predictions demanded a political and visible kingdom in Palestine, with Jerusalem for its capital, and its ritual the old Law. The kindgom of Jesus is not of this world. The ten tribes—have they come back to the home of their fathers? They have perished and are swallowed up in the tide of the nations, no one knowing the place of their burial. The kingdom of the two tribes soon went to the ground. These are notorious facts. The Jews are right when they say their predicted Messiah has not come. Does the Old Testament foretell a suffering Saviour, his kingdom not of this world; crucified; raised from the dead? The idea is foreign to the Hebrew Scriptures. Well might a Jew ask, "Wilt thou at this time restore the kingdom to Israel?" To trust the uncertain record of the New Testament, Jesus was slow to accept the name of the Messiah; he knew the "people would take him by force and make him a king." But what means the triumphal entry into Jerusalem? He forbids his disciples to speak of his Messiahship—"See that thou tell no man of it;" lets John draw his own inference, whether or not he must "look for another;" thinks Simon Peter could only find it out by inspiration. Was it that

[1] Many chapters of Isaiah have been shown to be spurious. The passages, Chapter xli.—lxvi., xiii. xiv., xxiii.—xxvii., xxxiv. xxxv., are of this character.

he knew he was not the Messiah of the prophets, and so never formally assumed the title ; but, knowing that he was a true deliverer, far greater than their impossible Messiah, first suffered the name to be affixed to him, and then made the most of the popular Idea ?   Or, was he himself mistaken ? It concerns us little ; but this remains, that he was much more than the Jews looked for.   The Jewish Christians mistook the matter ; Paul would prove that he was the Messiah of the prophets.   Mistakes in Theology, like bits of glass in a kaleidoscope, are repeated again and again, in fantastic combinations.[1]

III. *The Writings.*

Under this head are comprised the remaining books of the Old Testament.   Here is the dramatic poem of Job, a work of surprising beauty, and full of truth.   But its author denies the immortality of the soul, and though he attempts " to justify the ways of God to man," he yet leaves the question as undecided as he found it.

In the Psalms we have beautiful prayers, mixed up with their local occasions ; penitential hymns, songs of praise, expressions of hope, faith, trust in God, that have never been surpassed.   The devotion of some of these sweet lyrics is beyond praise.   But at the same time here are the most awful denunciations that speech ever spoke.   In the following passage the writer denounces his enemies.[2] " Set thou a wicked man over him.   Let Satan stand at his right hand ; when he shall be judged, let him be condemned, and let his prayer become sin.   Let his days be few ; let another take his office. Let his children be fatherless, and his wife a widow. Let his children be continually vagabonds and beg. . . . Let there be none to extend mercy unto him, neither let there be any to favour his fatherless children."   These are the words of a man angry and revengeful.   The Psalms abound with similar impre-

---

[1] See De Wette, Dogmatik, § 137—142 ; Opuscula, I. p. 23—31 ; the numerous Christologies of modern times, and the introductions to the Old Testament.   See also Strauss, Life of Jesus, § 60—68 ; Hennell, ubi sup. Chap. i. ii. and xii. xiii. ; Bretschneider, Dogmatik, § 30, 34, (p. 356, et seq.,) § 137, (p. 166, et seq.) ; Hahn, Knapp, Hase, Wegscheider, &c., and Hengstenberg's Christology.

[2] Ps. cix. 6, et seq.   See also Ps. cxxxvii.

cations. To maintain they came directly from the God of
love is to forget Reason, Conscience, and Religion, which
teach us to love our enemies, to pray for them that persecute us.

The book of Proverbs and the Song of Songs speak for
themselves, and neither need nor claim any more inspiration than other collections of Proverbs or Oriental amatory
Idyls. The latter belongs to the same class with the writings of Anacreon. The somewhat doubtful book of Eccle-
siastes seems to be the work of a sceptic. He denies the
immortality of the soul with great clearness; thinks wisdom and folly are alike vanity. Though he concludes most
touchingly in praise of virtue on the whole, and declares
the fear of God and keeping his commandments is the
whole duty of man, yet this conclusion is vitiated by the
former precept, "Be not righteous overmuch." The La-
mentations of Jeremiah have as little claim to inspiration.[1]

The historical books of this division present some peculiarities. Ezra and Nehemiah are valuable historical documents, though implicit faith is by no means to be placed
in them. The book of Esther is entirely devoid of religious
interest, and seems to be a romance designed to show that
the Jews will always be provided for. The brief book of
Ruth may be an historical or a fictitious work.

The book of Daniel is a perfect unique in the Old Testament. It professes to have been written by a captive Jew,
at Babylon, in the beginning of the sixth century before
Christ; it contains accounts of surprising miracles, dreams,
visions, men cast into a den of lions and a furnace of fire,
yet escaping unhurt; a man transformed to a beast, and
eating grass like an ox for some years, and then restored
to human shape; a miraculous and spectral hand writing
on the palace wall; grotesque fancies that remind us of
the Arabian Nights, and the Talmud.[2] To judge from internal evidence, it was written in the first part of the
second century, perhaps about one hundred and eighty-
seven years before Christ, in the time of Antiochus Epiph-
anes. The author seems to have a political and moral end

[1] See Leclerc's Five Letters concerning the Inspiration, &c., London, 1690;
and on the other hand, William Lowth's Vindication of the Divine Authority,
&c., Lond., 1699; and Gaussen, Horne, and Stuart, ubi sup.
[2] See De Wette, Vol. II. § 257, p. 505, note a, and Pliny, VIII. 34.

in view, and to write for the encouragement of his countrymen, perhaps designing his work should pass for what it
is, a politico-religious romance.[1]

All of these books hitherto mentioned seem written by
earnest men, with no intention to deceive. Their manly
honesty is everywhere apparent. But the book of Chronicles is of a very different character. Here is an obvious
attempt on the writer's part to exalt the character of orthodox kings, and depress that of heretical kings; to bring
forward the Priests and the Levites, and give everything
a ceremonial appearance. This design will be obvious to
any one who reads the stories in Chronicles, and then
turns to the parallel passages in Samuel and Kings.[2] To
take but a single instance: the writer of the book of
Samuel gives an account of David; tells of his good and
evil qualities; does not pass over his cruelty, nor extenu-
ate his sin. But in Chronicles there is not a word of this:
nothing of the crime of imperial adultery; nothing of
Nathan's rousing apologue, and Thou-art-the-man. The
thing speaks for itself.

Now if these books have any divine authority, what
shall we do with such contradictions; deny the fact? We
live too long after Dr Faustus for so easy a device. Shall
we say, with a modern divine, the true believer will accept
both statements with the same implicit faith? This also
may be doubtful.

To look back upon the field we have passed, it must be
confessed that the claims made for the Old Testament
have no foundation in fact; its books, like others, have a
mingling of good and evil. We see a gradual progress of
ideas therein, keeping pace with the civilization of the
world. Vestiges of ignorance, superstition, folly, of unre-
claimed selfishness, yet linger there. Fact and fiction are
strangely blended; the common and miraculous, the divine and the human, run into one another. We find rude
notions of God in some parts, though in others the more
lofty. Here, the moral and religious sentiment are in-
sulted; there, is beautiful instruction for both. Human

[1] See De Wette, Vol. II. § 253, et seq.
[2] The passages are conveniently arranged for this purpose, side by side, in
Jahn's edition of the Hebrew Bible. De Wette, § 189, et seq.

imperfections meet us everywhere in the Old Testament. The passions of man are ascribed to God. The Jews had a mythology as well as the Greeks : they transform law into miracles ; earth into a dream-land ; it rains manna for eight and thirty years, and the smitten rock pours out water. We see a gradual progress in this as in all mythologies : first, God appears in person ; walks in the garden in the cool of the day ; eats and drinks ; makes contracts with his favourites ; is angry, resentful, sudden and quick in quarrel, and changes his plans at the advice of a cool man. Then it is the Angel of God who appears to man. It is deemed fatal for man to see Jehovah. His messenger comes to Manoah, and vanishes in the flame of the sacrifice ; the angel of Jehovah appears to David. Next it is only in dreams, visions, types, and symbols that the Most High approaches his children. He speaks to them by night ; comes in the rush of thoughts, but is not seen. The personal Form, and the visible Angel, have faded and disappeared as the daylight assumed its power. The nation advanced ; its Religion and mythology advanced with it. Then again, sometimes God is represented as but a local deity ; Jacob is surprised to find him in a foreign land : next he is only the God of the Hebrews. At last, the ONLY LIVING AND TRUE GOD.

There is a similar progress in the notions of the service God demands. Abraham must offer Isaac ; with Moses, slain beasts are sufficient ; Micah has outgrown the Mosaic form in some respects, and says, " Shall Jehovah be pleased with thousands of rams ; shall I give the first-born of my body for the sin of my soul ? what doth Jehovah require of thee, but to do justly and to love mercy and to walk humbly with thy God ? " A spiritual man in the midst of a formal people saw the pure truth which they saw not. Does the Old Testament claim to be master of the soul ? By no means ; it is only a phantom conjured up by superstition that scares us in our sleep. Does the truth it contains make it a miraculous book ? It is poor logic which thinks what is *false* can cease to be false, though never so many wonders are wrought in its defence.[1]

---

[1] On the Old Testament, its authors' inspiration, &c., see some valuable remarks in Spinoza, Tract. theol. polit. Ch. I.—X. XII. XIII. See Norton, Vol. II. Append. D, and his Letter to Blanco White in Thom, ubi sup. Vol. II. p.

CHAPTER III.

AN EXAMINATION OF THE CLAIMS OF THE NEW TESTAMENT TO BE A DIVINE, MIRACULOUS, OR INFALLIBLE COMPOSITION.

LET us look the facts of the New Testament also in the face. Some men are glad to abandon the Old Testament to the Jews, but fear to look into the foundation of the Christian Scriptures, lest it also be found sandy. Does much depend on the New Testament? Then the more carefully must its claims be examined. Truth courts the light, its deeds never evil. Are the writings of the New Testament divine, miraculous, and infallible compositions; if the Old Testament fail—the only infallible rule of religious faith and practice? Such is the prevalent opinion with us.[1] After what was said above respecting the points to be proved before such a conclusion could be admitted, it becomes less difficult to decide this question. The general remarks respecting the inspiration of the Old Testament apply also to the New,[2] and need not be repeated. Bearing these in mind, let us subject these writings to the same test. To do this we must examine the works themselves. This general thesis may be affirmed : All the writings in the New Testament, as well as the Old, contain marks of their human origin, of human weakness and imperfection.

Now in the New Testament, as in the Old, we have spurious works mixed with the genuine. To separate the former from the latter, is not an easy work, perhaps not possible, at this day. However there are some books of

250, et seq. See also Ewald, Gesch. des Volkes Israel, &c., Gött. 1843, et seq.; B. I. Vorbereitung : all the six laborious volumes are rich in historical results.

[1] See Faustus Socinus, De Auctoritate Sac. Script., Ch. I. where he defends the Scripture against Christians; and Ch. II. against the not Christians.

[2] See above, B. IV. ch. i. and ii.

unquestionable genuineness, and others whose spurious character is almost demonstrated. Modern criticism and ancient authority seem to decide that the Epistle to the Hebrews is not the work of Paul, but of some unknown author; that the second Epistle of Peter is not from that apostle, but from one who, as Scaliger said, "abused his leisure time;" the second and third of John, the Epistles of James and Jude, are not from the apostolic persons whose names they bear; and that the book of the Revelation is not the work of John the Evangelist. Serious objections have been brought against some other epistles, many of which appear. to be well founded, and against some of the Evangelists alluded to already.

Then if the above remarks be correct, there are seven works in the New Testament whose claim to apostolical authority was anciently doubted with good reason. These disputed writings may be neglected in the present examination.[1] If the other writings, whose claim to an apostolic origin is supposed to be stronger, are not found miraculous and infallible, still less shall be expected of these. The rest of the New Testament may be divided into the epistolary and the historical writings.

I. Of the Epistolary Writings of the New Testament.

These are the oldest Christian documents; the works of Paul, Peter, and John, the most illustrious of the early disciples, the "chiefest apostles," and most instrumental in founding the Christian church. If any of the early Christians received miraculous inspiration, it must be the apostles; if any of the apostles, it must be one, or all, of these three. To determine their claims, the works of the three may be examined together, for the sake of brevity.

Now at the first view of these fifteen epistles, it does not appear that any miraculous inspiration was required to write these more than the letters of St Cyprian or Fenelon. They contain nothing above the reach of human faculties,

---

[1] The *non-apostolical* origin of these seven books is by no means *fixed* and agreed upon by all the critics. There is better evidence for the Johannic origin of the Revelation, than the 4th Gospel. See, who will, the discussions in the Introductions of Michäelis, Hug, De Wette, and the numerous monograms on these points. See above, p. 162, note.

and to *assume* a miraculous agency is contrary to the inductive method, to say the least of it.

Do the writers ever claim a peculiar and miraculous inspiration ? The furthest from it possible. Paul speaks of his inspiration, but admits that, of all Christians, "No man can say Jesus is the Lord," that is, Christianity is true, "but by the Holy Ghost." He refers wisdom, faith, eloquence, learning, skill in the interpretation of tongues, ability to teach, or heal diseases, to inspiration : "All these worketh that one and selfsame spirit." [1] The Spirit of Christ was in all Christian hearts ; they all received the "Spirit of God." That was Paul's view of inspiration. He and his fellow-apostles were servants that helped others to believe. He had the gift of teaching in a more eminent degree, and enjoyed a greater "abundance of revelations," and therefore taught. John carries the doctrine of the universal inspiration of Christians still further.

Now, if the apostles had this miraculous and peculiar inspiration, and through modesty did not state it, they must yet have known the fact. But it is notorious they taught not in the name of any private inspiration, but in that of Jesus.[2]

But even if the apostles claimed miraculous and infallible inspiration, and taught with authority they pretended to derive therefrom, still their claim could not be granted, for, if infallibly inspired, they must be ready for all emergencies. Now a practical question arose in a novel case which was a test of their inspiration : Should they admit the Gentiles to Christianity ? The book of Acts relates, that Peter required a special and miraculous vision to enlighten him on this head. He seems surprised to find that "God is no respecter of persons," but will allow all religious men of any nation to become Christians.[3] Had he been miraculously inspired before, to what purpose the vision ?

If the apostles were infallibly inspired, they could not

---

[1] Cor. xii. 1, et seq.

[2] This point has been ably touched by Spinoza, Tract. theol. polit. chap. xi. ed. Paulus, Vol. I. p. 315, et seq. From him both Leclerc, Sentimens de quelques Théologiens, &c., and Rich. Simon, (Hist. Crit. du V. T.,) seem to have drawn some of their stores. See also the acute remarks of Lessing, Werke, ed. Carlsruhe, 1824, Vol. XXIV. p. 84, et seq.

[3] Acts x. 1, et seq.

disagree on any point. Now another question comes up : Shall the Gentiles keep the old ceremonial Law of Moses, and be circumcised ? [1] It would seem that men of common freedom of thought, who had heard the teaching of Jesus, would not need miraculous help to decide so plain a question. If they had the alleged inspiration, each must know at once how to decide, and all would decide in the same way without consultation. But such was not the fact ; they were divided on this very question—plain as it is— and held a meeting of the Christians ; the "apostles and elders came together *to consider* this matter." It was not a plain case, there was "much disputing" about it. Peter, Barnabas, and Paul, spoke against the Law ; James, as chairman of the meeting, sums up the matter before putting the question, takes a middle ground, proposes a resolution that all the Mosaic ritual should not be imposed upon the Gentile converts, but only a few of its prohibitions, which he reckons "necessary things." He comes to this conclusion, not by special inspiration—of which no mention is made in the meeting—but from Peter's statement of facts, and from a passage in the Prophet who says, that "all the Gentiles might seek after the Lord." The question was put ; the chairman's motion prevailed ; a circular was drawn up in the name of the Holy Spirit and the assembly, and sent to the Churches. But Paul and Peter seem to have disregarded it, one going beyond, the other falling short of its requisitions.

Then, again, the apostles differed on some points. Paul and Barnabas had a sharp contention, and separated.[2] Could infallible men fall out ? Paul had little respect for those "that were apostles before him," and "withstood Peter to the face."[3]

These Apostles were mistaken in several things ; in their interpretation of the Old Testament, as any one may see by examining the passages cited by Peter in the Acts,[4] or the writings of Paul.[5] They were all mistaken in this capital doctrine : That Jesus would return to Judea, the

---

[1] Acts xv. 1, et seq.   [2] Acts xv. 39.
[3] Gal. i. 11—ii. 14. See Middleton's Reflections on the dispute between Peter and Paul, Works, Vol. II.
[4] Acts ii. 14—21, 25—34, iii. 18, 21—24, iv. 25, 26, et al.
[5] Gal. iv. 24, et seq. ; 1 Cor. x. 4, et seq., et al.

general resurrection and judgment take place, and the
world be destroyed within a very few years, during the
lifetime of the Apostles. This is a very strongly marked
feature in their teaching.[1] From the doubtful epistle ascribed to Peter, it seems that as times went by and the
world continued, scoffers very naturally doubted the truth
of this opinion,[2] but were assured it would hold good.

II. *Of the Historical Writings of the New Testament.*

Here we have, apparently, though I think not really,
the works of Matthew and John, two of the immediate
disciples of Jesus, and of Mark and Luke, the companions
of Peter and Paul. The first question is, have we really
the works of these four writers? It is a question which
can by no means be readily and satisfactorily answered in
the affirmative. However, it cannot be entered upon in
this place;[3] but admitting, in argument, the works are
genuine, at the first view, there seems no need of miraculous inspiration in the case of honest men wishing to
relate what they had seen, heard, or felt. It is not easy
to see why miraculous and infallible inspiration was
needed to write the memoirs of Jesus and the Acts of the
Apostles more than the memoirs of Socrates, or the Acts
of the Martyrs. The writers never claim such an inspiration.
Matthew and Mark never speak of themselves as writers;
Luke refers to certain " eye-witnesses and ministers of the
Word " as his authority for the facts of the Gospel. John
claims it as little as the others, though an unknown
writer, at the end of his Gospels, testifies to the truth of
the narrative.[4]

But even if they made this claim, so often made for them,

---

[1] See the essay of Mr Norton on this point, in Statement of Reasons, &c., p.
297, et seq.. and De Potter, ubi sup. Vol. I. p. cxl. et seq.

[2] 2 Pet. iii. 4, et seq.

[3] On the affirmative side, see Paley, Evidences, Pt. I. ; the masterly Treatise
of Mr Norton, Genuineness of the Gospels; Prof. Stuart's Review of it in Bib.
Rep. for 1837-8; and Lardner's Credibility, &c. See, on the other side, the
popular but important remarks of Hennel, ubi sup. ch. iii.—vi. See also
Strauss, Glaubenslehre, § 15 ; and the Life of Jesus, by Strauss, Theile,
Neander, &c. &c. ; the Introductions of Hug, De Wette, and Credner. Bruno
Baur's Kritik der evang. Geschichte des Johannes, 1840, and der Synoptiker,
1841. See above, the references B. III. ch. ii. at end.

[4] Luke i. 1, et seq. (See Acts i. 1, et seq.) John xxi. 24.

it could not be granted, for their testimony does not agree. The Jesus of the Synoptics differs very widely from the Jesus of John, in his actions, discourses, and general spiritual character, as much as the Socrates of Xenophon from that of Plato. This point was early acknowledged by Christian Fathers. But not to dwell on a general disagreement, nor to come down to the perpetual and well-known disagreement in minute details, there is a most striking difference between the genealogies of Jesus as given by Matthew and Luke. Both agree that Jesus was descended from David by the Father's side; but Matthew counts twenty-five ancestors between David and Joseph, the husband of Mary, and Luke enumerates forty ancestors, of whom thirty-eight are never mentioned by Matthew; one derives his descent from the illustrious Solomon, the other from the obscure Nathan; one makes Nazareth Joseph's dwelling-place, the other Bethlehem. They disagree, likewise, in numerous particulars of the early history, such as the miraculous appearance of the star, the Magi, the flight into Egypt, the songs, the angels, and the dreams.[1] Yet notwithstanding these genealogies both agree that Jesus had no human father, a fact never referred to by Mark or John, by Peter or Paul, nor in the recorded words of Jesus himself, or the people about him, who took him for the son of Joseph the carpenter. If he had no human father, how was he descended from David? Are we to believe a miracle so surprising, on the doubtful statement of two men whom we know nothing of, but who contradict themselves and one another, and relate the strongest marvels? Is it a part of Religion to believe such stories? What else would we believe on such evidence? It were easy to point out other disagreements in the words, and actions, and predictions ascribed to Jesus; in the accounts of his resurrection and the impossible events of his subsequent history, but it is not needed for the present purpose.[2] The book of the Acts, of a my-

---

[1] See these discrepancies ably stated by Mr Norton, ubi sup. p. liii. et seq.; and Strauss, Life of Jesus, § 19—38; and the popular statement in Harwood, ubi sup. p. 20, et seq.; Hennel, ubi sup. ch. iii. v.; Middleton, Reflections; on the Variations in the Gospels, Works, Vol. II. See Weisseler's attempt to reconcile these genealogies, Stud. und Krit. für 1845, p. 361, et seq. Compare the Apocryphal Gospels.

[2] See, who will, Evanson, Dissonance of the Evangelists, Gloucester, 1805;

thical and legendary character, requires no special examination.

This, however, must be admitted, that the facts of the case will not warrant the claim of miraculous and infallible inspiration that is made for them ; and that we are to examine with great caution before we accept their statements, which, in detail, have often but a low degree of historical credibility.[1]

These facts cannot be hushed up, nor put out of sight; we must look them in the face. They have pained already many a breaking heart, which could not separate the truth of Religion from the errors of the Christian record—felt with groans that could not be uttered. It need not be so. Christianity is one thing ; the Christian documents a very different matter. In them, as in the Old Testament, there is a mythology ; the natural and the supernatural are confounded. The Gospels cannot be taken as historical " authorities," until a searching criticism has separated their mythological and legendary narratives from what is purely a matter-of-fact. Some attempt to remove the difficulty by striking out the offensive passages,[2] and others by explaining them away, and still claim miraculous infallibility for all the rest, which the writers never claim for themselves nor allow one another. Let us rest on things as they are ; not try to base our Church on things that are not.

It may be asked : If there is no foundation of fact for the miraculous part of the narrative, why did the writers dwell so much on this part ? The question may be asked in the case of the catholic miracles ; those of St Bernard ; of witchcraft and possessions before named. It is at least difficult to determine what lay at the bottom of the matter. But this is a fixed point, that Devils, Ghosts, and Witches only appear where they were previously believed in, and there they continually appear ; "imagination bodies forth the forms of things not seen." The Catholic sees the Virgin, and the Mormonite finds miracles to-day. Will

Strauss, § 132—142 ; Wolfenbüttel, Fragment. Ueber Auferstehungsgeschichte, and the numerous replies.

[1] On the Credibility of Historians, see Arnold, Introduct. Lect. on Mod. Hist., Lond. 1843, Lect. VIII. See the valuable remarks of Grote, History of Greece, London, 1849, Vol. I.

[2] See Norton, Vol. I. p. liii. et seq.

not the same cause—whatever be it—help to explain the visions of Paul, the angels, and miracles of the New Testament? It is not many years since the divines of New England made collections of accounts of the devil appearing to men. If a religious teacher should appear at the time and place as Jesus appeared, it would be surprising, almost beyond belief, if miraculous tales were not connected with his birth, life, and death. Antiquity is full of sons of God, and wonder-workers. The story of Lazarus, and even that of the Ascension, is not without its parallels.

But if all the charges against the New Testament are true, what then? Why, this: honest men; noble, pious, simple-hearted men; the zealous Apostles of Christianity; the first to espouse it; willing to leave all, comfort, friends, life for its sake, after all, were but men, such as are born in these days, fallible, like ourselves; often in intellectual and moral error; they shared, like us, the ignorance and superstition of the times, and though earnest in looking saw not all things, but, as the wisest of them said, "through a glass darkly," and made some confusion among things they did see. Do we ask miraculous evidence to prove that Jesus lived a divine life? We can have no such testimony. We know that if he taught Absolute Religion, his Christianity is absolutely true; that if he did not teach it, still Absolute Religion remains, the everlasting Rock of Faith, in spite of the defects of historical evidence, or the limitations of this or that man. Has the New Testament exaggerated the greatness and embellished the beauty of Jesus? Measure his religious doctrine by that of the time and place he lived in, or that of any time and any place! Yes, by the doctrine of eternal truth. Consider what a work his words and deeds have wrought in the world; that he is still the Way, the Truth, and the Life to millions; that he is reckoned a GOD by the mass of Christians, his Word their standard of truth, his Life the Ideal they see too far above them in the Heavens for their imitation; remember that though other minds have seen further, and added new truths to his doctrine of Religion, yet the richest hearts have felt no deeper, and added nothing to the sentiment of Religion; have set no loftier aim, no truer method than his of PER-

FECT LOVE TO GOD AND MAN, and then ask, Have the Evangelists overrated him ? We can learn but few facts about Jesus ; but measure him by the shadow he has cast into the world ; no, by the light he has shed upon it, not by things in which Hercules was his equal, and Vishnu his superior. Shall we be told, Such a man never lived ; the whole story is a lie ? Suppose that Plato and Newton never lived ; that their story is a lie. But who did their works, and thought their thought ? It takes a Newton to forge a Newton. What man could have fabricated a Jesus ? None but a Jesus.

CHAPTER IV.

THE ABSOLUTE RELIGION INDEPENDENT OF HISTORICAL DOCUMENTS—THE BIBLE AS IT IS.

THIS doctrine of the infallible inspiration of the Scriptures has greater power with Christians at this day than in Paul's time. In the first ages of Christianity each apostle was superior to the Old Testament. There were no Scriptures to rely on, for the New Testament was not written, and the Old Testament was hostile. The Law stood in their way, a law of sin and death ; the greatest prophets were inferior to John the Baptist, and the least in the Christian kingdom was greater than he ;[1] all before Jesus were "thieves and robbers" in comparison. Yet Christianity stood without the New Testament. It went forward without it ; made converts and produced a wondrous change in the world. The Old Testament was the servant, not the master of the early Christians. Each church used what it saw fit. Some had the whole of the Old Testament ; some but a part ; others added the Apocrypha, for there was no settled canon " published by authority, and appointed to be read in churches." So it

---

[1] The opinion of some disciples about the excellence of that kingdom may be seen in Irenæus, Lib. II. Ch. 33, where he speaks of the Vine-Stocks.

was with the New Testament. Some received more than we, others less. Such men as Justin, Ignatius, Clement of Alexandria, and Origen, refer to some other books, just as they quote the New Testament. The canon of the New Testament was less certain than the Old. Men followed usage, tradition, or good sense in this matter, and at last the present collection was fixed by authority. But by what test were its limits decided? Alas, by no certain criterion.[1]

Let us look at things as they are. Here is a collection of ancient books, spurious and genuine, Hebrew and Greek. The one part belongs to a mode of worship, formal and obsolete; the other to a religion, actual, spiritual, still alive. The one gives us a Jehovah jealous and angry; the other a Father full of love. Each writer in both divisions proves by his imperfections that the earth did not formerly produce a different race of men. They contradict one another, and some relate what no testimony can render less than absurd; but yet all taken together, spite of their imperfections and positive faults, form such a collection of religious writings as the world never saw, so deep, so divine. Are not the Christian Gospels and the Hebrew Psalms still often the best part of the Sunday service in the church? Truly there is but one Religion for the Jew, the Gentile, and the Christian, though many theologies and ceremonies for each.

Now, unless we reject this treasure entirely, one of two things must be done: either we must pretend to believe the whole, absurdities and all; make one part just as valuable as the other, the Law of Moses as the Gospel of Jesus, David's curse as Christ's blessing,—and then we make the Bible our master, who puts Common Sense and Reason to silence, and drives Conscience and the religious Element out of the Church: or else we must accept what is true, good, and divine therein; take each part for what it is worth; gather the good together, and leave the bad to itself—and then we make the Bible our servant and helper, who assists Common Sense and Reason, stimulates

[1] On the use of the New Testament in the early times, see Credner, Beiträge zur Einleit. in biblischen Schriften, Ch. I. p. 1—90; Münscher, Handbuch der Dogmengeschichte, Vol. I. § 30—84; Augusti, Christlichen Archäologie, Vol. VI. p. 1—244; and De Wette, Vol. I. § 18—29.

Conscience and Religion, co-working with them all. A third thing is not possible.

Which shall be done?   The practical answer was given long ago; it has always been given, except in times of fanatical excitement.   Because there is chaff and husks in the Bible, are we to eat of them, when there is bread enough and to spare?   Pious men neglect what does not edify.[1]   Who reads gladly the curses of the Psalmist; chapters that make God a man of war, a jealous God, the butcher of the nations?   Certainly but few; let them be exhorted to repentance.   Men cannot gather grapes of thorns, grasp them never so lovingly; honest men will leave the thorns, or pluck them up.   Now Criticism— which the thinking character of the age demands—asks men to do consciously and thoroughly what they have always done imperfectly and with no science but that of a pious heart; that is, to divide the word rightly; separate mythology from history, fact from fiction, what is religious and of God from what is earthly and not of God; to take the Bible for what it is worth.   Fearful of the issue we may put off the question a few years; may insist as strongly as ever on what we know to be false; ask men to believe it, because in the records, and thus drive bad men to hypocrisy, good men to madness, and thinking men to "infidelity;" we may throw obstacles in the way of Religion and Morality, and tie the millstone of the Old and New Testaments about the neck of Piety as before. We may call men "Infidels and Atheists," whom Reason and Religion compel to uplift their voice against the idolatry of the Church; or we may attempt to smooth over the matter, and say nothing about it, or not what we think.   But it will not do.   The day of Fire and Fagots is ended; the toothless "Guardian of the Faith" can only bark.   The question will come, though alas for that man by whom it comes.

Other religions have their sacred books, their Korans, Vedas, Shasters, which must be received in spite of Reason, as masters of the soul.   Some would put the Bible on the same ground.   They glory in believing whatever is

---

[1] See Augustine, Doct. Christiana, Lib. I. C. 39, who says a man, supported by Faith, Hope, and Charity, does not need the Bible except to teach others with.

prefaced with a Thus-saith-the-Lord; but then all superiority of the Bible over these books disappears for ever; the daylight gives place to the shadow; the Law of Sin and Death casts out the Law of the Spirit of Life. Let honest Reason and Religion pursue their own way.

CHAPTER V.

CAUSE OF THE FALSE AND THE REAL VENERATION FOR THE BIBLE.

THE indolent and the sensual love to have a visible master in spiritual things, who will spare them the agony of thought. Credulity, Ignorance, and Superstition conjure up phantoms to attend them. Some honest men find it difficult to live nobly and divine; to keep the well of life pure and undisturbed, the inward ear always open and quick to the voice of God in the soul. They see, too, how often the ignorant, the wicked, the superstitious, and the fanatical confound their own passions with the still small voice of God; they see what evil, deep and dreadful, comes of this confusion. Such is the force of prejudice, indolence, habit, they find it sometimes difficult to distinguish between right and wrong; they love to lean on the Most High, and the Bible is declared His word. They say, therefore, by their action, Let us have some outward rule and authority, which, being infallible, shall help the still smallness of God's voice in the heart; it will bless us when weak; we will make it our master and obey its voice. It shall be to us as a God, and we will fall down and worship it. But alas, it is not so. The word of God—no Scripture will hold that. It speaks in a language no honest mind can fail to read. Such seem the most prominent causes that have made the Bible an Idol of the Christians.

No doubt it will be said, " such views are dangerous, for

the mass of men must always take Authority for Truth, not Truth for Authority." But are they not true? If so the consequences are not ours; they belong to the Author of truth, who can manage his own affairs, without our meddling. Is the wrong way safer than the right? No doubt it was reckoned dangerous to abandon the worship of Diana, of the cross, the saints and their reliques; but the world stands, though " the image that fell down from Jupiter" is forgotten. If these doctrines be true, men need not fear they shall have no " standard of religious faith and practice." Reason, Conscience, Heart, and Soul still remain; God's voice in Nature; His Word in Man. His Laws remain ever unchanged, though we set up our idols or pluck them down. We still have the same guide with Moses and David, Socrates and Zoroaster, Paul and John and Luther, Fenelon, Taylor, and Fox; yes, the same guide that led Jesus, the first-born of many brothers, in his steep and lonely pilgrimage.

This doctrine takes nothing from the Bible but its errors, which only weaken its strength; its truth remains, brilliant and burning with the light of life. It calls us away from each outward standard to the eternal truths of God; from the letter and the imperfect Scripture of the Word to the living Word itself. Then we see the true relation the Bible sustains to the soul; the cause of the real esteem in which it is held is seen to be in its moral and religious truths; their power and loveliness appear. These have had the greatest influence on the loftiest minds and the lowliest hearts for eighteen hundred years. How they have written themselves all over the world, deepest in the best of men! What greatness of soul has been found amid the fragrant leaves of the Bible, sufficient to lead men to embrace its truths, though at the expense of accepting tales which make the blood curdle!

Take the Bible for what is true in it, and the first chapter of Genesis is a grand hymn of creation, a worthy prelude of the sublime chants that follow; it sings this truth: The World was not always; is not the work of chance, but of the living God; all things are good, made to be blest. The writer—who, perhaps, never thought he was writing " an article of faith "—if he were a Jew, might superstitiously refer the Sabbath to the time of creation and the agency of God, just as the Greek refers one festival to Hercules and another to Bacchus. Then oriental Piety comes beautiful from the grave hewn in the rock by our dull Theology; utters her word of counsel and hope; sings her mythological poem, and warms the heart, but does not teach theology, or physical science.

The sweet notes of David's prayer; his mystic hymn of praise, so full of rippling life; his lofty Psalm, which seems to unite the warbling music of the wind, the sun's glance, and the rush of the lightning; which calls on the mountain and the sea, and beast, and bird, and man, to join his full heart,—all these shall be sweet and elevating, but we shall leave his pernicious curse to perish where it fell.

The excellence of the Hebrew devotional hymns has never been surpassed. Heathenism, Christianity, with all their science, arts, literature, bright and many-coloured, have little that approach these. They are the despair of imitators; still the uttered prayer of the Christian world. Tell us of Greece, whose air was redolent of song; its language such as Jove might speak; its sages, heroes, poets, honoured in every clime,—they have no psalm of prayer and praise like these Hebrews, the devoutest of men, who saw God always before them, ready to take them up when father and mother let them fall.

Some of the old prophets were men of stalwart and robust character, set off by a masculine piety that puts to shame our puny littleness of heart. They saw Hope the plainest when danger was most imminent, and never despaired. Fear of the people, the rulers, the priests, could not awe them to silence, nor gold buy smooth things from the prophet's tongue. They left Hypocrisy, with his weeds and weepers, and feigning but unstained handkerchief, to follow the coffin he knew to be empty, and went their own way, as men. What shall screen the guilty from the prophet's word? Even David is met with a Thou-art-the-man. What if they were stoned, imprisoned, sawn asunder? It was a prophet's reward. They did not prophesy smooth things; they gave the truth and took blows, not asking love for love. If these men are set up as masters of the soul, Justice must break her staff

over their heads.   But view them as patriots whom danger aroused from the repose of life; as pious men awakened by concern for the public virtue, and nobler men
never spoke speech.

Out from the heart of Nature rolled
The burdens of the Bible old.

Little needs now be said of the New Testament, of the
simple truth that rustles in its leaves, its parables, epistles,
where Paul lifts up his manly voice, and John, or whoso
wrote the words, pours out the mystic melody of his faith.
Why tell the deep words of Jesus?   Have we exhausted
their meaning? The world—has it outgrown Love to God
and Man?   They still act in gentle bosoms, giving strength
to the strong, and justice and meekness and charity and
faith to beautiful souls, long tried and oppressed.   There
is no need of new words to tell of this.

Now it is not in nature to respect the false, and yet
reverence the true.   Call the Bible master—we do not see
the excellence it has.   Take it as other books, we have its
Beauty, Truth, Religion, not its deformities, fables, and
theology.   We shall not believe in ghosts, though Isaiah
did: nor in devils, though Jesus teach there are such.
We shall see the excellence of Paul in his manly character,
not in the miracles wrought by his apron; the nobleness
of Jesus, in the doctrine he taught and the life he lived,
not in the walk on the water or the miraculous draughts
of fish.   We shall care little about the "endless genealogies and old-wives' fables," though still deemed essential by many—but much for being good and doing good.
Our faith—let him shake down the Andes who has an arm
for that work.

On the other hand, he that accepts the monstrous prodigies of the Gospels; is delighted to believe that Jesus
had divine authority for laying on forms, and damning all
but the baptized; that he gave Peter authority to bind
and loose on earth and in heaven; commanded his disciples to make friends of "the mammon of unrighteous-
ness," to tease God, as an unjust judge, into compliance,
with vain repetitions—can he accept the Absolute Religion?
It is not possible, for a long time, to make serious things
of trifles, without making trifles of serious things.   Cannot

drunkenness be justified out of the Old Testament; the very Solomon advising the poor man to drown his sorrows in wine? Jeremiah curses the man that will not fight.[1] Is not Sarah commended by the Fathers of the church, and Abraham by the Sons? Men justify slavery out of the New Testament, because Paul had not his eye open to the evil, but sent back a fugitive! It is dangerous to rely on a troubled fountain for the water of life.

The good influence of the Bible, past and present, as of all religious books, rests on its religious significance. Its truths not only sustain themselves, but the mass of errors connected therewith. Truth can never pass away. Men sometimes fear the Bible will be destroyed by freedom of thought and freedom of speech. Let it perish if such be the case. Truth cannot fear the light, nor are men so mad as to forsake a well of living water. All the free-thinking in the world could not destroy the Iliad; how much less the truths of the Bible. Things at last will pass for their true value. The truths of the Bible, which have fed and comforted the noblest souls for so many centuries, may be trusted to last our day. The Bible has already endured the greatest abuse at the hands of its friends, who make it an idol, and would have all men do it homage. We need call none our Master but the Father of All. Yet the Bible, if wisely used, is still a blessed teacher. Spite of the superstition and folly of its worshippers, it has helped millions to that fountain where Moses and Jesus, with the holy-hearted of all time, have stooped and been filled. We see the mistakes of its writers, for though noble and of great stature, they saw not all things. We reject their follies; but their words of truth are still before us, to admonish, to encourage, and to bless. From time to time God raises up a prophet to lead mankind. He speaks his word as it is given him; serves his generation for the time, and falls at last, when it is expedient he should give way to the next Comforter whom God shall send. But mankind is greater than a man, and never dies. The experience of the past lives in the present. The light that shone at Nineveh, Egypt, Judea, Athens, Rome, shines no more from those points; it is everywhere. Can Truth decease, and a good idea once made real ever

---

[1] Proverbs xxxvi. 6, et seq.; Jer. xlviii. 10.

perish? Mankind, moving solemnly on its appointed road, from age to age, passes by its imperfect teachers, guided by their light, blessed by their toil, and sprinkled with their blood. But Truth, like her God, is before and above us for ever. So we pass by the lamps of the street, with wonder at their light, though but a smoky glare; they seem to change places and burn dim in the distance as we go on; at last the solid walls of darkness shut them in. But high over our head are the unsullied stars, which never change their place, nor dim their eye. So the truths of the Scriptures will teach for ever, though the record perish and its authors be forgot. They came from God, through the Soul of Man. They have exhausted neither God nor the Soul. Man is greater than the Bible. That is one ray out of the sun; one drop from the infinite ocean. The inward Christ, which alone abideth for ever, has much to say which the Bible never told, much which the historical Jesus never knew. The Bible is made for Man, not Man for the Bible. Its truths are old as the creation, repeated more or less purely in every tongue. Let its errors and absurdities no longer be forced on the pious mind, but perish for ever; let the Word of God come through Conscience, Reason, and holy Feeling, as light through the windows of morning. Worship with no master but God, no creed but Truth, no service but Love, and we have nothing to fear.

BOOK V.

"When the Church, without temporal support, is able to do her great works upon the unforced obedience of man, it argues a divinity about her. But when she thinks to credit and better her spiritual efficacy, and to win herself respect and dread, by strutting in the false vizard of worldly authority, it is evident that God is not there, but that her apostolic virtue is departed from her, and hath left her key-cold; which she perceiving, as in a decayed nature, seeks to the outward fermentations and chafings of worldly help and external flourishes, to fetch, if it be possible, some motion into her extreme parts, or to hatch a counterfeit life with the crafty and artificial heat of jurisdiction. But it is observable, that so long as the Church, in true imitation of Christ, can be content to ride upon an ass, carrying herself and her government along in a mean and simple guise, she may be, as he is, a Lion of the tribe of Judah, and in her humility all men, with loud hosannas, will confess her greatness. But when, despising the mighty operation of the Spirit by the weak things of this world, she thinks to make herself bigger and more considerable by using the way of civil force and jurisdiction, as she sits upon this Lion, she changes into an Ass, and instead of Hosannas, every man pelts her with stones and dirt."—MILTON.— *The Reason of Church Government urged against Prelacy,* Chap. III.

BOOK V.

CHAPTER I.

CLAIMS OF THE CHRISTIAN CHURCH.

THE Catholic church, and most if not all the minor Protestant churches, claim superiority over Reason, Conscience, and the religious Element in the individual soul, assuming dominion over these, as the State justly assumes authority over the excessive passions and selfishness of men. Now since the former are not, like the latter, evils in themselves, the Church, to justify itself, must denounce them either as emanations from the devil, or at best as uncertain and dangerous guides. The churches make this claim of superiority, either distinctly in their creeds and formularies of faith, claiming a divine origin for themselves, or by implication, in their actions, when they condemn and blast with curses one who differs from them in religious matters, and teaches doctrines they disapprove. In virtue of this assumed superiority the Christian Church, as a whole, denies what it calls "salvation" to all out of the Christian Church—excepting some of the Jews before Christ—though their life be divine as an angel's. How often have Socrates and that long line of noble men who do honour to Greek and Roman antiquity been damned by hirelings of the Church! The Catholic church denies salvation to all out of its pale, and in general each church of the straiter and more numerous sects confirms the damnation of all who think more liberally.   Men who expose to scorn the folly of their assumptions, the Bayles, the Humes, the Voltaires ; men who will not accept their pretensions, the Newtons, the Lockes, the Priestleys, the Channings, have their warrant of eternal damnation made out and sealed ; not because their life was bad, but their faith not orthodox !   Supported by this claim of superiority on the churches' part, canonized Ignorance may blast Learning ; ecclesiastical Dulness condemn secular Genius ; and surpliced Impiety, with shameless forehead, may damn Religion, meek and thoughtful, who out of the narrow church, walks with beautiful feet on the rugged path of mortal life, and makes real the kingdom of Heaven.

For many centuries it has been a heresy in the Christian churches to believe that any man out of their walls could expect less than damnation in the next world ; it is still a heresy.   It is taught with great plainness by the majority of Christians, that God will damn to eternal torments the majority of his children, because they are not in any of the Christian churches.[1]   If we look into the value of this claim of superiority, we shall find the foundation on which it rests.   It must be either in the Idea of a Church, or in the Fact of the Christian Church receiving this delegated power from a human or a divine founder.

I. *Of the Idea of a Church.*

We do not speak, except figuratively, of a Church of Moses or Mahomet.   It seems to be necessary to the idea of a visible and historical Church, that there should be a model-man for its central figure, around whom others are to be grouped.   He must be an example of the virtues Religion demands ; an incarnation of God, to adopt the phrase of ancient India, which has since become so prevalent among the Christians.   Now Moses, viewed as a mythological character, and Mahomet, as an historical

[1] For the opinion of the Catholics on this point, see *instar omnium* Bossuet, Hist. des Variations, Liv. II. et al.; for that of the Protestants, see their various confessions, &c., conveniently collected in Niemeyer, Collectio Confessionum in Ecclesiis reformatis, Lips. 1840; Hahn, ubi sup. § 103 and 143; Bretschneider, ubi sup. Vol. II. § 204, p. 174, et seq.   But see Hase, Huttorus redivivus, § 88.

person, were not model-men, but miraculous characters whose relation to God and perfection of life each faithful soul might not share, for it was peculiar to themselves. Their character was not their own work. It was made for them by God, and therefore they could not be objects of imitation. It would be impious madness in the Mussulman or the Jew, to aim at the perfections of the great prophet who stood above him.

Now there is this peculiarity of the greater part of Christians, that while they affirm Jesus to be God, by the divine side, they yet claim him as a model-man, on the human side, and so call him a God-man.[1] About this central figure, the Christian Church is grouped. The fourth Gospel represents him as the Way, the Truth, and the Life, for all men. The churches also assume that he is to be imitated. But they assume this in defiance of logic, for Jesus is represented as born miraculously, endowed with miraculous powers, and separated from all others by his peculiar relation to God, in short, as a God-man. Of course he must be a model only to other God-men, who are born miraculously, endowed and defended as he was; he is no model to men born of flesh and blood, who have none but human powers. But he is the only God-man, and so no model to any one. Still more if the Christian churches view him as the infinite God with all His Infinity, dwelling in the flesh, it is absurd to make him a model for men. But the churches have rarely stopped at an absurdity. They "call things that are not as if they were." Yet since the life of Jesus appears so entirely human in his friendships, sorrows, love, prayer, temptation, triumph, and death, and the Apostles now and then represent him as the great example—the churches could not forbear making him the model-man. Hence the homilies of the Preacher; the disquisition of the Schoolmen; the glorifying treatise of the Mystic; the painting of the Artist, giving us his Triumph, Transfiguration, Farewell Meeting, and Crucifixion—all aim to bring the Great Exemplar distinctly before human consciousness, in the most prominent

---

[1] This term *God-man* is of Heathen origin, and involves a contradiction as much as the term *Circle-triangle*. The common mistake seems to arise from taking a *figure of speech for a matter-of-fact*, which leads to worse confusion in *Theology* than it would in *Geometry*.

scenes of his life, and always as a man, that the lesson of divinity might not be lost.

Now if he be this model man, and the churches are but assemblies of men and women grouped about him, to be instructed by his words, and warned by his example, it is not easy to see what authority they naturally have over the individual soul.

II. *Of the Fact of the Christian Churches.*

If Jesus were but a wise and good man, no word of his could have authority over Reason and Conscience. At best, it could repeat their oracles, and therefore he could never found an institution which should be Master of the Soul. But even if he were what the churches pretend, it does not appear that he has given this authority to any on earth. If we may credit the Gospels, Jesus established no organization; founded no church in any common sense of that term. He taught wherever men would listen; to numbers in the synagogue, temple, and fields; to a few in the little cottage at Bethany, and in the fisher's boat. He gave no instruction to his disciples to found a church; he sent them forth to preach the glad tidings to all mankind : the Spirit within was their calling and authority; Jesus their example; God their guide, protector, and head. In all the ministrations of Jesus, there is nothing which approaches the formation of a church. What was freely received was to be given as freely. Baptism and the Supper were accidents. He appointed no particular body of men as teachers, but sent forth his disciples, all of them, to proclaim the truth. The twelve had no actual authority over others; no preëminence in spreading the Gospel. Had they a right to bind and to loose ? Let Paul answer the question.[1] The first martyr, the most active Evangelist, and the greatest Apostle were not of the twelve. Excepting Peter, James, and John, the rest did little that we know of.[2] Did Jesus say—as Matthew relates—that

[1] Galat. i. ii. et al.; Strauss, ch. v.; Schwegler, Nachapost. Zeitalter, Tüb. 1846, Vol. I. p. 114, et seq.; Baur, Paulus der Apostel; Stuttgart, 1846, p. 104, et seq.

[2] See in Gieseler, Text-Book of Eccles. Hist., Philad. 1836, Vol. I. § 25—27.

he would found a church on Simon Peter ? It must have been a sandy foundation.[1] Paul did not fear to withstand him to the face. Jesus appointed neither place nor day for worship. All the commands of the decalogue are reinforced in the New Testament, excepting that which enjoins the Sabbath ; all the rest are natural laws. Religion with Jesus was a worship in spirit and in truth ; a service at all times and in every place. He fell back on natural Religion and Morality, demanding a divine life, purity without and piety within ; but he left the When, the Where, and the How to take care of themselves. A Church, in our sense of the term, is not so much as named in the Gospels. But Religion, above all emotions, brings men together. Uniting around this central figure, bound by the strongest of ties, the spiritual sympathies fired with admiration for the great soul of Jesus, relying on his authority, there grew up, unavoidably, a body of men and women. These the Apostles call the Church of Christ. Religion, as it descends into practice, takes a concrete form, which depends on the character and condition of the men who receive it : hence come the rites, dogmas, and ceremonies which mark the Church of this or that age and nation.

The Christian Church may be defined as a Body of Men and Women united in a common regard for Jesus, assembling for the purposes of worship and religious instruction. It has the powers delegated by individuals who compose it.[2]

[1] Math. xvi. 18, 19. See the various opinions of interpreters of this passage so improperly thrust into the mouth of Jesus, in De Wette, Exegetische Handbach zur N. T. See Origen's ingenious gloss.

[2] See the various opinions of the Catholics and Protestants on this point collected in Winer, Comparativ Darstellung der Lehrbegriffs, Leip. 1837, § 19, on the formation of the church. See much valuable matter in Ritschl, Die Entstehung der Altkatholischen Kirche, Bonn, 1850, Buch II.

CHAPTER II.

THE GRADUAL FORMATION OF THE CHRISTIAN CHURCH.

IN the earliest times of Christianity there were no regular systems of doctrine, to bind men together. The truths of natural Religion, the special forms of Judaism, and a somewhat indefinite belief in Jesus, were the cardinal points and essentials of Christianity. The public religious service seems perfectly free. Where the spirit of the Lord was, there was liberty. No one controlled another's freedom. The much vaunted "form of sound words" was notoriously different with different teachers. Paul, who came late to Christianity, boasts that he received his doctrine straightway from God, not from those "who were apostles before him," whom he seems to hold in small esteem. The decision of the council at Jerusalem, even if it ever took place, did not bind him. The practical side of Christianity was developed more than the theoretical. The effect of the truth proclaimed with freedom, was soon manifest; for the errors and superstition still clinging to the mind of the apostles could not chain mankind. Love increased; Christianity bore fruit; the Church spread wide its arms. It emancipated men from the yokes of the ancient sacerdotal class; but there was a fierce struggle in the new congregations before the Jewish forms could be given up. The Christians were "a royal priesthood;" all were "kings and priests," appointed to offer a "spiritual sacrifice." The apostles who had seen Jesus, or understood his doctrine, naturally took the lead of men they sought to instruct. As the number of Christians enlarged, some organization was needed for practical purposes. The pattern was taken from the Jewish Synagogue, which claimed no divine authority; not from the Temple, whose officers made such a claim. Hence there were elders and deacons.

One of the elders was an overseer, like the " Speaker " in a legislative assembly. But all these were chosen by the people, and as much of the people after their choice as before. There was no clergy and no laity ; all were sons of God, recipients of inspiration from him. The Holy Ghost fell upon all, the same in kind, only divine in degree and mode of manifestation. The wish of Moses was complied with, and God put his spirit upon each of them ; the prediction of Joel was fulfilled, and their sons and their daughters prophesied ; the word of Jeremiah had come to pass, and God put his Law in their inward parts, and wrote it on their heart, and they all knew the Lord from the least to the greatest. They were "anointed of God," and "knew all things ; " they "needed not that any man should teach them." Christ and God were in all holy hearts. The overseer, or bishop, claimed no power over the people ; he was only first among his peers ; the greatest only because the servant of all. Even Apollos, Cephas, Paul, who were they but servants, through whom others believed ? The bishop had no authority to bind and loose in heaven or earth ; no right to enforce a doctrine. He was not the standard of faith ; that was " the Mind of the Lord," which He would reveal to all who sought it. There was no monopoly of teaching on the part of the elders. A bishop, says the author of the Epistle to Timothy, " must be able to teach," not the only teacher, not necessarily a preacher at all; but a minister of silence as well as speech. Inspiration was free to all men. "Quench not the Spirit ; " " prove all things ; " " hold fast what is good ; " " covet earnestly the best gifts,"—these were the watchwords. Under Fetichism, all could consult their God, and be inspired ; miracles took place continually. Under Polytheism, only a few could come to God at first hand ; they alone were inspired, and miracles were rare. Under Christian Monotheism, God dwelt in all faithful hearts ; old covenants and priesthoods were done away, and so all were inspired.[1]

<hr />

[1] On the state of the early Church, and the Bishops, Elders, and Deacons, which is still a matter of controversy, see Campbell, Lectures on Ecc. Hist., Lec. I.—XIII.; Gieseler, ubi sup. § 29 ; Mosheim, ubi sup. Book I. Art. II. chap. ii. ; Neander, Allg. Geschichte der Christlichen Religion, Hamb. 1835, Vol. I. Part 1. chap. ii.; Gibbon, Chap. XV. ; Schleiermacher, Geschichte der Christlichen Kirche, Berlin, 1840, p. 86, et seq. Among the modern writers Mil-

The New Testament was not written, and the Old Testament was but the shadow of good things to come, and since they had come, the children of the free woman were not to sit in the shadow, but to stand fast in the liberty wherewith Christ had made them free. Man, the heir of all things, long time kept under task-masters and governors, had now come of age and taken possession of his birthright. The decision of a majority of delegates assembled in a council, bound only themselves.

Then the body of men and women worshipping in any one place was subject neither to its own officers, nor to the Church at large ; nor to the Scriptures of the Old or the New Testament. No man on earth, no organization, no book was master of the Soul. Each Church made out its canon of Scripture as well as it could.[1] Some of our canonical writings were excluded, and apocryphal writings used in their stead. Indeed, respecting this matter of Scripture, there has never been a uniform canon among all Christians. The Bible of the Latin differs from that of the Greek Church, and contains thirteen books the more. The Catholic differs from the Protestant ; the early Syrians from their contemporaries ; the Abyssinians from all other churches, it seems. Ebionites would not receive the beginning of Matthew and Luke ; the Marcionites had a Gospel of their own. The Socinians, and perhaps others, left off the whole of the Old Testament,[2] or counted it unnecessary. The followers of Swedenborg do not find a spiritual sense in all the books of the canon. Critics yearly make inroads upon the canon, striking out whole books or obnoxious passages, as not genuine. In the first ages of Christianity, the Bible was a subordinate thing. In modern times it has been made a vehicle to carry any doctrine the expositor sees fit to interpret into it.[3] The first preachers of Christianity fell back on the authority of

man takes the other side. History of Christianity, Lond. 1840, Book II. chap. ii. p. 63, et seq. See the recent works of Gfrörer, Hase, Schwegler. Baur, Schliemann, Ritschl, Staudenmaier, Rothensee, Hilgenfeld, &c.,—Stanley and Jowett and Martineau.

[1] See in Eusebius, H. E. III. 39. the use that Papias makes of Tradition ; he stood on the debatable ground between the Bible and Tradition, and continued to *mythologize.* Ewald, Jahrbücher for 1854, Ch. XXXIII.

[2] See Faustus Socinus, ubi sup. p. 271, et al.

[3] See, on this point, some ingenious remarks of Hegel, Philosophie der Religion, Vol. I. p. 29, et seq.

Jesus; appealed to the moral sense of Mankind; applied the doctrines of Christianity to life as well as they could, and with much zeal, and some superstition and many mistakes, developed the practical side of Christianity much more than its theoretical side.

But even in the Apostles, Christianity had lost somewhat of its simplicity, much of the practical character which marks the teaching of Jesus in the Synoptics. The doctrine of Paul was far removed from the doctrine of Jesus. It was not plain Religion and Morality coming from the absolute source, and proceeding by the absolute method to the absolute end. It is taught on the "authority of Christ." The Jews must believe he was the Messiah of the prophets. "Salvation" is connected with a belief in his person. "Neither is there salvation by any other," says the author who takes the name of Peter; the fourth Gospel makes Jesus declare "No man cometh unto the Father but by me," "all that ever came before me are thieves and robbers." The Jewish doctrine of "Redemption" and reconciliation by sacrifice appears more or less in the genuine works of the Apostles, and very clearly in the Epistle to the Hebrews. We may explain some of the obnoxious passages as "figures of speech," referring to the "Christ born in us;" but a fair interpretation leaves it pretty certain the writers added somewhat to the simpler form of Jesus, though they might not share the gross doctrines since often taught in their name. Christ is in some measure a mythological being even with Paul, —he was with the Jews in the desert, and assisted at the creation. The Jesus of history fades out and the Christ of fiction takes his place. The Pharisaic doctrine of the resurrection of the body appears undeniably; a local heaven and a day of judgment, in which Jesus is to appear in person and judge the world, are very clearly taught. The fourth Gospel speaks of Jesus as he never speaks of himself; the Platonic doctrine of the Logos appears therein. We may separate the apostolic doctrine into three classes, the Judaizing, the Alexandrine, and the Pauline, each differing more or less essentially from the simple mode of Religion of the Synoptics.[1] Already with the

[1] The Epistle to the Hebrews and the earlier Apocryphal Gospels and Epistles are valuable monuments of the opinions of the Christians at the time they

Apostles Jesus has become in part deified, his personality confounded with the infinite God.[1] Was it not because of the very vastness and beauty of soul that was in him? The private and peculiar doctrines of the early Christians appear in strange contrast with the gentle precepts of love to man and God, in which Jesus sums up the essentials of Religion. But, alas, what is arbitrary and peculiar in each form of worship, is of little value ; the best things are the commonest, for no man can lay a new foundation, nor add to the old, more than the wood, hay, and stubble of his own folly. The great excellence of Jesus was in restoring natural Religion and Morality to their true place ; an excellence which even the Apostles but poorly understood.[2]

In their successors Christianity was a very different thing, and in the course of a few years,—alas, a very few, —it appeared in the mass of the Churches, an idle mummery ; a collection of forms and superstitious rites. Heathenism and Judaism with all sorts of superstitious absurdities in their train, came into the Church. The first fifteen bishops of Jerusalem clung to the most obnoxious feature of Judaism. Christianity was the stalking-horse of ambition. A man stepped at once from the camp to the Bishop's mitre, and brought only the piety of the Roman Legion into the Church. The doctrine of many a Christian writer was less pure and beautiful than the faith of Seneca and Cicero, not to name Zoroaster, Pythagoras, and Socrates. After less than a century there was a distinction between clergy and laity. The former ere long became ' Lords over God's heritage," not " ensamples unto the flock." They were masters of the doctrine ; could bind and loose on earth and in heaven. The majority in a council bound the minority, and the voices of the clergy determined what was " the mind of the Lord." Thus the clergy became the Church, and were set above Reason and Conscience in the individual man. They were chosen by

were written. It is a curious fact that *circumcision* was rigidly enforced by the Bishops in the Church at Jerusalem for more than a century after the death of Christ ; many of the laity also were circumcised. Sulpitius Severus, Lib. II.

[1] See Dorner and Baur ; also Mass. Quarterly Review, Vol. III. Art. V., on the Christologies of N. T.

[2] See the impartial remarks of Schlosser, respecting the origin and subsequent fate of Christianity, in his Geschichte der alten Welt, Vol. III. Pt. i. p. 249—274, Pt. ii. p. 110—129, 381—416.'

themselves, and responsible to none on earth. Private inspiration was reckoned dangerous. Freedom of conscience was forbidden; he who denied the popular faith was accursed. The organization of the Church was then copied from the Jewish ·temple, not the synagogue. The minister was a priest, and stood between God and the people; the Bishop, an high-priest after the order of Aaron, his kingdom of this world. He was the "Successor of the Apostles;" the Vicegerent of Christ. Men came to the clerical office with no Religious qualification.[1] Baptism atoned for all sins, and was sometimes put off till the last hour, that the Christian might give full swing to the flesh, and float into heaven at last on the lustral waters of baptism. Bits of bread from the "Lord's table" were a talisman to preserve the faithful from all dangers by sea and land. Prayers were put up for the dead; the cross was worshipped; the bones of the martyrs could work miracles, cast out devils, calm a tempest, and even raise the dead. The Eucharist was forced into the mouths of children before they could say, "my father, and my mother." The sign of the cross and the "sacred oil" were powerful as Canidia's spell. In point of toleration the Christians went backward for a time, far behind the Athenians and men of Rome.[2] The clergy assumed power over Conscience; power to admit to Heaven, or condemn to hell; and not only decided in matters of mummery, whereof they made "divine service" to consist, but decreed what men should believe in order to obtain eternal life; an office the sublimest of all the sons of men, modest because he was great, never took upon himself. They collected the writings of the New Testament, and decided what should be the "Standard of Faith," and what not. But their canon was arbitrary, including some spurious books of small value, and rejecting others more edifying. However, they allowed some latitude in the interpretation of the works they had canonized. But next they went further, and developed systematically the doctrines of Scripture, on points deemed the most important, such as

[1] The histories of Synesius and Ambrose afford a striking picture of the clerical class in their time.
[2] See the writings of Tertullian and Cyprian, passim, for proofs of what is said above.

the "nature of God" and Christ. Thus the "mind of the Lord" was determined and laid down, so that he might read that ran. The mysticism of Plato, and the dialectic subtleties of the Stagirite, afforded matter for the pulpit and councils to discuss.

This method of deciding dark questions by plurality of votes has always been popular in Christendom. In some things the majority are always right; in some always wrong. The four hundred prophets of Baal have a "lying spirit" in them; Micaiah alone is in the right. The college of Padua and the Sorbonne would have voted down Galileo and Newton, a hundred to one; but what then? Majority of voices proves little in morals or mathematics. A single man in Jerusalem on a certain time had more moral and religious truth than Herod and the Sanhedrim. Synods of Dort and assemblies of Divines settle nothing but their own opinions, which will be reversed the next century, or stand, as now, a snare to the conscience of pious men.

In the early times of Christianity, the teachers in general were men of little learning, imbued with the prejudices and vain philosophies of the times; men with passions, some of them quite untamed, notwithstanding their pious zeal. In the first century no eminent man is reckoned among the Christians. But soon doctrines, that played a great part in the heathen worship, and which do not appear in the teaching of Jesus, were imposed upon men, on pain of damnation in two worlds. They are not yet extinct. Rites were adopted from the same source. The scum of idolatry covered the well of living water. The Flesh and the Devil sat down at the "Lord's Table" in the Christian Church, and with forehead unabashed, pushed away the worthy bidden guest. What passed for Christianity in many churches during the fourth and a large part of the third century was a vile superstition. The image of Christ was marred. Men paid God in Cæsar's pence. The shadows of great men, Pythagoras, Socrates, Plato; yes, the shades of humbler men, of name unknown to fame, might have come up, disquieted like Samuel, from their grave, and spit upon the superstition of the Christians defiling Persia, and Athens, and Rome. It deserved the mockery it met. Christianity was basely corrupted long before it gained the Roman Palace. Had it not been depraved, when would it have reached king's courts; in the time of Constantine, or of Louis XIV.? The quarrels of the Bishops; the contentions of the councils; the superstition of the laymen and the despotism and ambition of the clergy in general; the ascetic doctrine taught as morality; the monastic institutions with their plan of a divine life, are striking signs of the times, and contrast wonderfully with that simple Nazarene and his lowly obedience to God and manly love of his brothers.

Yet here and there were men who fed with faith and works the flame of piety, which, rising from their lowly hearth, streamed up towards heaven, making the shadows of superstition and of sin look strange and monstrous as they fell on many a rood of space. These were the men who saved the Sodom of the Church. Did Christianity fail? The Christianity of Christ is not one thing and human nature another. It is human Virtue, human Religion, man in his highest moments; the effect no less than the cause of human development, and can never fail till man ceases to be man. Under all this load of superstition the heart of faith still beat. How could the world forget its old institutions, riot, and sin, in a moment? It is not thus the dull fact of the world's life yields to the Divine Idea of a man. The rites of the public worship; the clerical class; the stress laid on dogmas and forms; all this was a tribute to the indolence and sensuality of mankind. The asceticism, celibacy, mortification of the body, contempt of the present life; the hatred of all innocent pleasure; the scorn of literature, science, and art,— these are the natural reaction of mankind, who had been bid to fill themselves with merely sensual delight. The lives of Mark Antony, Sallust, Crassus; of Julius Cæsar, Nero, and Domitian, explain the origin of asceticism and monastic retirement better than folios will do it. The writings of Petronius Arbiter, of Appuleius and Lucian, render necessary the works of Tertullian, Cyprian, Jerome, and John of Damascus. Individuals might come swiftly out of Egyptian darkness into the light of Religion, but the world moves slow, and oscillates from one extreme to the opposite.[1] For a time the leaven of Christianity seemed lost in the lump of human sin; but it was doing its great work in ways not seen by mortal eyes. The most profound of all revolutions must require centuries for its work. The good never dies. The Persecutions directed by tyrannical emperors against the new faith, only helped the work. What is written in blood is widely read and not soon forgot. Could the "holy alliance" of Ease, Hypocrisy, and Sin put down Christianity, which proclaimed the One God, the equality and brotherhood of all men? Did Force ever prevail in the long run against Reason or Religion? The ashes of a Polycarp and a Justin sow the earth for a Cadmean harvest of heroes of the soul; a man leaving wife and babes and dying a martyr's death—this is an eloquence the dullest can understand. If a fire is to spread in the forest let all the winds blow upon it. Even a bad thing is not put down by abuse. However, to see the earnest of that vast result Christianity is destined to work out for the nations, we must not look at king's courts, in Byzantium or Paris; not in the chairs of bishops, noble or selfish; not at the martyr's firmness when his flesh is torn off, for the unflinching Tuscarora surpasses "the noble army of martyrs" in fortitude; but in the common walks of life, its every-day trials; in the sweet charities of the fireside and the street; in the self-denial that shares its loaf with the distressful; the honest heart which respects others as itself. Looking deeper than the straws of the surface we see a stream of new life is in the world, and, though choked with mud, not to be dammed up.

The history of Christianity reveals the majestic pre-eminence of its earthly founder. In him amid all his Messianic expectations, there shines a clear religious light— Love to God, Love to Man. Come to the later times of the Apostles, the sky is overcast with dogmatic clouds, and doubtful twilight begins. Take another step, and the darkness deepens. Come down to Justin Martyr, it is deeper still; to Irenæus, Tertullian, Cyprian; to the times of the Council of Nice; read the letters of Ambrose, Jerome, Augustine, the Apologies of Christianity, the fierce bickerings of strong men about matters of no mo-

[1] But see how reluctantly Synesius comes to the duties of a bishop. Ep. 105, cited in Hampden, Bampton Lectures, Lond. 1837, p. 407, et seq.

ment,—we should think it the midnight of the Christian Church, did we not know that after this "woe was past," there came another woe ; that there was a refuge of lies remaining where the blackness of darkness fell, and the shadow of death lingered long and would not be lifted up.

It is not necessary to go into the painful task of tracing the obvious decline of Christianity, and its absorption in the organization of the Church, which assumed the Keys of Heaven, and bound and tortured men on earth. It is beautiful to see the free piety of Paul, amid all his dogmatic subtleties,—a man to whom the world owes so much,[1]—and the happy state of the earlier churches ; when no one controlled another, except by Wisdom and Love ; when each was his own priest, with no middle-man to forestall inspiration, and stand between him and God ; when each could come to the Father, and get truth at first hand if he would. Jesus would break every yoke, but new yokes were soon made, and in his name. He bade men pray as he did ; with no mediator, nothing between them and the Father of all ; making each place a temple and each act a divine service. With the doctrines of his Religion on their tongue ; the example of Jesus to stimulate and encourage them ; the certain conviction that Truth and God were on their side ; going into the world of men sick of their worn-out rituals, and hungering and thirsting after a religion they could confide in, live and die by ; having stout hearts in their bosoms which danger could not daunt, nor gold bribe, nor contempt shame, nor death appal, nor friends seduce—no wonder the Apostles prevailed ! An earnest man, though rude as Böhme, and Bunyan, and Fox, even in our times, coming in the name of Religion, speaking its word of fire, and appealing to what is deepest and divinest in our heart, never lacks auditors. How the zeal of the Mormons makes converts. No wonder the Apostles conquered the world. It were a miracle if they had not put to flight "armies of the aliens," the makers of "silver shrines," and "them that sold and bought in the temple." Man moves man the world round, and Religion multiplies itself as the Banian tree. Men with all the science of the nineteenth century, but no Religion, can scarce hold a village together, while every re-

[1] See Parker, ubi sup., p. 165, et seq.

ligious fanatic, from Mahomet to Mormon, finds followers plenty as flowers in summer, and true as steel. Can no man divine the cause ?

Blessed was the Christian Church while all were brothers. But soon as the Trojan Horse of an organized priesthood was dragged through the ruptured wall, there came out of it, stealthily, men cunning as Ulysses, cruel as Diomed, arrogant as Samuel, exclusive and jealous, armed to the teeth in the panoply of worldliness. The little finger of the Christian priesthood was found thicker than the loins of their fathers—the flamens of Jupiter, Quirinus, the Levitical priests of Jehovah. Then Belief began to take the place of Life ; the priest of the man ; the Church of home ; the Flesh and the Devil of the Word and the Holy Spirit. Divine service was mechanism ; Religion priestcraft ; Christianity a thing for kings to swear by, and to help priests to wealth and fame. But a seed remained that never bowed the knee to the idol. Righteous men, they were cursed by the Church, and blessed by the God of Truth. We are to blame no class of men, neither the learned who were hostile to Christianity, nor the priest who assumed this power for the loaves and fishes' sake ; they were men, and did as others, with their light and temptations, would have done. Looking with human eyes, it is not possible to see how the evil could have been avoided. The wickedness long intrenched in the world ; that under-current of sin which runs through the nations ; the low civilization of the race ; the selfishness of strong men, their awful wars ; the hideous sins of slavery, polygamy, the oppression of the weak ; the power of lust, brutality, and every sin,—these were obstacles that even Christianity could not sweep away in a moment, though strongest of the historic daughters of God. Men could sail safely for some years in the light of Jesus, though seen more and more dimly. But as the stream of time swept them further down, and the cold shadow from mountains of hoary crime came over them anew, they felt the darkness. Let us judge these men lightly. Low as the Christian Church was in the third, fourth, fifth, and sixth centuries, it yet represented the best interests of mankind as no other institution. Individuals but not societies rose above it, and soared away to the Heaven of Peace, amid its cry of excommunication. Let us give the Church its due.

Now as no institution exists and claims the unforced homage of men unless it have some real, permanent excellence, in virtue of which alone it holds its place, being hindered, not helped, by the accidental error, falsity, and sin connected therewith; and since the Christian Church has always stood, in spite of its faults, and filled such a place in human affairs as no other institution, it becomes us to look for the Idea it represents, knowing there must be a great truth to stand so long, extend so wide, and uphold so much that is false.

CHAPTER III.

THE FUNDAMENTAL AND DISTINCTIVE IDEA OF THE CHRISTIAN CHURCH—DIVISION OF THE CHRISTIAN SECTS.

ALL forms of conscious religion have this common point, an acknowledged sense of dependence on God, and each has some special peculiarity of its own, which distinguishes it from all others. Now the essential peculiarity of Christianity is, indeed, that moral and religious character already spoken of;[1] but the formal and theoretic peculiarity, which contradistinguishes it from all other religions, is this doctrine:—That God has made the highest revelation of himself to Man through Jesus of Nazareth. This doctrine—which does not proceed from the absolute character, but from the historical origin of Christianity—is the common ground on which all Christian sects, the Catholic and the Quaker, the Anabaptist, the Rationalist, and the Mormon, are agreed. But as this is logically affirmed by all theoretical Christians, it is as logically denied by all not theoretical Christians. Thus the Jews and Mahometans think their prophets superior to Jesus. When we find a man who is a higher "incarnation of God;" one who teaches

[1] Above, Book III. Ch. iii.

and lives out more of Religion and Morality than Jesus, we are bound to admit that fact, and then cease to be theoretical Christians. Men may now be essential and practical Christians, if they regard Christianity as the Absolute Religion and live it out; or if they live the Absolute Religion and give it no name, though not theoretical, may still be essential Christians.

This distinctive character of Christianity appears in various forms in the different sects. Thus some call Jesus the Infinite God; others the First of Created Beings; others a miraculous Being of a mixed nature, and hence a God-man, the identity of Man and God; others still, a mortal man, the most perfect Representation of Goodness and Religion. These may all be regarded, excepting the last, as more or less mythological statements of this distinctive doctrine.

Now if Christianity be taken for the Absolute Religion, with this theoretical peculiarity, and developed in a man, it has an influence on all his active powers. It affects the Mind, he makes a Theology; the Conscience, he lives a Manly Life; the Imagination, he devises a Symbol, rite, penance, or ceremony. The Theology, the Life, and the Symbol, must depend on the natural endowments and artificial culture of the individual Christian, and as both gifts and the development thereof differ in different men, it is plain that various sects must naturally be formed, each of which, setting out from the first principle common to all religions, and embracing the great theoretical doctrine of Christianity, which distinguishes it from all not-Christian religions, has, besides, a certain peculiar doctrine of its own which separates it from all other Christian sects. These sects are the necessary forms Religion takes in connection with the varying condition of men. The Christian Church as a whole is made up of these parties, all of whom taken together, with their Theologies, Life, and Symbols, represent the amount of absolute Religion which has been developed in Christendom, in the speculative, practical, or æsthetic way. To understand the Christian Church, therefore, we must understand each of its parties, their truth and error, their virtue and vice, and then form an appreciation of the whole matter.

In making the estimate, however, we may neglect such

portions of the Christian Church as have had no influence
on the present development of Christianity amongst us.
Thus we need not consider the Greek and Oriental churches
after the sixth century, as their influence upon the rest of
Christendom ceased to be considerable, in consequence of
the superior practical talents of the Western churches.[1]
The remaining portions may be classified in various ways;
but, for the present purpose, the following seems the best
arrangement, namely :

I. THE CATHOLIC PARTY.
II. THE PROTESTANT PARTY.
III. THOSE NEITHER CATHOLICS NOR PROTESTANTS.

These three will be treated each in its turn.

CHAPTER IV.

THE CATHOLIC PARTY.

THE Catholic Church is the oldest, and in numbers still
the most powerful of all Christian organizations. It grew
as the Christian spirit extended among the ruins of the
old world, by the might of the truth borne in its bosom
overpowering the old worship, the artifice of priests, the
selfishness of the affluent, the might of the strong, the
cherished forms of a thousand years, the impotent armies
of purple kings. It rose from small beginnings. No one
knows who first brought Christianity to Rome; nor who
planted the seed of that hierarchic power which soon became a tree, and at length a whole forest, stretching to
the world's end, enfolding chapels for the pious, and dens
for robbers. The practical spirit of old Rome came into
the Church. Its power grew as Christian freedom declined. The mantle of that giant genius, which made the
seven-hilled city conqueror of the world; the belt of power
which girt the loins of her mighty men, Fabius, Regulus,

[1] See Sermons of Theism, &c., Introduction.

Cicero, Cæsar, passed to the Christian bishops, as that genius fled from the earth, howling over his crumbled work.   The spirit of those ancient heroes came into the Church ; their practical skill ; their obstinate endurance ; their power of speech with words like battles ; their lust of power ; their resolution which nothing could overturn, or satisfy.   The Greek Christians were philosophic, literary ; they could sling stones at a hair's-breadth.   In the early times they had all the advantage of position ; "the chairs of the apostles ; " the Christian Scriptures written in their tongue.   Theirs were the great names of the first centuries, Polycarp, Justin, the Clements, Origen, Eusebius, Athanasius, Basil, the Gregories, Chrysostom. But the Latin Church had the practical skill, the soul to dare, and the arm to execute : its power therefore advanced step by step.   Its chiefs were dexterous men, with the coolness of Cæsar, and the zeal of Hannibal.   Ambrose, Jerome, Augustine, would have been powerful men anywhere—in the court of Sardanapalus, or a college of Jesuits.   They brought the world into the Church.   'Twas the world's gain, but the Church's loss.   The Emperor soon learned to stoop his conquering eagles to the spiritual power, which shook the capital.   The Church held divided sway with him.   The spiritual sceptre was wrested from his hands.   Constantine fled to Byzantium as much to escape the Latin clergy as to defend himself from the warriors of the North.[1]

Now the Catholic Church held to the first truths of Religion and of Christianity, as before shown.   Its peculiar and distinctive doctrine was this, that God still acts upon and inspires mankind, being in some measure immanent therein.   This doctrine is broad enough to cover the world, powerful enough to annihilate the arrogance of any Church.   But the Roman party limited this doctrine by adding, that God did not act by a natural law, directly on the mind and conscience, heart and soul, of each man, who sought faithfully to approach Him, but acted miracu-

---

[1] See the external causes of the superiority of the Roman Church, in Rehm, Geschichte des Mittelalters, Vol. I. p. 516, et seq.   Constantine established public worship on Fridays and Sundays in his army, appointing Priests and Deacons, and providing a Tent for religious purposes in every *Numerus*. Sozomen, H. E. I. C. 8.

lously, through the organization of the Church on its members and no others ; and on them, not because they were men, but instruments of the Church ; not in proportion to a man's gifts, or the use of his gifts, but as he stood high or low in the Church. The humblest priest had a little inspiration, enough to work the greatest of miracles ; the bishop had more ; the Pope, as head of the Church, must be infallibly inspired, so that he could neither act wrong, think wrong, nor feel wrong.

The Absolute Religion and Morality necessarily sets out from the absolute source, the spirit of God in the soul revealing truth. The Catholic Church, on the contrary, starts from a finite source, the limited work of inspired men, namely, the Traditional Word preserved in Scripture and the unscriptural tradition, both written and not written. But then, laying down this indisputable truth, that a book must be interpreted by the same spirit in which it is written, and therefore that a book written by miraculous and superhuman inspiration can be understood only by men inspired in a similar way, and limiting the requisite inspiration to itself, it assumed the office of sole interpreter of the Scriptures ; refused the Bible to the laymen, because they, as uninspired, could not understand it, and gave them only its own interpretation. Thus it attempted to mediate between mankind and the Bible.

Then again, relying on the unscriptural tradition preserved in the Fathers, the Councils, the organization and memory of the Church, it makes this of the same authority as the Scriptures themselves, and so claims divine sanction for doctrines which are neither countenanced by " human Reason," as true, nor " divine Revelation," as contained in the Bible. This is a point of great importance, as it will presently appear.

Now the Catholic Church was logically consistent with itself in both these pretensions. Each individual Church, at first, received what Scripture it saw fit, and interpreted the Word as well as it could. Next the synods decreed for the mass of Churches both the canon of Scripture and the doctrine it contained. The Catholic Church continued to exercise these privileges. Then again, taking the common notion, the Church had a logical and speculative basis for its claim to inspiration, though certainly none in

point of fact. If God miraculously inspired Jesus to
create a new religion, Peter, Paul, and John to preach it,
and Matthew, Mark, and Luke to record the words and
works of Christ and of the Christians, when did the miraculous inspiration cease? With the Apostles, or their successors; the direct, or the remote? Did it cease at all?
It did not appear. Besides, how could the inspired works
be interpreted except by men continually inspired; how
could the Church, founded and built by miraculous action,
be preserved by the ordinary use of man's powers? Were
Jude and James inspired and Clement and Ambrose left
with no open vision? Such a conclusion could not come
from a comparison of their works. Did not Jesus promise
to be with his Church to the end of the world? Here
was the warrant for the assumptions of the Catholic party.
So, with logical consistency, it claimed a perpetual, miraculous, and exclusive inspiration, on just as good ground as
it allowed the claim of earlier men to the same inspiration;
it made Tradition the master over the soul, on just the
same pretension that the Bible is made the only certain
rule of faith and practice. As the only interpreter of
Scripture, the exclusive keeper of tradition, as the vicar
of God, and alone inspired by Him, it stood between man
on the one side, and the Bible, Antiquity, and God, on
the other side. The Church was sacred, for God was immanent therein; the world profane, deserted of Deity.

The Church admits three sources of moral and religious
truth, namely:—
1. The Scriptures of the Old and New Testament and
Apocrypha. It declares these are good and wise, but ambiguous and obscure, and by themselves alone incomplete,
not containing the whole of the doctrine, and requiring an
inspired expositor to set forth their contents.
2. The unscriptural Tradition, oral and written. This
is needed to supply what is left wanting through the imperfection of Scripture, and to teach the more recondite
doctrines of Christianity, such as the Trinity, Redemption,
the Authority of the Church, Purgatory, Intercession, the
use of Confession, Penance, and the like, and also to explain the Scriptures themselves. But Tradition also is imperfect, ambiguous, full of apparent contradictions, and

impossible for the laity to understand, except through the inspired class, who alone could reconcile its several parts.

3. The direct Inspiration of God acting on the official members of the Church; that is, on its councils, priests, and above all on its infallible head.

The Church restricted direct inspiration to itself, and even within its walls the action of God was limited, for if an individual of the clerical order taught what was hostile to the doctrine of the Church, or not contained therein, his inspiration was referred to the Devil, not God, and the man burned, not canonized. Thus inspiration was subjected to a very severe process of verification even within the Church itself. It forbids mankind to trust Reason, Conscience, and the religious Element; to approach God through these, and get truth at first hand, as Moses, Jesus, and the other great men of antiquity had done. For this the layman must depend on the clergy, and the clergyman must depend on the whole Church, represented by the Fathers or Councils, and idealized in its head. Thus the Church was the judge of the doctrine and the practice; invested with the Keys of Heaven and Hell; with power to bind and loose, remit sins, or retain them, and authority to demand absolute submission from the world, or punish with fagots and hell men who would not believe as the Church commanded. In this way it would control private inspiration. But not to leave the heretics hopeless, or drive them to violence, it assumes the right to restore them, and pardon their sins, on condition of submission and penance. The Saviour, the Martyrs, the Saints, had not only expiated their own sins, but performed works of supererogation, and so established a sinking fund to liquidate the sins of the world. This deposit was at the disposal of the Church, who could therewith, aided by the intercession of the beatified spirits, purchase the salvation of a penitent heretic, though his sins were as crimson.

The Church assumed mastery over all souls. The individual was nothing; the Church was all. Its power stood on a miraculous basis; its authority was derived from God. The humblest priests, in celebrating the mass, performed a miracle greater than all the wonders of Jesus, for he only changed water into wine, and fed five thousand men with five loaves; but the priest, by a single word, changed bread and wine into the flesh and blood of Almighty God.   It styles itself God's vicegerent on earth, and as Jesus was a temporary and partial incarnation of the deity, so itself is a perfect and eternal incarnation thereof.   Thus the Christian Church became a Theocracy. It was far more consistent than the Jewish Theocracy, for that allowed private inspiration; and therefore was perpetually troubled by the race of prophets, who never allowed the priests their own way, but cried out with most rousing indignation against the Levites and their followers, and refused to be put down.   Besides, the Jewish Theocracy limited infallibility to God and the Law, which was to be made known to all, and though inspired could be easily understood by the simple son of Israel : it never claimed that for the Priesthood.

Now there are but two scales in the balance of power : the Individual who is ruled, and the Institution that governs, here represented by the Church.   Just as the one scale rises, the other falls.   The spiritual freedom of the individual in the Church is contained in an angle too small to be measurable.   Did men revolt from this iron rule ?   There was the alternative of eternal damnation, for all men were born depraved, exposed to the wrath of God ; their only chance of avoiding hell was to escape through the doors of the Church.   Thus men were morally compelled to submit for the sake of its "redemption."   Did they throw themselves on the mercy of the Holy Ghost, penitent for their disobedience of the Church ?   They were told that mercy was at the Church's disposal.   Did they make the appeal to Scripture, and say, as in Adam all die, so in Christ shall all be made alive ; that he had expiated all their sins ?   The Church told them their exegesis of the passage was wrong, for Christ only expiated their inherited sin, not the actual sins they had committed, and for which they must smart in hell, atone for in purgatory, or get pardoned by submitting to the vicar of God, and going through the rites, forms, fasts, and penances he should prescribe, and thus purchase a share of the redemption which Christ and the saints by their works of supererogation had provided to meet the case.   This doctrine was taught in good faith, and in good faith received.[1]

[1] See, who will, Rehm, ubi sup. Vol. II. p. 541, et seq., and Vol. III. p. 1,

I. *The Merits of the Catholic Church.*

As we look back upon the history of the Church and see the striking unity of that institution, we naturally suppose its chiefs had a regular plan; but such was not the fact. The peculiar merit of the Catholic Church consists in its assertion of the truth, that God still inspires mankind as much as ever; that He has not exhausted himself in the creation of a Moses, or a Jesus, the Law, or the Gospel, but is present and active in spirit as in space: admitting this truth, so deep, so vital to the race—a truth preserved in the religions of Egypt, Greece, and Rome, and above all in the Jewish faith—clothing itself with all the authority of ancient days; the word of God in its hands, both tradition and Scripture; believing it had God's infallible and exclusive inspiration at its heart, for such no doubt was the real belief, and actually, through its Christian character, combining in itself the best interests of mankind, no wonder it prevailed. Its countenance became as lightning. It stood and measured the earth. It drove asunder the nations. It went forth in the mingling tides of civilized corruption and barbarian ferocity, for the salvation of the people,—conquering and to conquer; its brightness as the light.

It separated the spiritual from the temporal power, which had been more or less united in the theocracies of India, Egypt, and Judea, and which can only be united to the lasting detriment of mankind. This was a great merit in the Church; one that cannot be appreciated in our days, for we have not felt the evil it aimed to cure. The Church, in theory, stood on a basis purely moral; it rose in spite of the State; in the midst of its persecutions. At first it shunned all temporal affairs, and never allowed a temporal power to be superior to itself. The department of political action belonged to the State; that of intellectual and religious action, the stablest and strongest of power,—to the

et seq., for the political aspect of the Roman Church; Guizot, Histoire de la Civilization, &c., Leçon II.—VI. X.—XII.; Hallam, State of Europe during the Middle Ages, ch. vii., and the admirably candid remarks thereon in his Supplementary notes. Gibbon, ubi sup. ch. xv. xvi. xviii. xxi. Comte, ubi sup. Vol. V., Leçon LIV. LV., who in some respects surpasses all his predecessors.

Church.   Hence its care of education; hence the influence it exerted on literature.   We read the letters of Ambrose and Augustine and find a spirit all unknown to former times.[1]   Tertullian could oppose the whole might of the State with his pen.   That fierce African did not hesitate to exhibit the crimes of the nation.   The Apologetists assume a tone of spiritual authority surprising in that age.

The Church set apart a speculative class, distinct from all others, including the most cultivated men of their times.   It provided a special education for this class, one most admirably adapted, in many points, for the work they were to do.   Piety and genius found here an asylum, a school, and a broad arena.   Thus it had a troop of superior minds, educated and pious men, who could not absorb the political power, as the sacerdotal class of India, Egypt, and Judea had done; who could not be indifferent to the social and moral condition of mankind, as the priesthood had been in Greece and Rome.   Theoretically, they were free from the despotism of one, and the indifference of the other.   The public virtue was their peculiar charge.

Ancient Rome was the city of organizations, and practical rules.   Nowhere was the Individual so thoroughly subordinated to the State.   War, Science, and Lust, of old time, had here incarnated themselves.   The same practical spirit organized the Church, with its Dictator, its Senate, and its Legions.   The discipline of the clerical class, their union, zeal, and commanding skill, gave them the solidity of the Phalanx, and the celerity of the Legion. The Church prevailed as much by its organization as its doctrine.   What could a band of loose-girt apostles, each warring on his own account, avail against the refuge of Lies, where Strength and Sin had intrenched themselves, and sworn never to yield?   An organized Church was demanded by the necessities of the time; an association of soldiers called for an army of saints.[2]   A sensual people required forms, the Church gave them; superstitious rites, divination, processions, images, the Church—obdurate as steel when occasion demands, but pliant as molten metal

---

[1] See this point ably though briefly treated in Schlosser, ubi sup. Vol. III. Pt. iii. p. 102—151, and iv. p. 25—75.   See also Pt. ii. p. 167, et seq.
[2] See Guizot and Comte.

when yielding is required—the Church allowed all this. Its form grew out of the wants of the time and place.

Was there no danger that the priesthood, thus able and thus organized, should become ambitious of wealth and power? The greatest danger that fathers should seek to perpetuate authority for their children. But this class of men, cut off from posterity by the prohibition of marriage, lived in the midst of ancient and feudal institutions, where all depended on birth; where descent from a successful pirate, or some desperate freebooter, hard-handed and hard-hearted, who harried village after village, secured a man elevation, political power, and wealth; the clergy were cut off from the most powerful of all inducements to accumulate authority. In that long period from Alaric to Columbus, when the Church had ample revenues; the most able and cultivated men in her ranks, so thoroughly disciplined; the awful power over the souls of men, far more formidable than bayonets skilfully plied; with an acknowledged claim to miraculous inspiration and divine authority, were it not for the celibacy of the Christian priesthood—damnable institution, and pregnant with mischief as it was—we should have had a sacerdotal caste, the Levites of Christianity, whose little finger would have been thicker than the loins of all former Levites; who would have flayed men with scorpions, where the priestly despots of Egypt and India only touched them with a feather, and the dawn of a better day must have been deferred for thousands of years. The world is managed wiser than some men fancy. "Surely the wrath of man shall praise Thee, and the remainder of wrath shalt thou restrain," said an old writer. The remedy of inveterate evils is attended with sore pangs. These wretched priests of the middle ages bore a burden, and did a service for us, which we are slow to confess.

The Church, reacting against the sensuality and excessive publicity of the heathen world, in its establishment of convents and monasteries, opened asylums for delicate spirits that could not bear the rage of savage life; afforded a hospital for men sick of the fever of the world, worn-out and shattered in the storms of State, who craved a little rest for charity's sweet sake, before they went where the wicked cease from troubling, and the weary are at rest.

Among the sensual the Saint is always an Anchorite;
Religion gets as far as possible from the world.[1] Rude
men require obvious forms and sensible shocks to their
roughness. The very place where the Monks prayed and
the Nuns sang, was sacred from the ruthless robber. As
he drew near it, the tiger was tame within him; the mail-
ed warrior kissed the ground, and Religion awoke for the
moment in his heart. The fear of hell, and reverence for
the consecrated spot, chained up the devil for the time.

Then the Church had a most diffusive spirit; it would
Christianize as fast as the State would conquer; its missionaries were found in the courts of barbarian monarchs,
in the caves and dens of the savage, diffusing their doctrine and singing their hymns. Creating an organization
the most perfect the world ever saw; with a policy wiser
than any monarch had dreamed of, and which grew more
perfect with the silent accretions of time; with address to
allure the ambitious to its high places, and so turn all
their energy into its deep wide channel; with mysteries to
charm the philosophic, and fill the fancy of the rude; with
practical doctrines for earnest workers, and subtle questions, always skilfully left open for men of acute discern-
ment; with rites and ceremonies that addressed every sense,
rousing the mind like a Grecian drama, and promising a
participation with God through the sacrament; with wisdom enough to bring men really filled with Religion into
its ranks; with good sense and good taste to employ all
the talent of the times in the music, the statues, the paint-
ings, the architecture of the temple, thus consecrating all
the powers of man to man's noblest work; with so much
of Christian truth as the world in its wickedness could not
forget,—no wonder the Church spread wide her influence;
sat like a queen among the nations, saying to one GO, and
it went, to another COME, and it came.

Then, again, its character, in theory, was kindly and
humane. It softened the asperity of secular wars; forbid
them in its sacred seasons; established its Truce of God,
and gave a chance for rage to abate. Against the King,
it espoused the cause of the People. Coming in the name
of one " despised and rejected of men," " a man of sorrows
and acquainted with grief;" of a man born in an ox's crib,

[1] To illustrate this point see, *instar omnium*, the works of St Bernard.

at his best estate not having where to lay his head; who died at the hangman's hand, but who was at last seated at the right hand of God, and in his low estate was deemed God in humiliation come down into the flesh, to take its humblest form, and show He was no respecter of persons, —the Church did not fail to espouse the cause of the people, with whom Christianity found its first adherents, its apostles, and defenders. With somewhat in its worst days of the spirit of him who gave his life a ransom for many, with much of it really active in its best days, and its theory at all times, the Church stood up, for long ages, the only bulwark of freedom; the last hope of man struggling but sinking as the whelming waters of barbarism whirled him round and round. It came to the Baron, haughty of soul, and bloody of hand, who sat in his cliff-tower, a hungry giant; who broke the poor into fragments, ground them to powder, and spurned them like dust from his foot; it came between him and the captive, the serf, the slave, the defenceless maiden, and stayed the insatiate hand. Its curse blasted as lightning. Even in feudal times, it knew no distinction of birth; all were "conceived in sin," "shapen in iniquity," alike the peasant and the peer. The distinction of birth, station, was apparent, not real. Yet were all alike children of God, who judged the heart, and knew no man's person; all heirs of Heaven, for whom prophets and apostles had uplifted their voice; yes, for whom GOD had worn this weary, wasting weed of flesh, and died a culprit's death. Then while nothing but the accident of distinguished birth, or the possession of animal fierceness, could save a man from the collar of the thrall, the Church took to her bosom all who gave signs of talent and piety; sheltered them in her monasteries; ordained them as her priests; welcomed them to the chair of St Peter; and men who from birth would have been companions of the Galilean fisherman, sat on the spiritual throne of the world, and governed with a majesty which Cæsar might envy, but could not equal. Priests came up from no Levitical stock, but the children of captives and bondmen as well as prince and peer. When northern barbarism swept over the ancient world; when temple and tower went to the ground, and the culture of old time, its letters, science, arts, were borne

off before the flood,—the Church stood up against the
tide; shed oil on its wildest waves; cast the seed of truth
on its waters, and as they gradually fell, saw the germ send
up its shoot, which growing while men watch and while
they sleep, after many days, bears its hundred-fold, a
civilization better than the past, and institutions more be-
neficent and beautiful.

The influence of the Church is perhaps greater than
even its friends maintain. It laid its hand on the poor and
down-trodden; they were raised, fed, and comforted. It
rejected, with loathing, from its coffers, wealth got by ex-
tortion and crime. It touched the shackles of the slave,
and the serf arose disenthralled, the brother of the peer.
It annihilated slavery, which Protestant cupidity would
keep for ever.[1] It touched the diadem of a wicked king,
and it became a crown of thorns; the monarch's sceptre
was a broken reed before the crosier of the Church.[2] Its
rod, like the wand of Moses, swallowed up all hostile rods.
Like God himself, the Church gave, and took away, rendering no reason to man for its gifts or extortions. It sent
missionaries to the east and the west, and carried the
waters of baptism from the fountains of Nubia to the roaring Geysers of a Northern isle. It limited the power of
kings; gave religious education to the people, which no
ancient institution ever aimed to impart; kept on its
sacred hearth the smouldering embers of Greek or Roman
thought; cherished the last faint sparkles of that fire Pro-
metheus brought from Gods more ancient far than Jove.
It had ceremonies for the sensual; confessionals for the

[1] See, in Comte, ubi sup. Vol. V. p. 407, et seq., some Reflections on the
milder Character of Slavery in *Catholic* America. compared with Slavery in
Protestant America; and yet Comte is hardly a Theist. For the influence of
Christianity on Slavery, see the accounts of Paulinus, Deogratias, Patiens, and
Synesius, in Schlosser, Vol. III. Part III. p. 284, et seq. Gibbon, in his
heartless way, passes over with scarce a notice, the beautiful Christianity
brought into Rome, and its influence on the condition of slaves. Hallam makes
but a one-sided appreciation of the Catholic church, and it seems to me has not
done justice to its merits. But see what ample amends he makes in the supplementary notes. Bp England, Letters to Hon. John Forsyth, Balt. 1844,
labours to show that the Catholic church has been the uncompromising *Friend*
of Slavery. He certainly makes out a strong case, *though not without a little*
suppression of the Truth, as it seems to me.

[2] See an early instance of the collision between the spiritual and temporal
power in the case of Ambrose, Archbishop of Milan, and the Queen Justina, in
Fleury, ubi sup. Liv. XVIII. Chap. 32, et seq., and also in Gibbon, Chap.
XXVII.

pious—needed and beautiful in their time—labours of love
for the true-hearted; pictures and images to rouse devotion in the man of taste; temples whose aspiring turrets
and sombre vaults filled the kneeling crowd with awe; it
had doctrines for the wise; rebukes for the wicked;
prayers for the reverent; hope for the holy, and blessings
for the true. It sanctified the babe, newly-born and welcome; watched over marriage with a jealous eye; fostered
good morals; helped men, even by its symbols, to partake
the divine nature; smoothed the pillow of disease and
death, giving the Soul wings, as it were, to welcome the
death-angel, and gently, calmly, pass away. It assured
masculine piety of its reward in Heaven; told the weak
and wavering, that divine beings would help him, if faithful. In the honours of canonization, it promised the most
lasting fame on earth; generations to come should call the
good man a blessed saint, and his name never perish while
the Christian year went round. Heroism of the Soul took
the place of boldness in the Flesh. It did not, like Polytheism, deify warriors and statesmen—Attila, Theodosius,
Clovis, their kingdom was of this world; but it canonized
martyrs and saints, Polycarp, Justin, Ambrose, Paulinus,
Bernard of Clairvaux.[1]

Such were some of the excellences, theoretical or practical, of the Church. This hasty sketch does not allow more
particular notice of them.

II. *The Defects and Vices of the Catholic Party.*

But the Church had vices, vast and awful to the thought.
As its distinctive excellence was to proclaim the continu-
ance of inspiration, so its sacramental sin was in limiting
this inspiration to itself, thus setting bounds to the Spirit
of God and the Soul of Man. Who shall say to the Infinite
God, Hitherto shalt Thou come, but no further; Thou hast
inspired Moses and Jesus, the Apostles, and the Church;
well done! now rest from thy work, and speak no more,
except as we prescribe? The Church did say it.
The wondrous mechanism of the Church and much of

---

[1] Canonization among the Catholics seems to come from the same root with
the Apotheosis of the Polytheists. Both, no doubt, exerted an influence on
men who asked a recompense for being good and religious.

its power came from this false assumption, that it alone had the Word of God. So its organization was based on a lie, and required new lies to uphold, and prophets of lies to defend it. Its servants, the priests, became proud of spirit. The only keepers of Scripture and Tradition; the only recipients of inspiration, they forbid free inquiry as of no use; stifled Conscience as only leading men into trouble; and excommunicated Common Sense, who asked "terrible questions," calling for the title-deeds of the Church. They went further, and forbid the bands between Reason and Religion; and when the parties insisted on the union, turned them both out of doors with a curse. The laity must not approach God, as the clergy; must only commune with Him "in one kind." The Church forgot God grants inspiration to no one except on condition he conforms to the divine law, living pure and true, and grants it only in proportion to his gifts and his use thereof: so, relying on the office and "apostolical succession" for inspiration, the priests lived shameless and wicked lives, rivalling Sardanapalus and Domitian in their cruelty and sin. They forgot that God withholds inspiration from none that is faithful; so they stoned the prophets who rebuked their lies and published their sin; they shamefully entreated men whom God sent of his errands to these unworthy husbandmen. They became spiritual tyrants, forcing all men to utter the same creed, submit to the same rite, reverence the same symbol, and be holy in the same way.

In its zeal to separate the spiritual power from temporal hands it took what was not its own—power over men's bodies; and made laws for the State.[1] In its haste to give preëminence to spiritual things, it made its offices a bribe, greater than the State could give. The honour of sainthood—what was the fame of king and conqueror to that? It promised the rewards of high clerical office, and even of canonization, to the most mercenary and cruel of men, whose touch was pollution. Its list of saints is full of knaves and despots. The State was taken into the Church, —a refractory member. The Flesh and the Devil were baptized; "took holy orders;" governed the Church in some cases, but were still the Flesh and the Devil, though

---

[1] See Hallam, ubi suprà, Chap. VII.

called by a Christian name. That divine man, whose name is ploughed into the world, said, If a man smite the one cheek, turn the other; but if a man lifted his hand or his voice against the Church,—it blasted him with damnation and hell. Christ said his kingdom was not of this world; so said the Church at first, and Christians refused to war, to testify in the courts, to appear in the theatres, and foul their hands with the world's sin. But soon as there was an organized priesthood, to defend themselves from the tyranny of the State, to exercise authority over the souls of men, power on the earth became needed. One lie leads to many. What the Church first took in self-defence it afterwards clung to and increased, and was so taken up with its earthly kingdom, it quite forgot its patrimony in Heaven; so it played a double game, attempting to serve God, and keep on good terms with the Devil. But it was once said, "no man can serve two masters." Unnatural, spiritual power could not be held without temporal authority to sustain it; so the Church took fleshly weapons for its carnal ends. Monks raised armies; Bishops led them; God was blasphemed by prayers to aid bloodshed. The Church sold her garment to buy a sword.

The Church was the exclusive vicar of God; she must have "the tonnage and poundage of all freespoken truth." To accomplish this end and establish her dogmas, she slew men, beginning with Priscillian and "the six Gnostics," in the fourth century, at Triers, and ending no one knows where, or when, or with whom.[1] It had such zeal for the "unity of the faith," that it put prophets in chains; asked the sons of God if they were "greater than Jacob." It made Belief take the place of Life. It absolved men of their sins, past, present, and future. Emancipated the clergy from the secular law, thus giving them license to sin. It sold heaven to extortioners for a little gold, and built St Peter's with the spoil. It wrung ill-gotten gains out of tyrants on their death-bed; devoured the houses of widows and the weak; built its cathedrals out of the spoil

[1] See the story, in Sulpitius Severus, Hist. Sac. Lib. II. ch. 50, 51. Fleury, ubi suprà, Liv. XVII. ch. 56, 57, and XVIII. ch. 29, 30. The Pope, St Leo, commended the action, but Gregory of Tours and Ambrose of Milan condemned it. Idacius and Ithacius, the two bishops who caused the execution, were expelled from their office by the popular indignation. See Jerome, Illust. Virorum, C. 122, et seq.

of orphans, thus literally giving a stone when bread was asked for, as St Bernard honestly called it.[1] It was greedy of gold and power, and at one time had well-nigh half the lands of England held in mortmain. It absolved men from oaths; broke marriages; told lies; forged charters and decretals; burned the philosophers; corrupted the classics; altered the words of the Fathers; changed the decisions of the Councils, and filled Europe with its falsehood.[2] It has fought the most hideous of wars; evangelized nations with the sword; laid kingdoms under interdict to gratify its pride.

The Church boasts of its uniform doctrine, but it changes every age; of its peaceful spirit, but who fought the crusades, the wars of extermination in Switzerland, France, the Low Countries? To whom must we set down the ecclesiastical butchery that filled Europe with funeral piles? It quarrelled with the temporal power, and built up institutions of tyranny to suppress truth; kept the Bible to itself; made the Greek Testament a prohibited book; brought dead men's bones into the temples, for the living to worship, and worked lying wonders to confirm false doctrine. It loved the night of the Dark Ages, and clung to its old dogmas.

The Church came at length to be a colossus of crime, with a thin veil of hypocrisy drawn over its face, and that only. The vow of purity its children took, became a license for sin. The corruptest of courts was the court of the Pope. What reverence had the Archbishops for the doctrine of the Church? Cardinal Bembo bid Sadolet not read St Paul, it would spoil his taste. In early ages the Apostles were the devoutest of men; in later days their "successors" were steeped to the lips in crime.[3]

---

[1] Dante touchingly complains of the evil which Constantine brought on the church *by the gifts which the first wealthy Pope received of him!* Inferno, XIX. 115, et seq.

[2] See instances of this forgery in Hallam, ubi sup. Ch. VII. p. 391, et seq. et al., ed. Paris; Daillé, on the right Use of the Fathers, &c., London, 1841, passim.; Middleton, ubi suprà. But see, on the side of the Church, Bossuet, Defense de la Tradition et des Saints Peres, and Manzoni, Osservazioni sulla Morale Cattolica, Firenze, 1835.

[3] See Hallam, ubi sup. Ch. VII. De-Potter loves to dwell on the faults of the church, for which there is sufficient opportunity; Neander, as much too lenient, errs on the other side. Much information in a popular form may be found in M. Roux-Ferrand, Histoire des Progrès de la Civilization en Europe,

For centuries, the Church, like the Berserkers of northern romance, seemed to possess the soul and strength of each antagonist it slew. But its hour struck. The work it required ten centuries to mature, stood in its glory not one. Each transient institution has a truth, or it would not be ; an error, or it would stand for ever. The truth opens men's eyes ; they see the error and would reject it. Then comes the perpetual quarrel between the Old and the New. "Every battle of the warrior," says an ancient prophet, "is with confused noise, and garments rolled in blood ; " but the battle of the Church was a devouring flame.

In the time of Boniface VIII., or about the end of the fourteenth century, an eye that read the signs of the times, and saw the cloud and the star below the horizon, could have foretold the downfal of the Church. Its brightest hour was in the day of Innocent III. A wise Providence governs the affairs of men, and never suffers the leaf to fall till the swelling bud crowds it off. Out of the ashes of the old institution there springs up a new being, soon as the world can give it place. No institution is normal and ultimate. It has but its day, and never lasts too long nor dies too soon. Judaism and Heathenism nursed and swaddled mankind for Christianity, which came in the fulness of time. The Catholic Church rocked the cradle of mankind. In due season, like a jealous nurse, assiduous and meddlesome, but grown ill-tempered with age and disgust of new things, she yields up with reluctance her rebellious charge, whose vagaries her frowns and stripes will not restrain ; whose struggling weight, her withered arms are impotent to bear ; whose aspiring soul her anicular and maudlin wit cannot understand. Her promise will not coax ; nor her baubles bribe ; nor her curses affright him more. The stripling child will walk alone.

The Protestant "Reformation" came from the action of Ideas which had not justice done them in the Catholic Church, just as the Christian Reformation from Ideas not sufficiently represented in Judaism and Heathenism. It did not, more than the other, come all at once. There was "Lutheranism" before Luther, as Christianity before

6 vols. 8vo, Paris, 1833—1841, Vol. I. II., Leçons X.—XII., Vol. III. ch. iv.—vi., Vol. IV. ch. v.—vii., et al., and Mrs Child's Religious Ideas, N. Y. 1855, Vols. II. and III.

Christ.   Slowly the ages prepared for both, for each was a point in the development of man.   The Church educated men to see her faults ; gave them weapons to attack her. The Reformation was long a gathering in the bosom of the Church itself.[1]   Athanasius had his Arius to contend with.   There was always some Paul of Samosata, some Theodore of Mopsuestia, some Peter of Bruis, or Henry of Lausanne, to trouble the church.   In the twelfth century it took all the miracles of Clairvaux and the leanness of its Abbot, to put down the heretics, who would come up again. Was there not Waldo in France, Arnold of Brescia in the papal state, John Huss at Constance, and Wicliff in England, and all of them at no great distance of time ? Faustus and Gutenberg did more for the Reformation than the Diet at Worms.   Luther, and Zwingle, and Calvin, and the host of great men who grew in their shadow, were only the heralds that blew the trumpet of the Reformation ; its prize-fighters, not directors of the movement.   It was the God of nations that moved the world's heart.   The Spirit only culminated in Luther and his friends.   It burned in holy souls in Bohemia and Languedoc, and the valleys of the Pyrenees, and the mountains of Tyrol ; it breathed in lofty minds at Paris, Saxony, Padua, London, Rome itself.   Every learned Greek the Turks frighted from Constantinople, or Italian wealth lured to the queen of cities ; every manuscript of the Classics, the Fathers, the Councils, the Scriptures which found deliverance from the moles and the bats ; every improvement in law, science, and art ; every discovery in Alchemy or Astrology ; every invention from the mariner's compass to monk Schwartz's gunpowder, was an agent of the Reformation.   We find Reformers, from the time of Marcion to John Wessel. Some tried, as in the time of Jesus, to put new wine in old bottles, but losing both, looked round for new things. That long train of Mystics, from Dionysius the Areopagite to Meister Eckart of Strasburg, prepared for the work which Luther built up with manly shouting.

To sum up the claim of this party ; the Catholic Church

---

[1] Ranke in his Die römischen Päbste, &c. im. 16, und 17 Jarhhundert, gives abundant proof of this reformatory movement in the church itself.   See particularly Vol. I. B. II., but the tale of ecclesiastical *crime* is even more distinctly told.

is based on the assumption that God inspires that Church, miraculously and exclusively. This assumption is false. Though the oldest organization in the world, it has no right over the soul of man.[1]

CHAPTER V.

THE PROTESTANT PARTY.

THE distinctive idea of Protestantism is this : the canonical Scriptures of the Old and New Testaments are the direct Word of God, and therefore the only Infallible Rule of religious Faith and Practice. It logically denied that an inspired man was needed to stand between mankind and the inspired Word. Each man must consult the Scriptures for himself; expound them for himself, by the common rules of grammar, logic, and rhetoric. Each man, therefore, must have freedom of conscience up to this point, but no further. God was immanent in the Scriptures; not in the Church. The ecclesiastical tradition was no better than other traditions. It might, or it might not, be true. The Catholic Church had no miraculous inspiration.

Now it was a great step for the human race to make this assertion in the sixteenth century; it demanded no little manhood to do so at that time. Where were the men who had made it in the sixth, and all subsequent centuries ?

---

[1] See, who will, the Roman doctrine thoroughly attacked in the ponderous folio of Joh. Gerhard, Confessio Catholica, &c. &c., Frankfort, 1679; and the superficial and somewhat one-sided Essay of M. Bouvet, Du Catholicisme, du Protestantisme, et de la Philosophie en France, Paris, 1840. But see the attack of Simmichius on Protestantism, Confessionistarum Goliathismus profligatus, &c. &c., Louvan, 1667. Many of the most important claims of the Catholic Church, that of Supremacy in temporal affairs, Infallibility in spiritual matters, and the Right to enforce doctrines, are abandoned by an able Catholic writer, J. H. Von Wessenberg, the late bishop of Constance. See his Die grossen Kirchenversammlungen des 15ten und 16ten Jahrhundert, Const. 1840, 4 vols. 8vo.

Their bones and their disgrace paved the highway on which Luther walked as a giant to a fame world-wide and abiding. At first the work of the Protestants, like that of all the Reformers, was negative, exposing the errors and sins of the Catholic party; clearing the spot on which to erect their Church; fighting with words and blows. In the war of the giants, sore strokes must be laid on. The ground shook and the sky rang with the quarrel. "God will see," said stout Martin, "which gives out first, the Pope or Luther." The Church thundered and lightened from the seven-hilled city looking with a frown towards Saxony. Luther gave back thunder for thunder, scorn for scorn. Did the Church condemn Luther? He paid it back in the same pence. The Church says, "Luther is a heretic, and should be burned had we skill to catch him." Luther declares, "The Pope is a wolf possessed with the devil, and we ought to raise the hue and cry, and tear him to pieces without judge or jury."

I. *The Merit of Protestantism.*

Its merit as a Reformation was both negative and positive. It was right in declaring the Roman Church, with its clergy, cardinals, councils, popes, no more inspired than other men, and therefore no more fit than others to keep Tradition, expound Scripture, and hold the keys of Heaven; nay, more, that by reason of their prejudice, ignorance, sloth, ambition, crime, and sin in general, they had less inspiration, for they had grieved away the Spirit of God. It was right in denying the authority of the Church in temporal matters; in declaring that its tradition was no better than other tradition, nay, was even less valuable, for the Church had told lies in the premises, and the fact was undeniable. The Protestants justified their words in this matter by exposing the weak points of the Church, its lies, false doctrines, and wicked practices; its arrogance and worldly ambition; the disagreement of the popes; the contradictions of the councils and fathers, and the crimes of the clergy, who make up the Church. It was right in examining the canon of Scripture, casting off what was apocryphal, or spurious; in demanding that the laity should have the Bible and the Sacraments in full, and claim the right to interpret Scripture, reject tradition, relics, saints, and have nothing between them and Christ or God. It was right in demanding freedom of conscience for all men, up to the point of accepting the Scriptures.[1] This was no vulgar merit, but one we little appreciate. The men who fight the battle for all souls, rarely get justice from the world.

II. *The Vice and Defect of Protestantism.*

Its capital vice was to limit the power of private inspiration, and, since there must be somewhere a standard external or within us, to make the Bible Master of the Soul. Theoretically, it narrowed the sources of religious truth, and instead of three, as the Catholics, it gave us but one; though practically it did more than the Catholics, for it brought men directly to one fountain of truth.[2] Now if the Catholic had an undue reverence for the organized Church, so had the Protestant for the Scriptures. Both sought in the world of concrete things an infallible source and standard of moral and religious truth. There is none such out of human consciousness; neither in the Church, nor the Bible. Both must be idealized to support this pretension. Accordingly as the one party idealized the Church; assumed its divine Origin, its Infallibility, and the exclusive Immanence of God therein; so the other assumed the divine origin of the Scriptures, their Infallibility, and the exclusive Immanence of God in them. Has either party proved its point? Neither is capable of proof. As the Catholic maintained, in the very teeth of notorious facts, that there was no contradiction in the doctrines of the

---

[1] It is not necessary to cite the proofs of the above statements from the Reformers, as they may be seen in the dogmatical writers so often referred to before. However, the most significant passages may be found collected in Harles, Theologische Encyclopädie und Methodologie, Leips. 1837, Chap. III. IV. The early Reformers differ in opinion as to the authority of the Bible. It is well known with what freedom and contempt Luther himself spoke of parts of the canon, and the stories of miracles in the Gospels and Pentateuch. But his own opinion fluctuated on this as on many other points. He cared little for Matthew, Mark, and Luke. Indeed, it would not require a very perverse ingenuity to make out, from the Reformers, a *Straussianismus ante Straussium.*

[2] This is, logically speaking, the fundamental principle of the Reformers, though qualifications of it may be found in Luther, Melancthon, Zwingle, and Calvin, which detract much from its scientific rigour. But still the principle was laid down at the bottom of the Protestant fabric, and is yet a stone of stumbling and rock of offence to free men.

19 *

Church, its popes and councils, and more eminent Fathers ;
in the very face of Reason, that all its doctrines were true
and divine ; so did the Protestant, in the teeth of facts
equally notorious, deny there was any contradiction in the
doctrines of the Bible, its prophets, evangelists, apostles ;
in the very face of Reason, declared that every word of
Scripture was the word of God, and eternally true !   Nay,
more, the Protestants maintained that the record of Scripture was so sacred, that a divine Providence watched over
it and kept all errors from the manuscript.   What a cry
the Protestants made about the " various readings."
Could Cappellus get his book on the textual variations of
the Old Testament printed under Protestant favour ?   A
perpetual miracle, said Protestantism, kept the text of the
Old Testament and New Testament from the smallest accident.   But that doctrine would not stand against the noble
army of various readings—thirty thousand strong.

"Where there is no vision, the people perish."   The
Protestants, denying there was inspiration now as in Paul's
time, yet knowing they must have religious truth or
the Word of God, clung like dying men to the letter of the
Bible, as their only hope.   The words of the Bible had
but one meaning, not many ; that was to be got at by
the usual methods—pious and honest study of the gram-
matical, logical, rhetorical sense thereof.[1]   With its word,
man must stop, for he has reached the fountain-head.
But has the word of God become a letter ; is all truth
in the Bible, and is no error, no contradiction therein ?
Was the doctrine once revealed to the saints, revealed
once for all ?   Is the Bible a Finality, and man only provisional ?   So said Protestantism.   This was its vice.
But God has set one thing against another, so that all
work together for good.   It was a great step to get back
to the Bible, and freedom of conscience, and good sense in
its exposition.

Protestantism wrought wonders, and overthrew the magi-

---

[1] Chemnitz, Loci communes, Pt. III. p. 235, et al., denounces the doctrine of
the Church, that the Bible was " imperfect, insufficient, ambiguous, and obscure."
Luther and Melancthon condemn the old practice of *allegorizing* Scripture.
See the passages collected in Harles, ubi sup. p. 133, et seq., and the dogmatical
writers above referred to, Strauss, Glaubenslehre, § 12, 13, Seckendorf, De
Lutheranismo, &c., ed. 1688, p. 10, 38, 130, 74.   But on the other side, see
Gazzaniga, ubi sup. Vol. I. p. 171, et seq.

cians in the Egypt of the Church. It saw the ecclesiastical Pharaoh and his host in the Red Sea, with destruction opening its hungry jaws to devour them. But it had a mixed multitude in its own train, and left the people in the wilderness, wandering like the Gibeonites, with no power to get bread from Heaven, or water from the living rock. Its Jethros were philologists who knew nothing of the spiritual land of hills and brooks, and milk and honey. Its leaders—men noble as Moses, men of vast soul, and Herculean power to do and suffer, to speak and be silent —had a Pisgah view of the land of promise, and wished God would put his spirit on all the people; but they died and gave no sign. The nations are still wandering in the desert; carrying the Sanctuary, the Ark, the Table of the Law; sometimes sighing after the leeks and garlics left behind; now and then worshipping a calf of gold, of parchment, or spoken wind; murmuring and rebellious; with here and there a Korah, Dathan, and Abiram rising up in their ranks, clouds enough, but with no Moses nor Pillar of Fire. Still, God be praised, we are no longer slaves under the iron bondage of the Church. They were MEN who dared to come out, those heroes of the Reformation. This Protest against the Roman Church was one of the noblest the world ever saw; perhaps never surpassed but once, and then by a single soul, big as yesterday, to-day, and for ever. Stout-hearted Martin Luther, with his face rugged, homely, and honest, with a soul of fire, and words like cannon-shot, a heart that feared neither Pope nor Devil, and a living faith which sang in his dungeon,— "The Lord our God is a castle strong,"—the greatest of the prophets and the "chiefest of apostles" seems little to him. We may thank God and take courage, remembering that such men have been, and may be. There is no tyranny like the spiritual—that of soul over soul; no heroism like that which breaks the bonds of such tyranny. You shall find men thick as acorns in autumn, who will wade neck-deep in blood, and charge up to the cannon's mouth, when it rains shot as snow-flakes at Christmas. Such men may be had for red coats and dollars, and "fame." It requires only vulgar bravery for that, and men who are "food for powder." But to oppose the institution which your fathers loved in centuries gone by; to sweep off the altars, forms, and usages that ministered to your mother's piety, helped her bear the bitter ills and cross of life, and gave her winged tranquillity in the hour of death ; to sunder your ties of social sympathy ; destroy the rites associated with the aspiring dream of childhood, and its earliest prayer, and the sunny days of youth—to disturb these because they weave chains, invisible but despotic, which bind the arm and fetter the foot, and confine the heart; to hew down the hoary tree under whose shadow the nations played their game of life, and found in death the clod of the valley sweet to their weary bosom,—to destroy all this because it poisons the air and stifles the breath of the world—it is a sad and a bitter thing ; it makes the heart throb, and the face, that is hard as iron all over in public, weeps in private, weak woman's tears it may be. Such trials are not for vulgar souls ; they feel not the riddle of the world. The vulgar Church—it will do for them, for it bakes bread, and brews beer. Would you more? No. That is enough for blind mouths. Duty, Freedom, Truth, a divine Life, what are they ? Trifles no doubt to monk Tetzel, the Leos and the Bembos, and other sleek persons, new and old. But to a heart that swells with Religion, like the Atlantic pressed by the wings of the storm, they are the real things of God, for which all poor temporalities of fame, ease, and life are to be cast to the winds. It is needful that a man be true ; not that he live. Are men dogs, that they must be happy ? Luther dared to be undone.

The sacramental error of Protestantism in restricting private judgment to the doctrines of the Bible, was in part neutralized by admitting freedom of individual conscience, and therefore the right and the duty to interpret the Bible. Here it allowed great latitude. Each man might determine by historical evidence his own canon of Scripture, in some measure, and devise his own method of interpretation. Yet the old spirit of the Church was still there, to watch over the exegesis. The Bible was found very elastic, and therefore hedges were soon set about it in the shape of symbolical books, creeds, thirty-nine articles, catechisms, and confessions of faith, which cooped up the soul in narrower limits. But these formularies, like the Scriptures, were found also indefinite, and would hold the most opposite doctrines, for though the schoolmen doubted whether two similar spirits could occupy at once the same point of space, it is put beyond a doubt that two very dissimilar doctrines may occupy the same words at the same time. Taking "substance for doctrine," any creed may be subscribed to, and a solemn ecclesiastical farce continue to be enacted, as edifying if not so entertaining as the old Miracle-plays. That was popular advice for theologians which the old Jesuit gave: "Let us fix our own meaning to the words, and then subscribe them." The maxim is still "as good as new."

This new and exclusive reverence for the Bible led to popular versions of it; to a hard study of its original tongues; and a most diligent examination of all the means interpreting its words. Here a wide field was opened for critical study, which even yet has not been thoroughly explored. A host of theological scholars sprang up, armed to the teeth with Greek and "the terrible Hebrew," and attended by a Babylonian legion of oriental tongues and rabbinical studies,—scholars who had no peers in the Church, at least, since the time of Jerome, who translated, so he says, the book of Tobit from the Chaldaic in a day! But this study led to extravagance. Sound principles of interpretation were advanced by some of the Reformers, but they were soon abandoned. Thus, to take a single example: Luther, Zwingle, and Melancthon said, A passage of Scripture can have but one meaning.[1] It is unquestionably true. But certain doctrines must be maintained, and defended by Scripture; therefore if this could not be done by the natural meaning of Scripture, a secondary sense or a type must be sought. Of course it was found. The old allegorical way of interpretation was bad, but this typical improvement and doctrine of secondary senses was decidedly worse.[2] In the hands of both Protestant and Catholic interpreters, the Bible is clay, to be turned into any piece of ecclesiastical pottery the case may require;

[1] Luther himself did not always adhere to this rule in explaining the Old Testament.
[2] See Strauss, Leben Jesu, § 3, 4; Palfrey, ubi sup. Vol. II. Lect. xxxiii.; Rosenmüller, Handbuch für Literatur der bib. Kritik. &c., Vol. IV. p. 1, et seq.

persecuted in one sense they flee into another. It is a very Proteus, and takes all forms at pleasure. Now it is a river placid as starlight, then a lion roaring for his prey. Job went through some troubles in his life, as the poem relates; but even death has not placed him where the wicked cease from troubling, and the weary are at rest. Professors and critics have handled him more sorely than Satan, his friends, or his wife. They have made him "sin with his lips;" his saddest disease he has caught at their hands; his greatest calamity was his exposition. "Oh that mine adversary had written a book," said the patient man. Did he wish to explain it? Then is he rightly treated, for the explainers have ploughed upon his back; they made long their furrows. Moses, says the Hebrew Scripture, was the most tormented of all the earth, but his trials in the wilderness were nothing to his sufferings on the rack of exegesis. The Critics and Truth have disputed over him as the Devil and Michael, but not without railing. The prophets had a hard time of it in their day and generation; but Jeremiah was put into his darkest dungeon by Christian scholars; Isaiah was never so painfully sawn asunder as by the interpreters, to whom facts are as no facts, and one day as a thousand years, in their chronology. Jonah and Daniel were never in such fatal jeopardy as at the present day. A choleric man in the Psalms could not curse his foes, but he uttered maledictions against "the enemies of the Church;" nor speak of recovering from illness, but "he predicts an event which took place a thousand years later." A young Hebrew could not write an Anacreontic, but he spoke "of the Church and Christ." Nay, Daniel, Paul, and John must predict the "abomination of Rome;" all the great events as they take place, and even the end of the world, in the day some fanatical interpreter happens to live. Is the Bible the Protestant standard of faith? Then it is more uncertain than the things to be measured. The cloud in Hamlet is not more variable than the "infallible rule" in the hands of the interpreters. The best things are capable of the worst abuse. Alas, when shall Science and Religion have their place with the sons of men?

Now since Protestantism denied the Immanence of God

in the Church, as such, and flouted the claim to inspiration when made by any modern, it is plain there could be no one Authoritative Church; all qualitatively were equal, resting on the same foundation. Then admitting freedom of judgment, within the limits of the Bible, and great latitude in expounding that; not very often burning men for heresy,—though cases enough in point might easily be cited,—and encouraging great activity of mind, it led to diversity of opinions, sentiments, and practice. This began in the Reformers themselves. Religion took different shapes in Ulrich von Hutten and John Calvin. Men obeyed their natural affinities, and grouped themselves into sects, each of which recognizing the great principle of all Religion; the special doctrine of Christianity; the peculiar dogma of Protestantism has also some distinctive tenet of its own. Soon as the outward pressure of Papal hostility was somewhat lightened, these conflicting elements separated into several Churches. Now neglecting those, with which we in New England have little to do, the rest may be divided into two parties, namely :—

I. Those who set out from the idea that God is a Sovereign.

II. Those who set out from the idea that God is a Father.

The theology and ethics, the virtue and vice, of each require a few words.

I. *The Party that sets out from the Sovereignty of God.*

This party takes the supernatural view before pointed out. It makes God an awful king. The universe shudders at his presence. The thunder and earthquake are but faint whispers of his wrath, as the magnificence of earth and sky is but one ray out from the heaven of his glory. He sits in awful state. Human flesh quails at the thought of Him. It is terrible to fall into his hands, as fall we must. Man was made not to be peaceful and blessed, but to serve the selfishness of the All-King, to glorify God and to praise him. Originally, Man was made pure and upright. But in order to tempt beyond his strength the frail creature he had made, God forbid him the exercise of a natural inclination, not evil in itself. Man disobeyed the arbitrary command. He " fell." His first sin brought on him the eternal vengeance of the all-powerful King; hurled him at once from his happiness; took from him the majesty of his nature; left him poor, and impotent, and blind, and naked; transmitting to each of his children all the " guilt " of the primeval sin. Adam was the " federal head of the human race." " In Adam's fall we sinned all." Man has now no power of himself to discern good from evil, and follow the good. His best efforts are but " filthy rags " in God's sight; his prayer an " abomination." Man is born " totally depraved." Sin is native in his bones. Hell is his birthright. To be anything acceptable to God he must renounce his " nature," violate the law of the soul. He is a worm of the dust, and turns this way and that, and up and down, but finds nothing in Nature to cling by and climb on.

God is painted in the most awful colours of the Old Testament. The flesh quivers while we read, and the soul recoils upon itself with suppressed breath, and ghastly face, and sickening heart. The very Heavens are not clean in his sight. The grim, awful King of the world, " a jealous God visiting the iniquities of the fathers upon the children;" " angry with the wicked every day," and " keeping anger for ever;" " of purer eyes than to behold iniquity," he hates Sin, though he created it, and Man, though he made him to fall, " with a perfect hatred." Vengeance is his, and he will repay. He must therefore punish Man with all the exquisite torture which infinite Thought can devise, and Omnipotence apply; a Creditor, he exacts the uttermost farthing; a King, upheld by his fury, the smallest offence is high-treason, the greatest of crimes. His code is Draconian; he that offends in one point is guilty of all; good were it for that man he had never been born; extremest vengeance awaits him; the jealous God will come upon him in an hour when he is not aware, and will cut him asunder. Hence comes the doctrine of " eternal damnation," a dogma which Epicurus and Strato would have called it blasphemy to teach.

But God, though called personal, is yet infinite. Mercy therefore must be part of his nature. He desires to save man from the horrors of hell. Shall he change the nature of things? That is impossible. Shall he forgive all mankind outright? The infinite King forgive high-treason! It is not consistent with divine dignity to forgive the smallest violation of his perfect law. A sin, however small, is "an infinite evil." He must have an infinite "satisfaction." All the human race are sinners, by being born of woman. The damning sin of Adam vests in all their bones. They must suffer eternal damnation to atone for their inherited sin, unless some "substitute" take their place.

Now it has long been a maxim in the courts of law,—whence many forensic terms have been taken and applied to theology,—especially since the time of Anselm—that a man's property may suffer in the place of his person, and since his friends may transfer their property to him, they may suffer in his place "vicarious punishment."[1] Thus before Almighty God, there may be a substitute for the sinner. This doctrine is a theological fiction. It is of the same family with what are called "legal fictions" in the courts, and "practical fictions" in the street: a large and ancient family it must be confessed, that has produced great names. But no man can be a substitute for another, for sin is infinite and he finite. Though all the liquid fires of hell be poured from eternity on the penitent head of the whole race, not a single sin, committed by one man, even in his sleep, could be thereby atoned for. An infinite "ransom" must be paid to save a single soul. God's "Mercy" overcomes his "Justice," for Man deserves nothing but "damnation," He will provide the ransom. So he sent down his Son to fulfil all the law—which man could not fulfil,—realize infinite goodness, and thus merit the infinite reward, and then suffer all the tortures of infinite sin, as if he had not fulfilled it, and thus prepare a ransom for all; "purchasing" their "salvation." Thus men are saved from hell, by the "vicarious suffering" of the Son. But this would leave them in a negative state; not bad enough for hell; not good enough for Heaven. The "merits" of the Son, as well as his sufferings, must be set down to their account, and thus man is elevated to Heaven by the "imputed righteousness" of the Son.

But how can the Son achieve these infinite merits and

---

[1] "Qui non habet in crumena, luet in cute," is a maxim; and its converse holds good in theology.

endure this infinite torment and "redeem" and "save" the race? He must be infinite, and then it follows; for all the actions of the Infinite are also infinite, in this logic. But two Infinites there cannot be. The Son, therefore, is the Father, and the Father the Son. God's Justice is appeased by God's Mercy. God "sacrifices" God for the sake of men. Thus the infinite "satisfaction" is accomplished; with God, God has paid God the infinite ransom, for the infinite sin; the "sacrifice" has been offered; the "atonement" completed; "we are bought with a price;" "as in Adam all die, so in Christ shall all be made alive."[1]

Now in the very teeth of logic this system under consideration maintains that God did not thus purchase the redemption of all, for such "forgiveness" would ill comport with his dignity. Therefore certain "conditions" are to be complied with, before man is entitled to this salvation. God knew from all eternity who would be saved, and they are said to be "elected from before the foundation of the world," to eternal happiness. God is the cause of their compliance—for men have no free-will,—hence "fore-ordination;" they are not saved by their own merit, but each by Christ's—hence "particular redemption;" having no will, they must be "called" and moved by God, and if elected must be sure to come to him—hence "effectual calling;" if to be saved, they must certainly continue in "grace"—hence the "perseverance of the saints." The salvation of the "elect," the damnation of the non-elect, is all effected by the "decrees of God;" the "agency of the Holy Spirit," the "satisfaction of Christ," all is a work of "divine grace."

The doctrine of the "Trinity" has always been connected with this system. It does not embrace three Gods, as it has been often alleged, but one God in three persons, as the Hindoos have one God in thirty million persons, and the Pantheists one God in all persons and all things. The Father sits on the throne of his glory; the Son, at his right hand, "intercedes" for man; the Holy Spirit "proceeds" from the Father and the Son, "calls" the saints and makes them "persevere." This doctrine of a Trinity covers a truth, though it often conceals it. Its

[1] See Theism, &c., Sermons III. IV.

religious significance—the same with that of Polytheism—seems to be this; God does not limit himself within the unity of his essence, but incarnates himself in man—hence the Son; diffuses himself in space and in spirit, works with men both to will and to do—hence the Holy Ghost.[1]

1. *Merits of this Party.*

This party has great practical merits. The doctrine sketched above shows the hatefulness of sin, the terrible evils it brings upon the world. Alas, it need not look long to see them. It shows Man at first the child of God; holding daily intercourse with the Father; enjoying the raptures of Heaven on earth, but by one step, cast out, degraded, lost, undone! It shows the world full of sweet sunshine, truth, beauty, love, till Sin entered, and then—"the trail of the Serpent is over it all." It tells how sin benumbs the mind, palsies the heart, and shuts out wisdom at every entrance, bringing death to the intellect, death to the affections, death to the soul. The great Enemy of men is the child of sin. It tells Man he is the son of God, fallen from his high estate, and crushed by the Fall; but he may yet return. Christ will bind up his wounds; wash away all sin, with his blood, and he may start anew. It encourages men who are steeped in sin; tells them they may yet return. It says, "Come unto Christ." But alas, the wounded man, with no freedom, must wait till the Holy Ghost, like the good Samaritan, bind up his wounds and bid him rise and walk. If he is of the elect, the invitation will come, and each hopes he is of that blessed company.

One excellence comes out of its very defect: it thinks none can be saved but by accepting Christianity, a knowledge of which comes though the letter of the Bible. Therefore it is indefatigable in sending Bibles and missionaries the world over. If they do little good where they go, the very purpose and effort are good. A man is always warmed by the smoke of his own generous sacrifice.

It recommends an austere morality. It calls on men to repent; addresses rousing sermons to the fears of the wicked, and stirs men whom higher motives would not

[1] See Miscellanies, Art. XII., and Sermon of the Relation of Ecclesiastical Institutions, &c.

move—men who ask pay for goodness. It has a deep reverence for God ; and counts religion a reality ; insists on a right heart. It watches over sin with a jealous eye. Coming from a principle so deep as reverence for God ; believes it has all of truth in the lids of the Bible ; confiding in the intercession and atonement of Christ ; setting before the righteous the certainty of God's aid if they are faithful, to assure their perseverance, and promising all the rewards of heaven, it makes men strong, very strong. We see its influence, good and bad, on some of the fathers of New England, in their self-denial, their penitence, their austere devotion, the unconquerable daring, the religious awe which marked those iron men.

2. *The Vices of this Party.*

If it have great merits, it has great faults, which come from its peculiar doctrine, while its merits have a deeper source. It makes God dark and awful ; a judge not a protector ; a king not a Father ; jealous, selfish, vindictive. He is the Draco of the Universe ; the Author of Sin, but its unforgiving avenger. Man must hate the picture it makes of God. He is the Jehovah of the book of Numbers, more cruel than Odin or Baal. He punishes sin—though its Author—for his own glory, not for Man's benefit and correction. All the lovely traits of divine character it bestows upon the Son ; he is mild and beautiful as God is awful and morose. Men rush from the Father ; they flee to the Son. Its religion is Fear of God, not love of him, for Man cannot love what is not lovely.

This system degrades Man. It deprives him of freedom. It makes him not only the dwarf of himself—for the actual man is but the dwarf of the ideal and possible man—but a being hapless and ill-born ; the veriest worm that crawls the globe. To take a step toward Heaven he must deny his nature, and crucify himself. He is born totally depraved, and laden besides with the sins of Adam. He can do nothing to recover from these sins ; the righteousness of Christ is the only ground of the sinner's justification ; this righteousness is received through "faith," which is "the gift of God," and so "salvation is wholly of grace." The salvation of Man is wrought for him, not by him. It logically annihilates the difference between good and evil, denying the ultimate value of a manly life. It takes out of the pale of humanity its fairest sons, prophets, saints, apostles, Moses, Jesus, Paul, and makes their character miraculous, not manly. It tears off the crown of royalty from Man, makes Jesus a God; does not tell us we are born sons of God, as much as Jesus, and may stand as close to God. It does not tell of God now, near at hand, but a long while ago. It makes the Bible a tyrant of the soul. It is our master in all departments of thought. Science must lay his kingly head in the dust; Reason veil her majestic countenance; Conscience bow him to the earth; Affection keep silence when the priest uplifts the Bible. Man is subordinate to the apocryphal, ambiguous, imperfect, and often erroneous Scripture of the Word; the Word itself, as it comes straightway from the fountain of Truth, through Reason, Conscience, Affection, and the Soul, he must not have. It takes the Bible for God's statute-book; combines old Hebrew notions into a code of ethics; takes figures for fact; settles questions in Morals and Religion by texts of Scripture! It can justify anything out of the Bible. It wars to the knife against gaiety of heart; condemns amusement as sinful; sneers at Common Sense; spits upon Reason, calling it "carnal;" appeals to low and selfish aims—to Fear, the most selfish and base of all passions. Fear of hell is the bloody knout with which it scourges reluctant flesh across the finite world, and whips him smarting into Heaven at last. It does not know that goodness is its own recompense, and vice its own torture; that judgment takes place daily, and God's laws execute themselves. Shall I be bribed to goodness by hope of Heaven; or driven by fear of hell? It makes men do nothing from the love of what is good, beautiful, and true. It asks, Shall a man love goodness as a picture, for itself? Its divine life is but a good bargain. It makes a day of judgment; heaven and hell to begin after death, while goodness is Heaven, and vice Hell, now and for ever.

It makes Religion unnatural to men, and of course hostile; Christianity alien to the soul. It paves Hell with children's bones; has a personal Devil in the world, to harry the land, and lure or compel men to eternal woe. Its God is diabolical. It puts an Intercessor between God and Man; relies on the Advocate. Cannot the Infinite love his frail children without teasing? Needs He a chancellor, to advise Him to use forgiveness and mercy? Can men approach the Every-where present only by attorney, as a beggar comes to a Turkish king? Away with such folly. Jesus of Nazareth bears his own sins, not another's. How can his righteousness be "imputed" to me! Goodness out of me is not mine; helps me no more than another's food feeds or his sleep refreshes me. Adam's sin,—it was Adam's affair, not mine.

This system applies to God the language of kings' courts, trial, sentence, judgment, pardon, satisfaction, allegiance, day of judgment. Like a courtier it lays stress on forms—baptism, which in itself is nothing but a dispensation of water; the Lord's Supper, which of itself is nothing but a dispensation of wine and bread. It dwells in professions of faith; watches for God's honour. It makes men stiff, unbending, cold, formal, austere, seldom lovely. They have the strength of the Law, not the beauty of the Gospel; the cunning of the Pharisee, not the simplicity of the Christian. You know its followers soon as you see them; the rose is faded out of their cheeks; their mouths drooping and sad; their appearance says, Alas, my fellow-worm! there is no more sunshine, for the world is damned! It is a faith of stern, morose men, well befitting the descendants of Odin, and his iron peers; its Religion is a principle, not a sentiment; a foreign matter imported into the soul, by forethought and resolution; not a native fountain of joy and gladness, leaping up in winter's frost and summer's gladness, playing in the sober autumn or the sunshine of spring. Its Christianity is frozen mercury in the bosom of the warm-hearted Christian, who, by nature, would go straight to God, pray as spontaneous as the blackbird sings, love a thousand times where he hated not once, and count a divine life the greatest good in this world, and ask nothing more in the next. The Heaven of this system is a grand pay-day, where Humility is to have its coach and six, forsooth, because she has been humble; the Saints and Martyrs, who bore trials in the world, are to take their vengeance by shouting "Hallelujah, Glory to God," when they see the anguish of their old persecutors, and the "smoke of their torment ascending up for ever and ever." Do the joys of Paradise pall on the pleasure-jaded sense of the "Elect?" They look off in the distance to the tortures of the damned, where Destruction is naked before them, and Hell hath no covering; where the Devil with his angels stirreth up the embers of the fire which is never quenched; where the doubters, whom the Church could neither answer nor put to silence; where the great men of antiquity, Confucius, Budha, Hermes, Zoroaster, Pythagoras, Anaxagoras, Socrates, Plato, Aristotle; where the men, great, and gifted, and glorious, who mocked at difficulty, softened the mountains of despair, and hewed a path amid the trackless waste, that mortal feet might tread the way of peace; where the great men of modern times, who would not insult the Deity by bowing to the foolish word of a hireling priest—where all these writhe in their tortures, turn and turn and find no ray, but yell in fathomless despair; and when the Elect behold all this, they say, striking on their harps of gold, "Aha! We are comforted and Thou art tormented, for the Lord God Omnipotent reigneth, and our garments are washed white in the blood of the Lamb."

This system exists nowhere in its perfection; that is, only ideal. It is incarnated imperfectly in many forms. But it is the groundwork of the Popular Theology of New England.[1] It appears variously modified in all the chief denominations of North America and Great Britain. No one of all the sects which represents it but has great excellencies in spite of this hateful system. Each of them is doing a good but imperfect work. A rude nation must have a rude doctrine. Yet such is the system on which they rest their Theology. Though their Religion, say what they will, comes from no such quarter. This system is older than Protestantism, and is the child of many fathers. However it is continually approaching its end. The battering-ram which levelled the philosophy of the Stagirite and the schoolmen, will beat, ere long, on the Theology of the Church, and how shall it stand? It is based on a lie, and that lie undermined. A man who

[1] I have been careful not to cite authorities lest *individual churches* or *writers* should be deemed responsible for the sin of the mass. But *I have not spoken without book.*

loves wife and child, and would die any death to save a friend, will be slow to believe in total depravity; he that sees a swarm of bees in summer, or hears the blackbird sing in his honeysuckle, will not believe God is a devil, though all the divines in the Church quote the Fathers and Scriptures to prove it. God speaks truth always; will the pulpit prevail against Him? The sands of this Theology are numbered, and its glass shaken.

II. *The Party that sets out from the Paternity of God.*

This system makes God not a King but a Father and Mother, infinite in power, wisdom, and love. His love rays out in every direction, seeking to bless the all of things. The world, its overarching heavens, its ocean, its mountains, its flowers that brighten in the sunbeam; the crimson and purple that weave a lustrous veil for the face of Day, at the rising and decline of light; the living things of earth, beast, bird, fish, insect, so full of happiness that the world hums with its joy,—all these it counts but a whisper of God's goodness, though all which these babbling elements can teach. It sees the same in the Bible, for it will see itself, and walks in the shade of its own halo of glory, and so treads on rainbows where it steps.

This doctrine of God's goodness is a mighty truth, poorly apprehended as yet, though destined to a great work, and development which shall never end. Men can only see in God what is in themselves. Their conception of God cannot transcend their own ideal stature of spirit. Since goodness is not active in most men, nor love predominant, they see God as Power to be feared; at best as Wisdom to be reverenced; not as Goodness to be loved; nor can they till themselves become lovely.

1. *The Merits of this Party.*

The merits of this system are very great. It makes goodness the cause of all. God made the world to bless it. His love flowed forth a celestial stream that sparkles in the sky, surrounding the world. Apparent evils are but good in disguise, save only sin, and this Man brings on himself, through the imperfection of his nature, progressive and free. Goodness is infinite, but sin and evil finite. It sees a perfect system of optimism everywhere. The infinite Love must desire the best thing, the infinite Wisdom devise means for that end, and the infinite Power bring about the result. All things are overruled for good at the last. Sin is a point which mistaken men pass through in their development. Suffering is Man's instructor. It was good for Isaiah and Stephen and Paul to bear the burdens they bore; Affliction is success in a mask. It makes the world look fair and the face joyful. It hears the word of Love even in the voice of the earthquake and the tread of the pestilence. Evil is not ultimate but transient. It tells man of his noble nature; his lofty duty; his fair destination if faithful. It makes Religion natural to Man; bids him obey its law and be blessed; not to be good or do good for fear of Hell or hope of Heaven, but for itself. It would not have men fear God —the Religion of the Old Testament; but love him—the Religion of the New Testament. It tells us we are made for progressive goodness here, and Heaven hereafter. It denies original sin, or admitting that, makes it of no effect, for Christ has restored all to their first estate; thus avoiding the logical absurdity of the last form. Its Hell is not eternal, for the Infinite Love of God must make the whole of existence a blessing to each man. God is so lovely that we flee, as children, to his arms, a refuge from all the troubles, follies, and sins of life. It shows this uncontainable goodness in earth and sea and sky; in the prophets and apostles, sent to bless; in Jesus, the noble man who came to help the world—to seek and save the lost. It fills the soul with tranquillity, peace, and exceeding trust in God. Serenely the man goes about his duties; is not borne down with his cross, though never so weighty; looks on and smiles, fearing no evil but error and lack of faith. As he looks back, he sees an end of his perfection, but does not despair at the broadness of the divine law, though his steps totter in this infancy of his being, for he sees worlds open before him, where a stronger sunlight and a purer sky await him; where Reason, Conscience, the Affections, and the Soul shall finish their perfect work, and he shall not be weary with his walk, nor faint though he runs.

This system allows no ultimate evil, as a background of God; believes in no vindictive punishment. The woes of sin are but its antidote. Suffering comes from wrong-doing, as well-being from virtue. If there be suffering in the next world, it is, as in this, but the medicine of the sickly soul. It allows no contradiction between God's Justice and Mercy. We require to be reconciled with Him, not He with us. We love Him soon as seen. It makes religion inward; of the life and heart; the Son's service, not the Slave's; a sentiment, as well as principle; an encouragement no less than a restraint. God seeks to pour himself into the heart, as the sun into the roses of June. These are no vulgar merits.[1]

2. *The Defects and Vices of this Party.*

So far as this system is derived from its fundamental Idea, it has no defect nor vice, for the Idea is absolute and answers to the fact that God is good. But the absurdities of other forms mingle their pestilent breath with the fragrance of truth; and the party that poorly espouses this divine idea has its defects. Men do not see the sinfulness of sin; underrate the strength of human passion, cupidity, wrath, selfishness, intrenched in the institutions of the world, and belonging to the present low stage of civilization. They reflect too little on the evil that comes from violating the law of God; overlook the horrors of outraged conscience, and do not remember that suffering must last as long as error, and man only can remove that from himself. They are not sufficiently zealous to do good to others, in a spiritual way.

This party has also its redundancies. It has taken much from the ungrateful doctrines of the darker system. Its followers rely on Authority, as all Protestants have done. They make a man depend on Christ, who died centuries ago—not on himself, who lives now; forgetting that it is not the death of Jesus that helps us, but the death of Sin in our heart; not the life of Jesus, the personal Christ, however divine, but the life of Goodness, Holiness, Love, in our own heart. A Christ outside the man is nothing; his divine life nothing. God is not a magician to blot sin

[1] Theism, &c., Sermons V.—X.

out of the soul, and make men the same as if they had never sinned. Each man must be his own Christ, or he is no Christian.

No sect has fully developed the doctrine that is legitimately derived from this absolute Idea. When its time comes it will annihilate this poor theology of our time, and give Man his birthright. Some have attempted the work in all ages, and shared the fate of men before their time. Their bones lie mouldering in many a spot, accursed of men. They bore a prophet's mission, and met his fate. Their seed has not perished out of the earth.

This doctrine in some measure tinges the faith of all sects with its rosy light. It abates the austerity of the Calvinist, the exclusiveness of the Baptist; does a great work in the camp of the Methodist. All Churches have some of it, from the Episcopalian to the Mormonite, though in spite of their theology. There is something so divine in Religion, that it softens the ruggedest natures, and lets light even into theology. The sects, however, which chiefly rely upon it, are the Universalists, the Restorationists, and Unitarians. But how poorly they do their work; with what curtains of darkness do they overcloud the holy of holies! What poor ineptitudes do they offer us in the midst of the sublimest doctrines; how does the timid littleness of their achievement, or endeavour, stand rebuked before Absolute Religion; before the motto on the banner of Christianity: GOD IS LOVE! What despair of Man, of Reason, of Goodness; what bowing and cringing to tradition! Are not men born in our time as of old, or has a race of Liliputs and Manikins succeeded to Moses, Socrates, Jesus, and Paul? But this must pass. The two former have at their basis the old supernatural theology, and differ from the strictest sect mainly in their exegesis; they would believe anything which the Bible taught. They are, however, doing a great work. But the latter are of more importance in this respect, and, though few in numbers, deserve a notice by themselves.

Of the Unitarians, and their present Position.

At first the "Unitarian heresy," as it was presumptuously called, was a protest against the unreasonable and unscriptural doctrines of the Church; a protest on the part of Reason and Conscience; an attempt to apply good sense to theology, to reconcile Knowledge with Belief, Reason with Revelation, to humanize the Church. Its theology was of the supernatural character mingled with more or less of naturalism and spiritualism. It held to the first positive principles of the Reformation—the Bible and Private Judgment. Contending, as it must, with the predominant sects, then even more arrogant and imperious than now—perhaps not knowing so well the ground they stood on—its work, like most Reformations, was at first critical and negative. It was a " Statement of Reasons for not believing" certain doctrines, very justly deemed not scriptural. Thus it protested against the Trinity, total depravity, vindictive and eternal punishment, the common doctrines of the satisfaction of Christ, the malevolent character ascribed to God by the popular theology. It recommended a deep, true Morality lived for its own sake; perhaps sometimes confounded Morality with Piety. To make sure of Heaven, it demanded a manly life, laying more stress on the character than the creed; more on honesty, diligence, charity, than on grace before meat, or morning and evening prayers. In point of moral and religious life, as set forth in the two Great Commands, its advocates fear no comparison with any sect. It was not boastful, but modest, cautious, unassuming; mindful of its own affairs; not giving a blow for a blow, nor returning abuse—of which there was no lack—with similar abuse. It had a great work to do, and did it nobly. The spirit of reformers was in its leading men. The sword of polemic theology rarely fell into more just and merciful hands. But the time has not come to celebrate with due honour the noble heart, the manly forbearance, the Christian heroism of those who have gone where the weary are at rest, or who yet linger here. They fought the battle like Christian scholars, long and well. The sevenfold shield of Orthodoxy was clove asunder, spite of its gorgon head. Its terrible spear, with its " five points," was somewhat blunted.

Thus far Unitarianism was but carrying out the principles of the Protestant Reformation, to get at the pure doctrines of Scripture, which was still the standard of faith. Some, it seems, silently abandoned the divine and infallible character of the Old Testament—as Socinus had done—but clung strongly as ever to that of the New Testament, while they admitted the greatest latitude in the criticism and exegesis of that collection. The Unitarians were at first the most reasonable of sectarians. The Bible was their creed. Thinking men, who would conclude for themselves, say the Church what it might say, naturally came up to Unitarianism. Hence its growth in the most highly cultivated portion of the New World, and the most moral, it has been said. Men sick of the formality, the doctrines, the despotism of other sects ; disgusted with the sophistry whose burrow was in the Church ; pained at the charlatanry which anointed dulness sometimes showed, as the clerical mantle blew aside, by chance—these also came up to the Unitarians. Besides these, perhaps men of no spiritual faith, who hated to hear hell mentioned, or to have piety demanded, came also, hoping to have less required of them. Pious men, hungering and thirsting after truth—men born religious, found here their home, where the Mind and the Soul were both promised their rights. This explains the growth of the sect. The Unitarians, seeing the violence, the false zeal, of other sects, the compassing of sea and land to make a proselyte, went, it may be thought, to the opposite extreme, in some cases. They were called " cold," and were never accused of carrying matters too fast and too far, and pushing Religion to extremes. They were never good fighters, unless when occasion compelled. They stood on the defensive, and never crossed their neighbour's borders, except to defend their own. They thought it better to live down an opponent, than to talk him down, or even hew him down,—the old theological way of silencing an adversary whom it was difficult to answer.

Still, however, it seems there always were in their ranks men who thought freedom was too free ; that " there must be limits to free inquiry," even within the canon ; and Unitarians must have a " creed." [1] Others began to look into the mythology of the Old Testament, and to talk very freely about the imperfections in the New Testament. Some even doubted if the whale swallowed Jonah.

[1] It has since been made, and such a creed !

" Biblical criticism " opened men's eyes, and " terrible
questions " were asked ; great problems were coming up
which Luther never anticipated, for mankind has not stood
still for three centuries, but has studied science and history, and learned some things never known before.

At length the negative work was well over, and the
hostile forces of other sects were withdrawn, or the war
changed into an armed neutrality, at most "a war of
posts." The " Christian name," however, is not yet
allowed the Unitarians by their foes, and a hearty male-
diction, a sly curse, or a jealous caution, shows even at
this day the spirit that yet keeps its " theological odium,"
venomous as before. It is no strange thing for Unitarians
to be pronounced Infidels, and remanded to Hell by their
fellow Christians ! Now the time has come for Unitarianism—representing the movement party in theological
affairs—to do something ; develope the truth it has borne,
latent and unconscious, in its bosom. It is plain what the
occasion demands. Good sense must be applied to Theology, Religion applied to life, both to be done radically,
fearlessly, with honest earnestness ; assumptions must be
abandoned ; the facts sought for ; their relation and their
law determined, and thus truth got at. Did the early
Reformers see all things ; are we to stop where they
stopped, and because they stopped ? All false assumptions must be laid aside. The very foundation of Protestantism—the infallibility of Scripture—is that a Fact, or a
No-Fact ? But this is just the thing that is not done ;
which Unitarianism is not doing. The Trojan horse of
sectarian organization is brought into the citadel with the
usual effect upon that citadel. The " Unitarian sect " is
divided. There is an " Old School," and a " New School,"
as it is called, and a chasm between them, not wide, as
yet, but very deep. " The Old School " holds, in part, to
the first principles of the Reformation ; sees no further ;
differs theoretically from the " Orthodox " party, in exegesis, and that alone ; like that is ready to believe anything which has a Thus-saith-the-Lord before it, at least
if we may judge from the issue so often made ; its Christianity rests on the Authority of Jesus ; that on the authority of his miracles ; and his miracles on the testimony
of the Evangelists. Therefore it is just as certain there is

a God, or an immortal soul, and religious duties, as it is certain that Jesus raised Lazarus from the dead, or that John wrote the fourth Gospel and never made a mistake in it! It has somebody's word for it. But whose? Its religious doctrine is legitimated only by the sensations of the apostles. This party says, as the Unitarian fathers never said: There must be limits to free inquiry; we must not look into the grounds of religious belief, lest they be found no grounds; "where ignorance is bliss 't is folly to be wise!" The old landmarks must not be passed by, nor the Bible questioned as to its right to be master over the soul. Christianity must be rested on the authority of Christ, and that on the miracles, and the words of the New Testament. We must not inquire into their authority. If there is a contradiction between the Word of the New Testament and Reason, why the "Word" must be believed in spite of Reason, for we can be much more certain of what we read than of what we know!

Thus the old school assumes a position abhorred by primitive Unitarianism, which declared that free inquiry should never stop but with a conviction of truth. Unitarianism, as represented by the majority of its adherents, refuses to fall back on Absolute Religion and Morality, with no reliance on Form, Tradition, Scripture, personal Authority. It creeps behind texts, usage, and does not look facts in the face. The cause, in part, is plain as noonday. It is connected with a poor and sensual philosophy, the same in its basis with that which gave birth to the selfish system of Paley, the scepticism of Hume, the materialism of Hobbes, the denial of the French Deists; the same philosophy which drives other sects in despair to their supernatural theory. This cuts men off from direct communion with God, and curtails all their efforts. Unitarianism, therefore, is in danger of becoming a truncated supernaturalism, its apex shorn off; all of supernaturalism but the supernatural. With a philosophy too rational to go to the full length of the supernatural theory, too sensual to embrace the spiritual method and ask no person to mediate between man and God, it oscillates between the two; humanizes the Bible, yet calls it miraculous; believes in man's greatness, freedom, and spiritual nature, yet asks for a Mediator and Redeemer, and says, "Christ established a new relation between Man and God;" it admits man can pray for himself, and God hear for himself, and yet prays "in the name of Christ," and trusts an "intercessor." It censures the traditionary sects, yet sits itself among the tombs, and mourns over things past and gone; believes the humanity of Jesus, that he was a model-man for us all, yet his miraculous birth likewise and miraculous powers, and makes him an anomalous and impossible being. It blinds men's eyes with the letter, yet bids them look for the spirit; stops their ears with texts of the Old Testament, and then asks them to listen to the voice of God in their heart; it reverences Jesus manfully, yet denounces all such as preach Absolute Religion and Morality, as he did, on its own authority, with nothing between them and God, neither tradition nor person. Well might a weeping Jeremiah say of it, "Alas for thee, now hast thou forsaken the promise of thy youth, the joy of thine espousals!" or with the son of Sirach, "How wise wast thou in thy youth, and as a flood filled with understanding. Thy soul covered the whole earth; thy name went far unto the islands, and for thy peace thou wast beloved; the countries marvelled at thee for thy songs and proverbs, and parables, and interpretations; but by thy body wast thou brought into subjection; thou didst stain thine honour, so that thou broughtest wrath upon thy children, and was grieved for thy folly!" It has not kept its faith. It clings to the skirts of tradition, which, "as a scarecrow in a garden of cucumbers—keepeth nothing." It would believe nothing not reasonable, and yet all things scriptural; so it will not look facts in the face, and say, This is in the Bible, yes, in the New Testament, but out of Reason none the less. So with perfect good faith, it "explains away" what is offensive: "This is not in the canon. That is a false interpretation." To such a proficiency has this art of explaining away been carried that the Scripture is a piece of wax in the Unitarian hand, and takes any shape: the Devil is an oriental figure of speech; Paul believed in him no more than Peter Bayle; the miraculous birth of Jesus, the ascension in the body, the stories of Abraham, Jonah, Daniel, are "true as symbols not as facts;" Moses and Isaiah never speak of Jesus in the Law and the Prophets, yet Jesus is right when he says they did; David in the Psalm is a sick man, speaking only of himself, but when Simon Peter quotes that Psalm, the inspired king is predicting Jesus of Nazareth![1] These things are notorious facts. If the Athanasian Creed, the thirty-nine articles of the English church, and the Pope's bull "Unigenitus," could be found in a Greek manuscript, and proved the work of an "inspired" apostle, no doubt Unitarianism would in good faith explain all three, and deny they taught the doctrine of the Trinity or the fall of man. The Unitarian doctrine of inspiration —can any one tell what it is?

But let the sect be weighed in an even balance, its theological defects be set off against the vast service it has done, and is still doing for morals and religion. But this is not the place for its praise. Of the "new school" of Unitarians, if such it may be called, embracing as it does men of the greatest possible diversity of religious sentiment and opinion—it is not decorous to speak here.

Now Unitarianism must do one of two things, affirm the great doctrines of Absolute Religion—teaching that man is greater than the Bible, ministry, or church, that God is still immanent in mankind, that man saves himself by his own and not another's character, that a perfect manly life is the true service, and the only service God requires, the only source of well-being now or ever—it must do this, or cease to represent the progress of man in theology, and then some other will take its office; stand God-parent to the fair child it has brought into the world, but dares not own.[2]

To sum up what has been said:—we see that the Catholic and the Protestant party both start with a false assumption, the Divinity of the Churches, or that of the Bible; both claim mastery over the Soul; but both fail to give or allow the Absolute Religion. Both set bounds to Man,

---

[1] Dr Palfrey's work on the Old Testament by one of its most distinguished scholars, finds small favour with this party, though, excepting the valuable works of Dr Geddes above referred to, it is the only attempt ever made in the English tongue to look the facts of the Old Testament manfully in the face!

[2] The above was written in 1841, since then the American Unitarians, as a Body, have retreated still further back, siding with Mediæval Theology and American Slavery.

which must be reached if they are not already. Both represent great truths, out of which their excellence and power proceed, but both great falsehoods, which impoverish their excellence. Each is too narrow for the Soul; should the persons who sit in these Churches rise to the stature of men, they must carry away roof and steeple, for Man is greater than the Churches he allows to tyrannize over him.

CHAPTER VI.

OF THE PARTY THAT ARE NEITHER CATHOLICS NOR PROTESTANTS.

THIS party has an Idea wider and deeper than that of the Catholic or Protestant, namely, that God still inspires men as much as ever; that he is immanent in spirit as in space. For the present purpose, and to avoid circumlocution, this doctrine may be called SPIRITUALISM. This relies on no Church, Tradition, or Scripture, as the last ground and infallible rule; it counts these things teachers, if they teach, not masters; helps, if they help us, not authorities. It relies on the divine presence in the Nature of Man; the eternal Word of God, which is TRUTH, as it speaks through the faculties he has given. It believes God is near the soul, as matter to the sense; thinks the canon of revelation not yet closed, nor God exhausted. It sees him in Nature's perfect work; hears him in all true Scripture, Jewish or Phœnician; feels him in the aspiration of the heart; stoops at the same fountain with Moses and Jesus, and is filled with living water. It calls God Father and Mother, not King; Jesus brother, not Redeemer; Heaven home; Religion nature. It loves and trusts, but does not fear. It sees in Jesus a man living manlike, highly gifted, though not without errors, and living with earnest and beautiful fidelity to God, stepping thousands of years before the race of men; the profoundest religious genius God has raised up, whose words and works help us to form and develope the idea of a complete religious man. But he lived for himself; died for himself; worked out his own salvation, and we must do the same, for one man cannot live for another more than he can eat or sleep for him. It is no personal Christ, but the Spirit of Wisdom, Holiness, Love, that creates the well-being of men; a life at one with God. The divine incarnation is in all mankind.

The aim it proposes is a complete union of Man with God, till every action, thought, wish, feeling, is in perfect harmony with the divine will. The "Christianity" it rests in is not the point Man goes through in his progress, as the Rationalist, not the point God goes through in his development, as the Supernaturalist maintains; but Absolute Religion, the point where Man's will and God's will are one and the same. Its Source is absolute, its Aim absolute, its Method absolute. It lays down no creed; asks no symbol; reverences exclusively no time nor place, and therefore can use all time and every place. It reckons forms useful to such as they help; one man may commune with God through the bread and the wine, emblems of the body that was broke, and the blood that was shed, in the cause of truth; another may hold communion through the moss and the violet, the mountain, the ocean, or the Scripture of suns, which God has writ in the sky; it does not make the means the end; it prizes the signification more than the sign. It knows nothing of that puerile distinction between Reason and Revelation; never finds the alleged contradiction between Good Sense and Religion. Its Temple is all space; its Shrine the good heart; its Creed all truth; its Ritual works of love and utility; its Profession of faith a manly life, works without, faith within, love of God and man. It bids man do duty, and take what comes of it, grief or gladness. In every desert it opens fountains of living water; gives balm for every wound, a pillow in all tempests, tranquillity in each distress. It does good for goodness' sake; asks no pardon for its sins, but gladly serves out the time. It is meek and reverent of truth, but scorns all falsehood, though upheld by the ancient and honourable of the earth. It bows to no idols, of wood or flesh, of gold or parchment, or spoken wind; neither Mammon, neither the Church, nor the Bible, nor yet Jesus, but God only. It takes all helps it can get; counts no good word profane, though a heathen spoke it; no lie sacred, though the greatest prophet had said the word. Its redeemer is within; its salvation within; its heaven and its oracle of God. It falls back on perfect Religion; asks no more; is satisfied with no less. The personal Jesus is its encouragement, for he helps reveal the possible of man. Its watchword is, BE PERFECT AS GOD. With its eye on the Infinite, it goes through the striving and the sleep of life; equal to duty, not above it; fearing not whether the ephemeral wind blow east or west. It has the strength of the Hero; the tranquil sweetness of the Saint. It makes each man his own priest; but accepts gladly him that speaks a holy word. Its prayer in words, in works, in feeling, in thought, is this, Thy will be done; its Church that of all holy souls, the Church of the first-born, called by whatever name.[1]

Let others judge the merits and defects of this scheme. It has never organized a Church; yet in all ages, from the earliest, men have, more or less freely, set forth its doctrines. We find these men among the despised and forsaken. The world was not ready to receive them. They have been stoned and spit upon in all the streets of the world. The "pious" have burned them as haters of God and man; the "wicked" called them bad names and let them go. They have served to flesh the swords of the Catholic Party, and feed the fires of the Protestant. But flame and steel will not consume them. The seed they have sown is quick in many a heart; their memory blessed by such as live divine. These were the men at whom the world opens wide the mouth and draws out the tongue and utters its impotent laugh; but they received the fire of God on their altar, and kept living its sacred flame. They go on the forlorn hope of the race; but Truth puts a wall of fire about them and holds the shield over their head in the day of trouble. The battle of Truth seems often lost, but is always won. Her enemies but erect the bloody scaffolding were the workmen of God go up and down, and

---

[1] It is unnecessary to enlarge on this scheme, since so much has been said of it already. See Book I. ch. vii. § 3, and Book II. ch. viii., and Book III. ch. v. vi.

with divine hands build wiser than they know. When the scaffolding falls the temple will appear.

CHAPTER VII.

THE FINAL ANSWER TO THE QUESTION.

Now then, if it be asked, what relation the Church sustains to the religious Element, the answer is plain: The Soul is greater than the Church. Religion, as Reason, is of God; the Absolute Religion, and therefore eternal, based on God alone; the Christian Churches, Catholic and Protestant, are of men, and therefore transient. Let them say their say; man is God's child, and free of their tyranny; he must not accept their limitations, nor bow to their authority, but go on his glorious way. The Churches are a human affair quite as much as the State; ecclesiastical, like political institutions, are changeable, human, subject to the caprices of public opinion. The divine right of kings to bear sway over the Body, and the divine right of the Churches to rule over the Soul, both rest on the same foundation—on a LIE.

The Christian Church, like Fetichism and Polytheism, like the State, has been projected out of man in his development and passage through the ages; its several phases correspond to Man's development and civilization, and are inseparable from it. They are the index of the condition of Man. They bear their justification in themselves. They could not have been but as they were. To censure or approve Catholicism, or Protestantism, is to censure or approve the state of the race which gave rise to these forms; to condemn Absolute Religion, called by whatever name, is to condemn both Man and God.

Jesus fell back on God, aiming to teach absolute Religion, absolute Morality; the truth its own authority, his works his witness. The early Christians fell back on the authority of Jesus; their successors, on the Bible, the work of the apostles and prophets; the next generation on the Church, the work of apostles and fathers. The world retreads this ground. Protestantism delivers us from the tyranny of the Church, and carries us back to the Bible. Biblical criticism frees us from the thraldom of the Scripture, and brings us to the authority of Jesus. Philosophical Spiritualism liberates us from all personal and finite authority, and restores us to GOD, the primeval fountain, whence the Church, the Scriptures, and Jesus have drawn all the water of life, wherewith they fill their urns. Thence, and thence only, shall mankind obtain Absolute Religion and spiritual well-being. Is this a retreat for mankind? No, it is progress without end. The race of men never before stood so high as now; with suffering, tears, and blood they have toiled, through barbarism and war, to their present height, and we see the world of promise opening upon our eye. But what is not behind is before us.

Institutions arise as they are needed, and fall when their work is done. Of these things nothing is fixed. Institutions are provisional, man only is final. Corporeal despotism is getting ended; will the spiritual tyranny last for ever? A will above our puny strength, marshals the race of men, using our freedom, virtue, folly, as instruments to one vast end—the harmonious development of Man. We see the art of God in the web of a spider, and the cell of a bee, but have not skill to discern it in the march of Man. We repine at the slowness of the future in coming, or the swiftness of the past in fleeing away; we sigh for the fabled "Millennium" to advance, or pray Time to restore us the Age of Gold. It avails nothing. We cannot hurry God, nor retard him. Old schools and new schools seem as men that stand on the shore of some Atlantic bay, and shout, to frighten back the tide, or urge it on. What boots their cry? Gently the sea swells under the moon, and, in the hour of God's appointment, the tranquil tide rolls in, to inlet and river, to lave the rocks, to bear on its bosom the ship of the merchant, the weeds of the sea. We complain, as our fathers; let us rather rejoice, for questions less weighty than these have in other ages been disposed of only with the point of the sword, and the thunder of cannon—put off, not settled.

If the opinions advanced in this Discourse be correct, then Religion is above all institutions, and can never fail; they shall perish, but Religion endure; they shall wax old as a garment; they shall be changed, and the places that knew them shall know them no more for ever; but Religion is ever the same, and its years shall have no end.

THE CONCLUSION.

"Changes are coming fast upon the world. In the violent struggle of opposite interests, the decaying prejudices that have bound men together, in the old forms of society, are snapping asunder, one after another. Must we look forward to a hopeless succession of evils, in which exasperated parties will be alternately victors and victims, till all sink under some one power, whose interest it is to preserve a quiet despotism? Who can hope for a better result, unless the great lesson be learnt, that there can be no essential improvement in the condition of society, without the improvement of men as moral and religious beings; and that this can be effected only by religious TRUTH? To expect this improvement from any form of false religion, because it is called religion, is as if, in administering to one in a fever, we were to take some drug from an apothecary's shelves, satisfied with its being called medicine."—ANDREWS NORTON.—*Statement of Reasons, &c.* Preface. p. xxii.—xxxiii.

"What greater calamity can fall upon a nation than the loss of Worship? Then all things go to decay. Genius leaves the temple to haunt the senate or the market. Literature becomes frivolous. Science is cold. The eye of youth is not lighted by the hope of other worlds, and age is without honour. In the Soul let the redemption be sought. In one soul, in your soul, there are resources for the world. The stationariness of religion, the assumption that the age of inspiration is passed, that the Bible is closed; the fear of degrading the character of Jesus, by representing him as a man, indicate with sufficient clearness the falsehood of our theology. It is the office of a true teacher, to show us that God is, not was; that he speaketh, not spake. The true Christianity—a faith like Christ's in the infinitude of man—is lost. None believeth in the soul of man, but only in some man, or person, old and departed."—RALPH WALDO EMERSON.—*Address in Divinity College, &c.*, p. 24, 25.

THE CONCLUSION.

I. OF THE POPULAR THEOLOGY.

THEOLOGY is the science of Religion. It treats of Man, God, and the Relation between Man and God, with the duties which grow out of that relation. It is both queen and mother of all science; the loftiest and most ennobling of all the speculative pursuits of Man. But the popular theology of this day is no science at all, but a system of incoherent notions, woven together by scholastic logic, and resting on baseless assumptions. The pursuit thereof in the ecclesiastical method does not elevate. There is in it somewhat not holy. It is not studied as science, with no concern except for the truth of the conclusion. We wish to find the result as we conceived it to be; as Bishop Butler has said, " People habituate themselves to let things pass through their minds, rather than to think of them. Thus by use they become satisfied merely with seeing what is said, without going any further." Our Theology has two great Idols, the BIBLE and CHRIST; by worshipping these, and not God only, we lose much of the truth they both offer us. Our theology relies on assumptions, not ultimate facts; so it comes to no certain conclusions; weaves cobwebs, but no cloth.

The popular Theology rests on these main assumptions; the Divinity of the Churches, and the Divinity of the Bible. What is the value of each? It has been found convenient to assume both. Then it has several important aphorisms, which it makes use of as if they were established truths, to be employed as the maxims of geometry, and no more to be called in question. Amongst these are the following : Man under the light of nature is not capable of discovering the moral and religious truth needed for his moral and religious welfare ; there must be a personal and miraculous mediator between each man and God ; a life of blameless obedience to the law of Man's nature will not render us acceptable to God, and insure our well-being in the next life ; we need a superhuman being to bear our sins, through whom alone we are saved ; Jesus of Nazareth is that superhuman, and miraculous, and sin-reconciling mediator ; the doctrine he taught is Revealed Religion, which differs essentially from Natural Religion ; an external and contingent miracle is the only proof of an eternal and necessary truth in Morals or Religion ; God formerly transcended the laws of Nature and made a miraculous revelation of some truth ; he does not now inspire men as formerly.   Each of these aphorisms is a gratuitous assumption, which has never been proved, and of course all the theological deductions made from the aphorisms, or resting on these two main assumptions, are without any real foundation.   Theologians have assumed their facts, and then reasoned as if the fact were established, but the conclusion was an inference from a baseless assumption.   Thus it accounts for nothing.   "We only become certain of the immortality of the soul from the fact of Christ's resurrection," says Theology.   Here are two assumptions : first, the fact of that resurrection ; second, that it proves our immortality.   If we ask proof of the first point, it is not easy to come by ; of the second, it is not shown.   The theological method is false ; for it does not prove its facts historically, or verify its conclusions philosophically.   The Hindoo theory says, the earth rests on the back of an Elephant, the Elephant on a Tortoise.   But what does the Tortoise rest upon ?   The great Turtle of popular theology rests on—an assumption.   Who taught us the infallible divinity of the Bible, or the Churches ?   "Why, we always thought so. We inherited the opinion, as land, from our fathers, to have and to hold, for our use and behoof, for ourselves, and our heirs for ever.   Would you have a better title ?   We are regularly ' seized ' of the doctrine ; it came, with the divine right of kings, from our fathers, who by the grace of God, burnt men for doubting the truth of their theology ! " This is the defence of the popular theology. We have freedom in civil affairs, can revise our statutes, change the administration, or amend the constitution. Have we freedom in theological affairs, to revise, change, amend a vicious theology ? We have always been doing it, but only by halves, not looking at the foundation of the matter. We have applied good sense to many things, Agriculture, Commerce, Manufactures, and with distinguished success ; not yet to Theology. We make improvements in science and art every year. Men survey the clouds, note the variations of the magnetic needle, analyze rocks, waters, soils, and do not fear truth shall hurt them though it make Hipparchus and Cardan unreadable. Our Method of theology is false no less than its assumptions. What must we expect of the conclusion ? What we find.

If a school were founded to teach Geology, and the professors of that science were required to subscribe the geological symbol of Aristotle or Paracelsus, and swear solemnly to interpret facts by that obsolete creed, and maintain and inculcate the geological faith as expressed in that creed, in opposition to Wernerians, Bucklandians, Lyellians, and all other geological " heresies," ancient or modern ; if the professors were required to subscribe this every five years, and no pupil was allowed the name of Geologist, or permitted peacefully to examine a rock, unless he professed that creed, what would men say to the matter ? No one thinks such a course strange in theology ; our fathers did so before us. In plain English, we are afraid of the truth. " God forbid," said a man famous in his day, " that our love of truth should be so cold as to tolerate any erroneous opinion "—but our own. Any change is looked on with suspicion. If the drift-weed of the ocean be hauled upon the land, men fear the ocean will be drank up, or blown dry ; if the pine-tree rock, they exclaim, the mountain falling cometh to nought. How superstitiously men look on the miracle-question, as if the world could not stand if the miracles of the New Testament were not real !

The popular theology does not aim to prove Absolute Religion, but a system of doctrines made chiefly of words. Now the problem of theology is continually changing. In the time of Moses it was this : To separate Religion from

the Fetichism of the Canaanites, and the Polytheism of the
Egyptians, and connect it with the doctrine of one God.
No doubt Jannes and Jambres exclaimed with pious horror,
What, give up the Garlic and the Cats which our fathers
prayed to and swore by! we shall never be guilty of that
infidelity.   But the Priesthood of Garlic came to an end,
and the world still continued, though the Cats were not
worshipped.   In the time of Jesus, the problem was, to
separate Religion from the obsolete ritual of Moses.   We
know the result; the Scribes and Pharisees were shocked
at the thought of abandoning the ritual of Moses!   But
the ritual went its way.   In the time of Luther a new problem arose; to separate Religion from the forms of the
Catholic church.   The issue is well known.   In our times
the problem is to separate Religion from whatever is finite,
church, book, person, and let it rest on its Absolute
Truth.[1]   Numerous questions come up for discussion: Is
Christianity Absolute Religion? What relation does Jesus
bear to the human race?   What relation does the Bible
sustain to it?   We have nothing to fear from truth, or for
truth, but everything to hope.   It is about Theology that
men quarrel, not about Religion; that is but one.

II. OF THE POPULAR CHRISTIANITY.

Coming away from the theology of our time, and looking at the public virtue, as revealed in our life, political,
commercial, and social, and seeing things as they are, we
must come to this conclusion; either Christianity—considered as the Absolute Religion—is false and utterly detestable, or else modern society, in its basis and details, is
wrong, very wrong.   There is no third conclusion possible.
Religion demands a divine life; society one mean and
earthly.   Religion says—its great practical maxim—We
that are strong ought to bear the burdens of the weak;
society, We that are strong must make the weak bear our
burdens, and do this daily.   The strong do not always
compel the weak as heretofore, with a sword, nor violently
bind them mainly in fetters of iron; they compel with an
idea, and chain with manacles unseen, but felt.   Men most
eminent in defence of the popular theology are loudest in

[1] See Miscellanies, Art. XII.

support of American Slavery. Hell and Slavery are their favourite dogmas! Who does the world's work; he that receives most largely the world's good? It needs not that truisms be repeated. Now it is a high word of Christianity, he that is greatest shall be your servant. What is the corresponding word of society? Everybody knows it. Do we estimate greatness in this way, by the man's achievements for the public welfare? Oh no, we have no such vulgar standard! Men of "superior talents and cultivation," do we expect them to be great by serving mankind? Nay, by serving themselves!

Religion is love of God and Man. Is that the basis of action with us? A young man setting out in life, and choosing his calling, says this to himself: How can I get the most ease and honours out of the world, returning the least of toil and self-denial? That is the philosophy of many a life; the very end of even what is called the "better class" of society. Who says, This will I do; I will be a man, a whole complete man, as God made me; take care of myself, but serve my brother, counting my strength also HIS, not merely his MINE; I will take nothing from the world which is not honestly, truly, manfully earned? Who puts his feet forward in such a life? We call such a man a FOOL. Yes, Jesus of Nazareth is a fool, tried by the penny-wisdom of this generation. We honour him in our Sunday talk; hearing his words, say solemnly as the parasites of Herod, "It is the voice of a God, not of a man!" and smite a man on both cheeks, who does not cry Amen. But all the week long, we blaspheme that great soul, who speaks though dead, and call his word, a Fool's talk. That is the popular Christianity. We pray as well as the old Pharisee, "Lord, we thank thee we are not as other men, as the Heathen Socrates, who knew nothing, as the 'Infidel,' who cannot believe contradictions and absurdities. We say grace before meat; attend to all the church-ordinances; can repeat the creed, and we believe every word of both thy Testaments; O Lord, what wouldst thou more? We have fulfilled all righteousness."

Alas for us! We have taken the name of Jesus in our Church, and psalm-singing. We can say "Lord, Lord, no man ever spake as thou." But our Christianity is talk; it is not in the heart, nor the hand, nor the head, but only in the tongue. Could that great man, whose soul bestrides the world to bless it, come back again, and speak in bold words, to our condition, follies, sins, his denunciation and his blest beatitudes, rooting up with his "Woe-unto-you, Hypocrites," what was not of God's planting, and calling things by right names—how should we honour him? As Annas, and Caiaphas, and their fellows honoured that "Galilean, and no prophet,"—with spitting and a cross. But it costs little to talk and to pray.

A divine manliness is the despair of our Churches. No man is reckoned good who does not believe in sin, and human inability. We seem to have said :—"Alas for us! We defile our week-days by selfish and unclean living; we dishonour our homes, by low aims and lack of love; by sensuality and sin. We debase the sterling word of God in our soul; we cannot discern between good and evil, nor read Nature aright; nor come at first-hand to God; therefore let us set one day apart from our work; let us build us a house which we will enter only on that day trade does not tempt us; let us take the wisest of books, and make it our oracle; let it save us from thought, and be to us as a God; let us take our brother to explain us this book, to stand between us and God; let him be holy for us, pray for us, represent a divine life. We know these things cannot be, but let us make believe." The work is accomplished, and we have the Sabbath, the Church, the Bible, and the Ministry; each beautiful in itself, but our ruin, when made the substitutes for holiness of heart and a divine life.

In Absolute Religion we have what is wide as the East and the West; deep and high as the Nadir and Zenith; certain as Truth, and everlasting as God. But in our life we are heathens. He that fears God becomes a prey. To be religious, with us, in speech and action, a man must take his life in his hand, and be a lamb among the wolves. Does our Christianity enter the counting-room; the senate-house; the jail? Does it look on ignorance and poverty, seeking to root them out of the land? The religious doctrine of work and wages is a plain thing; he that wins the staple from the maternal earth; who expends strength, skill, taste, on that staple, making it more valuable; who aids men to be healthier, wiser, better, more holy, he does a service to the race; does the world's work. To get commodities won by others' sweat, by violence and the long arm, is Robbery, the ancient Roman way; to get them by cunning and the long head, is Trade, the modern Christian way. What say Reason and Jesus to that? No doubt the Christianity of the Pulpit is a poor thing. Words cannot utter its poverty; it is neither meat nor drink; the text saves the sermon. But the Christianity of daily life, of the street, that is still worse, the whole Bible could not save it. The history of society is summed up in a word; Cain killed Abel: that of real Religion also in a word; Christ died for his brother.

From ancient times we have received two priceless treasures: The Sunday, as a day of rest, social meeting, and religious instruction; and the institution of Preaching, whereby a living man is to speak on the deepest of subjects. But what have we made of them? Our Sabbath—what a weariness is it; what superstition defiles its sunny hours! And Preaching—what has it to do with life? Men graceless and ungifted make it handiwork; a sermon is the Hercules-pillar and *ultima Thule* of dulness. The Popular Religion is unmanly and sneaking. It dares not look Reason in the face, but creeps behind tradition and only quotes. It has nothing new and living to say. To hear its talk one would think that God was dead, or at best asleep. We have enough of Church-going, a remnant of our fathers' veneration, which might lead to great good; reverence still for the Sabbath, one of the best institutions the stream of time has brought us; we have still admiration for the name of Jesus. A soul so great and pure could not have lived in vain. But to call ourselves Christians after his kind of Religion, while we are keeping slaves and stoning prophets—may God forgive that mockery! Are men to serve God by lengthening the creed and shortening the commandments; making long prayers and devouring the weak; by turning Reason out of doors and condemning such as will not believe our Theology, nor accept a priest's falsehood in God's name?

Religion is Life. Is our Life Religion? No man pretends it. No doubt there are good men in all Churches, and out of all Churches; there have been such in the hold of pirate-ships and robbers' dens. I know there are good men and pious women, and I would go leagues long to sit down at their blessed feet and kiss their garments' hem; but what are the mass of us? Disciples of Absolute Religion? Christians after the fashion of Jesus of Nazareth? No! only Christians in tongue. It is an imputed righteousness that we honour; not ours, but borrowed of Tradition; an "historical Christianity" that was, but is no more. A man is a Christian if he goes to meeting in a fashionable place; pays his pew-tax; bows to the parson; believes with his sect; is good as other people. That is our religion; what is lived, what is preached; "like people, like priest," was never more true.

It is not that we need new forms and symbols, or even the rejection of the old. Baptism and the Supper are still beautiful and comforting to many a soul. A spiritual man can put spirit upon these. To many they are still powerful auxiliaries. They commune with God now and then—through bread and wine, as others hold converse with Him for ever, through the symbols of Nature, the winds that wake the "soft and soul-like sound" of the pine tree; through the earliest violets of spring and the last leaf of autumn; through calm and storm, and stars and blooming trees, and winter's snows and summer's sunshine. A religious man never lacks symbols of its own, elements of communion with God. What we want is the SOUL of Religion, Religion that thinks and works; its SIGN will take care of itself.

With us Religion is a nun; she sits, of week days, behind her black veil, in the meeting-house; her hands on her knees; making her creed more unreadable; damning "infidels" and "carnal Reason;" she only comes out in the streets of a Sunday, when the shops are shut, and temptation out of sight, and the din of business is still as a baby's sleep. All the week nobody thinks of that joyless vestal. Meantime strong-handed Cupidity, with his legion of devils, goes up and down the earth, and presses Weakness, Ignorance, and Want, into his service; sends

Bibles to Africa on the deck of his ship, and Rum and Gunpowder in the hold, knowing that the Church he pays will pray for "the outward bound." He brings home, most Christian Cupidity, images of himself God has carved in ebony; to enslave and so Christianize and bless the sable son of Ethiopia! Verily we are a Christian people; zealous of good-works; drawing nigh unto God—with our lips! Lives there a savage tribe our sons have visited, that has not cause to curse and hate the name of Christians, who have plundered, polluted, slain, enslaved their children? Not one the wide world round, from the Mandans to the Malays. If there were but half the Religion in all Christendom, that there is talk of it during a "Revival," in a village; at the baseness, political, commercial, social baseness daily done in the world, such a shout of indignation would go up from the four corners of earth, as should make the ears of Cupidity tingle again, and would hustle the oppressor out of creation.

The Poor, the Ignorant, the Weak, have we always with us; inasmuch as we do good unto them, we serve God; inasmuch as we do it not unto the least of them, we blaspheme God and cumber the ground we tread on. Was there no meaning in that old word, "He that knew his Lord's will and did it not, shall be beaten with many stripes?" They are already laid upon us. Religion meant something with Paul; something with Jesus; what does it mean with us? A divine life from infancy to age; divine all through? Oh, no; a cheaper thing than that; it means talk, creed-making, and creed-believing, and creed-defending. We Christians of the "nineteenth century" have many "inventions to save labour;" among them a process by which "a man is made as good a Christian in five minutes as in fifty years." Behold Christianity made easy! Do men love Religion and its divine life, as Gain and Trade? Is it the great moving principle with us; something loved for itself; something to live by? Oh, no. Nobody pretends it.

No wonder "ministers cannot bear to hear the truth spoken;" five minutes' talk will not weigh down fifty years' work, save in the Church's balance. The Christianity of the Churches stands at the corner of the street, and

bellows till all rings again from Cape Sable to the Lake of
the Woods, if a single " heretic " lifts up his voice, though
never so weak, in the obscurest corner of the earth; but
Giant Sin may go through the land with his hideous rout;
may ride rough-shod over the poor, and burn the standing
corn and poison the waters of the nation, and shake the
very Church till the steeple rock—and there shall not a
dog wag his tongue. When did the Christianity of the
churches leave a heresy unscathed; when did it ever denounce a popular sin—the desolation of intemperance, our
butchery of the Indians, the soul-destroying traffic in the
flesh and blood of men " for whom Christ died ? " These
things need no comment. They tell their own tale.
Where is the infidelity of this age? Read the sectarian
newspapers. We have a theological Religion to defend
with tracts, sermons, ministers, and scandal. It needs all
that to defend it.

No wonder young men, and young women too, of the
most spiritual stamp, lose their reverence for the Church,
or come into it only for a slumber, irresistible, profound,
and strangely similar to death. What concord hath freedom with slavery? Talent goes to the world, not the
churches. No wonder Unbelief scoffs in the public print :
" beside what that grim wolf, with privy paw, daily de-
vours apace, and nothing said; " there is an unbelief,
worse than the public scoffing, though more secret, which
needs not be spoken of. No wonder the old cry is raised,
" The Church in danger," as its crazy timbers sway to and
fro if a strong man treads its floors. But what then?
What is true never fails. Religion is permanent in the
race; Christianity everlasting as God. These can never
perish, through the treachery of their defenders, or the
violence of their foes. We look round us, and all seems to
change ; what was solid last night, is fluid and passed off
to-day ; the theology of our fathers is unreadable ; the
doctrine of the middle-age " divines " is deceased like
them. Shall our mountain stand? " Everywhere is in-
stability and insecurity." It is only men's heads that swim ;
not the stars that run round. The Soul of man remains
the same ; Absolute Religion does not change ; God still
speaks in Mind and Conscience, Heart and Soul ; is still

immanent in his children. We need no new forms; the old, Baptism and the Supper, are still beautiful to many a man, and speak blessed words of religious significance. Let them continue for such as need them. We want real Christianity, the absolute Religion, preached with faith and applied to life; Being Good and Doing Good. There is but one real Religion; we need only open our eyes to see that; only live it, in love to God, and love to Man, and we are blest of Him that liveth for ever and ever.

THE END.

JOHN CHILDS AND SON, PRINTERS.

WORKS BY THE EDITOR.

AN ESSAY ON INTUITIVE MORALS.—Vol. I. Theo
of Morals. 2nd edition, 12mo. Trübner & Co.

AN ESSAY ON INTUITIVE MORALS.—Vol. II. Re
gious Duty. (Out of print, and shortly to be re-published.)

PAMPHLETS.

THE WORKHOUSE AS AN HOSPITAL.

FRIENDLESS GIRLS, AND HOW TO HELP THEM

FEMALE EDUCATION, AND HOW IT WOULD BE
     AFFECTED BY UNIVERSITY EXAMINATIONS. Emily Faith
     full & Co.

IN THE PRESS—

ESSAYS ON THE PURSUITS OF WOMEN.—Re
     printed from Fraser's and Macmillan's Magazines. 1 vol. 8vo. Emily
     Faithfull & Co.